Modeling and Texturing Techniques with 3ds Max 2017®: The Ultimate Beginner's Guide

ROC

and

Elizabeth VT

RISING POLYGON

Modeling and Texturing Techniques with 3ds Max 2017 - The Ultimate
Beginner's Guide

Copyright © Rising Polygon

Book Code: RPO8C

Edition: 2nd Edition

ISBN: 978-1539666042

Web: www.risingpolgon.co

Author Email: rconor@risingpolgon.co

Contents

Index

This page is intentionally left blank

Acknowledgements

Thanks to:

Everyone at Autodesk [www.autodesk.com].
Everyone at Microsoft [www.microsoft.com].

Thanks to all great digital artists who inspire us with their innovative VFX, gaming, animation, and motion graphics content.

And a very special thanks to wonderful CG artists of London, UK.

Finally, thank you for picking up the book.

About the Author

Rising Polygon, founded by **Ravi Conor** aka **ROC, Elizabeth VT**, and **Gordon Fisher** is a group of like-minded professionals and freelancers who are specialized in advertising, graphic design, web design and development, digital marketing, multimedia, exhibition, print design, branding, and CG content creation.

ROC has over a decade of experience in the computer graphics field and although he is primarily a shading and texturing artist, he is also experienced in the fields of Dynamics, UVMapping, Lighting, and Rendering. Along side 3ds Max, ROC has experience with VRay, Maya, FumeFX, Mudbox, Mari, Photoshop, xNormal, UVLayout, Premiere, and After Effects.

Elizabeth is primarily an Android App developer. She is passionate about computer graphics and has an experience of over 6 years with 3ds Max, Maya, Photoshop, and Blender.

Gordon Fisher is the back bone of Rising Polygon and handles operations, finance, and accounts.

You can contact authors by sending an e-mail to the following Email ID: **rconor@risingpolygon.co.**

Preface

Why this Book?

The **Modeling and Texturing Techniques with 3ds Max 2017 - The Ultimate Beginner's Guide, 2nd Edition** textbook offers a hands-on exercises based strategy for all those digital artists who have just started working on the 3ds Max and interested in learning modeling and texturing in 3ds Max. This brilliant guide takes you step-by-step through the whole process of modeling and texturing. From the very first pages, the users of the book will learn how to effectively use 3ds Max for hard surface modeling and shading surfaces.

What you need?

To complete the examples and hands-on exercises in this book, you need 2017 version of Autodesk 3ds Max.

What are the main features of the book?

- The book is written using 3ds Max 2017 in an easy to understand language.
- Polygon and Spline modeling techniques covered.
- All modifiers explained.
- Shading and texturing techniques covered.
- 65 Hands-on exercises to hone your skills.
- Detailed coverage of tools and features.
- Additional tips, guidance, and advice is provided.
- Important terms are in bold face so that you never miss them.
- Support for technical aspect of the book.
- 3ds Max files and textures used are available for download from the accompanying website.

Is this book is available in e-Book format?

Yes. You can download the color e-Book from the Amazon's Kindle store.

How This Book Is Structured?

This book is divided into following units:

Unit MI1 - Introduction to 3ds Max - I

- Navigating the workspace
- Customizing the interface
- Understanding various UI components

- Working with the file management commands
- Setting preferences for 3ds Max
- Understanding workspaces
- Understanding the enhanced menu system
- Working with viewports
- Setting preferences for the viewports
- Creating objects in the scene
- Selecting objects
- Using the navigational gizmos
- Moving, rotating, and scaling objects
- Getting help
- Per-view Preferences, Creative Market Store, Asset Library, Print Studio, and Game Exporter

Unit MI2 - Introduction to 3ds Max - II
- Working with templates
- Creating clones and duplicates
- Understanding hierarchies
- Working with the **Scene** and **Layer** Explorers
- Understanding the **Mirror** tool, the **Select and Place** tool, and the **Select and Manipulate** tool
- Working with the Align tool and the Array tool
- Working with precision and drawing aids
- Understanding modifiers, and normals

Unit MM1 - Working with Geometric Primitives and Architectural Objects
- Creating and modifying Standard Primitives
- Creating and modifying Extended Primitives
- Working with the Architectural objects
- Setting the project folder
- Using the **Align** and **Mirror** tools
- Creating clones
- Using the **Scene Explorer**
- Creating a group
- Setting grid spacings
- Using **Transform Type-In** dialog
- Using **Array** dialog
- Specifying units for the scene

Unit MM2: Working with Polygons
- Working with the polygon modeling tools
- Using the polygon modeling techniques
- Selecting polygon sub-object

- Transforming sub-objects
- Soft selecting sub-objects

- Working with the **Graphite Modeling Tools**
- Selecting sub-objects
- Creating models using the tools available in the **Ribbon**

- Generate planar and 3d surfaces
- Paths and shapes for the loft components
- Generate extrusions
- Generate revolved surfaces
- Define motion path for animations

- Using modifiers
- Stack display
- Object-space modifiers vs World-space modifiers
- How transform affects modifiers
- Deformers

- Compact Material Editor
- Slate Material Editor

- General/Scanline materials
- General maps

- Autodesk Materials
- Arch & Design Material
- Physical Material

Examination Copies

Books received as examination copies are for review purposes only and may not be made available for student use. Resale of the examination copies is prohibited. If you want to receive this book as an examination copy, send the request from your official e-mail id to us using the **Contact** page of from our website.

Electronic Files

Any electronic file associated with this book are licensed to the original user only. These files can not be transferred to a third party. However, the original user can use these files in personal projects without taking any permission from **Rising Polygon**.

Trademarks

3ds Max is the registered trademarks of **Autodesk Inc. Windows** is the registered trademarks of **Microsoft Inc.**

Disclaimer

Access to Electronic Files

This book is sold via multiple sales channels. If you don't have access to the resources used in this book, you can place a request for the resources by visiting the following link: *bhttp://bit.ly/resources-rp*.

Customer Support

At **Rising Polygon**, our technical team is always ready to take care of your technical queries. If you are facing any problem with the technical aspect of the book, navigate to *http://bit.ly/contact-rp* and let us know about your query.

Reader Feedback

Your feedback is always welcome. Your feedback is critical to our efforts at **Rising Polygon** and it will help us in developing quality titles in the future. To send the feedback, visit *http://bit.ly/contact-rp*.

Errata

We take every precaution while preparing the content of the book but mistakes do happen. If you find any mistake in this book general or technical, we would be happy that you report it to us so that we can mention it in the errata section of the book's online page. If you find any errata, please report them by visiting the following link: *http://bit.ly/contact-rp*. This will help the other readers from frustration. Once your errata is verified, it will appear in the errata section of the book's online page.

Contact Author

Stay connected with us through Twitter (**@risingpolygon**) to know the latest updates about our products, information about books, and other related information. You can also send an e-mail to author at the following address: **rconor@risingpolygon.co**.

This page is intentionally left blank

Unit MI1: Introducing 3ds Max - I

Welcome to the latest version [2017] of **3ds Max**. In any 3D computer graphics application, the first thing you encounter is interface. Interface is where you view and work with your scene. The 3ds Max's interface is intuitive and highly customizable. You can make changes to the interface and then save multiple 3ds Max User Interface [UI] settings using the **Workspaces** feature. You can create multiple workspaces and switch between them easily.

In this release, Autodesk has modernized the interface using streamlined new icons. However, the icons look somewhat similar to the previous version. If you are long time user of 3ds Max, you will not have difficulties in identifying them. Autodesk has also refined the typography for a cleaner look.

In this unit, I'll describe the following:

- Understanding workspaces
- Navigating the workspace
- Customizing the interface
- Understanding various UI components
- Working with the file management commands
- Setting preferences for 3ds Max
- Understanding the enhanced menu system
- Working with viewports
- Setting preferences for the viewports
- Creating objects in the scene
- Selecting objects
- Using the navigational gizmos
- Moving, rotating, and scaling objects
- Getting help
- Per-view Preferences, Creative Market Store, Asset Library, Print Studio, and Game Exporter

Note: Interface Customization

By default, 3ds Max starts with a dark theme [white text on the dark gray background]. This is good for those digital artists who spend hours working on 3ds Max, however, the default theme is not good for printing. I have customized the theme so that the captures appear fine when book is printed. You can easily switch between the custom color themes from the **Choose initial settings for tool options and UI layout** *dialog. To open this dialog, choose* **Custom UI and Default Switcher** *from the* **Customize** *menu.*

The 3ds Max's interface is now **HDPI** [High Dots Per Inch] aware. Now, Windows scaling is correctly applied when interface appears on high DPI monitors and laptops. If you are working on a ultra-high resolution monitor, the 3ds Max's icons may appear small. You can scale the interface from the Windows control panel. Here's the process on Windows 7.

RMB click on your **Desktop** and choose **Screen Resolution** from the popup menu. On the window displayed, choose **Make text and other items larger or smaller**. Now, you can choose a preset value from the page [see Figure F1]. If you want to create a custom text size, click **Set custom size (DPI)** from the left of the page [see Figure F1]. Now, click drag the scale on the **Custom DPI Setting** dialog to change the scale [see Figure F2]. Click **OK** to accept the settings.

When you first time open the 3ds Max application, you will see the **Select your initial 3ds Max experience** window [see Figure F3]. You can set default template for your 3ds Max scenes from this window. Select the desired template and then click **Continue** to open the default workspace with the **Welcome Screen** [see Figure F4]. There are three panels available in the **Welcome Screen: Learn, Start**, and **Extend**.

The content of the **Start** panel appears by default in the **Welcome Screen**. From the **RECENT FILES** section of this panel, you can open the recent files you have worked on. Also, you can look for files on your storage device by clicking the **Browse** button. On the right of the **Start** panel, you will see some templates in the **START-UP TEMPLATES** section and a link to open the **Template Manager**. You can use the **Template Manager** to inspect and edit existing templates.

F3

F4 Show this Welcome Screen at startup

Learn   Start   Extend

To create a new scene, choose a template and then click **New Using Selected Template**. A new scene will be created with the settings specified by that template. I will explain templates in details in the **Unit MI2**. The **Learn** panel [see Figure F5] contains list of **1-Minute Startup Movies** that you can view to learn the basics of some 3ds Max features. When you select a movie from the list, you are taken to a web page where the movie is being played. In the **More Learning Resources** section, there are four links for navigating to 3ds Max Learning Channel, what's new page, learning path page, and downloading the sample content.

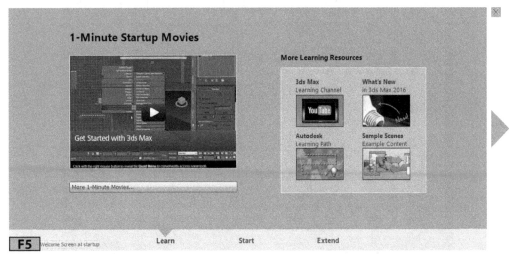

The **Extend** panel [see Figure F6] features ways to extend capabilities of 3ds Max. This panel displays featured apps from the **Autodesk Exchange Store**. It also contains list of useful Autodesk resources.

Note: Welcome Screen

*If you don't want to see the **Welcome Screen** when next time you open 3ds Max, turn off **Show this Welcome Screen at startup**. You can bring back the screen anytime by choosing **Welcome Screen** from the **Help** menu.*

Close the **Welcome Screen** to view the default UI of 3ds Max [refer Figure F7].

Notice, I have marked different components of the UI with numbers to make the learning process easier. In 3ds Max, commands and tools are arranged in groups so that you can find them easily. For example, all viewport navigation tools are grouped together on the bottom-right corner of the interface [marked as 12 in Figure F7]. The 3ds Max interface can be divided into 12 sections. I have marked those sections in Figure F7. Table 1 summarizes the numbers and the sections of the UI they represent.

Table 1: 3ds Max interface overview

No.	Item	Description
1	Application Button	On clicking this button, the **Application** menu appears. This menu contains file management commands.
2	Quick Access Toolbar	This toolbar gives access to the file handling and undo/redo commands. It also contains a drop-down that lets you switch among different workspaces.
3	Main Toolbar	This toolbar provides many commonly used tools.
4	The Ribbon	The **Ribbon** contains many tools for modeling and painting in the scene. Also, here you will find tools for adding people to populate a scene.
5	Scene Explorer	The **Scene Explorer** lets you view, sort, filter, and select objects in a scene. You can also use it to rename, delete, hide, and freeze objects. It is also used to create and amend object hierarchies.
6	Status Bar Controls	The **Status Bar** contains the prompt and status information about the scene. The Coordinate Transform Type-In boxes in the **Status Bar** let you transform the objects manually.

7	Viewport Label Menus	These menus let you change the shading style for the viewport. They also contain other viewport related commands and features.
8	Time Slider	Allows you to navigate along the timeline.
9	Viewports	Viewports let you view your scene from multiple angles. They also allow you to preview lighting, shading, shadows, and other effects.
10	Command Panel	The **Command Panel** is the nerve center of 3ds Max. It contains six panels that you can use to create and modify objects in 3ds Max.
11	Create and Play Back Animation	These controls affect the animation. This area also contains buttons to playback animation in the viewports.
12	Viewport Navigation	These buttons allow you to navigate your scene [Active Viewport].
13	Rollout	Rollouts are used to change properties of the object in 3ds Max.

There are some other elements of the interface that are not visible in the default UI. These elements appear when you run a command from the **Main** toolbar or menu, or choose an option from the RMB click menu. Here's is the quick rundown to those elements:

■ **Floating Toolbars**: There are quite a few floating toolbars available in 3ds Max. To access these toolbar, RMB click on a gray area on the toolbar to open a popup menu [see Figure F8] containing the options for invoking the floating toolbars. The popup menu shown in Figure F8 displayed when I RMB clicked on the gray area below the **Named Selection Sets** drop-down on the **Main** toolbar. The area is marked with an arrow in Figure F8. When I chose **MassFx Toolbar** from the popup menu, the floating **Mass FX Toolbar** appeared [see Figure F9].

■ **Quad Menus**: Whenever you RMB click in an active viewport [except on a viewport label], 3ds Max opens a **Quad** menu at the location of the mouse pointer. The **Quad** menu can display up to four quadrants [see Figure F10] with various commands and allows you to work efficiently as the commands in the menu are context-sensitive. The **Quad** menu is the quickest way to find commands.

Figure F10 shows a **Quad** menu which appeared when I RMB clicked on an **Editable Poly** object in the viewport.

■ **Caddy Controls**: A caddy control in 3ds Max can be described as **"in-canvas"** interface that comprises a dynamic label and an array of buttons superimposed over a viewport. You can use the standard mouse operations such as clicking and dragging to change the values in the spinners.

The changes you made are immediately updated in the viewport. The **Chamfer** caddy control shown in Figure F11 appeared when I selected edges of a box and then clicked **Chamfer's** settings button on the **Command Panel**.

■ **Dialogs, Windows, and Editors**: Some of the commands in 3ds Max opens dialogs, editors, and windows. Some of these elements have their own menu bars and toolbars. Figure F12 shows the **Slate Material Editor**. You can use the **M** hotkey to open this editor.

Note: Spinners
*Spinners are found everywhere in 3ds Max [I have marked **U** and **V** spinners with black rectangle in Figure F12]. Spinners are controllers that you will touch on regular basis. They allow you to quickly amend numerical values with ease. To change the value in a spinner, click the up or down arrow on the right of the spinner. To change values quickly, click and drag the arrows. You can also type a value directly in the spinner's field.*

Tip: Fast and slow scroll rate in a spinner
*Press and hold **Alt** and then click–drag the spinner's up or down arrow for a slower numerical scroll rate. Hold **Ctrl** for the faster scroll rate. RMB click on a spinner to set it to its default value.*

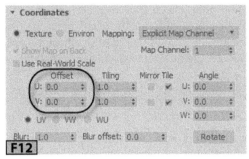

F12

Note: Numerical Expression Evaluator

If the type cursor is located inside a spinner and you press Ctrl+N, the Numerical Expression Evaluator appears [see Figure F13]. This evaluator lets you calculate the value for the spinner using an expression. For example, if you type 30+50 in this evaluator's field and click Paste, 80 appears in the associated spinner.

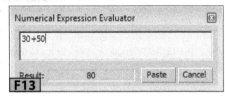

F13

Note: Modeless dialogs, controls, windows, and editors

Quite a few dialogs in 3ds Max are modeless meaning the dialog doesn't need to be closed in order to work on other elements of the interface. A good example of modeless dialog is the Slate Material Editor. You can minimize the editor and continue working on the scene. Other modeless dialogs that you would frequently use are Transform Type-In dialogs, Caddy controls, Render Scene dialog, and so forth.

Tip: Toggling the visibility of all open dialogs

You can toggle visibility of all open dialogs by using the Ctrl+~ hotkeys.

UI Components

The following section presents what you need to know about 3ds Max UI.

Caption Bar

The **Caption** bar is another name for the **Title** bar. It is the topmost element in the 3ds Max UI [see Figure F14].

F14

The **Title** bar hosts the **Application** button, **Quick Access Toolbar**, **Workspaces** drop-down, and **InfoCenter**. It also displays the name of the current 3ds Max file.

Quick Access Toolbar

This toolbar provides most commonly used file-management commands as well as commands for **Undo** and **Redo**. It also contains a drop-down that allows you to switch between different workspaces. Table 2 summarizes the interface of the **Quick Access Toolbar**.

Table 2: The Quick Access Toolbar interface		
Item	**Icon**	**Description**
New Scene		Click to create a new scene.

Open File		Click to open a saved file from the storage.
Save File		Click to save file to the disk.
Undo Scene Operation		Click to undo the previous operation. Click the arrow on the right of the button to open a list of previous operations performed in the scene. Hotkeys: **Ctrl+Z**.
Redo Scene Operation		Click to redo the previous operation. Hotkeys: **Ctrl+Y**.
Project Folder		Click to open the **Browse For Folder** dialog to set a project folder for the scene.
Workspaces drop-down list	Workspace: Default	Click to open the options available for managing and switching workspaces.
Quick Access toolbar drop-down		Click to display options to manage the **Quick Access Toolbar**.

Q. Can I remove a button from the Quick Access Toolbar?

Yes. RMB click on a button on the toolbar and then choose **Remove from Quick Access Toolbar** [see Figure F15]. You can also add any button from the **Ribbon** to the **Quick Access Toolbar** by RMB clicking on the button and then choosing **Add To Quick Access Toolbar** [see Figure F16].

Q. Is there any place in the UI from where I can access file management commands?

Yes. You can access file management commands from the **Application** menu. To open the menu, click the **Application** button. You can also open the menu using the **Alt+F** hotkeys. When you press **Alt+F**, 3ds Max superimposes hotkeys on the corresponding **Application** menu items [see Figure F17].

Now, for example, if you want to reset the scene, press **Atl+F+R**. To open the **Preferences** dialog, press **Alt+F+C**. To exit 3ds Max, press **Alt+F+X**.

Q. What's the function of the Reset command?

This command clears all data as well resets 3ds Max settings such as viewport configuration, snap settings, **Material Editor**, background image, and so forth. If you have done some customization during the current session of the 3ds Max, and you execute the **Reset** command, all startup defaults will be restored according to the setting stored in the **maxstrat.max** file.

Q. How can I use maxstart.max?

You can use this file to make the changes you would like to see at the startup. Start 3ds Max and make the adjustments. Then, save file in the **scenes** folder with the name **maxstrat.max**.

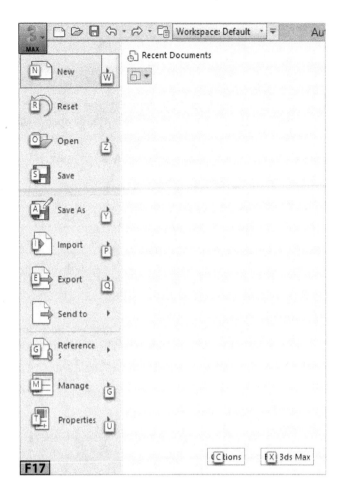

Note: Templates

If you reset the scene, it will also affect the template that you had used to open the scene. The template will be reset back to its default settings.

Q. How can I change the undo levels?

You can change it from the **Preferences** dialog. By default, 3ds Max allows only **20** levels for the undo operations. To change it, choose **Preferences** from the **Customize** menu. On the **General** panel of the dialog, you can set **Levels** from the **Scene Undo** group.

Q. What's the use of the Preferences dialog?

The **Preferences** dialog contains options that 3ds Max offers for its operations. 3ds Max behaves according to the options you set in the **Preferences** dialog. You have just seen an example how you can change the undo levels. If you increase the number of levels, you force 3ds Max to obey that setting. The **Preferences** dialog comprises many panels with lots of options that you can use.

Tip: The Preferences dialog

*You can also open the **Preferences** dialog by clicking **Options** from the **Application** menu.*

Q. Can I undo all commands in 3ds Max?

No. You cannot undo commands such as saving a file or using the **Collapse** utility. If you know an action cannot be undone, first hold you scene by choosing **Hold** from the **Edit** menu [Hotkeys: **Ctrl+H**]. When you want to recall, choose **Fetch** from the **Edit** menu [Hotkeys: **Alt+Ctrl+F**].

Q. Why do I need a project folder?

When you work on a project, you have to deal with many scenes, texture files, third party data, rendering, material libraries, and so forth. If you don't organize the data for the project, it would be very difficult for you to manage the assets for the project. The project folder allows you to organize all your files in a folder for a particular project. You can also set a project by choosing **Manage | Set Project Folder** from the **Application** menu.

Q. What is the Workspaces feature?

This feature allows you to quickly switch between the different arrangement of panels, toolbars, menus, viewports, and other interface elements. Figure F18 shows the UI when **Default with Enhanced Menu** workspace is chosen. Choose **Reset To Default State** from the **Workspaces** drop-down to rest the workspace to the saved settings of the active workspace. On choosing the **Manage Workspaces** from the **Workspaces** drop-down, the **Manage Workspaces** dialog appears [see Figure F19] from where you can switch, add, edit, and delete workspaces.

Q. What are enhanced menus?

3ds Max offers two types of menu systems for the menu bar: **Standard** menu [default] and the **Enhanced** menu. The menu bar is located directly under the main interface window's **Title** bar.

The default menu system follows the standard **Windows** conventions. When you click on a menu item on the menu bar, a pulldown menu appears. The menu in Figure F17 appeared when I clicked **Edit** on the menu bar. Notice that hotkeys are displayed next to some of the commands. You can use these hotkeys to execute the command without invoking the menu. For example, to select all objects in a scene, you can press **Ctrl+A**. Not all the commands are available all the time. These commands are context-sensitive. If a command is not available, it is grayed out in the menu, for example, see the **Fetch** command in Figure F20. If a black triangle appears [for example, the **Selection Region** command in the **Edit** menu] on the next to a menu command, it indicates that a sub-menu exists. Place the mouse pointer on the command to view the sub-menu.

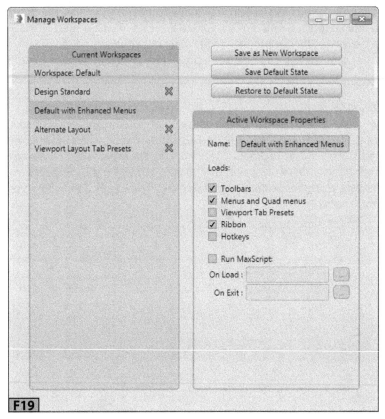

F19

Tip: Menu hotkey
*You can use the keyboard [**Alt** key] to invoke a pulldown menu. Press **Alt**, 3ds Max displays the hotkey with an underline for the menu items. For example, to invoke the **Edit** pull-down menu, press **Alt+E**. Similarly, for the **Customize** menu, press **Alt+U**.*

Tip: Hiding menu bar
*If for some reason, you want to hide the menu bar, RMB click on the menu bar then click **Show Menu Bar** from the pop-up menu. To recover the menu back, click on the arrow located on the right of the **Workspaces** drop-down [see Figure F21] and then choose **Show Menu Bar**. You can also hide menu bar from the **Quick Access Toolbar** menu.*

The **Enhanced** menu system provides some additional features such as configurable display, link to relevant help topics, enhanced tool tips, and drag and drop menu categories. You can also search for the menu commands. The image at the left of Figure F22 shows standard **Rendering** menu whereas the image at the right of Figure F22 shows enhanced **Rendering** menu.

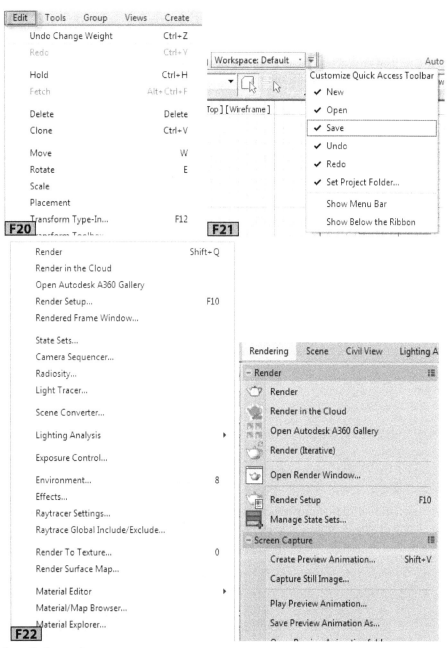

Tip: Toggling Enhanced menu

*You can toggle the enhanced menu by using the **Enhanced Menu** command. To access this command, press **X** to open the **Search All Action** dialog and then type **enh** in the field available in this dialog [see Figure F23]. The **Enhanced Menus** command appears in the list. Click it to open the enhanced menu sytem.*

Here's is a quick run down to the various functions available for the **Enhanced** menu system:

■ You can collapse or expand each panel in a menu. When collapsed, a **+** icon appears on the title bar. When expanded a **-** icon appears on the title bar [refer Figure F24]. When you position the mouse pointer on the title bar of a collapsed menu, a sub-menu appears with the content of the collapsed menu [refer Figure F24].

Note: Restoring menu settings
3ds Max remembers all settings of collapsed or expanded states of the menu and it restores them when you reopen 3ds Max.

■ You can view the content of a menu as icon, text, or icon+text. To toggle the view mode, click on the icon at the top-right end of the title bar [see Figure F25].

■ To view the detailed tooltip that provides a brief description of a menu command, position the mouse pointer on the menu option, a tool tip appears [see Figure F26]. If you want to see help documentation about the command under the mouse pointer, press **F1**.

■ You can also float a menu panel or submenu. Drag the title bar of the panel away from the menu to make it a floating panel [see Figure F27].

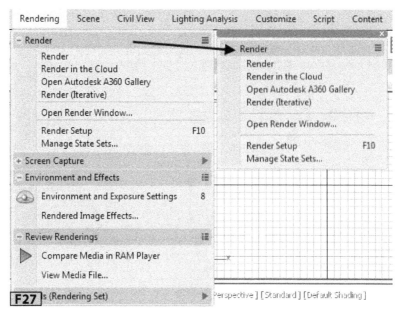

■ You can also merge the floating panels. Drag title bar of a panel to the bottom or top of the target panel, a blue line appears [see the image at the left of Figure F28]. Release the mouse button to dock the two panels [see the image at the right of Figure F28].

■ You can also search a menu command from the menu. Type the name of the command when the menu is active. A text box appears at top of the menu when you start typing. As you type, menu shows the command matching with the string you have typed [see Figure F29].

Viewports

In 3ds Max, you will be doing most of the work in viewports. Viewports are openings into 3D space you work. A viewport represents 3D space using the **Cartesian** coordinates system. The coordinate are expressed using three numbers such as **[10, 10, 20]**. These number represent points in 3D space. The origin is always at **[0, 0, 0]**. By default, 3ds Max displays a four viewport arrangement: **Top**, **Front**, **Left**, and **Perspective**. The **Top**, **Front**, and **Left** are known as orthographic views. 3ds Max provides many options to change the viewport as well as the layout. Using multiple viewports can help you visualize the scene better.

Q. What do you mean by an Orthographic View?

Most of the 3D designs created using computer relies on the 2D representation of the designs. Some examples of the 2D representations are maps, elevations, and plans. Even to create a character model, you first design it on paper [front, side, and back views] [see Figure F30] and then create 3D model using these designs.

F30

Note:

Blueprint Courtesy: *http://www.the-blueprints.com*

In laymen terms, you can think of the orthographic views as flat, or straight on. The orthographic views are two dimensional views. Each dimension is defined by two world coordinate axes. Combination of these two axes produce three sets of orthographic views: **Top and Bottom, Front and Back**, and **Left and Right**. Figure F31 shows a model in three orthographic views [**Top, Right**, and **Left**] and in **Perspective** view.

F31

You can change a viewport to various orthographic views using the controls available in the **Point-Of-View (POV)** viewport label menu. The **Perspective** view on the other hand closely resembles with the human view. In 3ds Max there are three ways to create a perspective view: Perspective view, camera view, and light view.

Q. Can you tell me little more about Viewport Label menus and how can I change a viewport to the orthographic views?

Notice on top-left corner of a viewport, there are three labels. Figure F32 shows labels on the **Perspective** viewport. Each label is clickable [click or RMB click]. When you click on any of the labels, a popup menu appears.

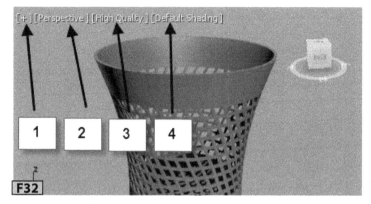

The left most menu is the **General Viewport** label menu [marked as 1], in the middle is the **Point-Of-View [POV]** viewport label menu [marked as 2], and on the right is **Lights and Shadows** viewport label menu [marked as 3]. The right most menu is the **Shading** viewport label menu [marked as 4]. The **General Viewport** label menu comprises controls for overall viewport display or activation. It also gives you access to the **Viewport Configuration** dialog. The **POV Viewport** label menu provides options mainly for changing the viewports. To change a viewport, for example, to change the **Top** viewport to **Bottom** viewport, make sure the **Top** viewport is active and then click or RMB click on the **POV Viewport** label menu. Now, choose **Bottom** from the menu. You can also use the hotkey **B**. Table 3 summarizes the hotkeys that you can use to change the viewports.

Table 3: The hotkeys for switching the viewports	
View	**Hotkey**
Top	I
Bottom	B
Front	F
Left	L
Camera	C
Orthographic	U
Perspective	P

The **Lights and Shadows** menu lets you adjust the behavior of the lights and shadows in the viewport. You can also adjust quality settings from this menu.

The **Shading Viewport** menu lets you control how objects are displayed in the viewport. I will discuss the options in this menu later in the unit.

Q. What is active viewport?

An active viewport is where all actions take place in 3ds Max. One viewport is always active in 3ds Max marked with a highlighted border. To switch the active viewport, you can use any of the three mouse buttons. It is recommended that you use the middle mouse button for making a viewport active as LMB and RMB clicks are also associated with other command in 3ds Max.

When viewports are not maximized, you can press the **Windows** key and **Shift** on the keyboard to cycle the active viewport. When one of the view is maximized, pressing **Windows** key and **Shift** displays the available viewports [see Figure F33] and then you can press **Shift** repeatedly with the **Windows** key held down to cycle among viewports. When you release the keys, the chosen viewport becomes the maximized viewport.

[Perspective] [High Quality]
Use Win+Shift for Viewport Cycling

F33

You can save an active viewport in the internal buffer and later restore it. It useful when you want to frame a shot in any view other than a camera view. One view each can be saved for the following viewports: **Top**, **Bottom**, **Left**, **Right**, **Front**, **Back**, **Orthographic**, and **Perspective**. To save an active view, for example the **Perspective** view, activate it with the zoom level you want to save and then choose **Save Active Perspective View** from the **Views** menu. To restore the view, make the **Perspective** view active and then choose **Restore Active Perspective View** from the **Views** menu. The saved active view is saved with the scene file.

Q. How can I change the viewport configuration like the one shown in Figure F31?

The **Viewport Layouts** bar lets you quickly switch among different types of viewport layouts. This bar generally docked on the left of the viewports [see Figure F34]. If it is not visible, RMB click on the **Main** toolbar and then choose **Viewport Layout Tabs** [see Figure F35]. To change the layout, click on the arrow on the bar to open a flyout and then click on the desired layout to make it active. You can also change the layout using the **General Viewport** label menu. Click on the label and then choose **Configure Viewports**. The **Viewport Configuration** dialog appears [see Figure F36]. Select the **Layout** panel and then choose the desired layout. Now, click **OK** to accept the changes.

Customize...

✓ Command Panel
✓ Ribbon
✓ Viewport Layout Tabs
　 Brush Presets
✓ Main Toolbar
　 Axis Constraints
　 Layers
　 State Sets
　 Extras
　 Render Shortcuts
　 Snaps
　 Animation Layers
　 Containers
　 MassFX Toolbar

F34

F35

F36

Q. I can see a grid in each viewport, how can I use it?

The grid you see in each viewport is one of the three planes [along the X, Y, and Z axes] that intersect at the right angles to each other at a common point called **origin** [X=O, Y=O, and Z=O]. The three planes based on the world coordinate axes are called **home grid**. To help you easily position objects on the grid, one plane of the home grid is visible in each viewport. The grid acts as a construction plane when you create objects on it.

Tip: Turning off grid
*You can turn off the grid in the active viewport by pressing the **G** hotkey.*

Command Panel

The **Command Panel** is the nerve center of 3ds Max. It comprises of six panels that give you access to most of the modeling tools, animation features, display choices, and utilities. Table 4 summarizes the panels in the **Command Panel**.

Table 4: Different panels in the **Command Panel**	
Panel	**Description**
Create	Contains controls for creating object such as geometry, lights, cameras, and so forth.
Modify	Contains controls for editing objects as well as for applying modifiers to the objects.
Hierarchy	Contains controls for managing links in the hierarchy, joints, and inverse kinematics.
Motion	Contains controls for animation controllers and trajectories.
Display	Contains controls that lets you hide/unhide objects. It also contains display options.
Utilities	Contains different utility programs.

Rollouts

Most of the controls in the **Command Panel** live inside rollouts. A rollout is a group of controls, a section of the **Command Panel** that shows parameters of the selected object. You can collapse the rollouts. When you collapse them, only the title bar of the rollout appears. Figure F37 shows the **Parameters** rollout of the **Box** primitive in the **Modify** panel of the **Command Panel**.

Once you create a box in the viewport, you can modify its parameters such as **Length** and **Width** using the **Parameters** rollout. Each rollout has a title bar that you can click to collapse or expand the rollout. You can also change the default position of the rollout by dragging the dots located on the right of the title and dropping on another place when a blue line appears [see Figure F38].

By default, the rollout occupies a single column space in UI. However, you can increase the numbers of columns by dragging the left most edge of the panel. You can create as many columns as you want [see Figure 35] as long the screen real state is available. Multiple columns are helpful when you are working with an object with which many rollouts are associated.

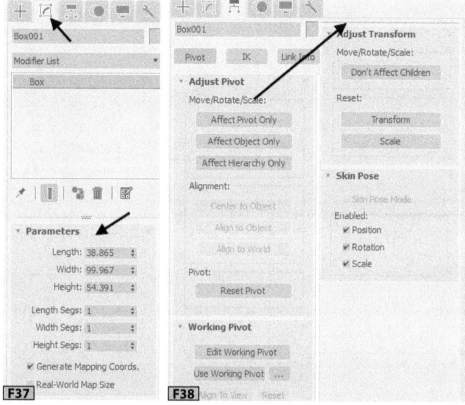

F37   **F38**

If you RMB click on a rollout [**on the empty gray area**], a popup menu appears [see Figure F39]. This popup allows you to open or close all rollouts at once, or close the rollout on which you RMB clicked.

In the bottom section of the popup menu, you will see a list of rollouts available for the selected object. No tick appears for the collapsed rollouts.

If you have changed order of the rollouts, you can rest the order by choosing **Reset Rollout Order** from the bottom of the menu.

If you have expanded the **Command Panel** to more than one column and you RMB click on a rollout, only those rollouts appear on the popup menu that are in the column [see Figure F40].

Tip: The default value for the spinners
*The nature of the spinners in 3ds Max is persistence meaning that value specified for the spinners remains set for the current spinners. For example, if you created a **Sphere** primitive with **64** segments. When you create the next sphere, the value **64** will be default for it. To reset spinners to their default values, choose **Reset** from the **Application** menu.*

Main Toolbar

The **Main** toolbar comprises commonly used tools and dialog. Table 5 summarizes the tools available in the **Main** toolbar.

Item	Icon	Description
Table 5: The **Main** toolbar interface overview		
Undo/Redo		Undo reverses the last command. Redo reverses the last undo command.
Select and Link		Defines the hierarchical relationship [links] between two objects.
Unlink Selection		Removes the hierarchical relationship between two objects.
Bind to Space Warp		Attaches the current selection to a space warp or vice versa.
Selection Filter List		Limits the selection to specific types and combinations of objects.

Select Object		Selects objects and sub-objects. Hotkey: **Q**.
Select by Name		Allows you to select specific objects from a list of objects using the **Select from Scene** dialog. **Hotkey: H.**
Selection Region Flyout		Allows you to select objects within a region using different methods. You can create different marquee shapes using the options available in this flyout.
Window/Crossing Selection Toggle		Switch between window and crossing methods for selection.
Select and Move		Selects and moves objects. Hotkey: **W**.
Select and Rotate		Selects and rotates objects. Hotkey: **E**.
Select and Scale		Selects and scales objects. Hotkey: **R** to cycle.
Select and Place Flyout		Position an object accurately on the surface of another object.
Reference Coordinate System	Local ▼ View Screen World Parent Local Gimbal Grid Working Local Aligned Pick	Specifies the coordinate system used for a transformations (Move, Rotate, and Scale).

Use Center Flyout		Specifies geometric centers for scale and rotate transformations.
Select and Manipulate		Select objects and allows editing of the parameters for certain objects, modifiers, and controllers by dragging "manipulators" in viewports.
Keyboard Shortcut Override Toggle		Allows you to toggle between using only the "Main User Interface" hotkeys or using both the main hotkeys and hotkeys for groups such as Edit/Editable Mesh, Track View, NURBS, and so on.
2D Snap, 2.5D Snap, 3D Snap		Specify the snap types. Hotkey: **S** to cycle.
Angle Snap Toggle		Enables angle increment snap for rotation. It allows you to snap rotations to certain angles. Hotkey: **A**.
Percent Snap Toggle		Toggles increments scaling of objects by the specified percentage. Hotkeys: **Shift+Ctrl+P**.
Spinner Snap Toggle		Sets the single-click increment or the decrement value for all of the spinners in 3ds Max.
Edit Named Selection Sets		Displays the **Edit Named Selections** dialog, letting you manage named selection sets of sub-objects
Named Selection Sets	Create Selection Se ▼	Allows you to name a selection set and recall the selection for later use.
Mirror		Enables you to move and clone selected objects while reflecting their orientation.
Align Flyout		Gives you access to six different tools for alignment. Hotkeys: Align [**Alt+A**], and Normal Align [**Alt+N**].

Toggle Scene Explorer		Toggles the **Scene Explorer**.
Toggle Layer Explorer		Toggles the **Layer Explorer**.
Toggle Ribbon		Expands or collapses the **Ribbon**.
Curve Editor (Open)		Opens the **Track View - Curve Editor**.
Schematic View (Open)		Opens the **Schematic View** window.
Material Editor flyout		Opens the **Material Editor** that provides functions to create and edit materials and maps.
Render Setup		Opens the **Render Setup** dialog. Hotkey: **F10**.
Rendered Frame Window		Opens the **Rendered Frame Window** that displays rendered output.
Render Production		Renders the scene using the current production render settings without opening the **Render Setup** dialog.
Render Iterative		Renders the scene in iterative mode without opening the **Render Setup** dialog.
ActiveShade		Creates an **ActiveShade** rendering in a floating window.
Render in the cloud		Uses the **A360 Cloud** to render your scene.
Open Autodesk A360 Gallery		Opens a web page that showcases **A360 Cloud** renderings.

Docking and Floating Toolbars

3ds Max allows you to dock and float toolbars. You have already seen an example of the floating toolbar [**Mass FX Toolbar**]. By default, the **Main** toolbar is docked below the menu bar. If you want to undock it, position the mouse pointer in the double vertical lines located at the extreme left of the **Main** toolbar [also available at the extreme right]; the shape of the mouse pointer changes [see Figure F41]. Now, click and drag away and drop when the shape of the mouse pointer changes to a window icon [see Figure F42] to float the **Main** toolbar. Once the toolbar appears as a floating panel [see Figure F43], you can resize it as you resize any other panel on **Windows** operating system.

You can doc the **Main** toolbar back to its last position by double clicking on the title of the floating panel. Similarly, you can float any toolbar, window, or panel [like **Command Panel**, **Scene Explorer**, and **Ribbon**] in 3ds Max.

Tip: Main toolbar visibility toggle
*You can quickly toggle the display of the **Main** toolbar by using the **Alt+6** hotkeys.*

If you RMB click on the title of a floating toolbar, window, or panel. Or, on the vertical or horizontal lines of a toolbar, window, or panel; a pop menu appears with the options to doc that element [see Figure F44].

These options allow you to doc an element on the top, bottom, left, or the right of the interface. However, you can rearrange the interface elements as per you need. For example, if you are a leftie, you would like the **Command Panel** on the left and the **Scene Explorer** on the right. For example, to doc the **Command Panel** on the left, position the mouse pointer on the top right corner of the panel until the shape of the pointer changes [see Figure F45].

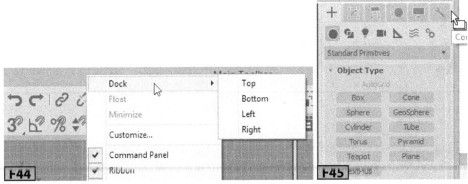

Drag the **Command Panel** to the left of the **Scene Explorer** when the shape of the cursor changes to the one shown in Figure F46 to doc the **Command Panel** on the left [see Figure F47].

Tip: Resetting Workspace
*After experimenting with the rearrangement of panels, you can reset the original positions of the elements by choosing **Reset to Default State** from the **Workspaces** drop-down.*

Note: Quick Access Toolbar
*The **Quick Access Toolbar** and **InfoCenter** toolbar cannot be undocked from the 3ds Max UI.*

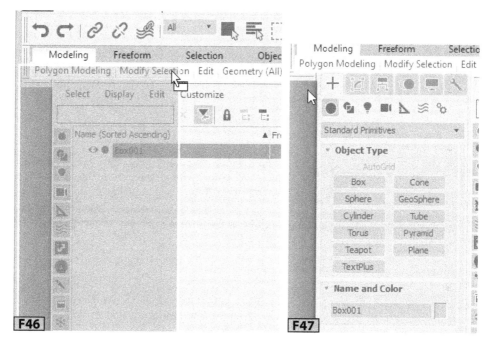

F46   F47

Main Toolbar Flyouts

You might have noticed a small triangle on the lower right corner of some buttons in the **Main** toolbar. Click on hold on such a button to expand a flyout with additional buttons. Figure F48 shows the **Selection Region** flyout.

Ribbon

Ribbon [see Figure F49], is available below the **Main** toolbar. The **Ribbon** appears in collapsed state by default. To expand it, double-click on it. You can toggle the display of the **Ribbon** by clicking **Toggle Ribbon** from the **Main** toolbar.

F48

It contains many tabs. The content in the tabs is depended on the context. The items displayed may vary according to the selected sub-objects. I will cover **Ribbon** in a later unit in the book.

F49

Most of the tools are only visible in the **Ribbon** when you are editing a poly object. You will learn about **Ribbon** and poly modeling techniques in a later unit.

Animation and Time Controls

The animation controls are found on the left of the **Viewport Navigation** controls [see Figure F50].

Two other controls that are vital to animation are **Time Slider** and **Track Bar** [see Figure F51]. These controls are available below the viewports. The **Time Slider** works with the **Track Bar** to allow you to view and edit animation. The sliders shows the current frame and the total number of frames in the range. The **Track Bar** shows the frame numbers and allows you to move, copy, and delete keys.

F50

F51

Table 6 summarizes the animation controls.

Table 6: The animation controls

Item	Icon	Description
Auto Key Animation Mode, Set Key Animation Mode		The Auto Key Animation Mode toggles the keyframing mode called **Auto Key**. Set Key Animation Mode allows you to create keys for selected objects individual tracks using a combination of the **Set Keys** button and **Key Filters**.
Selection List		Provides quick access to **Named Selection Sets** and track sets.
Default In/Out Tangents for New Keys		This flyout provides a quick way to set a default tangent type for new animation keys.
Key Filters		Opens the **Set Key Filters** dialog where you can specify the tracks on which keys are created.
Go To Start		Moves the time slider to the first frame of the active time segment.
Previous Frame/Key		Moves the time slider back one frame.
Play/Stop		The Play button plays the animation in the active viewport. You can stop the playback by clicking on the button again.
Next Frame/Key		Moves the time slider ahead one frame.
Go To End		Moves the time slider to the last frame of the active time segment.
Current Frame (Go To Frame)		Displays the number or time of the current frame, indicating the position of the time slider.
Key Mode		Allows you jump directly between keyframes in your animation.
Time Configuration		Open the **Time Configuration** dialog that allows you to specify the settings for the animation.

Viewport Navigational Controls

The **Viewport Navigation Controls** are located at the right end of the status bar [see Figure F52].

F52

The controls in the **Viewport Navigational Controls** depend on the type of viewport [Perspective, orthographic, camera, or light] active. Some of the buttons have a little black triangle at the right bottom corner. The arrow indicates that there are some hidden buttons exist. To view them, press and hold the LMB on the button. When a button is active, it is highlighted, to deactivate it, press **ESC**, choose another tool, or RMB click in a viewport.

Table 7 shows the controls available for all viewports. Table 8 shows the controls available for perspective and orthographic views. Table 9 shows the controls available for the camera views. Table 10 shows the controls available for the camera views.

Table 7: The viewport navigational controls available for all viewports		
Item	**Icon**	**Description**
Zoom Extents All, Zoom Extents All Selected		Allow you to zoom selected objects or all objects to their extent in the viewport.
Maximize Viewport Toggle		It switches any active viewport between its normal size and full-screen size. Hotkeys: **Alt+W**.

Table 8: The viewport navigational controls available for perspective and orthographic views		
Item	**Icon**	**Description**
Zoom		Allows you to change the magnification by dragging in a Perspective or orthographic viewport. Hotkeys: **Alt+Z**. You can also use the bracket keys, [and].
Zoom All		Allows you adjust view magnification in all Perspective and orthographic viewports at the same time.
Zoom Extents/Zoom Extents Selected		**Zoom Extents** centers all visible objects in an active Perspective or orthographic viewport until it fills the viewport. Hotkeys: **Ctrl+Alt+Z**. Zoom Extents Selected centers a selected object, or set of objects. Hotkey:**Z**.
Field-of-View Button (Perspective) or Zoom Region		**Field-of-View** adjusts the amount of the scene that is visible in a viewport. It's only available in the Perspective viewport. Hotkeys: **Ctrl+W**. **Zoom Region** magnifies a rectangular area you drag within a viewport.
Pan View		**Pan View** moves the view parallel to the current viewport plane. Hotkeys: **Ctrl+P**.
Walk Through		Allows you to move through a viewport by pressing arrow keys. Hotkey: **Up Arrow**.
Orbit, Orbit Selected, Orbit Sub-Object		**Orbit** rotates the viewport and uses the view center as the center of rotation. Hotkeys: **Ctrl+R**. **Orbit Selected** uses the center of the current selection as the center of rotation. **Orbit Sub-object** uses the center of the current sub-object selection as the center of rotation.

Table 9: The viewport navigational controls available for camera views

Item	Icon	Description
Dolly Camera, Target, or Both		This flyout replaces the **Zoom** button when the **Camera** viewport is active. Use these tools to move camera and/ or its target along the camera main axis.
Perspective		It performs a combination of FOV and Dolly for target cameras and free cameras.
Roll Camera		Rotates a free camera around its local Z-axis.
Field-of-View Button		Adjusts the amount of the scene that is visible in a viewport
Truck Camera		Moves the camera parallel to the view plane.
Walk Through		Allows you move through a viewport by pressing a set of shortcut keys.
Orbit/Pan Camera		**Orbit Camera** rotates a camera about the target. **Pan Camera** rotates the target about the camera.

Table 10: The viewport navigational controls available for light views

Item	Icon	Description
Dolly Light, Target, or Both		Moves the light or its target or both along the light's main axis, toward or away from what the light is pointing at.
Light Hotspot		Allows you adjust the angle of a light's hotspot.
Roll Light		Roll Light rotates the light about its own line of sight (the light's local Z axis).
Light Falloff		Adjusts the angle of a light's falloff.
Truck Light		Moves a target light and its target parallel to the light view, and moves a free light in its XY plane.
Orbit/Pan Light		Rotates a light about the target. **Pan Light** rotates the target about the light.

Interaction Mode Preferences

If you are an **Autodesk Maya** user then it's good news for you that you can change the interaction mode to **Maya**. The **Interaction Mode** panel of the **Preferences** dialog box [see Figure F53] allows you to set the mouse and keyboard shortcut according to **3ds Max** or **Maya**.

When you set **Interaction Mode** to **Maya**, most of the shortcuts and mouse operations behave as they do in **Autodesk Maya**.

| Radiosity | Animation | Inverse Kinematics | Gizmos | MAXScript | Containers |
| General | Files | Viewports | Interaction Mode | Gamma and LUT | R |

Interaction

Set my mouse and keyboard interaction to:

| 3ds Max ▼ | For 3ds Max Only ▼ |

☐ Enable Touch Navigation

F53

Here's the list:

- Pressing **Spacebar** maximizes the viewport that is beneath the mouse pointer.
- **Shift+Click** adds or removes from the selection. **Ctrl+Click** removes from the selection.
- The **Orbit** tools are not available in in the orthographic views.
- **Alt+Home** switches to the default perspective view.
- **Alt+LMB** drag to rotate the view. **Alt+MMB** drag to pan the view. **Alt+RMB** drag to zoom in or out in the view.

Table 11 shows a comparison between **3ds Max** and **Maya** hotkeys.

Table 11: The comparison between 3ds Max and Maya hotkeys		
Function	**3ds Max**	**Maya**
Maximize Viewport Toggle	Alt+W	Spacebar
Zoom Extents Selected	Z	F
Zoom Extents All	Shift+Ctrl+Z	A
Undo Viewport Operation	Shift+Z	Alt+Z
Redo Viewport Operation	Shift+Y	Alt+Y
Play Animation	/	Alt+V
Set Key	K	S
Group	None	Ctrl+G
Editable Poly Repeat Last Operation	;	G

Getting Around in 3ds Max

In the previous section, you have seen various components of the 3ds Max's UI. Don't get hung up on all the buttons, commands, menus, and options. It was a quick tour of the interface to get your feet wet. The more time you spent on **Unit MI1** and **Unit MI2**, easier it will be for you to understand rest of the units.

Creating Objects in the Scene

You can't do much with a blank scene. You need some objects in the scene in order to work on them. 3ds Max offers a wide range of standard objects. Let's start with creating some geometry in the scene.

Start 3ds Max, if not already running. Press **Alt+F+R** to open the 3ds Max message box. Click **Yes** to reset the scene.

Notice there are several panels in the **Command Panel: Create, Modify, Hierarchy, Motion, Display,** and **Utilities.** Position the mouse pointer on a panel's icon; a tooltip appears showing the name of the panel. The **Create** panel comprises of the following basic categories: **Geometry, Shapes, Lights, Cameras, Helpers, Space Warps,** and **Systems.** Each category is farther divided into sub-categories.

Notice in [see Figure F54] the **Create** panel [marked as 1], the **Geometry** button [marked as 2] is active. Below that button you will see a drop-down [marked as 3] that contains the **Geometry** sub-categories 3ds Max offers. Notice the **Standard Primitives** is selected by default in the drop-down.

Below the drop-down there is **Object Type** rollout [marked as 4]. There are ten buttons in this rollout. When you click on one of the buttons, the corresponding tool gets active and then you can create an object in the scene interactively using the mouse or by entering precise values using the keyboard.

Let's create an object from the **Standard Primitive** sub-category. Ensure you are in the **Command Panel | Create** panel | **Geometry** category | **Standard Primitives.** Now, click on **Box** in the **Object Type** rollout. Notice four rollouts appears in the **Create** panel: **Name and Color, Creation Method, Keyboard Entry,** and **Parameters.**

The **Keyboard Entry** rollout is collapsed whereas the other two are in the expanded state. Expand the **Keyboard Entry** rollout by clicking on the title bar of the rollout. Set **Length** to **50, Width** to **50,** and **Height** to **10.** Click **Create.** You need to press **Enter** or **Tab** after typing the values. Congratulations, you have created your first object in 3ds Max [see Figure F55].

You have not changed values of the **X, Y,** and **Z** controls in the **Keyboard Entry** rollout. As a result, the box is created at the origin of the home grid [0, 0, 0].

Also, notice the name of the object [**Box001**] in the **Name and Color** rollout. Every time you create an object in the scene, 3ds Max assigns it a default name. Collapse the **Keyboard Entry** rollout. On the **Parameters** rollout, change **Length** and **Width** to **100.**

Notice the box in the scene resizes as per the new dimensions you have set for the **Length** and **Width** controls. The change occurs because still **Box** is active in the **Object Type** rollout. If you select any other tool, then you would not be able to modify values from the **Create** panel.

F55

Then, how to change the parameters? Well, once you select any other tool, you can change values for controls from the **Modify** panel [panel available on the right of the **Create** panel]. Click the **Modify** panel [see Figure F56] and notice the **Parameters** rollout appears there. Change **Height** to **20**.

F56

Change **Length Segs**, **Width Segs**, and **Height Segs** to **2** each. Notice the change is reflected on the object in the viewport.

Notice the white brackets around the box in the **Perspective** viewport. These are selection brackets that show the bounding box of the object. I am not a big fan of the selection brackets and don't find them very useful. Press **J** to get rid of the selection brackets. In order to change values for controls of an object from the **Parameters** rollout, the object must be selected in the viewport. I will cover selection methods later in the unit.

Click the **General Viewport** label in the **Perspective** viewport and choose **Configure Viewports** from the popup menu. In the **Viewport Configuration** dialog that appears, choose the **Layout** tab and then click on the layout button highlighted with white borders in Figure F57. Now, click **OK** to change the viewport layout [see Figure F58].

You have just changed the viewport layout. The **Top**, **Front**, and **Left** viewports are stacked over each other on the left and on the right you will see enlarged **Perspective** viewport. I frequently change viewport layout as per my needs. In this book, especially in hands-on exercises, if you find a different viewport layout in captures, this is the place from where you can change it. I have not written this process in hands-on exercises.

MMB click on the **Left** viewport to make it active. Press **B** to change it to the **Bottom** viewport. Press **L** to change it to the **Left** viewport. As discussed earlier, the options for changing the viewport are available in the **Point-Of-View [POV]** viewport label menu. Now onward, I will refer **Point-Of-View [POV]** viewport label menu as **POV** viewport label menu.

Notice the label for the **Shading Viewport** label reads **Realistic**. Click on the **Shading Viewport** label to display the **Shading Viewport** label menu. The options in this menu allow you to define the shading style for the viewport. The default shading style is **Realistic**. **Realistic** displays textures geometry realistically. Also, the shading and lighting in the viewport is of high quality. **Shaded** smoothly shades the geometry in the viewport using the **Phong** shader. **Facets** displays faceted geometry. It ignores the smooth group settings of the geometry.

Consistent Colors shows the raw color in the viewport ignoring lighting. **Edged Faces** shows the edges of the face. Figure F59 shows the teapot in **Realistic**, **Shaded**, **Facets**, **Consistent Colors**, and **Edged Faces** shading modes, respectively. The hotkeys for **Realistic** and **Edged** Face modes are **Shift+F3** and **F4**, respectively. You can toggle these modes using **Shift+F3** and **F4** hotkeys.

F59

Hidden Line hides the faces and vertices whose normals are pointing away from the viewport. Shadows are unavailable in this mode. **Wireframe** displays objects in wireframe mode. The hotkey for toggling the **Wireframe** mode is **F3**. **Bounding Box** displays the edges of the bounding box of the geometry. **Clay** displays geometry in an uniform terracotta color. Figure F60 shows the teapot in the **Hidden Line**, **Wireframe**, **Bounding Box**, and **Clay** modes, respectively.

F60

My favorite shading mode for modeling is **Clay** with **Edges Faces** and I have extensively used it in this book.

Press **Ctrl+S** to open the **Save File As** dialog and then type the name of the file in the **File name** text box and click **Save** to save the file. Now, if you want to open this file later, choose **Open** from the **Application** menu to open the **Open File** dialog. Navigate to the file and then click **Open** to open the file. If you want to save an already saved file with different name, choose **Save As** from the **Application** menu. You can also save a copy to the previous version of 3ds Max, choose **Save As** from the **Application** menu to open the **Save File As** dialog. In this dialog, choose the appropriate option from the **Save as type** drop-down [see Figure F61]. Click **Save** to save the file.

F61

Tip: Incremental Save

When you are working on a file, I highly recommend that you save different versions of it. If the current version gets corrupt, you can always fall back to a previous version of the file. 3ds Max allows you to save the file incrementally. In the Save File As dialog, click + on the left of Save to save the file with a name ending in a number greater than the current number displayed with the file name. For example, if the current name is x1.max, clicking + will save file with the name x02.max.

Tip: Quick Access Toolbar

You can also open and save files using the options available in the Quick Access Toolbar.

Selecting Objects

Selecting objects is an important process before you perform any action on an object or objects. Selection in 3ds Max works on the noun-verb terminology. You first select the object (**the noun**) and then execute a command (**the verb**). 3ds Max provides a wide variety of tools for selecting objects. The **Selection** commands and functions are found in the following areas of interface:

- Main toolbar
- Edit menu
- Quad menu
- Tools menu
- Track View
- Display panel
- Modify panel
- Ribbon
- Schematic View
- Scene Explorer

Selecting Objects using Main toolbar Selection Buttons

The buttons available on the **Main** toolbar provides direct means of selection. These buttons are: **Select Object**, **Select by Name**, **Select and Move**, **Select and Rotate**, **Select and Scale**, and **Select and Manipulate**. To select an object, click on one of the selection buttons on the **Main** toolbar. Position the mouse pointer on the object that you want to select. The shape of the pointer changes to a small cross if the object is eligible for the selection. Click on the object to select it and de-select any selected object.

Note: Valid surface for selection
*The valid selection zone for the surface depends on the type of the object you are selecting and shading mode of the viewport in which you are selecting the object. In **Shaded** mode, any visible area of the surface is valid selection zone whereas in the **Wireframe** mode any edge or segment of the object is valid including the hidden lines.*

Adding and Removing Objects from the Current Selection

To extend a selection [adds objects to the existing selection], press and hold **Ctrl** while you make selections. For example, if you have selected two objects and you want to add third object to the selection, press and hold **Ctrl** and click on the third object to add it to the selection. To remove an object from selection, press and hold **Alt** and click on the object that you want to remove from the selection.

Inverting Selection

To invert the selection, choose **Select Invert** from the **Edit** menu. The hotkeys for this operation are **Ctrl+I**. For example, if you have total five objects in the scene and three of them are selected. Now, to select the remaining two objects and terminating the current selection, press **Ctrl+I**.

Selecting All Objects

To select all objects, choose **Select All** from the **Edit** menu or press **Ctrl+A**.

Locking the Selection

When the selection is locked, you can click-drag mouse anywhere in the viewport without losing the selection. To lock a selection, click **Selection Lock Toggle** [see Figure F62] from the **Status Bar** or press **Spacebar**. Press **Spacebar** again to unlock the selection.

Deselecting an Object

To deselect an object, click on another object, or click on an empty area of the viewport. To deselect all objects in a scene, choose **Select None** from the **Edit** menu.

Selecting by Region

The region selection tools in 3ds Max allow you to select one more object by defining a selection region using mouse. By default, a rectangular region is created when you drag the mouse. You can change the region by picking a region type from the **Region** flyout [see Figure F63] **Main** toolbar.

Note: Using Ctrl and Alt

*If you draw a selection region with the **Ctrl** held down, the affected objects are added to the selection. Conversely, if you hold down **Alt**, the affected objects are removed from the selection.*

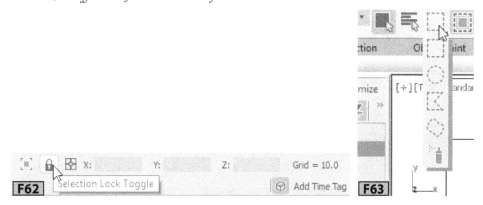

Table 12 lists the types of region selection. Figure F61 shows the rectangular, circular, fence, lasso, and paint marquee selections, respectively.

Table 12: The region selection types

Type	Description
Rectangular	Allows you select objects using the rectangular selection region.
Circular	Allows you select objects using the circular selection region.
Fence	Allows you to draw an irregular selection region.
Lasso	Allows you to draw an irregular selection region with single mouse operation.
Paint	Activates a brush. Paint on the objects to add them to the selection.

Note: Changing the Brush Size

*You can change the brush size from the **Preferences** dialog. RMB on the **Paint Selection** type to open the dialog. In the **General** panel | **Scene Selection** area, you can set the brush size by specifying a value for the **Paint Selection Brush Size** control. The default value for this control is **20**.*

The button on the right of the **Region Selection** flyout is a toggle button. It allows you to specify whether to include objects touched by the region border. This button affects all region selection methods I have described above. The default state of the button is **Crossing**. It selects all objects that are within the region and crossing the boundary of the region [see Figure F65]. The other state of the button is **Window**. It selects only those objects that are completely within the region [see Figure F66].

Select By Name

On clicking the **Select By Name** button on the **Main** toolbar, the **Select From Scene** dialog appears [see Figure F67]. It allows you to select objects by their assigned names.

To select objects by name, click **Select By Name** on the **Main** toolbar or press **H** to open the **Select From Scene** dialog. It lists all the objects in the scene. Click on the names of one or more objects to select them and then click **OK** to select the object and close the dialog and select the highlighted objects. Use **Ctrl+click** to highlight more than one entry in this dialog.

Tip: Quickly selecting an object
To select a single object, double-click on its name to select it and close the Select By Name dialog.

Named Selection Sets

You can name a selection in 3ds Max and then recall the selection by choosing their name from a list. To assign a name to the selection, select one or more objects or sub-objects in the scene. Click on the **Named Selection** field [see Figure F68] on the **Main** toolbar to activate a text box and then type a name for your selection set. Press **Enter** to complete the operation.

F67

F68

Caution: Case sensitive names
The names you enter for the selection are case-sensitive.

To retrieve a named selection set, click the **Named Selection Sets** list's arrow. Choose the desired name from the list. The corresponding objects are selected in the viewport. You can also select the selection sets from the **Named Selection Sets** dialog [see Figure F69]. To open this dialog, click **Edit Named Selection Sets** from the **Main** toolbar. Highlight the name of the set in this dialog and then click **Select Objects in Set** from the **Named Selection Sets** dialog's toolbar.

Using the Selection Filters

You can use the **Selection Filter** list [see Figure F70] to deactivate selection of all but a specific category by choosing category from this list. For example, if you select **Lights** from this list, you would be only select the light objects in the scene. To remove filtering, select **All** from this list.

F69

F70

Using the Navigation Controls

3ds Max provides two controls to navigate a viewport: **ViewCube** and **SteeringWheels**. These semitransparent controls appear on the upper right corner of a viewport and allow you to change the view without using any menu, command, or keyboard.

ViewCube

This gizmo [see Figure F71] provides a visual feedback to you about the orientation of the viewport. It also lets you quickly switch between the standard and orthographic views. The **ViewCube** does not appear in the camera, light, or shape viewport as well as in the special type of views such as **ActiveShade** or **Schematic**. When the **ViewCube** is inactive, the primary function of the **ViewCube** is to show the orientation of the model based on the north direction of the model. The inactive **ViewCube** remains in the semi-transparent state. When you position the mouse pointer on it, it becomes active.

F71

Tip: Toggling the visibility of the ViewCube
*Press **Ctrl+Alt+V** to toggle the **ViewCube's** visibility.*

If you hover the mouse pointer on top of the **ViewCube**, you will notice that faces, edges, and corners of the cube are highlighted. Click on the highlighted part of the cube; 3ds Max animates the viewport and orients it according to the clicked part of the cube. Click on the home icon on the **ViewCube** to switch to the default viewport orientation. You can also click and drag the ring to spin model around its current orientation.

To change the **ViewCube's** settings, RMB click on the **ViewCube** and choose **Configure** from the popup menu to open the **Viewport Configuration** dialog [see Figure F72] with the **ViewCube** panel active. From this panel you can change various settings for the **ViewCube**.

F72

Table 13 lists the other option available in the popup menu.

Option	Description
Table 13: The options available for **ViewCube** in the popup menu	
Option	**Description**
Home	Restores the home view.
Orthographic	Changes the current orientation to the orthographic projection.
Perspective	Changes the current orientation to the perspective projection.
Set Current View as Home	Defines the home view based on the current orientation.
Set Current View as Front	Defines the front projection based on the current projection.
Reset Front	Resets the front projection to its default view.
Configure	Opens the **Viewport Configuration** dialog.

Help	Launches the online help system and navigate to the **ViewCube's** documentation.

SteeringWheels

The **SteeringWheels** gizmo [see Figure F73] allows you to access different 2D and 3D navigation tools from a single tool. When you first start 3ds max, the **SteeringWheels** gizmo is not available. To enable this gizmo press **Shift+W**. When the wheel is displayed, you can activate it by clicking on one of its wedges. If you click drag a wedge, the current view changes. The navigation tools listed in Table 14 support click action.

F73

Table 14: The navigation tools	
Tool	**Function**
Zoom	Adjust the magnification of the view.
Center	Centers the view based on the position of the mouse pointer.
Rewind	Restores the previous view.
Forward	Increases the magnification of the view.

To close a wheel, you can use one of the following methods:

1. Press **Esc**.
2. Press **Shift+W** to toggle the wheel.
3. Click the small **x** button the upper right area of the wheel.
4. RMB click on the wheel.

Tip: Changing wheel's settings
*You can change the **SteeringWheels'** settings from the **SteeringWheels** panel of the **Viewport Configuration** dialog box [see Figure F74].*

There are other versions of the wheels available that you can activate from the **Wheel** menu. To open the menu, click on the down arrow on the bottom-right corner of the wheel. Table 15 lists those options.

Table 15: The options available in the **Wheel** menu.	
Option	**Function**
Mini View Object Wheel	Displays the mini version of the **View Object** wheel [see the first image in Figure F75].
Mini Tour Building Wheel	Displays the mini version of the **Tour Building** wheel [see the second image in Figure F75].
Mini Full Navigation Wheel	Displays the mini version of the **Full Navigation** wheel [see the third image in Figure F75].
Full Navigation Wheel	Displays the big version of the **Full Navigation** wheel [see the fourth image in Figure F75].

Basic Wheels	Displays the big versions of the **View Object** or **Tour Building** wheel [Figure F76].
Go Home	Restores the **Home** view.
Restore Original Center	Pans the view to the origin.
Increase Walk Speed	Doubles the walk speed used by the **Walk** tool.
Decrease Walk Speed	Cuts the walk speed by half used by the **Walk** tool.
Help	Navigates you to the online documentation of the steering wheels.
Configure	Opens the **Viewport Configuration** dialog that allows you set preferences for the wheel.

F74

F75

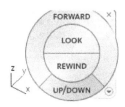

Zooming, Panning, and Orbiting Views using Mouse Scroll

To zoom in and out in the viewport, scroll the mouse wheel. It zooms in or out in steps and is equivalent to using bracket keys, [and]. If you want to gradually zoom, scroll the wheel with the **Ctrl+Alt** held down. Press and hold MMB and then drag the mouse pointer to pan the view. You can pan the viewport in any direction. To rotate the viewport press and hold **Alt+MMB** and then drag the mouse pointer.

Moving, Rotating, and Scaling Objects

The transformation tools [see Figure F77] in 3ds Max allow you to move, rotate, and scale an object[s]. A transformation is the adjustment position, orientation, and scale relative to the 3D space you are working in. 3ds Max provides four tools that allow you to transform the object: **Select and Move**, **Select and Rotate**, **Select and Scale**, and **Select and Place**. The **Select and Move**, **Select and Rotate**, and **Select and Scale** tools are generally referred as **Move**, **Rotate**, and **Scale** tools. Now onward, I will use these names.

To transform an object, click the **Move**, **Rotate**, or **Scale** button from the **Main** toolbar. Position the mouse pointer on the object[s]. If the object[s] is already selected, the shape of the cursor changes to indicate transform. If object[s] is not selected, the shape of the mouse pointer changes to a crosshair. Now, drag the mouse pointer to apply the transform. You can restrict the motion to one or two axes by using the transform gizmos. The transform gizmos are the icons displayed in the viewport. Figure F77 shows the **Move**, **Rotate**, and **Scale** gizmos, respectively.

Tip: Changing size of the gizmos
You can change the size of the gizmos by using the - and = keys on the main keyboard.

When no transform tool is active and you select objects, an axis tripod appears in the viewports [see Figure F78]. Each axis tripod consists of three lines labeled as **X**, **Y**, and **Z**. The orientation of the tripod indicates the orientation of the current reference coordinate system.

The point where the three lines meet indicates the current transform center and the highlighted red axis lines show the current axis constraints.

Each gizmo indicates axes by using three colors: **X** is **red**, **Y** is **green**, and **Z** is **blue**. You can use any of the axes handles to constrain transformation to that axis.

Tip: 1-minute learning movies
To more about transform tools, download the movies from the following link: http://download.autodesk.com/us/3dsmax/ skillmovies/index.html.

The transform commands are also available from the **Quad** menu. To transform an object using the **Quad** menu, RMB click on the selected object[s], choose the transform command from the **Quad** menu and then drag the object to apply the transform.

Tip: Cancelling transform
To cancel a transform, RMB click while dragging the mouse.

Using the Transform Type-In dialog

You can use the **Transform Type-In** dialog to precisely enter the transformation values. To transform objects using this dialog, if the **Move, Rotate**, or **Scale** tool is active, press **F12** to open the dialog or choose **Transform Type-In** from the **Edit** menu to open the associated **Transform Type-In** dialog. Figure F79 shows the **Move Transform Type-In, Rotate Transform Type-In**, and **Scale Transform Type-In** dialogs, respectively. You can enter both the absolute and relative transformation values in this dialog.

Tip: Transform Type-In dialog
*You can also open this dialog by RMB clicking on the tool's button on the **Main** toolbar.*

The controls in this dialog are also replicated in the **Status Bar**. You can use these **Transform Type-In** boxes on the **Status Bar** to transform the object. To switch between the absolute and relative transform modes, click the **Relative/Absolute Transform Type-In** button on the **Status Bar** [see Figure F80].

Getting Help

Autodesk provides rock solid documentation for 3ds Max. There are several places in the UI from where you can access different forms of help. The help options are listed in the **Help** menu [see Figure F81]. Click **Autodesk 3ds Max Help** from the **Help** menu to open the online documentation for 3ds Max. You can also download offline help from the Autodesk website and install on your computer. If you have a slow internet connection, you can download the offline help and use it. To access offline help, download and install it on your system. Press **Alt+U+P** hotkeys to open the **Preferences** dialog [refer Figure F82].

Choose the **Help** panel from the dialog and click **Browse** to open the **Browser For Folder** dialog. In this dialog, navigate to the directory where you installed help, generally, *C:\Program Files (x86)\Autodesk\ Help\3dsmax2017\en_us*. Click **OK** to close the dialog. Click **OK** from the **Preferences** dialog to close it. Now, when you press **F1**, 3ds Max will navigate you to the offline help.

Search Command

The search command feature was introduced in 2014 version of 3ds Max. This feature helps you finding a specific command. For example, if you are looking for the **Sunlight** tool but not sure where it is on the interface. Press **X** to open the **Search Command** text box and then type **Sun; SunLight** System appears in a list [see Figure F83]. Click on it, 3ds Max takes you to **Systems** category of the **Create** panel in the **Command Panel**.

InfoCenter Toolbar

The **InfoCenter** is located on the right of caption bar at the top-right of the UI [see Figure F84]. This toolbar allows you to access information about 3ds Max as well as other Autodesk products.

Table 16 shows the elements of this toolbar.

Table 16: The InfoCenter toolbar interface overview		
Element	**Icon**	**Description**
Search field	-	The search box is marked by arrow in Figure F81. You can use this search box to lookup information in the help documentation. This field supports wildcard characters such as * and ?.
Communication Center		Takes you to the **Communication Center** that displays announcements about product updates and other news.
Favorites		Click to view the **Favorite** panel.

Sign In		Allows you to access Autodesk 360 for mobility, collaboration, and online services of the cloud.
Autodesk Exchange Apps		Takes you to the Autodesk Exchange Application store.
Quick Help menu		Takes you to quick help menu which is a smaller version of the **Help** menu.

Hands-on Exercise

Before you start the exercise, let's first create a project folder for the hands-on exercise of this unit. You can proceed without creating a project folder but I highly recommend that you create one. The project folder allows you to keep your file organized.

Open the **Windows Explorer** and create a new directory with the name **max2017projects** in the **C** drive of your system. Start 3ds Max. From the **Application** menu, choose **Reset**. Click **Yes** from the dialog that opens.

From the **Application** menu, choose **Manage | Set Project Folder** to open the **Browse for Folder** dialog. Navigate to the **3dsmax2017projects** directory and then click **Make New Folder**. Create the new folder with the name **unit-mi1** and click **OK** to create the project directory.

Now, if you navigate to the **\max2017projects\unit-mi1** directory, you will see a number of sub-directories [see Figure E1].

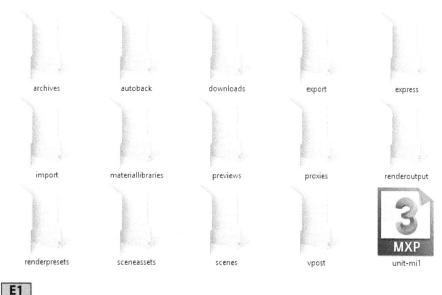

E1

What just happened?
*Here, I have set a project folder for the hands-on exercise of this unit. When you set a project folder for a scene, 3ds Max creates a series of folders such as **scenes**, **sceneassets**, and so forth. These folders are default locations for certain types of operations in 3ds Max. For example, the **scenes** folder is used when 3ds Max opens or saves scene files.*

*It is a good idea to reset the scene before you start new work because the **Open** command defaults to the folder where the previous scene was saved. After the reset operation, the **Open** command defaults to the **scenes** folder of the current project folder.*

The **unit-mi1** folder will contain all the data related to the hands-on exercise of this unit.

Exercise 1: Creating Simple Model of a House

OK, now it is time to work on the first exercise of the book. In this exercise, you will create a simple model of a house using the **Standard Primitives** [see Figure E2].

E2

Table E1 summarizes the exercise:

Table E1 - Creating a Simple Model of a House	
In this exercise, you will learn how to	• Reset 3ds Max settings • Create objects • Use navigational controls • Align objects • Undo and redo scene views • Use navigational gizmos • Use **Transform Type-In** boxes
Skill level	Beginner
Project Folder	**unit-mi1**
Time to complete	20 Minutes
Final exercise file	**umi1-hoe1-end.max**

Start 3ds Max. Choose **Reset** from the **Application** menu or press **Alt+F+R**. Click **Yes** on the **3ds Max** message box to reset the settings. Choose **Unit Setup** from the **Customize** menu to open the **Units Setup** dialog. Ensure that **Generic Units** in on in this dialog box and then click **OK** to close the dialog.

Click **Box** on the **Object Type** rollout in the **Command Panel** and then click-drag in the **Perspective** viewport to define the length and width of the box. Release the mouse button to define the length and width of the box. Release the LMB and then drag upward to define the height. Click to specify the height.

Press **J** to turn off the selection brackets and **F4** to turn on the **Edged Faces** mode. Now, click on the **Shading Viewport** label and choose **Clay** from the popup menu. Press **G** To turn off the grid. Press **G** again to turn it on. Drag the mouse pointer with the **MMB+Alt** held down to rotate the view. Drag the mouse pointer with the **MMB** held down to pan the view. Drag the mouse pointer with the **Ctrl+Alt+MMB** held down to zoom in or out of the view. You need to place the mouse pointer on the area for which you want to change the magnification.

Next, you will use the brackets keys to change the settings.

Place the mouse pointer on the area for which you want to change the magnification settings and then use the bracket keys **[** and **]** to change the level of magnification. MMB click on the **Perspective** viewport to make it active, if not already active. Press **Alt+W** to maximize the viewport. Click on the **Home** icon on the **ViewCube** to restore the home view. Alternatively, you can RMB click on the **ViewCube** and then choose **Home** from the **ViewCube's** menu. Press **Alt+W** again to restore the four viewport arrangement. Click drag the compass ring of the **ViewCube** to change the orientation of the viewport. Now, click-drag edges, corners, or faces of the **ViewCube** and experiment with various possibilities that **ViewCube** offers. When done, click on the **Home** icon to restore the view.

Press **Shift+Z** repeatedly to undo the scene view changes. Press **Shift+Y** to redo the scene view changes. Click on the **ViewCube's Home** icon to restore the home view. Press **Ctrl+P** to activate the **Pan View** tool and then drag in the viewport to pan the view. Now, press **Ctr+R** to activate the **Orbit** tool and drag in the viewport to rotate the view. Press **Q** to deactivate the **Orbit** tool and activate the **Select** tool. Press **Shift+W** to activate **StreeringWheels**. Click drag the **ZOOM** wedge to change the magnification level. Similarly, experiment with other wedges of the wheel. Press **Esc** to deactivate **SteeringWheels**.

Make sure **Box001** is selected in the viewport and then RMB click on the **Move** tool to open the **Move Transform Type-In** dialog. In the **Absolute:World** group of the dialog, RMB click on the spinners to set them to their default values which is **zero**. You will notice that the box is now placed at the origin in the viewports. The **Move Transform Type-In** dialog is a **modeless** dialog. You don't have to close it in order to work on the model we are creating in this exercise. Choose the **Modify** panel in the **Command Panel**. In the **Parameters** rollout, set **Length**, **Width**, and **Height** to **80**, **50**, and **70**, respectively, to change the size of the box. Press **Ctrl+Shift+Z** to zoom the box to its extents in all viewports [see Figure E3].

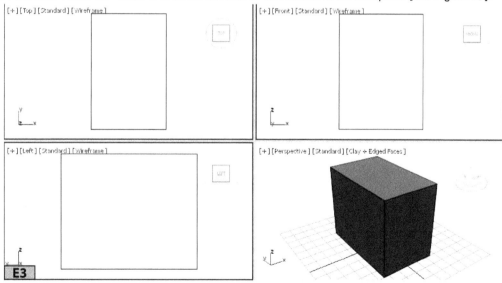

If you press **Z** the box will be zoomed in the active viewport only. Now, let's create door and windows of the house. Create another box in the **Perspective** viewport and then set its **Length, Width,** and **Height** to **23, 6,** and **40,** respectively [see Figure E4]. Ensure **Box002** and the **Move** tool selected and then enter **-25, -2.3,** and **-0.03** in the **Transform Type-In** boxes in the **Status Bar** [see Figure E5].

Create two windows using the **Box** primitive. Use the values **23, 6,** and **18** for the **Length, Width,** and **Height** spinners, respectively. Now, align the boxes [see Figure E6]. Ensure the **Box** tool is active and then turn on **AutoGrid** from the **Object Type** rollout. Position the mouse pointer on the **Box001**, an axis tripod shows up [see Figure E7]. Create a box on the **Box001**.

Ensure **Box005** is selected and then click **Align** ![icon] on the **Main** toolbar. Now, click **Box001** in the **Perspective** viewport to open the **Align Selection** dialog. In this dialog, set the values as shown in Figure E8 and click **OK** to align the boxes.

Ensure **Box005** is selected and then choose the **Modify** panel. On the **Parameters** rollout, set **Length, Width,** and **Height** to **91, 60,** and **2,** respectively [see Figure E9]. Choose the **Create** panel and ensure **Auto Grid** is on. Click **Pyramid** on the **Object Type** rollout and then create a pyramid on **Box005**. Align **Pyramid001** with **Box005**. Ensure **Pyramid001** is selected and then in the **Modify panel | Parameters** rollout, set **Width, Depth,** and **Height** to **60, 90,** and **46,** respectively [see Figure E10].

Now, let's create a chimney for the house.

On the **Create** panel, choose **Cylinder** from the **Object Type** rollout and create a cylinder in the **Perspective** viewport. In the **Modify panel | Parameters** rollout, set **Radius** and **Height** to **5** and **60,** respectively. Now, place **Cylinder001** on the roof using the **Move** tool [see Figure E11]. In the **Create** panel, choose **Cone** from the **Object Type** rollout and ensure **AutoGrid** is on. Create a cone on **Cylinder001**. Align **Cone001** and **Cylinder001**.

Align Selection (Box001)

Align Position (World):

☑ X Position   ☑ Y Position   ☐ Z Position

Current Object: Target Object:
○ Minimum   ○ Minimum
● Center   ● Center
○ Pivot Point   ○ Pivot Point
○ Maximum   ○ Maximum

Align Orientation (Local):

☐ X Axis   ☐ Y Axis   ☐ Z Axis

Match Scale:

☐ X Axis   ☐ Y Axis   ☐ Z Axis

Apply   OK   Cancel

E8

In the **Modify panel | Parameters** rollout, set **Radius 1**, **Radius 2**, and **Height** to **7.5**, **2**, and **13**, respectively [see Figure E12].

Choose **Select All** from the **Edit** menu to select all objects in the scene. Choose **Group** from the **Group** menu to open the **Group** dialog. In this dialog, type **House** in the **Group name** field and click **OK** to create a group. Press **Ctrl+S** to open the **Save File As** dialog. In this dialog, navigate to the location where you want to save the file. Type the name of the file in the **File name** text box and then click **Save** to save the file.

Practical Tests
Complete the following tests:

Test 1: Creating Text
Create the text [Love] as shown in Figure P1 using the **Box** primitive.

Test 2: Creating a Road Side Sign
Create a road side sign, as shown in Figure P2, using the **Box**, **Pyramid**, and **Box** primitives.

P2

Explore More

Per-view Preferences and Presets

We can define display quality settings for each viewport. For example, you can specify the rendering level [**Basic**, **Advanced**, and **DX**], Lighting and Shadow settings, ambient occlusion settings, and so forth. The Per-view Preferences and Presets can be accessed from the **Viewport Setting and Preference** dialog [see Figure EM1]. To open this dialog, choose **Per-View Preset** from the third viewport label menu or **Per-View Preference** from the fourth viewport label menu.

Creative Market Store

You can buy 3D assets from independent creators using the **Autodesk Creative Market Store**. To open the store, choose **Creative Market Store** from the **Content** menu to open the **Creative Market** in-application browser. You need to have an account with the store before you start using it. This store is same as their website which is available at the following address: *https://creativemarket.com/3d*.

Asset Library Application

You can download the application from the Autodesk site and the use it to navigate and download files from **Autodesk seek**. It allows you to quickly access 3D content on your local computer and network in a single view, making all content instantly searchable. You can also drag and drop scenes from your local hard drive. Once installed, you can launch the application from the Window **Start** menu or you can choose Launch **3ds Max Asset Library** from the **Content** menu. After you zero-in on a desired asset, you can control how the asset will integrate with scene through Xref, merge or replace.

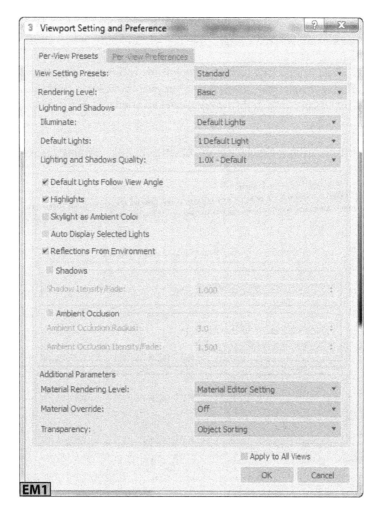

EM1

Sending Files to Print Studio

3ds Max allows you to send your 3D models to **Print Studio** which is a program for 3D printing. To access this feature, choose the **Application** button and then choose **Send to | Send to Print Studio** [see Figure EM2].

EM2

Game Exporter Utility

This utility [see Figure EM3] allows you to export the models and animations clips in **FBX** format to your game engine in a streamlined fashion. This utility is specifically designed for game users to export game assets more efficiently. This utility uses minimal amount of settings, as a result, you can easily export the model without changing too many settings. It also supports animation clips thus allows you to export multiple clips as a single FBX file or as multiple files. You can open this utility from the **Application** menu or **Utilities** panel:

- **Utilities** panel | **Utilities** rollout | **More** button | **Utilities** dialog | **Parameters** rollout | **Game Exporter** button
- **Application** menu | **Export** | **Game Exporter**

EM3

Summary

The unit covered the following topics:

- Understanding workspaces
- Navigating the workspace
- Customizing the interface
- Understanding various UI components
- Working with the file management commands
- Setting preferences for 3ds Max
- Understanding the enhanced menu system
- Working with viewports
- Setting preferences for the viewports
- Creating objects in the scene
- Selecting objects
- Using the navigational gizmos
- Moving, rotating, and scaling objects
- Getting help
- Per-view Preferences, Creative Market Store, Asset Library, Print Studio, and Game Exporter

This page intentionally left blank

Unit MI2: Introducing 3ds Max - II

In the previous unit, I covered the interface as well as the tools that allow you to transform objects in the viewport. In this unit, I will cover the tools and procedures that will help you immensely during the modeling process. You will know about various explorers as well as various precision tools that 3ds Max offers. I have also covered the procedures for creating clones, and duplicates.

In this unit, I will cover the following:

- Working with templates
- Creating clones and duplicates
- Understanding hierarchies
- Working with the **Scene** and **Layer** Explorers
- Understanding the **Mirror**, **Select and Place**, and **Select and Manipulate** tools
- Working with the **Align** and **Array** tools
- Working with precision and drawing aids
- Understanding modifiers, and normals

Working with Templates

Templates, introduced in 2016 version of 3ds Max allow you to create a base file that you can use to create new files based on a template. For example, if you regularly work on projects that consist of studio lighting, you can create a template with three point light setup, **mental ray** renderer, and HD resolution for rendering. The template will save you lot of time when you start working on a new project. The following information can be saved in templates:

- Scene and display units
- Renderer and rendering resolution
- Scene geometry, which can be animated
- The active workspace
- The order of rollouts
- The **ViewCube** settings
- Viewport layout and settings
- User paths

The start-up templates are available in the **Start** panel of the **Welcome Screen**. If the **Welcome Screen** is not visible, choose **Welcome Screen** from the **Help** menu. 3ds Max comes with some default templates that you can access from the **START-UP TEMPLATES** section of the **Start** panel. To start a new scene using a default template, double-click on a template preview. You can use a template by first selecting the preview icon and then clicking **New Using Selected Template**.

The Template Manager

Click **Open Template Manager** from the **Start** panel of the **Welcome Screen** to open the **Template Manager** dialog [see Figure F1]. At the left of the dialog, you will see the preview icons of the available templates. Place the mouse pointer on the icons to view the brief description of the template. Click on an icon to see its details at the right of the dialog. Click **Set as Default** to make the selected template default for the new scenes. The array of buttons available for **Thumbnail** control allows you to set a preview icon for the template. The controls to set scene file, project folder, and workspace are available below these buttons.

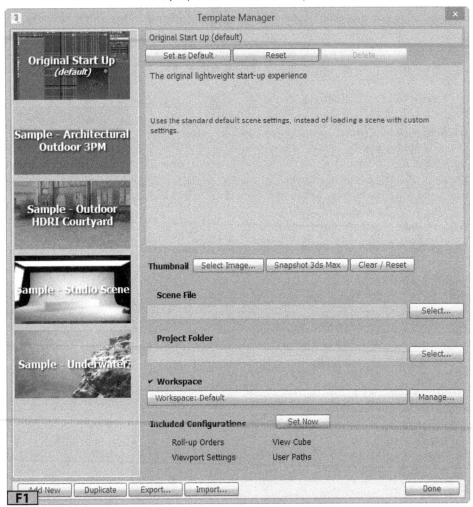

To create a new template, click **Add New** and then provide the required information at the right of the dialog. Click **Done** to create a new template and close the **Template Manager** dialog. To duplicate an existing template, select the template and then click **Duplicate**.

Creating Copies, Clones, and References

The general terms used for duplicating objects is **cloning**. To create a duplicate, clone, or reference, transform [move, rotate, or scale] the object with **Shift** held down. This process is generally called

Shift+Transform. There are some other tools such as the **Mirror** tool available in 3ds Max that allows you to create clones.

Q: What's is the difference between Copy, Instance, and Reference?

*There are three methods available in 3ds Max to clone the objects: **Copy**, **Instance**, and **Reference**. At geometry level, clones created using any method are identical. However, they behave differently when used with the modifiers such as **Bend** or **Twist**.*

*The **Copy** method allows you to create a completely different copy of the original object. If you modify the original object, it will have no effect on the other. The **Instance** method creates a completely interchangeable clone of the original. If you modify the original or the instance, the change will be replicated in both objects. The **Reference** method creates a clone dependent on the original upto the point when the object was created. If you apply a new modifier to the referenced object, it will affect only that object. Depending on the method used, the cloned objects are called copies, instances, or references.*

Cloning Techniques

3ds Max provides several techniques for creating clones. You can use any of these techniques on any selection. Here's the list:

- Clone
- Shift+Clone
- Snapshot
- **Array** tool
- **Mirror** tool
- **Spacing** tool
- **Clone and Align** tool
- Copy/Paste (**Scene Explorer**)

Table 1 summarizes these techniques:

Table 1: The list of cloning techniques	
Technique	**Description**
Clone	The easiest method for creating clones is to use the **Clone** command. To create clone using this command, select the object[s] that you want to clone and then choose **Clone** from the **Edit** menu or press **Ctrl+V**. The **Clone Options** dialog appears. Choose the method you want to use from the **Object** section of the dialog and then specify a name for the cloned object using **Name** text box and then click **OK** to create a clone. The clone will be superimposed on the original object at the same location. Use the **Move** tool to separate the two.
Shift+Drag	You can use this technique to clone objects while transforming them. This technique is most used technique for cloning objects. To clone and transform objects, click **Move**, **Rotate**, or **Scale** on the **Main** toolbar and then select an object, multiple objects, group, or sub-objects in a viewport. Hold down **Shift** and then drag the selection. As you drag the selection the clone is created, and transformed. Now, release **Shift** and mouse button to open the **Clone Options** dialog. Change the settings and click **OK** to create a clone.

Snapshot	You can use this feature to create an animated object over time. You can create a single clone on any frame or you can create clones on multiple frames along the animation path. The spacing between the clones is a uniform time interval.
Array	You can use the **Array** tool to create repeating design patterns for example, legs of a round coffee table, blades of a jet engine, text on the dial of a watch, and so forth. The **Array** command allows you to precisely control the transformations in 3D space.
Mirror	**Mirror** allows you to create a symmetrical copy along any combination of axes. This tool also provide an option "**No Clone**" that allows you to perform a mirror operation without creating clone.
Spacing Tool	This tool distributes objects along a path define by a spline. You can control the spacing between the objects.
Clone and Align Tool	This tool allows you to distribute the source objects to a selection of the destination objects. This tool is very useful when you work on an imported CAD file that contains lots of symbols. For example, you can replace the chair symbols in the CAD file with the actual chair geometry en masse.
Copy/Paste (Scene Explorer)	You can use the **Scene Explorer's Edit** menu command to copy paste nodes. The **Scene Explorer** should be in **Sort By Hierarchy** mode.

Working with the Mirror Tool

On clicking **Mirror** from the **Main** toolbar, the **Mirror** dialog appears [see Figure F2]. The controls in this dialog allow you to mirror the current selection about the center of the current coordinate system. You can also create a clone while mirroring a selection. To mirror an object, make a selection in a viewport. Click **Mirror** on the **Main** toolbar or choose **Mirror** from the **Tools** menu. In the **Mirror** dialog that appears, set the parameters and click **OK** [see Figure F3]. In Figure F3, I have selected the left leg of the robot and then used the **Mirror** dialog to create his right leg.

Notice in the **Mirror** dialog, there are two options at the top: **Transform** and **Geometry**. These options control how the **Mirror** tool treats the reflected geometry. **Transform** uses the legacy mirror method. This method mirrors any word-space-modifiers [**WSM**] effect. **Geometry** applies a **Mirror** modifier to the object and does not mirror any **WSM** effect.

Working with the Array Tool

The **Array** tool allows you to create an array of objects based on the current selection in the viewport. The **Array** button in not visible on the **Main** toolbar by default. The **Array** button is part of the **Extras** toolbar which is not visible by default. To make it visible, RMB click on a gray area of the **Main** toolbar and then choose **Extras** from the popup menu to display the **Extras** toolbar [see Figure F4].

To understand the functioning of this tool, reset 3ds Max and create a teapot in the scene. Ensure teapot is selected in a viewport and then choose **Array** from the **Tools** menu to open the **Array** dialog. Now, click **Preview** and set other parameters as shown in Figure F5. Notice in Figure F5, 3ds Max creates **4** copies of the teapot with **60** units distance between each copy. Notice total distance is now **300** units, as shown in **Totals** section of the dialog indicating that **5** copies of the teapot are taking up **300** units space along the **X** direction.

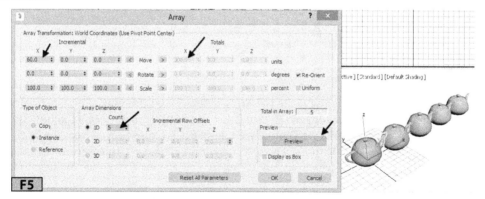

Now, if you want to distribute these teapots over a distance of say **400** units, click **>** on the right of the **Move** label and then set **X** to **400** [see Figure F6], the teapots are now spread over a distance of **400** units. Similarly, you can create an array using the **Rotate** and **Scale** transformations.

F6

Settings in Figures F7 and F8 show how you can create a 2D or 3D array, respectively, using the **Array** dialog.

F7

F8

You can also create a **360** degree array using the **Array** dialog. Reset 3ds Max and then create a **Teapot** primitive with radius **10** at the top edge of the grid [see Figure F9]. From the **Main** toolbar | **User Center** flyout, choose **Use Transform Coordinate Center** [see Figure F10]. Choose **Array** from the **Tools** menu to open the **Array** dialog. Now, specify the settings, as shown in Figure F11 to create 12 teapots in a full circle [360 degrees].

Working with the Spacing Tool

This tool allows you to distribute the selected objects along a spline or along the distance specified by two points. You can also control the spacing between two objects. This tool can be activated by choosing **Tools | Align | Spacing Tool** from the menu bar or choosing **Spacing Tool** from the **Array** flyout.

To distribute objects along a path, select the objects in the scene and then activate the **Spacing Tool** to open the **Spacing Tool** dialog [see Figure F12]. This dialog gives you two methods for selecting path: **Pick Path** and **Pick Points**. If you click **Pick Path**, place a cursor on a spline in the view and click to select the spline as path. Now, specify the number of objects you want to distribute and then choose a distribution algorithm from the drop-down available in the **Parameters** section [see Figure F13]. Turn on **Follow**, if you want to align the pivot points of the object along the tangents of the spline [see Figure F14].

If you click **Pick Points** from the **Spacing Tool** dialog, specify the path by clicking on two places in the viewport. When you are finished with the tool, 3ds Max deletes the spline.

Working with Clone and Align Tool

This tool lets you distribute the source objects based on the current selection to a selection of the target objects. You can activate this tool by choosing **Align | Clone and Align** from the **Tools** menu. Alternatively, choose **Clone and Align Tool** from the **Array** flyout.

F14

To use the **Clone and Align** tool, create four teapots and a cone in the viewport [see Figure F15]. Select cone in a viewport and then choose **Align | Clone and Align** from the **Tools** menu to open the **Clone and Align** dialog.

F15

In this dialog, click **Pick** and then click on each teapot to align the cone with the teapots [see Figure F16]. If you want to pick multiple destination objects at once, click **Pick List** to open the **Pick Destination Objects** dialog. In this dialog, select the objects and then click **Pick**.

Working With the Select and Place Tool

The **Select and Place** tool has been introduced in the 2015 release of 3ds Max. This tool is cousin of the **AutoGrid** option found in the **Object Type** rollout. However you can use it any time in your scene not just when you are creating an object. This tool can be activated by using one of the following four methods:

- Click the **Select and Place** icon on the **Main** toolbar.
- Choose **Placement** from the **Edit** menu.
- Press **Y** on the keyboard.
- RMB click on an object and then choose **Placement** from the **Transform** quadrant [see Figure F17].

F16

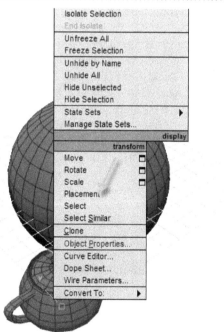

Isolate Selection
End Isolate
Unfreeze All
Freeze Selection
Unhide by Name
Unhide All
Hide Unselected
Hide Selection
State Sets ▶
Manage State Sets...
display

transform
Move ▫
Rotate ▫
Scale ▫
Placement
Select
Select Similar
Clone
Object Properties...
Curve Editor...
Dope Sheet...
Wire Parameters...
Convert To: ▶

F17

To place an object, you don't have to select it first. Pick the **Select and Place** tool, click on the object to select it and then drag to place on another object [see Figure F18].

As you drag the object, the orientation of the object changes based on the normals of the target object and object **Up Axis** settings. The contact position of the target surface will be the object's pivot. To change the **Up Axis** settings, RMB click on the **Select and Place** tool on the **Main** toolbar to open the **Placement Settings** dialog [see Figure F19] and then select the axis from the **Object Up Axis** button array.

When **Rotate** is active on the **Placement Settings** dialog, the translation of the object is prevented and object rotates around the local axis speci-fied with the **Object Up Axis** settings. **Use Base as Pivot** is useful in those cases when the pivot is not already located in the base of the object. **Pillow Mode** is very useful when you are trying to place an object on a target whose surface is uneven. This option prevents the intersection of the objects. When **Autoparent** is active, the placed object automati-cally becomes the child of the other object. This is a quick way to make parent-child relationship.

Note: Select and Rotate tool
*If you just want to rotate the object, you can use the **Select and Rotate** tool from the **Main** toolbar.*

There are some more goodies associated with this tool:

- You can clone an object while dragging it by pressing **Shift**.
- Hold **Ctrl** and then drag to position an object vertically along the **Up Axis**.
- You can prevent an object from rotating while you place it by holding **Alt**.

You can also place several objects at one go. You can either select the desired objects before picking the **Select and Place** tool or you can select additional objects using **Ctrl** when this tool is active. Each object will move according to its own pivot, unless objects are linked together.

Working With the Select and Manipulate Tool

The **Select and Manipulate** tool allows you to interactively edit the parameters of certain objects by dragging the manipulators in the viewports. The state of this tool is non-exclusive. You can manipulate objects as long as any of the select mode or one of the transform mode is active but if you want to select a manipulator helper, you must deactivate the **Select and Manipulate** tool. All those primitives with a **Radius** parameter have a built-in manipulator for the radius value. Let's see how it works:

Create a **Teapot** primitive in the scene. Pick the **Select and Manipulate** tool from the **Main** toolbar. A green ring appears beneath the teapot [see Figure F20]. Click drag the ring to interactively change the radius of the teapot. Click on **Select and Manipulate** on the **Main** toolbar to deactivate the tool. There are three types of custom manipulators available in 3ds Max: cone angle manipulator, plane angle manipulator, and slider manipulator. The cone angle manipulator is used by a spot light's **Hotspot** and **Falloff** controls. To create a cone angle manipulator, choose **Create** panel | **Helpers** | **Manipulators** and then click **Cone Angle**. Click drag in the viewport to create the helper [see Figure F21]. To change its parameters, go to **Modify** panel and change the values.

F20   F21

Now, let's work on a spot light to see this manipulator in action:

Create a **Teapot** primitive in the scene. Now create a spot light and place it as shown in Figure F22. Ensure the spot light is selected and then click **Select and Manipulate** from the **Main** toolbar. Two rings appear on the spot light [see Figure F23].

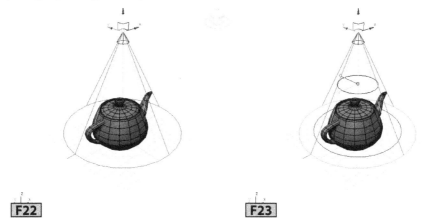

F22   F23

The inner ring controls **Hotspot** whereas the outer rings controls **Falloff**. Click drag to interactively change these parameters. The plane angle manipulator allows you to create a lever or joystick type shape. You can use its **Angle** parameter to create a custom control. You can use this control to drive parameter of another objects.

Let's see how it works, choose **Create** panel | **Helpers** | **Manipulators** and then click **Plane Angle**. In the **Front** viewport, click drag to create a shape [see Figure F24]. The **Plane Angle** manipulator always created vertically along the Y axis of the viewport in which you are creating it. Create a teapot in the **Perspective** viewport. Ensure the **Select and Manipulate** tool is not active and manipulator is selected. Choose **Wire Parameters** | **Wire Parameters** from the **Animation** menu. In the popup that appears, choose **Object (Plane Angle Manipulator)** | **Angle** [Figure F25]. A rubber band line appears. Click on the teapot.

In the popup that appears, choose **Object (Teapot)** | **Radius** [see Figure F26]. In the **Parameter Wiring** dialog, click **One-way connection** button and then the **Connect** button [see Figure F27] to make the connection. Now close the dialog.

Pick the **Select and Manipulate** tool and click drag the manipulator to interactively change the radius of the teapot. The third type of manipulator, **Slider**, which creates a graphic control in the viewport. You can wire its value to a parameter of another object within the scene.

Here's how:

Create a **Slider** manipulator in the **Front** viewport. Create a teapot in the **Perspective** viewport [see Figure F28].Wire the **Value** parameter to the **Radius** of the teapot as described above. Change the controls such as **Label**, **Minimum**, and **Maximum** values in the **Modify** panel [see Figure F29]. Pick the **Select and Manipulate** tool and drag the manipulator's **Adjust** control to interactively change the shape of the teapot. Figure F30 shows the components of a **Slider** control [1. Label, 2. Value, 3. Move, 4. Show/hide, 5. Slider bar, 6. Adjust value, and 7. Change width].

F28   F29

F30

Scene Explorer

The **Scene Explorer** [see Figure F31] is a modeless dialog in 3ds Max that you can use to view, sort, filter, and select objects. In addition, you can rename, delete, hide, and freeze objects. You can also create and modify and edit object properties en masse. Each workspace in 3ds Max comes with a different **Scene Explorer** with the same name as its workspace. The **Scene Explorer** is docked to the left of the viewports.

Several explorers in 3ds Max are different versions of the **Scene Explorer**. These includes: **Layer Explorer**, **Container Explorer**, **MassFX Explorer**, and **Material Explorer**. The **Scene Explorer** comes with many toolbars [see Figure F31]. Table 2 summarizes various toolbars available.

Table 2: The **Scene Explorer** toolbars	
Flag	**Toolbar**
1	Selection toolbar
4	View toolbar
5	Display toolbar
6	Find toolbar
7	Tools toolbar

Selection Toolbar

The **Scene Explorer** comes with two sorting modes: **Sort By Layer** mode and **Sort By Hierarchy** mode. You can use the **Sort By Layer** or **Sort by Hierarchy** button on the **Selection** toolbar [marked as 1 in Figure F31] to use these modes. The **Sort By Layer** button [marked as 2 in Figure F31] sets **Scene Explorer** to **Sort By Layer** mode. In this mode, you can use drag and drop feature for editing layers. Some other options are also available in this mode. The **Sort By Hierarchy** [marked as 3 in Figure F31] button allows you to edit hierarchies using drag and drop functionality.

If you click on an object in the **Scene Explorer**, the object is selected and the associated row in the explorer gets highlighted. To select multiple objects, click on objects with the **Ctrl** held down. Press **Ctrl+A** to select all objects, **Ctrl+I** to invert the selection, and **Ctrl+D** to deselect. These commands are also available at the right of the **Selection** toolbar [marked as 1 in Figure 31]. The **Selection Set** drop-down in the **Selection** toolbar lets you select objects using **Named Selection Sets**.

Tools Toolbar

The tools available in this toolbar are dependent on whether **Sort By Hierarchy** mode or **Sort By Layer** mode is active. When **Lock Cell Editing** is on, you cannot change any name or settings. The **Pick Parent** button is only available in the **Sort By Hierarchy** mode. It allows you to change the parent. To make an object parent, select one or more objects and then click **Pick Parent**. Now, select the object that you want parent of the selected object. The **Create New Layer** button is available in the **Sort By Layer** mode. When you click **Create New Layer**, a new layer is created and the selection is automatically added to this layer. The new layer you create becomes the active layer and any subsequent objects you create are added to this layer automatically. If an existing layer is selected, and you click **Create New Layer**, the new layer becomes child of the selected layer. The **Add to Active Layer** is available in the **Sort By Layer** mode only. When you click on this button, all selected objects and layers are assigned to the active layer. **Select Children** allows you to select all child objects and layers of the selected items.

Tip: Selecting children
Double-clicking on a parent layer or object selects the parent and all its children.

The **Make Selected Layer Active** button is available in the **Sort By Layer** mode only. When you click on this button, 3ds Max makes the selected layer the active layer. Alternatively, click on the layer icon to make it the layer active.

Display Toolbar

The **Display** toolbar allows you to display various categories in the **Scene Explorer**. It controls the type of objects that appear in the **Scene Explorer's** listing. You can also solo the category by clicking on one of the category button with **Alt** held down. You can also turn on or off the categories by choosing **Display | Object Types** from the **Scene Explorer's** menu bar.

View Toolbar

The **View** toolbar is located at the bottom-left corner of the **Scene Explorer**. This toolbar shows the name of the current **Scene Explorer**. When you click on the arrow located in this toolbar, a menu appears. This menu gives access to all local and global explorers.

Local and Global Scene Explorers

3ds Max comes with different **Scene Explorer** configurations. These configurations are available to every scene you create in 3ds Max. Therefore, they are referred to as **Global Scene Explorers**. On the other hand the **Local Scene Explorers** live within a single scene and saved/loaded with the scene. The options to make a **Local** explorer **Global** are available in the menu located on the **View** toolbar [see Figure F32].

Q. How to delete objects?

To delete one or more objects in the **Scene Explorer**, select them and then press **Delete** or RMB click on the list and then choose **Delete** from the **Quad** menu.

Q. How to hide and show objects?

Click the light bulb icon of the layer or object to hide. The light bulb icon turns gray. Click again to reveal.

Q. How to create hierarchies in the Sort By Hierarchy mode?

To make a parent, drag and drop the child objects' name or icon onto the object that you want to act as parent. To restore the child object to the top level, drag them to an empty area of the **Scene Explorer**. Alternatively, you can RMB click on them and then choose **Unlink** from the **Quad** menu. You can use the same techniques on the layers as well.

Q. How to freeze objects?

To freeze objects, click on the **Frozen** column of the object. Click again to unfreeze. If you want to freeze many objects, select them and then click on the **Frozen** column of any selected objects.

Q. How to change object properties?

To change the object properties, select one or more objects in the **Scene Explorer** and then RMB. Choose **Properties** from the **Quad** menu to open the **Object Properties** dialog. You can use this dialog to change the properties of the selected objects.

Q. How to rename an object?

Select the object and then RMB click. Choose **Rename** from the **Quad** menu and then type a new name for the object.

Tip: Renaming objects
Slowly double-click on the object name to rename the object if you don't want to use the **Quad** *menu.*

Q. Can I add more column next to the Frozen column?

Yes, you can. RMB click on any of the column head and then choose **Configure Columns** *[see Figure F33]* from the popup menu. The **Configure Column** window appears *[see Figure F34]*. Click on the name of the column in this window that you want to add. Figure F35 shows the **Has Material** column. A tick will appear in this column if the material has been assigned to the object.

Q. Can I search object by names?

Yes, you can search object by using the search text box available in the **Find** toolbar. Type the search sting and press **Enter**. For example, if you have many teapots in the scene and all have default names. Entering **tea** in the **search** field and then pressing **Enter** will select all teapots in the scene. You can also use the wild card characters **?** and ***** to create a broader search criteria.

Working with the Precision Tools

3ds Max comes with several tools and objects that allow you to position and align objects efficiently. Two tools [**Select and Place** tool, and **Select and Manipulate** tool] I have already discussed that let you align and position objects. You have also seen the use of some helpers that are used with the **Select and Manipulate** tool.

Using Units

The units define the measurement system for the scene. The default unit system in 3ds Max is **Generic**. Besides the **Generic** units, you can also use feet and inches units both decimal and fractional. The **Metric** system allows you to specify units from millimeters to kilometers. You can specify the unit system from the **Units Setup** dialog [see Figure F36]. You can open this dialog by choosing **Units Setup** from the **Customize** menu. On clicking **System Unit Setup** from this dialog, the **System Unit Setup** dialog appears from where you can specify the **System** units.

F36

Q. What is the difference between Scene Units and System Units?

The system units only affects how geometry appears in the viewports whereas the system units control the actual scale of the geometry.

Caution: System Units

*The system units should only be changed before you create your scene or import a **unitless** file. Do not change the system units in the current scene.*

If you change units for a scene, 3ds Max automatically changes the values for the controls. For example, if you are using **Centimeters**, and value in a spinner is **30 cm**, when you change units to **Decimal Inches**; 3ds Max will change the value to **11.811** inches. Now, if you type **50cm** in the spinner and press **Enter**, 3ds Max will change value to **19.685** inches. Similarly, if you type **2'** in the spinner, the value will be changed to **24.0** inches.

Using Grids

Grids are two dimensional arrays that you can use to position the objects accurately. You can use grids to visualize space, scale, and distance. You can use it as construction plane to create objects as well use it for snapping objects using the snap feature. I will discuss snap features later in this unit. 3ds Max provides two types of grids: **Home** grid and **Grid** objects.

Home Grid

The **Home** grid is defined by three intersecting planes along the world **X**, **Y**, and **Z** axes. These planes intersect at the origin defined by **0,0,0**. The **Home** grid is fixed, you cannot move or rotate it.

Tip: Home Grid

*Press **G** to toggle the visibility of the **Home** grid.*

Grid Object

The **Grid** object [see Figure F37] is a helper object that you can use to create a reference grid as per your needs. You can create as many **Grid** objects as you want in a scene. However, only one **Grid** object will be active at a time. When a **Grid** object is active, it replaces the **Home** grid in all viewports. You can rename and delete **Grid** objects like any other object. The **Grid** object is available in the **Helpers** category on the **Create** panel.

F37

Tip: Activating the Home grid and Grid object
*You can activate the **Home** grid by choosing **Grids and Snaps | Activate Home Grid** from the **Tools** menu. When you choose this command, it activates the **Home** grid in all viewports and deactivates the current active grid object. Similarly, you can activate a **Grid** object by choosing **Grids and Snaps | Activate Grid Object** from the **Tools** menu.*

Tip: Aligning a Grid object to the view
*To align a **Grid** object with the current view, choose **Grids and Snaps | Activate Grid Object** from the **Quad** menu. The **Grid** object is aligned and will be coplanar with the current view.*

Auto Grid

The **Auto Grid** feature lets you create objects on the surface of other objects. The **Auto Grid** option is available on the **Object Type** rollout of any category. It is also available in the **Extras** toolbar. When you activate this option, and drag the cursor on the surface of an object, a construction plane is created temporarily on the surface of object.

Tip: Select and Place tool
*The **Select and Place** tool discussed earlier provides a similar mechanism to align the objects.*

Aligning Objects

3ds Max provides six different tools for aligning the objects in a scene. These tools are available in the **Align** flyout on the **Main** toolbar.

Using with Align Tool

The **Align** tool in 3ds Max allows you to align the current selection to a target selection. You can pick the **Align** tool from the **Align** flyout on the **Main** toolbar. You can also activate this tool by choosing **Align | Align** from the **Tools** menu or by pressing **Alt+A**. Using this tool, you can align the position and orientation of the bounding box of a source object to the bounding box of a target object. A bounding box is the smallest box that encloses the extents (maximum dimensions) of an object. A bounding box appears when you set a viewport to non-wireframe mode. Figure F38 shows the extents of a teapot model.

F38

To show the bounding box, select the object and then press **J**. You can also enable display of the bounding boxes by turning on **Selection Brackets** from the **Viewport Setting and Preference** dialog | **Per-View Preferences** panel [see Figure F39]. Refer to Explore More section of **Unit MI1** for more information on **Viewport Setting and Preference** dialog.

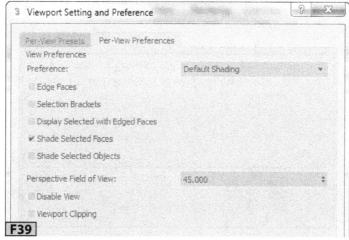

F39

Let's dive in and align some objects:

Create three boxes and assign them red, green, and blue colors [see Figure F40]. Use the following dimensions:

Red Box: Length=52, Width=61, and Height=32
Green Box: Length=35, Width=40, and Height=12
Blue Box: Length=50, Width=40, and Height=30

RMB click on the red box and choose **Object Properties** from the **Quad** menu. On the **General panel** | **Display Properties** group, turn on **See-Through**. This will help you better see the alignment process. Now let's center align the red and blue boxes along the **X** and **Y** axes. Make sure the red box is selected and then pick the **Align** tool from the **Main** toolbar. Click the blue box. On the **Align Selection dialog** | **Align Position (World) group**, turn on **X Position** and **Y Position**. Turn off **Z Position**. Make sure **Center** is on in the **Current Object** and **Target Object** groups. You will see that both the objects are center aligned [see Figure F41]. Click **OK** to accept changes.

F40   F41

Now, let's see how to place blue box on the top of the red box.

Select the blue box and then pick the **Align** tool from the **Main** toolbar. Click red box. We have already performed alignment along the **X** and **Y** axes. Therefore, turn off **X Position** and **Y Position** and turn on **Z Position**. You will see that now the blue box is at the center of the red box. Turn on **Maximum** from the **Target Object** group. Notice the blue box's center is aligned to the center of the red box [see Figure 42]. Now select **Pivot Point** from the **Current Object** group. The blue box sits on the top of the red box [see Figure F43]. Click **OK** to accept changes.

F42   F43

Now, let's align one corner of the green box with blue box.

Select the green box and then pick the **Align** tool from the **Main** toolbar. Click the blue box. Turn on **X Position**, **Y Position**, and **Z Position**. Turn on **Minimum** from the **Current Object** and **Target Object** groups [see Figure F44]. Click **OK** to accept changes. With the green box selected, click the blue box using the **Align** tool. Now, turn on **Z Position** and turn off **X Position** and **Y Position**. Turn on **Maximum** from the **Target Object** group and click **OK**. The boxes are now stacked over each other [see Figure F45].

F44   F45

Using the Quick Align Tool

The **Quick Align** tool instantly aligns an object with the target object. The hotkeys associated with this tool are **Shift+A**. To align an object, select the source object and press **Shift+A** to activate the tool. Now, click on the target object to align two objects [see Figure F46]. If the current selection contains a single object, this tool uses the pivot points of the two objects for alignment. If multiple objects are selected, the selection center of the source objects is aligned with the pivot of the target objects.

F46

Using the Normal Align Tool

This tool allows you to align the two objects based on the directions of the normals of the selected faces. The hotkeys associated with this tool are **Alt+N**. To understand functioning of this tool, create a sphere and teapot in the scene [see Figure F47]. Select the teapot, the source object in this case. Press **Alt+N** to activate the tool and then drag across the surface of the teapot, a blue arrow indicates the location of the current normal [see Figure F48]. Keep dragging on the surface until you find the normal you are looking for. Now, click and drag on the surface of the sphere until you find the normal to which you want to align the the source object. Release the mouse button the teapot gets aligned with the sphere [see Figure 49] and the **Normal Align** dialog opens. Using the controls available in this dialog you can offset the position and orientation of the teapot.

F47   F48   F49

Q. What are normals?

A normal is a vector that defines the inner and outer surfaces of a face in a mesh. The direction of the vector indicates the front [outer] surface of a face or vertex. Sometimes, normals are flipped during the modeling process. To fix this issue, you can use the **Normal** *modifier to flip or unify normals. Figure 50 shows the vertex and face normals, respectively.*

F50

Using the Place Highlight Tool

You can use this tool to align an object or light to another object so that its highlight [reflection] can be precisely positioned. To position a light to highlight a face, make sure the viewport that you want to render is active. Choose **Place Highlight** from the **Align** flyout and drag the mouse pointer on the object to place the highlight. Now, release the mouse button when the normal indicates the face on which you want to place the highlight [see Figure F51].

Note: Light type and highlights

With the omni, free spot, or directional light, 3ds Max displays face normal. With a target spotlight, 3ds Max displays target of the light and base of it's cone.

Using the Align Camera Tool

This tool lets you align the camera to a selected face normal. This tool works similar to the **Place Highlight** tool but it does not change the camera position interactively. You need to release the mouse button and then 3ds Max aligns the camera with the selected face.

Using the Align View Tool

When this tool is picked from the **Align** flyout, it opens the **Align to View** dialog that lets you align the local axis of the selection or sub-object selection with the current viewport [see Figure F52]. To use this tool, select the objects or sub-objects to align and then choose **Align to View** from the **Align** flyout. 3ds Max opens the **Align to View** dialog. Choose the options from the dialog as desired. If you want to flip the direction of alignment, turn on **Flip** on this dialog box.

Drawing Assistants

3ds Max provides several tools and utilities that help you in drawing objects with precession. Let's have a look.

F51   F52

Measuring Distances

The **Measure Distance** tool allows you to quickly calculate distance between two points. The calculated distance appears in the **Status Bar** in Scene [display] units. To measure distance, choose **Measure Distance** from the **Tools** menu. Now, click on the point in the viewport from where you want to measure the distance. Click again in the viewport where you want to measure to. The distance between the two points is displayed in the **Status Bar**.

The **Measure** utility available in the **Utilities** panel provides the measurement of a selected object or spline. To measure an object, select the object and then on the **Utilities** panel | **Measure** rollout, click **Measure**. The measurements are displayed in the **Measure** rollout [see Figure F53].

There is one more utility called **Rescale World Units** that you can use to rescale the word units. You can scale entire scene or the selected objects. To rescale an object, select it and then on the **Utilities** panel click **More** to open the **Utilities** panel. Select **Rescale World Units** from the dialog and then click **OK**. The **Rescale World Units** rollout appears in the **Utilities** panel. Click **Rescale** from this rollout to open the **Rescale World Units** dialog [see Figure F54].

Set **Scale Factor** in this dialog and then turn on **Scene** or **Selection** from the **Affect** section. Click **OK** to apply the scale factor to the selected object or to entire scene. For example, you specify **Scale Factor** as **2** and turn on **Selection** from the dialog, the selected object will be scaled to double of its current size.

Using Snaps

The Snap tools in 3ds Max allow you to precisely control the dimensions and placement of the objects when you create or transform them. You and invoke these tools using the **Snap** buttons available on the **Main** toolbar. You can also invoke these tools by choosing **Grids and Snaps** from the **Tools** menu.

2D Snap, 2.5 Snap, and 3D Snap

The hotkey for activating snap is **S**. The **2D Snap** tool snaps the cursor to the active construction grid including the geometry on the plane of the grid. The **Z** axis is ignored by this tool. The **2.5D Snap** tool snaps the cursor to the vertices or edges of the projection of an object onto the active grid. The **3D snap** is the default tool. It snaps the cursor directly to any geometry in the 3D space.

RMB click on snap toggle button to open the **Grid and Snap Settings** dialog [see Figure F55]. You can specify which type of snap of you want active from the **Snap** panel of this dialog box.

Fox example, if you want the cursor to snap to the pivot or vertices of the object, turn on **Pivot** and **Vertex** from this panel.

To see snap in action, turn on **Pivot** and **Vertex** from the **Grid and Snap Settings** dialog. Now, create a box and teapot in the viewport [see first image at the left of Figure F56].

Pick the **Move** tool from the **Main** toolbar and move the teapot to one of the vertex of the box or its pivot [see middle and right image in Figure F57].

Angle Snap Toggle

You can use the **Angle Snap Toggle** to rotate an object around a given axis in the increment you set. This snap toggle also works with the **Pan/Orbit** camera controls, **FOV** and **Roll** camera settings, and **Hotspot/Falloff** spotlight angles. The hotkey for invoking this toggle is **A**.

To rotate an object, click **Angle Snap Toggle** on the **Main** toolbar and then rotate the object using the **Rotate** tool. By default, the rotation takes place in five degree increments. You can change this default value by specifying a value for the **Angle** control in the **Options** panel of the **Grid and Snap Settings** dialog.

Percent Snap Toggle

The **Percent Snap Toggle** lets you control the increments of scaling by the specified percentage. The hotkey for invoking this toggle is **Shift+Ctrl+P**. The default percentage value is **10**. You can change this default value by specifying a value for the **Percent** control in the **Options** panel of the **Grid and Snap Settings** dialog.

Spinner Snap Toggle

This toggle allows you to set single-increment or decrement value for all the spinners in 3ds Max. The default value is **1**. To change this value, RMB click on **Spinner Snap Toggle** on the **Main** toolbar to open the **Preferences Settings** dialog. In the **Spinners** section of the **General** panel, specify a value for the **Snap** control.

Modifiers

The modifiers in 3ds Max provide a way to edit and sculpt objects. You can change shape of an object using the modifier's properties. Figure F58 shows the original box [first image] and the modified geometry after applying the **Bend**, **Twist**, and **Taper** modifiers, respectively.

You can apply modifiers from the **Modifier** drop-down available in the **Modify** panel of **Command Panel** [see Figure F59]. The modifier you apply to an object are stored in a stack called modifier stack.

F59

Practical Test

Complete the following test:

Test 1: Creating a Robo Model

Create a robot model, as shown in Figure P1, using the **Standard** primitives.

Hints:

- The primitives used in the model shown in Figure P1 are: **Box**, **Sphere**, **Cylinder**, **Pyramid**, **Cone**, **Torus**, and **Pipe**.
- The fingers are created using **Torus** primitives. Turn on **Slice On** the **Parameters** rollout of torus to create opening in the torus.
- Use **Auto Grid** and **Select and Place** features of 3ds Max to align and place body parts.
- Create one leg and then use the **Mirror** tool to create a copy on the other side. Apply same concept on eyes and hands. Create a group before applying the **Mirror** tool.
- Create layers for different parts in the **Layer Explorer**. For example, keep all geometries that make hand in the hands layer, and so forth.
- Try to use various features of the **Scene Explorer**.

P1

Summary
The unit covered the following topics:

- Working with templates
- Creating clones and duplicates
- Understanding hierarchies

- Working with the **Scene** and **Layer** Explorers
- Understanding the **Mirror**, **Select and Place**, and **Select and Manipulate** tools
- Working with the **Align** and **Array** tools
- Working with precision and drawing aids
- Understanding modifiers, and normals

Unit MM1: Working with Geometric Primitives and Architectural Objects

The 3D objects in the scene and the objects that are used to create them are known as geometries. Most of the 3D applications offer basic building blocks for creating geometries called geometric primitives. You can use these primitives and some modifiers to create basic models. In this unit, you will work with the **Standard** and **Extended** primitives as well as the **Architectural** objects.

In this unit, I'll describe the following:

- Creating and modifying **Standard** Primitives
- Creating and modifying **Extended** Primitives
- Working with the **Architectural** objects
- Setting the project folder
- Using the **Align** and **Mirror** tools
- Creating clones
- Using the **Scene Explorer**
- Creating a group
- Setting grid spacings
- Using **Transform Type-In** dialog
- Using **Array** dialog
- Specifying units for the scene

You can edit these geometric primitives at sub-object levels to create complex models. This process is known as surface modeling that I've covered in the next unit. In this unit, I will explain **Standard** and **Extended** primitives and how you can use them to create some basic models.

The geometric primitives in 3ds Max are divided into two categories: **Standard** primitives and **Extended** primitives. Let's first start exploring the **Standard** primitives.

Standard Primitives

3ds Max offers eleven standard primitives, see Figure F1. You can combine **Standard** primitives into more complex objects. You can then further refine them by using the modifiers. You can dynamically create primitives in the viewport using the mouse and most of the primitives can be generated by entering precise values using the keyboard. You can specify the parameters before creating the primitives and modify them later from the **Parameters** rollout in the **Modify** panel. Let's take a look at different **Standard** primitives.

Box

Box is the simplest of the primitives. You can use it to create rectangular as well as cubical geometries in 3ds Max [see Figure F2]. To create a **Box** primitive, on the **Create** panel, click **Geometry**, and then in the **Object Type** rollout, click **Box**. You can also choose **Box** from the **Standard** menu as well as from the **Enhanced** menu:

Standard Menu: Create menu | Standard Primitives | Box
Enhanced Menu: Objects menu | Primitives | Box

To create a box, click and drag in a viewport to specify the length and width of the box. Now, release the mouse button and drag the mouse up or down [without holding any button] to specify the height of the box and then click to complete the process.

Whenever you choose a tool from the **Object Type** rollout, the **Name and Color**, **Creation Method**, **Keyboard Entry**, and **Parameters** rollouts appear on the **Command Panel**. You can use these rollouts to specify the initial properties of the objects.

Tip: Navigating between the steps
*If you are creating a primitive that requires two or more steps [for example Cylinder or Torus], you can pan and orbit the viewport between the steps. To pan the viewport, MMB drag. To orbit, hold **Alt** and then MMB drag.*

Name and Color Rollout

The controls in the **Name and Color** rollout allow you to rename the objects and change their colors. Whenever you create an object, 3ds Max assigns it a default name and color. For example, if you reset the scene and create a box in the viewport, 3ds Max assigns it the name **Box001**. To change the name of the object, type a new name in the text box available in the **Name and Color** rollout. The color swatch to the right of the text box lets you change the color of the object.

On clicking the color swatch, the **Object Color** dialog appears. You can click on one of the color swatches and then click **OK** to assign the color to the object. If you want to specify a custom color, select a color swatch for **Custom Colors** and then click **Add Custom Colors**. In the **Color Selector : Add Color** dialog that appears, specify a color and then click **Add Color** to add the chosen color to the selected swatch in **Object Color** dialog. Now, click **OK** to close the dialog and apply selected color to the object.

Tip: Scene Explorer
*As discussed in Unit MI2, you can easily rename objects using the **Scene Explorer**.*

Creation Method Rollout

There are two controls available in this rollout: **Cube** and **Box**. **Box** creates a standard box primitive with different settings for length, width, and height. **Cube** creates a cube with equal width, height, and length. Creating a cube is one step operation. Click and drag the mouse pointer in the viewport to create a cube.

Parameters Rollout

The default settings in this rollout produce a box with one segment on each side. Table 1 summarizes the controls in the **Parameters** rollout.

Table 1: The controls in the **Box's Parameters** rollout	
Control	**Description**
Length, Width, Height	The **Length, Width**, and **Height** controls set the length, width, and height of the box, respectively. These controls also act as readouts when you interactively create a primitive.
Length Segs, Width Segs, Height Segs	The **Length Segs, Width Segs**, and **Height Segs** controls set the number of segments [divisions] along each axis of the object. You can set these parameters before and after the creation of the box. The default value for these parameters is **1, 1, 1**.
Generate Mapping Coords	**Generate Mapping Coords** is on by default. It generates coordinates for applying material to the box.
Real-World Map Size	**Real-World Map Size** control lets you create a material and specify the actual width and height of a 2D texture map in the **Material Editor**. The scaling values are controlled from the material's **Coordinate** rollout.

Note: Default values
Whatever values you specify for these controls become default for the current session.

Tip: Resolution
*If you are planning to use the modifiers such as **Bend** on a primitive, increase the values for the **Length Segs**, **Width Segs**, and **Height Segs** controls to get some extra resolution on the objects.*

Keyboard Entry Rollout

You can use the controls in this rollout to define both the size of the box as well as its position in 3D space in a single operation. The method for creating objects through keyboard is generally same for all primitives; differences might occur in the type and number of controls.

The **X**, **Y**, and **Z** controls define the position of the object. The default value is **0, 0, 0** which is center of the active grid.

Cone

You can use this primitive to create round upward or inverted cones [see Figure F3]. To create a cone, click **Cone** in the **Object Type** rollout. In the viewport, drag to define the base of the cone and then release mouse button. Now, move the mouse pointer up or down in the viewport to define the height.

The height can be negative or positive. Click to set the height. Move the mouse pointer to define the radius of the other end of the cone. If you want to create a pointed cone, set this radius to zero.

Creation Method Rollout

Two creation methods are available for the **Cone** primitive: **Edge** and **Center**. **Edge** draws a cone from edge to edge. **Center** draws from the center out.

Parameters Rollout

The default settings in this rollout produce a smooth cone with 24 sides, one cap segment and five height segments. Table 2 summarizes the controls in the **Parameters** rollout.

Table 2: The controls in the **Cone's Parameters** rollout	
Control	**Description**
Radius 1, Radius 2	**Radius 1** and **Radius 2** define the first and second radii of the cone. You can use these two controls to create pointed or flat-topped cones.
Height	**Height** sets the dimension of the cone along the central axis. If you set a negative value, the cone will be created below the construction plane.
Height Segments	**Height Segments** controls sets the number of divisions along the major axis of the cone.
Cap Segments	**Cap Segments** sets the number of concentric divisions in the top or bottom of the cone.
Sides	**Sides** determines the number of sides around the cone.
Smooth	**Smooth** is on by default. It blends the faces of the cone on rendering therefore producing smooth looking renders.
Slice From, Slice To	You can use the **Slice From** and **Slice To** controls to slice the cone. These two controls set the number of degrees around the local Z axis. To turn on these two controls, turn on **Slice On**.

Caution: Minimum and negative values
*If you specify negative values for **Radius 1** and **Radius 2**, these values will be converted to **0**. The minimum values for these controls is **0**.*

Note: Same value for Radius 1 and Radius 2
*If you specify a same values for **Radius 1** and **Radius 2**, a cylinder will be created. If these two values are close in size, an object is created which resembles the effect as if a **Taper** modifier is applied to a cylinder.*

Tip: Pointed cones
For improved rendering on smooth pointed cones, increase the number of height segments.

Sphere

You can use the **Sphere** primitive to create a full sphere, a hemisphere, slice of the sphere, or some part of a sphere [see Figure F4]. To create a sphere, on the **Create** panel, click **Geometry**, and then on the **Object Type** rollout, click **Sphere**.

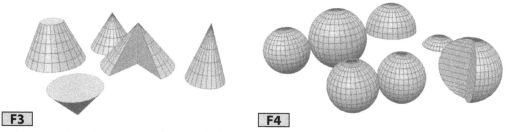

F3   F4

In the viewport, drag the mouse pointer to define the radius of the sphere, release mouse button to set the radius. To create a hemisphere, create the desired sphere of the desired radius and then set **Hemisphere** to **0.5** in the **Parameters** rollout.

Creation Method Rollout

There are two methods available for creating a sphere: **Edge** and **Center**. **Edge** draws the sphere from edge to edge. **Center** draws a sphere from center out.

Parameters Rollout

The default values in the rollout produce a smooth sphere with **32** divisions. Table 3 summarizes the controls in the **Parameters** rollout.

Table 3: The controls in the **Sphere's Parameters** rollout	
Control	**Description**
Radius	**Radius** specifies the radius of the sphere.
Segments	**Segments** controls the number of segments for the sphere.
Hemisphere	**Hemisphere** lets you create a hemisphere. It cuts off the sphere to create a partial sphere. You can use this control to create an animation in which the sphere will be cut off starting from its base to top.
Chop, Squash	**Chop** and **Squash** determine the number of vertices and faces when you create a hemisphere. **Chop** reduces the number of vertices and faces by chopping them out whereas **Squash** maintains the number of vertices and faces by squashing the geometry toward the top of the sphere. Figure F5 shows the effect of **Chop** [left] and **Squash** [right] on a hemisphere with **16** segments.
Base To Pivot	If you turn on **Base to Pivot**, the sphere moves upward along its local Z axis and places the pivot point at its base. Figure F6 shows the pivot at the center [left], which is default, and pivot at the base of the sphere [right].

[+][Perspective][Wireframe]

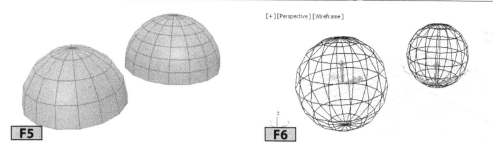

F5   F6

GeoSphere

You can use the **GeoSphere** primitive to create spheres and geo-hemispheres based on three classes of polyhedrons: **Tetra**, **Octa**, and **Icosa** [see Figure F7].

The **GeoSphere** primitive produces more regular shape than the **Sphere** primitive. Unlike the **Sphere** primitive, the geometry produced by the **GeoSphere** primitive has no poles which is an advantage is in certain modeling scenarios. Also, they appear slightly smoother than the standard sphere when rendered. To create a **GeoSphere**, on the **Create** panel, click **Geometry**, and then on the **Object Type** rollout, click **GeoSphere**. In the viewport, drag the mouse pointer to define the radius of the sphere, release mouse button to set the radius. To create a hemisphere, create the desired sphere of the desired radius and then check **Hemisphere** in the **Parameters** rollout.

Creation Method rollout

There are two methods available for creating a sphere: **Diameter** and **Center**. **Diameter** draws the geosphere from edge to edge whereas **Center** draws a geosphere from the center out.

Parameters Rollout

Table 4 summarizes the controls in the **Parameters** rollout.

Table 4: The controls in the **GeoSphere's Parameters** rollout	
Control	**Description**
Radius	**Radius** sets the radius of the geosphere.
Segments	**Segments** controls the number of faces in the geosphere.
Tetra, Octa, Icosa	The controls in the **Geodesic Base Type** group let you choose one of the regular polyhedrons for geosphere geometry. **Tetra** creates a four-sided tetrahedron. The facets can vary in shape and size. The geosphere can be divided into four equal segments. **Octa** creates an eight-sided tetrahedron. The facets can vary in shape and size. The geosphere can be divided into eight equal segments. **Icosa** creates a 20-sided tetrahedron. The facets are equal in size. The geosphere can be divided into any number of equal segments.

Cylinder

The **Cylinder** primitive creates a cylinder that can be sliced along its major axis [see Figure F8]. To create a cylinder, on the **Create** panel, click **Geometry**, and then on the **Object Type** rollout, click **Cylinder**. In the viewport, drag the mouse pointer to define the radius, release the mouse button to set the radius. Now, move the mouse pointer up or down to define the height, click to set it.

F7   F8

Parameters Rollout

The default controls in the **Parameters** rollout produce an **18** sided smooth cylinder with the five height segments, one cap segment, and the pivot point at its base. Table 5 summarizes the controls in the **Parameters** rollout.

Table 5: The controls in the **Cylinder's Parameters** rollout	
Control	**Description**
Radius	**Radius** sets the radius of the cylinder.
Height	**Height** defines the height of the cylinder along the cylinder's major axis.
Height Segments	**Height Segments** defines the number of divisions along the cylinder's major axis.
Sides	**Sides** sets the sides around the cylinder.
Cap Segments	**Cap Segments** sets the number of concentric divisions around top and bottom of the cylinder.

Tip: Resolution

*If you are going to use the cylinder with a modifier such as **Bend**, increase the number of height segments. If you are planning to modify the end of the cylinder, increase the number of cap segments.*

Tube

The **Tube** primitive produces a cylinder with a hole in it [see Figure F9]. You can use this primitive to use both round and prismatic tubes. To create a **Tube**, on the **Create** panel, click **Geometry**, and then on the **Object Type** rollout, click **Tube**. In the viewport, drag the mouse pointer to define the first radius, which can be either the inner or the outer radius of the tube, release the mouse button to set the first radius. Move the mouse pointer to create the second radius, and then click to set it. Move the pointer up or down to create the height [positive or negative] and then click to set the height of the tube.

Tip: Prismatic Tube

*To create a prismatic tube, set the number of sides to according to the type of the prismatic tube you want to create. Uncheck **Smooth** and create the tube.*

Parameters Rollout

Radius 1 and **Radius 2** are used specify the inside and outside radii of the tube. The larger among the two values defines the outside radius of the tube.

Torus

You can use the **Torus** primitive to create a doughnut like shape which is ring with the circular cross section [see Figure F10]. To create a torus, on the **Create** panel, click **Geometry**, and then on the **Object Type** rollout, click **Torus**. In the viewport, drag the mouse pointer to define a torus; the torus emerges from its center. Release the mouse button to set the radius of the torus ring. Now, move the mouse pointer to define the radius of the cross section, and click to complete the creation process.

Parameters Rollout

The default values in this rollout produce a smooth torus with **12** sides and **24** segments. The pivot point of the torus is located at the center of the torus on the plane which cuts through the center of the torus.

Rotation sets the degree of rotation. The vertices are uniformly rotated about the circle running through the center of the torus ring. **Twist** defines the degree of twist. 3ds Max twists the cross sections about the circle running through the center of the torus.

F9   F10

Caution: Twisting a close torus
*Twisting a close torus will create a constriction in the first segment. To overcome this, you can either twist the torus in the increments of 360 or turn on **Slice** and then set both **Slice From** and **Slice To** to 0.*

The controls in the **Smooth** group control the level of smoothing. The default **All** control produces smoothing on all surfaces of the torus. **Sides** smooths the edges between the adjacent segments thus producing smooth bands which run around the torus. **None** turns off the smoothing and produces prism-like facets on the torus. **Segments** smooths each segment individually and produces ring-like segments.

Pyramid
The **Pyramid** primitive is used to create a pyramid like shape with the square or rectangle face and triangular sides [see Figure F11]. To create a pyramid, on the **Create** panel, click **Geometry**, and then on the **Object Type** rollout, click **Pyramid**. In the viewport, drag the mouse pointer to define the base of the pyramid. Click to set it and then drag the mouse pointer up to define the height.

Tip: Constrain the base of the pyramid to a square
*To constrain the base of the pyramid to a square, drag with the **Ctrl** key held down.*

Plane
The **Plane** primitive creates a flat plane that you can enlarge to any size [see Figure F12]. To create a **Plane**, on the **Create** panel, click **Geometry**, and then on the **Object Type** rollout, click **Plane**. In the viewport, drag the mouse pointer to create a plane.

F11   F12

Parameters Rollout
The controls in the **Render Multipliers** group are used to set the multipliers at render time. You can use **Scale** to specify the factor by which both length and width will be multiplied at render time. **Density** specifies a factor by which the number of segments in both length and width are multiplied at the render time.

Teapot

The **Teapot** primitive is used to create a parametric teapot object [see Figure F12A]. This object is comprised of a lid, body, handle, and sprout. You can create the whole teapot [which is default] or combination of the parts. You can even control which parts to display after creation. To create a **Teapot**, on the **Create** panel, click **Geometry**, and then on the **Object Type** rollout, click **Teapot**. In the viewport, click and drag to define the radius. Release the mouse button to set the radius and create teapot. You can control which part of the teapot you want to create by turning on the required controls from the **Teapot Parts** group of the **Parameters** rollout.

TextPlus

The **TextPlus** primitive is used to create all-in-one text object. You can use this primitive to create an spline outline as well as solid, extruded beveled geometry. It allows you to apply different fonts and styles on a per-character basis and add animation and special effects. It is a very useful tool for producing motion graphics elements. To create the text, on the **Create** panel, click **Geometry**, and then on the **Object Type** rollout, click **TextPlus**. Click on the viewport to create the **TextPlus** object. If you want to create a region of text, click-drag in the viewport to define the region.

Layout Rollout

From this rollout, you can define the plane onto which you will type the text. The default plane is **XY** plane. Also, you can set whether you want to create a region of text or text just starting from a point [see Figure F13].

F12A   F13

Parameters Rollout

From this rollout, you can set the font and other global parameters such as tracking and leading for the text. If you click on **Open Large Text Window**, the **Enter Text** window appears [see Figure F14]. This window lets you easily type and format text. If you want to interactively change global parameters in viewport, click **Manipulate Text**, some symbols appear on the text in the viewport [see Figure F15]. You can use these symbols to manipulate the global parameters.

When you are manipulating the text, you can you use the following:

- To select more than one letter, use **Ctrl+click**.
- If you click a letter with **Shift** held down, the clicked letter will be selected, all other previously selected letters will be de-selected.
- The tracking symbols only appear when you select more than one letter.
- You can change font and font type for individual characters.
- When you select letters in the **Text** field, letters are also selected in the viewport [see Figure F16].

F14

F15

F16

To reset the parameters, click **Reset Parameters,** the **Reset Text** dialog appears [see Figure F17]. Select the options that you want to reset and then click **Reset.**

F17

Geometry Rollout
The controls in this rollout allow you to create depth using **Extrude** and **Bevel** functions.

Values As Strings
You can also use the **TextPlus** object to display value of a object's parameter in the viewport. You can also show any value that can be returned from a script or expression. The value will dynamically update in the viewport when it changes. To see this feature in action, create a **TextPlus** object in a viewport

and then type **radius:** in the **Text** field of the **Parameters** rollout. Create a sphere in a viewport. On the **Parameters** rollout of the **TextPlus** object, click **Set Value as Text** to open the **Edit Value As** Text dialog. In this dialog, select **Script** from the **Value Options** area [see Figure F18] and then click **Pick Value From Scene**. Now, click the scene and then choose **Object (Sphere)** | **Radius** from the popup [see Figure F19] to make the connection.

F18

F19

Select **Real Number** from the drop-down available in the **Display As** area and then set **Decimals** to **2**. Now, put the cursor at the end of the text typed in the **Text** field and click **Insert In Text** from the **Edit Value As Text** dialog. Close the dialog. The string **%[Value1]** is appended in the **Text** field [see Figure F20]. Now, if you change the value of **Radius** control, the value will be dynamically updated in the **TextPlus** object.

F20

Extended Primitives

Extended primitives are little complex than the **Standard** Primitives. 3ds Max offers thirteen extended primitives, see Figure F21. You can combine **Extended** primitives with the **Standard** primitives and modifiers to create refined models. You can dynamically create **Extended** primitives in the viewport using the mouse and most of the primitives can be generated by entering precise values using the keyboard. You can specify the parameters before creating the **Extended** primitives and

F21

modify them later from the **Parameters** rollout in the **Modify** panel. Let's take a look at the commonly used **Extended** primitives. Experiment with the primitives that are not covered in this section. They are straight forward and you can easily understand their parameters by changing them from the **Parameters** rollout.

Hedra

You can use this primitive to create different type of polyhedra objects [see Figure F22].

Table 6 summarizes the controls in the **Parameters** rollout.

Table 6: The controls in the **Hedra's Parameters** rollout	
Control	**Description**
Family Group	The controls in this group allows you to choose the type of polyhedral you want to create. **Tetra** creates a tetrahedron. **Cube/Octa** creates a cubic or octahedral polyhedron. **Dodec/Icos** creates a dodecahedron or icosahedron. **Star 1** and **Star 2** create two different star-shaped polyhedron.
Family Parameters Group	The **P** and **Q** controls in this group change the geometry back and forth between the vertices and faces. In Figure F23, the left polyhedron has **P** and **Q** values set to **0** each whereas the polyhedron on the right has the **P** and **Q** values set to **0.3** each. The combined value of **P** and **Q** can be equal to or less than **1**.
Axis Scaling Group	The **P**, **Q**, and **R** controls in this group allow you to push or pull the corresponding facets in or out. The polyhedron on the left in Figure F24 is created with the default parameters. For the polyhedron on the right, I have changed **Q** and **R** values to **120** and **150**, respectively. On clicking **Reset**, the axes return to their default values.
Vertices Group	The controls in this group determine the internal geometry of each facet of the polyhedron.
Radius	Sets the radius of the polyhedron.

Note: Creating Extended primitives
*To save some space, I am not writing the process to create the **Extended** primitives. You can easily create them using the standard click drag methods as done in the **Standard Primitives** section.*

F22   F23

ChamferBox

You can use this primitive to create a box with beveled or round edges [see Figure F25]. Most of the controls in the **Parameters** rollout are similar to that of the **Box** primitive. Table 7 lists the controls that are unique to **ChamferBox**.

F24   F25

Table 7: The controls in the **ChamferBox's Parameters** rollout

Control	Description
Fillet	Slices the edges of the box. Higher the value for this control, more refined fillet you will get.
Fillet Segs	Determines the number of segments in the filleted edges.
Smooth	Blends the display of faces of the box. As a result, when rendered, box appears smooth in the rendered results.

ChamferCylinder

This primitive creates a cylinder with beveled or rounded cap edges [see Figure F26].

F26

Most of the controls in the **Parameters** rollout are similar to that of the **Cylinder** primitive. Table 8 lists the controls that are unique to **ChamferCylinder**.

Table 8: The controls in the **Chamfer Cylinder's Parameters** rollout

Control	Description
Fillet	It chamfers the top and bottom cap edges of the cylinder. Higher the value, more refined fillet will be.
Fillet Segs	Determines the number of segments in the filleted edges of the cylinder.

Architectural Objects

3ds Max provides several architectural objects that you can use as a basic building blocks for architectural models such as home, offices, and so forth. Table 9 summaries the architectural objects that 3ds Max offers.

Table 9: The architectural objects	
Types	Objects
AEC Extended Objects	**Foliage**, **Railing**, and **Wall**
Stairs	**L-Type Stair**, **Spiral Stair**, **Straight Stair**, and **U-Type Stair**
Doors	**Pivot**, **Bifold**, and **Sliding**
Windows	**Awning**, **Casement**, **Fixed**, **Pivoted**, **Projected**, and **Sliding**

You can access all **AEC** objects from the **AEC Objects** sub-menu of the **Create** menu. You can also access these objects from the **Create** panel. Let's explore these objects.

Doors

The door objects allow you to quickly create a door. You can also set the door to be partially open even you can animate the opening. 3ds Max offers three types of doors. Table 10 summarizes these types.

Table 10: The door types	
Type	Description
Pivot	This door is hinged on one side only [see Figure F27]. You can also make the door double-door, each hinged on its outer edge.
Bifold	This door is hinged in the middle as well as in the side. You can use this object to model a set of double doors [see Figure F28].
Sliding	This type of door has a fixed half and a sliding half [see Figure F29].

F27

F28

F29

Tip: Navigating Viewport
*If while creating **AEC** objects, you need to navigate the interface between clicks, drag the **MMB** to pan the viewport, **Alt+MMB** drag to orbit the viewport, and **Alt+Ctrl+Scroll** to zoom the viewport.*

To create a door, click **Command Panel | Create** panel | **Geometry** and then choose **Doors** from the drop-down. In the **Object Type** rollout, choose the type of the door you want to create and then set the desired create options from the rollouts. Drag the mouse in the viewport to create first two points to define the width and angle of the base of the door. Now, release the mouse button and drag to define the depth of the door and click to set. Drag the mouse to define the height of the door and then click to finish.

Assigning Material to Doors

By default, 3ds Max assigns five different IDs to the door you create. The default **Door-Template Multi-Subobject** material is found in the **Ace Templates.mat** material library. Figure F30 shows the ID numbers and their associated parts in the door. 3ds Max does not assign a material to the door object. If you want to use the default material, you need to open the library in the **Material Editor** and then assign material to your object.

Table 11 summarizes the material IDs assigned to doors.

Table 11: The material IDs	
ID	**Component**
1	Font
2	Back
3	Inner Bevel. This ID is used for glazing when you set **Panels** to **Glass** or **Beveled**.
4	Frame
5	Inner Door

Tip: The Ace Template.mat library
*You can find this library at the following location: **C:\Program Files\Autodesk\3ds Max 2017\materiallibraries**.*

F30

The window objects in 3ds Max allow you to create the appearance of a window. You can also set the window to be partially open even you can animate the opening. 3ds Max offers six types of windows. Table 12 summarizes the window types.

Table 12: The window types	
Type	**Description**
Casement	Two door like sashes arrangement that can swing inward or outward [see Figure F31].
Pivoted	It pivots vertically or horizontally at the center of its sash [see Figure F32].
Projected	It has three sashes two of which open like awning in opposite directions [see Figure F33].
Sliding	It has two sashes one of which slides vertically or horizontally [see Figure F34].
Fixed	It does not open [see Figure F35].
Awning	It has a sash that is hinged at the top [see Figure F36].

To create a window, click **Command Panel | Create** panel | **Geometry** and then choose **Windows** from the drop-down. In the **Object Type** rollout, choose the type of the window you want to create and then create the window in the viewport using click-drag operations.

F31 F32
F33 F34
F35 F36

Assigning Material to Windows

By default, 3ds Max assigns five different IDs to the window you create. The default **Window-Template Multi-Subobject** material is found in the **Ace Templates.mat** material library. Figure F37 shows the ID numbers and their associated parts in the window. 3ds Max does not assign a material to the window object. If you want to use the default material, you need to open the library in the **Material Editor** and then assign material to your object.

F37

Table 13 summarizes the material IDs assigned to windows.

ID	Component
Table 13: The material IDs	
ID	**Component**
1	Front Rails
2	Back Rails
3	Panels. The Opacity is set to 50%.
4	Front Frame
5	Back Frame

Stairs

3ds Max allows you to create four different types of stairs. The following table summarizes the types of stairs.

Type	Description
Table 14: The stairs types	
Type	**Description**
Spiral Stair	It allows you to create spiral staircase. You can specify radius, and number of revolutions. You can also add stringers, center pole, and more to the stairs [see Figure F38].

Straight Stair	It allows you to create simple straight stairs [see Figure F39].
L-Type Stair	It lets you create the L-Type stairs [see Figure F40].
U-Type Stair	It lets you create the U-Type stairs [see Figure F41].

To create a stair, click **Command Panel | Create** panel | **Geometry** and then choose **Stairs** from the drop-down. In the **Object Type** rollout, choose the type of the stair you want to create and then create the stair in the viewport using click-drag operations.

Assigning Material to Stairs

By default, 3ds Max assigns five different IDs to the stairs you create. The default **Stairs-Template Multi-Subobject** material is found in the **Ace Templates.mat** material library. 3ds Max does not assign a material to the stairs object. If you want to use the default material, you need to open the library in the **Material Editor** and then assign material to your object.

Table 15 summarizes the material IDs assigned to stairs.

Table 15: The material IDs	
ID	Component
1	Treads of the stairs.
2	Front riser of the stairs.
3	Bottom, back, and sides of the risers of the stairs.
4	Center pole of the stairs.
5	Handrails of the stairs.
6	Carriage of the stairs.
7	Stringers of the stairs.

AEC Extended Objects

AEC stands for **Architecture Engineer Construction**. These objects are designed to for use in the architectural, engineering, and construction field. To create an **AEC** object, click **Command Panel | Create** panel | **Geometry** and then choose **AEC Extended** from the drop-down. In the **Object Type** rollout, choose the type of the object you want to create and then create the object in the viewport using click-drag operations.

Railing

This tool allows you to create railings in a 3ds Max scene. The railing object includes rails, posts, and fencing [see Figure F42]. You can create railing by specifying the orientation and height. You can also use a spline object to create railing along it. If you edit the spline, the railing object updates to follow the path. You can use railing object with the stair object to create a complete stair.

To create a railing, click **Command Panel | Create** panel | **Geometry** and then choose **AEC Extended** from the drop-down. In the **Object Type** rollout, click **Railing** and then create the stair in the viewport using click-drag operations.

F42

Assigning Material to Railings

By default, 3ds Max assigns five different IDs to the railings you create. The default **Rail-Template Multi-Subobject** material is found in the **Ace Templates.mat** material library. 3ds Max does not assign a material to the railing objects. If you want to use the default material, you need to open the library in the **Material Editor** and then assign material to your object. Table 16 summarizes the material IDs assigned to railings.

Table 16: The material IDs	
ID	Component
1	Lower rails

2	Posts of the railing
3	Solid fill of the railing
4	Top of the railing
5	Pickets of the railing

Foliage

You can use this tool to place various kinds of tree species in a scene [see Figures F43 and F44]. This tool can produce good looking trees efficiently. You can define height, density, pruning, seed, canopy display, and level of detail for the **Foliage** object.

F43

F44

To create a tree, click **Command Panel | Create** panel | **Geometry** and then choose **AEC Extended** from the drop-down. In the **Object Type** rollout, click **Foliage**. In the **Favorite Plants** rollout, either drag a tree to add to the scene or select the plant and then click on the viewport to place it. You can also double-click on a plant in the **Favorite Plants** rollout.

Tip: Placing plants in the scene
*You can use the **Spacing** tool to place plants along a path.*

Wall

The **Wall** tool is used to create walls [see Figure F45] in 3ds Max. The wall object is made up of three sub-object types: **Vertex**, **Segment**, and **Profile** that you can use to edit it.

You can create wall in any viewport but for vertical walls you should use a **Perspective**, **Camera**, or **Top** viewport. To create a wall, set the **Width** and **Height** parameters and then click in a viewport. Now, release the mouse button and then drag to specify the length, click again.

F45

If you want to create a single wall component, RMB, else continue clicking. To finish creating a room, click on an end segment; 3ds Max displays the **Weld Point** dialog. You can use the options in this dialog to either weld the two end vertices into a single vertex or you can keep the two end vertices distinct. **RMB** click to finish the wall.

Assigning Material to Walls

By default, 3ds Max assigns five different IDs to the walls you create. The default **Wall-Template Multi-Subobject** material is found in the **Ace Templates.mat** material library. 3ds Max does not assign a material to the wall object. If you want to use the default material, you need to open the library in the **Material Editor** and then assign material to your object.

Table 17 summarizes the material IDs assigned to the walls.

Table 17: The material IDs assigned to the walls	
ID	**Component**
1	Vertical ends of the wall.
2	Outside of the wall.
3	Inside of the wall.
4	Top of the wall, including any edges cut out of the wall.
5	Bottom of the wall.

Note: ID 2 and 3
The definitions of ID 2 and 3 is interchangeable because the inside and outside of the wall depend on your point-of-view and how you created the wall object.

Note: Inserting doors and windows in a wall
3ds Max automatically makes opening for doors and windows in a wall object. It also makes the linked doors and windows children of the wall object. To do this, directly create doors and windows on the wall by snapping to its faces, vertices, or edges.

Hands-on Exercises

From the **Application** menu, choose **Manage | Set Project Folder** to open the **Browse for Folder** dialog. Navigate to the **max2017projects** directory that you have created and then click **Make New Folder**. Create the new folder with the name **unit-mm1** and click **OK** to create the project directory.

Exercise 1: Creating a Sofa

In this exercise, you will model a sofa using the **Box** primitive [see Figure E1]. The following table summarizes the exercise:

E1

Table E1: Creating Model of a Sofa	
In this exercise, you will learn how to:	• Create simple geometry • Setup units and home grid settings • Use the **Align** tool • Use the **Mirror** tool • Create clones • Use the **Scene Explorer** • Create a group • Open and close a group
Skill level	Beginner
Time to complete	30 Minutes
Topics in the section:	• Specifying the Units for the Exercise • Creating One Seat Section of the Sofa • Creating Corner Section of the Sofa
Project folder	**unit-mm1**
Units	**US Standard – Decimal Inches**
Final exercise file	**umm1-hoe1-end.max**

Specifying the Units for the Exercise

From **Customize** menu choose **Units Setup**. In the **Units Setup** dialog that appears, select **US Standard** from the **Display Unit Scale** group. Next, choose **Decimal Inches** from the drop-down located below **US Standard** [see Figure E2] and then click **OK** to accept the change.

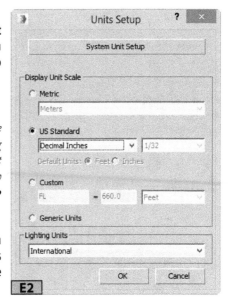

What just happened?

*Here, I have set the display units for the scene. The units that you set here are used to measure geometry in the scene. You can also set the lighting units using this dialog box. Apart from the display units, you can also set the system units that 3ds Max uses for the internal mechanism. To view controls available for changing system units, click **System Unit Setup** on the **Units Setup** dialog.*

It is important to understand the difference between the system and display units. The scene units only affect how geometry is displayed in the viewports whereas the system units control the actual scale of the geometry.

Caution: System Units

*The system units should only be changed before you create your scene or import a **unitless** file. Do not change the system units in the current scene.*

RMB click on any snap toggle button on the **Main** toolbar. In the **Grid and Snap Settings** dialog that opens, choose the **Home Grid** panel and then set **Grid Spacing** to **6**, **Major Lines every Nth Grid Line** to **12**, and **Perspective View Grid Extent** to **10**.

What Just Happened?

*The home grid provides a visual reference to the user. It helps in visualizing space, scale, and distance. Here, I have set **Grid Spacing** to **6**, the size of the smallest square of the grid. In the previous step, I have set the units to inches therefore the size of one grid space is equal to **6** inches. For example, if you create a box with width set to **24** inches, it will take **4** grid boxes.*

Close the **Grid and Snap Settings** dialog. From the **Application** menu, choose **Save** to open the **Save File As** dialog. In the **File name** text box type **umm1-hoe1-end.max** and then click **Save** to save the file.

Note: Saving Files

*I highly recommend that you save your work regularly by pressing **Ctrl+S**.*

Creating One Seat Section of the Sofa

On the **Create** panel ![+], click **Geometry** ![○], and then on the **Object Type** rollout, click **Box**. In the **Perspective** viewport, drag out a box of any size. Go to **Modify** panel ![], and on the **Parameters** rollout, set **Length** to **25.591**, **Width** to **25.591**, and **Height** to **1**. RMB click on the **Select and Move** tool ![+] on the **Main** toolbar to open the **Move Transform Type-In** dialog and then set **X** to **0**, **Y** to **0**, and **Z** to **11.42** in the **Absolute:World** group. Close the dialog. Click **Zoom Extents All** ![] to zoom on **Box001** in all viewports [see Figure E3].

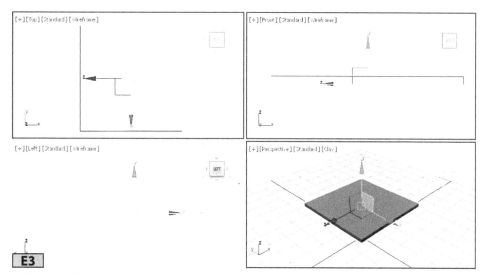

E3

What just happened?

*Here, I have set the position of the box using the **Transform Type-In** dialog [**Move Transform Type-In** dialog]. This dialog allows you to enter precise values for move, rotate, and scale transforms. To open this dialog, RMB click on **Select and Move** ✛ , **Select and Rotate** ↻ , or **Select and Scale** ▫ tool on the **Main** toolbar. You can also press **F12** while one of the aforesaid tools is active to open the dialog.*

Tip: Transform Type-In boxes

*You can also use the **Transform Type-In** boxes on the **Status Bar**. To transform objects, ensure they are selected. Type the values in the **Transform Type-In** boxes and then press **Enter**. You can toggle between the absolute transform and relative transform by clicking the **Absolute/Offset Mode Transform Type-In** button available to the left of the transform boxes.*

In the **Create** panel, click **Geometry**, and then in the **Object Type** rollout, click **Box**. Activate the **Top** viewport. Expand the **Keyboard Entry** rollout, and set **Length** to **25.591**, **Width** to **1**, and **Height** to **11.417**. Click **Create**. Click **Align** ▤ on the **Main** toolbar. Now, click **Box001**. In the **Align Selection** dialog that opens, set the controls shown in Figure E4. Click **OK** to accept the changes made [see Figure E5].

E4   E5

Align **Box001** and **Box002** using **Select and Move** [see Figure E6]. Click **Mirror** 🔛 on the **Main** toolbar to open the **Mirror** dialog. In this dialog, make sure **X** is selected in the **Mirror Axis** group. Select **Copy** from the **Clone Selection** group and then set **Offset** to **24.591**. Click **OK** to accept the changes made and create a mirror copy of **Box002** [see Figure E7].

E6   E7

Activate the **Top** viewport. On the **Create** panel, click **Geometry**, and then in the **Object Type** rollout, click **Box**. Expand the **Keyboard Entry** rollout and then set **Length** to **1**, **Width** to **25.591**, and **Height** to **25.984**. Click **Create** to create a box with the name **Box004**. Make sure **Box004** is selected. Activate the **Top** viewport. Click **Align** on the **Main** toolbar and then click **Box001**. In the **Align Selection** dialog that opens, set the controls shown in Figure E8 and click **OK** to align the objects [see Figure E9].

E8   E9

Activate the **Top** viewport. On the **Create** panel, click **Geometry**, and then on the **Object Type** rollout, click **Box**. Expand the **Keyboard Entry** rollout and then set **Length** to **1**, **Width** to **23.591**, and **Height** to **11.417**. Click **Create** to create a box with the name **Box005**. Next, align it as shown in Figure E10.

E10

Select **Box001** to **Box005** in the **Scene Explorer**. RMB click on the selection to open a **Quad** menu. Choose **Add Selected To | New Group** from the menu. In the **Group** dialog that opens, type the group name as **oneSeat** and click **OK**.

Creating Corner Section of the Sofa

Collapse **oneSeat** in the **Scene Explorer**, if no already collapsed, RMB click on it and select **Clone** from the **Quad** menu. In the **Clone Options** dialog that opens, select **Copy** from the **Object** group. Change the **Name** to **cornerSeat** and click **OK**.

In the **Perspective** viewport, move the **cornerSeat** to the right of **oneSeat**. Select **cornerSeat** in the **Scene Explorer**, from the **Group** menu, select **Open**. Select **Box008** from the **Scene Explorer**. Go to **Modify** panel, and then on the **Parameters** rollout, set **Height** to **25.984**. From the **Group** menu, select **Close**. Figure E11 shows the **cornerSeat** and **oneSeat**. Now, make various combinations of **oneSeat** and **cornerSeat** by making copies of them [see Figure F12]. Press **CTRL+S** to save the file.

Exercise 2: Creating a Coffee Table

In this exercise, you will model a coffee table using the **Cylinder** and **Torus** primitives [see Figure E1]. The following table summarizes the exercise:

Table E2: Creating Model of a Coffee Table	
In this exercise, you will learn how to:	• Create simple geometry • Setup units and home grid settings • Use the **Select and Place** tool
Skill level	Beginner
Time to complete	20 Minutes
Topics in the section:	• Specifying the Units for the Exercise • Creating the Coffee Table
Project Folder	**unit-mm1**
Units	**Metric - Centimeters**
Final exercise file	**umm1-hoe2-end.max**

Specifying the Units for the Exercise

Reset 3ds Max. From **Customize** menu choose **Units Setup**. In the **Units Setup** dialog that opens, select **Metric** from the **Display Unit Scale** group. Next, select **Centimeters** from the drop-down located below **Metric**, if already not selected. Click **OK** to accept the change. RMB click on any snap toggle button on the **Main** toolbar. In the **Grid and Snap Settings** dialog that opens, choose the **Home Grid** panel and then set **Grid Spacing** to **5**, **Major Lines every Nth Grid Line** to **10**, and **Perspective View Grid Extent** to **8**.

Close the **Grid and Snap Settings** dialog. From the **Application** menu, choose **Save** to open the **Save File As** dialog. In the **File name** text box type **umm1-hoe2-end.max** and click **Save** to save the file.

Creating the Coffee Table

In the **Create** panel, click **Geometry**, and then in the **Object Type** rollout, click **Cylinder**. Activate the **Top** viewport. Expand the **Keyboard Entry** rollout, and set **Radius** to **37.5** and **Height** to **2**. In the **Parameters** layout, set **Height Segments** to **1**, **Cap Segments** to **1**, and **Sides** to **63**. Click **Create** from the **Keyboard Entry** rollout.

On the **Create** panel, click **Geometry**, and then in the **Object Type** rollout, click **Torus**. Create a torus in the **Top** viewport. Go to **Modify** panel and then in the **Parameters** rollout set **Radius 1** to **37.5**, **Radius 2** to **1.581**, **Segments** to **100**, and **Sides** to **12**. Now, click **Select and Place** 🖱 tool on the **Main** toolbar and then drag torus onto the cylinder to align the two objects [see Figure E2]. If required, use the **Move** tool to align the two objects. Place the two objects at the origin as discussed earlier.

Select the torus and the cylinder and then activate the **Front** viewport by MMB clicking on it. Click **Select and Move** on the **Main** toolbar and then press **Shift**, move the selection down by **30** units along the negative **Y** direction. In the **Clone Options** dialog that appears, choose **Copy** from the **Object** group and click **OK** to create a copy of the selected object [see Figure E3].

In the **Create** panel, click **Geometry**, and then in the **Object Type** rollout, click **Cylinder**. Create a cylinder in the **Top** viewport. Go to **Modify** panel and then in the **Parameters** rollout set **Radius** to **1.2**, **Height** to **41**, **Height Segments** to **1**, and **Sides** to **18**. Next, make sure that **Select and Move** tool is active and then on the **Status Bar**, enter **-40.246**, **0**, and **-35.352** in the **Transform Type-In** boxes to place the cylinder [see Figure E4]. In the **Hierarchy** panel of the **Command Panel**, click **Use Working Pivot** from the **Working Pivot** rollout.

E2   E3

Choose **Array** from the **Tools** menu. Set the parameters in the **Array** dialog, as shown in Figure E5 and click **OK** to create two more copies of the cylinder [see Figure E6].

E4   E5

E6

Select all objects from the **Scene Explorer** and then choose **Group** from the **Group** menu. Name the group **coffeeTable**. Press **CTRL+S** to save the file.

Exercise 3: Creating a foot stool

In this exercise, you will model a foot stool using the **ChamferBox** and **OilTank** extended primitives [see Figure E1]. The following table summarizes the exercise:

Table E3: Creating a Foot Stool	
In this exercise, you will learn how to:	• Create extended primitives • Create clones
Skill level	Beginner
Time to complete	20 Minutes

Topics in the section:	• Specifying the Units for the Exercise • Creating the Stool
Project folder	**unit-mm1**
Units	**US Standard – Decimal Inches**
Final exercise file	**umm1-hoe3-end.max**

E1

Specifying the Units for the Exercise

Reset 3ds Max. From **Customize** menu choose **Units Setup**. In the **Units Setup** dialog that opens, select the **US standard** option from the **Display Unit Scale** group. Next, select **Decimal Inches** from the drop-down located below the **US standard** option, if already not selected. Click **OK** to accept the change.

RMB click on any snap toggle button on the **Main** toolbar. In the **Grid and Snap Settings** dialog that opens, choose the **Home Grid** tab and then set **Grid Spacing** to **3**, **Major Lines every Nth Grid Line** to **5**, and **Perspective View Grid Extent** to **5**. Close the **Grid and Snap Settings** dialog.

Creating the Stool

In the **Create** panel, click **Geometry**, and then choose **Extended Primitives** from the drop-down located below **Geometry**. In the **Object Type** rollout, click **ChamferBox**. Create a chamfer box in the **Top** viewport. Go to **Modify** panel and then in the **Parameters** rollout set **Length** to **24.8**, **Width** to **31.5**, **Height** to **5**, **Fillet** to **1.2**, and **Fillet Segs** to **5**. Rename the chamfer box to **baseGeo**.

Click **Select and Move** in **Main** toolbar and then enter **0** in all **Transform Type-In** boxes to place the box at the origin. Press **Shift+Ctrl+Z** to zoom the chamfer box to its extents. In the **Perspective** viewport, press **Shift** and drag **baseGeo** along the **+Z** axis about **5** units. In the **Clone Option** dialog that appears, make sure **Copy** is chosen from the **Object** group. Type **seatGeo** in the name text box and click **OK**. Go to **Modify** panel and then in the **Parameters** rollout set **Height** to **8**, **Fillet** to **0.72** and **Fillet Segs** to **3**. Align the boxes [see Figure E2].

In the **Create** panel, click **Geometry**, and then choose **Extended Primitives** from the drop-down located below **Geometry**. In the **Object Type** rollout, click **OilTank**. Create an oil tank in the **Top** viewport. Go to **Modify** panel and then in the **Parameters** rollout set **Radius** to **1.1**, **Height** to **5**, **Sides** to **25**, and **Cap Height** to **0.9**.

Rename oil tank as **legGeo** and then align it [see Figure E3]. Create three more copies of legGeo and align it viewports [see Figure E4].

[+][Perspective][Standard][Clay + Edged Faces]

E2

E3

E4

Exercise 4: Creating a Bar Table

In this exercise, you will model a bar table using the **ChamferBox** and **ChamferCyl** extended primitives [see Figure E1].

E1

The following table summarizes the exercise:

Table E4: Creating a Bar Table	
In this exercise, you will learn how to:	• Create extended primitives • Create clones • Apply **Bend** and **Taper** modifiers • Use the working pivot
Skill level	Beginner

Time to complete	40 Minutes
Topics in the section:	• Specifying the Units for the Exercise • Creating the Bar Table
Project folder	**unit-mm1**
Units	**US Standard – Decimal Inches**
Final exercise file	**umm1-hoe4-end.max**

Specifying the Units for the Exercise

Reset 3ds Max. From **Customize** menu choose **Units Setup**. In the **Units Setup** dialog that opens, select the **US standard** option from the **Display Unit Scale** group. Next, select **Decimal Inches** from the drop-down located below the **US Standard** option, if already not selected. Click **OK** to accept the change.

RMB click on any snap toggle button on the **Main** toolbar. In the **Grid and Snap Settings** dialog that opens, choose the **Home Grid** tab and then set **Grid Spacing** to **3**, **Major Lines every Nth Grid Line** to **5**, and **Perspective View Grid Extent** to **5**. Close the **Grid and Snap Settings** dialog.

Creating the Bar Table

In the **Create** panel, click **Geometry**, and then choose **Extended Primitives** from the drop-down located below **Geometry**. In the **Object Type** rollout, click **ChamferCyl**. Create a cylinder in the **Top** viewport. Go to **Modify** panel and then in the **Parameters** rollout set **Radius** to **13.78**, **Height** to **1.5**, **Fillet** to **0.15**, **Fillet Segs** to **5**, and **Sides** to **50**. Rename the cylinder as **topGeo**.

Click **Select and Move** in **Main** toolbar and then enter **0** in all **Transform Type-In** boxes to place **topGeo** at the origin. Create another chamfer cylinder in the **Top** viewport and rename it as **supportGeo**. Go to **Modify** panel and then in the **Parameters** rollout set **Radius** to **1.3**, **Height** to **38**, **Fillet** to **0**, **Fillet Segs** to **1**, and **Sides** to **18**. Now, align **topGeo** and **supportGeo** in viewports [see Figure E2].

In the **Create** panel, click **Geometry**, and then choose **Standard Primitives** from the drop-down located below **Geometry**. In the **Object Type** rollout, click **Tube**. Create a tube in the **Top** viewport. Place the tube at the origin. Go to **Modify** panel and then in the **Parameters** rollout set **Radius 1** to **4**, **Radius 2** to **1.3**, **Height** to **2**, and **Sides** to **50**. Rename tube as **tubeGeo** [see Figure E3].

In the **Create** panel, click **Geometry**, and then choose **Extended Primitives** from the drop-down located below **Geometry**. In the **Object Type** rollout, click **ChamferBox**. Create a box in the **Top** viewport. Go to **Modify** panel and then in the **Parameters** rollout set **Length** to **2.1**, **Width** to **12.8**, **Height** to **1.6**, **Fillet** to **0.1** and **Fillet Segs** to **6**. Rename the box as **legGeo**. From the **Object-Space Modifiers** section of the **Modifier** List, select **Taper**. In the **Parameters** layout, set **Amount** to **-0.64**. Set **Primary** to **X** in the **Taper Axis** area. Now, aline **legGeo** with **tubeGeo** [see Figure E4].

Create another chamfer box in the **Top** viewport. Go to **Modify** panel and then in the **Parameters** rollout set **Length** to **1.57**, **Width** to **5.6**, **Height** to **0.64**, **Fillet** to **0.07**, **Width Segs** to **32**, and **Fillet Segs** to **3**. From the **Object-Space Modifiers** section of the **Modifier List**, select **Bend**. In the **Parameters** layout, set **Angle** to **213**. Turn on **X** in the **Bend Axis** area [see Figure E5].

Create a chamfer cylinder in the **Top** viewport. Go to **Modify** panel and then in the **Parameters** rollout set **Radius** to **1.362**, **Height** to **1.72**, **Fillet** to **0.1**, **Fillet Segs** to **5**, and **Sides** to **50**. Align the cylinder with the box and then group them with the name **grpRoller**. Align **grpRoller** with **legGeo** [see Figure E6] and then group them as **grpLeg**. Ensure **grpLeg** is selected and activate the **Top** viewport. Select **Use Transform Coordinate Center** from the **Use Center** flyout the **Main** toolbar. Choose **Array** from the **Tools** menu. Now, set the values in the **Array** dialog, as shown in Figure E7, and then click **OK** to create **3** more copies [see Figure E8].

Practical Tests

Complete the following tests:

Test 1: Creating a Coffee Table

Create the coffee table model [see Figure P1] using the **Box** primitive.

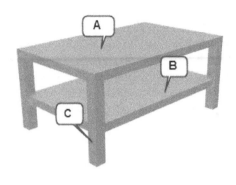

P1

Dimensions:
A: Length=35.433", Width=21.654", Height=1.5"
B: Length=34.037", Width=20.8", Height=1.5"
C: Length=2", Width=2", Height=13.78"

Test 2: Creating a 8-Drawer Dresser

Create the 8-drawer model [see Figure P2] using the **Box** primitive. Create the knobs using the **Sphere** and **Cylinder** primitives.

P2

Dimensions:
A: Length=65", Width=21", Height=1.5"
B: Length=2", Width=2", Height=35"
C: Length=60.76", Width=18.251", Height=30"
D: Length=27.225", Width=19.15", Height=11"
E: Length=27.225", Width=19.15", Height=7"
F: Length=12.871", Width=19.15", Height=5"

Create the foot stool model [see Figure P3] using the **ChamferCyl** and **Chamfer Box** primitives.

P3

Dimensions 3.6.1
A: *Radius=14", Height=5.91", and Fillet=0.32"*
B: *Radius=14", Height=7.5", and Fillet=0.74"*
C: *Length=1.651", Width=3.455", Height=1.496", and Fillet=0.087"*

Hint
*Check **Slice On** for the cylinders and set **Slice From** to **–180**. Apply the **Taper** modifier to the legs of the stool.*

Summary

In this unit, you have seen how you can quickly create models using the **Standard** and **Extended** primitives. You have also leaned about the **AEC** objects. You also got a chance to use the tools that I have covered in Unit MI1 and Unit MI2. Although, I have provided two exercises in this unit but you just don't stop here. Visit the **Ikea** website [*http://www.ikea.com*] and look for inspiration there. They provide the dimensions of the product along with the product features. For example, if you visit to the following link: *http://www. ikea.com/us/en/catalog/products/60128562*, you will be greeted by a **Glass-door** cabinet. Now, scroll down and choose the **Product Information** tab. Notice the dimensions [both in **inches** and **centimeters**] are mentioned under the **Product dimensions** area of the tab.

The unit covered the following topics:

- Creating and modifying **Standard** Primitives
- Creating and modifying **Extended** Primitives
- Working with the **Architectural** objects.
- Setting the project folder
- Using the **Align** and **Mirror** tools
- Creating clones
- Using the **Scene Explorer**
- Creating a group
- Setting grid spacings
- Using **Transform Type-In** dialog
- Using **Array** dialog
- Specifying units for the scene

Unit MM2: Working with Polygons

In Unit MM1, you have modeled objects using the **parametric** modeling techniques. In parametric modeling, you create primitives from the **Create** panel and modify their shapes using the creation parameters. Then, you transform the primitives using the transformation tools to create shape of the models. **Parametric** modeling is powerful and easy but it has some limitations when it comes to creating complex models. **Surface** modeling on the other hand is more flexible and allows you to create any object that you can imagine. Once you convert an object to an editable object such as an editable poly, editable mesh, editable patch, or NURBS object; 3ds Max provides specialized toolset to create the models. In this unit, I will explain the editable poly object.

In this unit, I'll describe the following:

- Working with the polygon modeling tools
- Using the polygon modeling techniques
- Selecting polygon sub-object
- Transforming sub-objects
- Soft selecting sub-objects

Editable Poly Object

The editable poly object is an editable object with five sub-object levels: **Vertex**, **Edge**, **Border**, **Polygon**, and **Element**. Sub-objects such as vertices and edges are the basic building blocks of an object. Vertices are points in 3D space. They define the structure for other sub-objects such as edges and polygons. An edge is a line connecting two vertices. The connection forms one side of the polygon. An edge cannot be shared by more than two polygons. Also, normals of the two polygons should be adjacent. When three or more edges combine together, they form a polygon. **Elements** are groups of contiguous polygons. A border can be described as the edge of a hole in the object. Figure F1 shows various sub-object levels available for the editable poly object.

Note: The editable poly objects vs editable mesh objects
*The editable poly object is similar to the edit mesh object with the only difference is that the edit mesh object comprises of **triangular** faces whereas the editable poly object comprises of polygons with any number of vertices.*

You can convert an object to an editable poly object by using one of the following methods:

1. Select an object in a viewport and then go to the **Modify** panel. Next, RMB click on the object entry in the stack display and then choose **Editable Poly** from the pop up menu displayed [see Figure F2].
2. Select the object in a viewport and then RMB click. Choose **transform** quadrant| **Convert To:** | **Convert to Editable Poly** [see Figure F3].
3. Apply a modifier to a parametric object that makes the object a poly object. For example, the **Turn to Poly** modifier.
4. Apply the **Edit Poly** modifier.

Tip: Exiting a Command
You can exit most of the poly editing commands by RMB clicking in a viewport.

Caution: Preserving the parametric nature of a primitive
*When you convert an object to an editable poly object, you lose all of its creation parameters. If you want to retain the creation parameters, use the **Edit Poly** modifier.*

Caution: Limitations of the Edit Poly modifier
*The **Edit Poly** modifier offers most of the capabilities of the **Editable Poly** object except the **Vertex Color Information**, **Subdivision Surface** rollout, **Weight** and **Crease** settings, and **Subdivision Displacement** rollout.*

Note: Graphite Modeling Tools

*The option to convert an editable poly is also available in the **Graphite Modeling Tools**. You will learn about these tools in a later unit.*

Selecting Sub-objects

You can select sub-objects using one of the following ways:

1. Expand the object's hierarchy [by clicking the arrow] from the stack display and then choose a sub-object level [see Figure F4]. The select sub-object will be highlighted in the stack display.
2. Click a selection button from the **Selection** rollout [see Figure F5].
3. RMB click on an object in a viewport and then choose the sub-object level from the upper left quadrant of the **Quad** menu displayed [see Figure F6].
4. Choose a selection or transform tool and then click on the sub-objects in a viewport using the standard selection techniques.

F4   F5   F6

Note: Adding and removing from the selection

*To select a vertex, edge, polygon, or element, click it. To add to the sub-object selection, press and hold **Ctrl** and click. You can also drag a selection region to select a group of sub-objects. To subtract from the sub-object selection, press and hold **Alt** and click. You can also drag a selection region to deselect a group of sub-objects.*

Tip: Locking selection

*Once you make the sub-object selection, you can lock the selection by pressing **Spacebar**. Locking the selection helps in unintentionally selecting other sub-objects. To release the lock, press **Spacebar** again.*

Tip: Keyboard shortcuts

*You can use the numeric keys from **1** to **5** to activate the **Vertex**, **Edge**, **Border**, **Polygon**, and **Element** sub-object levels, respectively. Press **6** to return to the **Object** level.*

Creating and Modifying Selections

The controls available in the **Selection** and **Soft Selection** rollouts let you access different sub-object levels as well as they give you ability to create and modify selections. Let's have a look at the tools available in these two rollouts.

Selection Rollout

There are five buttons at the top of the **Selection** rollout. These buttons allow you to select the sub-object levels. Table 1 summarizes function of these buttons:

Table 1: The sub-object buttons		
Button	**Interface**	**Description**
Vertex		Activates the **Vertex** sub-object level. Allows you to select the vertex beneath the mouse pointer. Draw a region selection to select the vertices within the region.
Edge		Activates the **Edge** sub-object level. Allows you to select the edge beneath the mouse pointer. Draw a region selection to select the edges within the region.
Border		Activates the **Border** sub-object level. Allows you to select a set of edges that borders a hole in the geometry. In other words, you can select the edges that are on the border.
Polygon		Activates the **Polygon** sub-object level. Allows you to select the polygon beneath the mouse pointer. Draw a region selection to select the polygons within the region.
Element		Activates the **Element** sub-object level. Allows you to select all contiguous polygons. Draw a region selection to select multiple elements within the region.

Note: Border edges

*If the concept of border edges is not clear to you, I would recommend a simple exercise. Create a **Cylinder** primitive in the scene and then convert it to **Editable Poly**. Select the **Polygon** sub-object level and then click on the top face of the cylinder to select it. Press **Delete** to delete the top face. Now, activate the **Border** sub-object level, and click on the border to select the border element [see Figure F7]. There is now only one border edge in the geometry that borders a hole in the cylinder.*

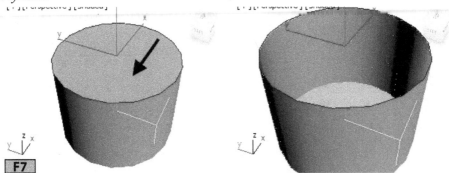

Working with Selection Sets

The **Named Selection Sets** list allows you to name a selection set [both at the object level as well as at the sub-object level] that you can recall later during the modeling process. For example, if you are modeling a face, you might want to select different sub-objects for various parts of the face. In such a case, you can create a selection set for a particular area of the face [nose, for example] and recall it later. It will save you lot of time as you do not have to recreate the selection later during the modeling process.

Keep the following in mind while working with the named selection sets:

- You can transfer sub-objects selection from one modifier to another. You can also transfer the sub-object selection from one level to another in the modifier stack.
- You can transfer named selection sets only between the same types of sub-objects. For example, you cannot transfer a **Vertex** selection to a **Face** selection.
- You are only allowed to transfer selection sets between the modifiers that work on the same geometry type. For example, you cannot transfer a selection set from an **Edit Spline** modifier to **Edit Poly** modifier.
- You can copy and paste selection sets between two modifiers assigned to two different objects. However, both modifiers should handle the same types of geometry.

To create a named selection set, select the objects or sub-objects that you want part of the set and then type the name of the selection set in the **Named Selection Sets** field [see Figure F8] of **Main** toolbar. Press **Enter** to create the selection set.

To recall a selection, select the name from the **Named Selection Sets** list. If you want to select more than one selection set from the list, press **Ctrl** while selecting names. To remove name from the selection, press and hold **Alt** and then click the name in the list.

Once you make a sub-object selection, you perform the following tasks.

- You can move, rotate, and scale sub-objects using standard transformation tools.
- You can apply the object-space modifiers.
- You can bind a space warp to the selection.
- If you have made the polygon selection, you can use the **Align**, **Normal Align**, and **Align To View** tools from the **Align** flyout of the **Main** toolbar.

Transforming a Sub-object Selection
If you are working with an editable object such as mesh, poly, patch, or spline, you can directly manipulate the selection using the transformations tools. However, if you are using a selection modifier such as **Mesh Select** or **Spline Select**, you need to use an **XFrom Modifier** to transform the selection. Here's how it works:

1. Create a polygon primitive such as **Box** and then convert to an **Editable Poly** object.
2. Make a sub-object selection and move it using the **Select and Move** tool. You will notice that

you can easily move the selection [see Figure F9]. Press **Ctrl+Z** to undo the last operation. Now, deselect everything. You can also press **6** on the main keyboard.

3. Apply the **Mesh Select** modifier [see Figure F10] and then make a selection. Notice that the transformation tools are inactive on the **Main** toolbar.

4. Apply the **XFrom** modifier to the object. Expand **XFrom** modifier in the stack display and select **Gizmo** [see Figure F11]. Now, you can move the selection as required.

Cloning Sub-objects

When you **SHIFT+Transform** [move, scale, or rotate] a sub-object selection, the **Clone Part of Mesh** dialog appears [see Figure F12]. This dialog gives you two options: **Clone to Object** and **Clone to Element**. When you select **Clone To Object**, 3ds Max creates a separate object comprises of the selected sub-objects. If you select **Clone to Element**, the selection is cloned and it becomes an element of the current object.

Converting Sub-Object Selections

If you make a sub-object selection, for example, a vertex selection, you can convert it to a different sub-object selection such as edge or face using the **Ctrl** and **Shift** keys:

- To convert a selection to a different sub-object selection, click on the sub-object level button in the **Selection** rollout with **Ctrl** held down [see Figure F13].
- If you press **Ctrl+Shift** while clicking the sub-object level button, only those sub-objects will be selected whose source components were originally selected [see Figure F14].
- If you press **Shift** while clicking the sub-object level button, only those sub-objects will be selected that border the selection [see Figure F15].

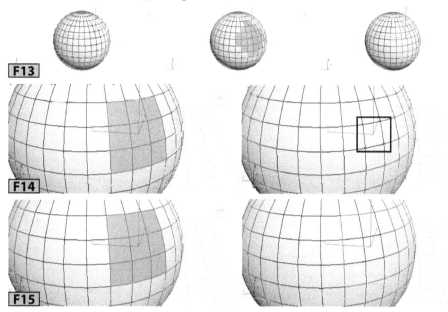

Note: Quad Menu

*The conversion commands are also available from the **Quad** menu. To convert a selection, RMB click and then choose the desired option from the upper left quadrant of the **Quad** menu with **Ctrl**, **Shift**, or **Ctrl+Shift** held down.*
Now, let's explore the other options available in the **Selection** rollout.

When **By Vertex** is on, you can select the sub-objects that share the clicked vertex [see Figure F16]. When **Ignore Backfacing** is on, you can only select those sub-objects that are facing you. When off, you can select any sub-object beneath the mouse pointer. When **By Angle** is on and you select a polygon, all neighboring polygons are also selected based on the angle value specified by the spinner on the right of **By Angle** [see Figure F17].

Shrink reduces the selection area by deselecting the outermost sub-objects [see Figure F18]. On the other hand, **Grow** expands the selection in all possible directions [see Figure F19].

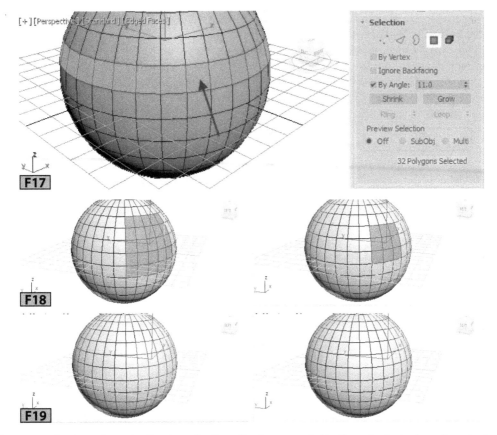

Ring lets you select an edge selection by selecting all edges parallel to the selected edges. To select an edge ring, select an edge[s] and then click **Ring** to select edges parallel to the selected edges [see Figure F20].

Tip: Quickly selecting a ring
*Select an edge and then click on another edge in the same ring with **Shift** held down.*

The spinner next to **Ring** allows you to move the selection in the either direction to other edges in the same ring. The left image in Figure F21 shows the two edges selected. When I clicked on the up arrow of the spinner the selection moved, as shown in the right image of Figure F21. This feature works with only the **Edge** and **Border** sub-object types.

Tip: Loop
If you have selected a loop, you can use the spinner to select the neighboring loop.

F21

Loop allows you to expand edge selection as far as possible. The selection only propagates through four-way junctions. To select a loop, select and edge and then click **Loop** [see Figure F22].

F22

Tip: Loop selection shortcut
*You can quickly select a loop by double-clicking on an edge. At **Vertex** and **Polygon** sub-levels, you can quickly select a loop by first selecting a sub-object and then **Shift** clicking another object of same type in the same loop [see Figure F23].*

Shift click here

F23

The spinner on the right of **Loop** allows you to move the selection in either direction to other edges in the same loop. If you have selected a ring, it allows you to move the ring selection. This feature works with the **Edge** and **Border** sub-objects.

The controls in the **Preview Selection** group allow you to preview a selection before actually selecting. When **Off** is on, no preview will be available. When **SubObj** is on, you can preview the selection at the current sub-object level. The preview appears in yellow color [see Figure F24].

When **Multi** is on, you can switch between various sub-object levels. For example, you place the mouse pointer on an edge, the edge highlights, and clicking on the edge activates the **Edge** sub-object level.

To select multiple sub-objects at current level, press and hold **Ctrl** and move [do not click] to add highlighted sub-objects to the preview. Now, to make the selection, click.

To remove sub-objects from the selection, move the mouse pointer over the selected sub-objects to highlight them in yellow. Now, press **Alt** and then click to deselect the sub-objects. The area below these controls displays information about the selected or highlighted polygons [see Figure F25].

F24 F25

Soft Selection Rollout

The controls in the **Soft Selection** rollout let you partially select the sub-objects in the vicinity of the selected sub-objects. As you transform the sub-objects, the sub-objects in the vicinity will be transformed smoothly [see Figure F26]. The fall off appears in the viewport as a color spectrum [**ROYGB**: red, orange, yellow, green, and blue]. The sub-objects that you explicitly select coded in red color.

F26

When **Edge Distance** is on, 3ds Max limits the selection to a certain number of edges specified by the spinner on right of **Edge Distance**. Figure F27 shows the selection with **Edge Distance** value set to **1** and **7**, respectively.

F27

When **Affect Backfacing** is on, those deselected faces whose normals face in the opposite direction to the average normal of the selected sub-objects are affected by the soft-selection. **Falloff** defines the distance in current units from the center to the edge of a sphere that defines the region of influence. The fall off curve appears below **Bubble**. **Pinch** affects the top point of the curve. **Bubble** lets you expand or shrink the falloff curve along the vertical axis. Experiment with these settings to get a better understanding of how these controls affect the falloff curve. **Shaded Face Toggle** displays a color gradient in the viewport [see Figure F28].

F28

The gradient represents the weight on the faces of the geometry. This feature is only available when you are working with editable poly or patch objects. **Lock Soft Selection** locks the soft selection to prevent any changes in the procedural selection.

The controls in the **Paint Soft Selection** group, let you paint soft selection on the object using a brush. Click **Paint** and then drag the mouse pointer on the surface to paint the selection. **Blur** lets you soften the edges of the selection whereas **Revert** reverses the selection.

Object Level

When no sub-object level is active, you are at the **Object** level. The controls available at the **Object** level are also available at all sub-object levels.

Edit Geometry Rollout

The **Edit Geometry** rollout provides global controls for modifying a poly object. Let's have a look at these controls:

Repeat Last

When clicked, 3ds Max repeats the most recently used command. For example, if you apply a command such as **Bevel** to some polygons and then want to apply the same settings to other set of polygons, select them and then click **Repeat Last**. The same bevel settings will be applied to the last selected polygons.

Caution: Which commands are repeated?

__Repeat Last__ does not repeat all commands, for example, transformations. To check which command in 3ds Max will repeat, hover the mouse pointer on __Repeat Last__. A tooltip appears indicating which command will be repeated when you click this button [see Figure F29].

Tip: Keyboard Shortcut

You can also use the keyboard shortcuts to repeat the last command. If you are using the __3ds Max__ mode, press semicolon (;) and if you are using the __Maya__ mode, press __G__.

Constraints

The controls in this rollout let you constrain the sub-objects transformations to edges, faces, or normals of the existing geometry. Table 2 summarizes the types of constraints.

Table 2: The **Constrains** types	
Type	**Description**
None	This is the default option. No constraints will be applied.
Edge	It constrains transformations to the edge boundaries [see Figure F30].
Face	It constrains transformations to the face boundaries.
Normal	It allows the transformations along the normals.

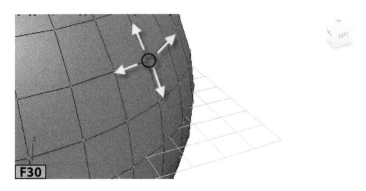

F30

Preserve UVs

When **Preserve UVs** is on, it allows you to edit the sub-objects without affecting the UV mapping [see Figure F31]. The image at the left of Figure F30 is the original vertex position. I scaled the selected vertices inward to show the function of **Preserve UVs**. The middle image shows the result when **Preserve UVs** is on. The image on at right of Figure F31 shows the result when **Preserve UVs** is off.

F31

Create

Allows you to create new geometry in the scene. The result produced by **Create** depends on which sub-object level is active. Table 3 summarizes the behavior of this command.

Table 3: Creating new geometry

Level	Description
Object, Polygon, Element	Adds polygons by clicking existing or new vertices.
Vertex	Adds vertices.
Edge, Border	Adds edges between the pairs of the non-adjacent vertices on the same polygon.

To create geometry, activate a sub-object level and then click **Create**. Now, in the active viewport click to create the geometry [see Figure F32].

F32

Collapse

It allows you to collapse contiguous selection of the vertices, edges, borders, or polygons by welding their vertices to a vertex. The welded vertex is placed at the center of the selection [see Figures F33 and F34].

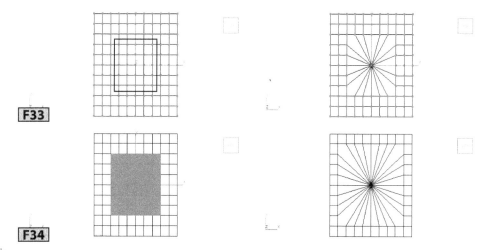

F33

F34

Attach

Attach allows you to attach other geometries to the selected poly object. To attach the objects, select a poly object and then click **Attach**. Now, click on the object that you want to attach; the **Attach** command remains active. If required, keep clicking on other objects to attach them to selected object. RMB click or click **Attach** again to terminate the command.

You can also attach splines, patch objects, and NURBS surfaces to a poly object. If you attach a non-mesh object it is converted to an editable format. It becomes an element of the poly object [see Figure F35].

F35

On clicking **Attach List** on the right of **Attach**, opens the **Attach List** dialog. You can use this dialog to attach multiple objects to the selected poly object.

Detach

Detach allows you to separate the selected sub-objects and corresponding polygons to an object or element. To detach sub-objects, select them and then click **Detach**. In the **Detach** dialog that appears, type the name of the object in the **Detach as** field and then click **OK**.

There are two controls in the **Detach** dialog that let you detach sub-objects as an element or a clone. These controls are **Detach To Element** and **Detach As Clone**, respectively. Turn on the required control and then click **OK**.

Slice Plane

This option is available at the sub-objects levels only. The controls in the group are known as knife tools. These tools subdivide along a poly plane [slice] or in a specific area [cut]. When you click **Slice Plane**, a gizmo appears in viewports. Also, **Slice** and **Reset Plane** controls become active in the rollout.

Transform the Gizmo in a viewport and then click **Slice** to create the edges where the gizmo intersects the edges [see Figure F36]. Click **Slice Plane** to deactivate the command. Click **Reset Plane** to reset the position of the gizmo.

If you turn on **Split**, 3ds Max creates double sets of vertices that allows you to create hole in the geometry [see Figure F37].

QuickSlice

QuickSlice allows you to quickly sub-divide a geometry without making adjustments to the gizmo. To slice a geometry, make a selection and then click **QuickSlice**. Now, drag the cursor in a viewport to create a slicing line. Release the mouse button to slice the selection [see Figure F38]. You can continue slicing the geometry or RMB click to exit the command.

You can use **QuickSlice** in any viewport including perspective and camera. 3ds Max also show you the preview of the slice before you commit the command.

Caution: Polygons and Elements
*If you are at **Polygon** or **Element** level, only selected sub-objects are sliced. If you want to slice entire object, use any sub-object level other than **Polygon** or **Element**.*

Cut

Cut allows you to subdivide polygons by creating edges from one polygon to another or within the polygons. It is available at the object level as well as at all sub-object levels. To create edges, click **Cut** and then click

MM2-14 Unit MM2: Working with Polygons

at the start point. Move the mouse pointer and then click on another point to create connected edges [see Figure F39]. You can continue moving and clicking to create the edges. RMB click to exit the command.

Tip: Mouse pointer

The shape of the mouse pointer shows the type of sub-object it is on. Figure F40 shows the shape of the mouse pointer when you are cutting to a vertex, edge, or polygon, respectively.

MSmooth

Applies smoothing to the selected area of the poly object [see Figure F41]. Click **Settings** on the right of **MSmooth** to open the **MSmooth** caddy control [see Figure F42] that allows you to adjust the settings used by the **MSmooth** command. Table 4 summarizes the **MSmooth** caddy control.

Table 4: The **MSmooth** caddy control

Control	Description
Smoothness	Smoothness in a poly mesh is created by adding polygons to it. **Smoothness** determines how sharp the corners of the mesh are. A value of **1** adds polygons to all vertices of the mesh. If you set **Smoothness** to **0**, no polygons will be created.
Separate by Smoothing Groups	When on, the polygons are created at the edges that share atleast one smoothing group.
Separate by Materials	When on, the polygons are created at the edges that share the material IDs.

Tessellate

It subdivides the polygons based on the tessellate setting that can be accessed by clicking **Settings** on the right of **Tessellate**. Figure F43 shows the **Tessellate** caddy control.

Table 5 summarizes the **Tessellate** caddy control.

Table 5: The Tessellate caddy control	
Control	**Description**
Type	There are two tessellation types available: **Edge** and **Face**. When **Edge** is selected, 3ds Max inserts vertices at the center of each edge and then connect them. The polygons created are the number of sides of the original polygon [see Figure F44]. On selecting the **Face** type, a vertex is created at the center of each polygon and then that vertex is connected to the original vertices. The number of polygons created are equal to the number of sides of the original polygon [see Figure F45].
Tension	It is available for only for the **Edge** type. It determines the edge tension value. A positive value pulls the edges outward whereas a negative value pulls them inward [see Figure F46].

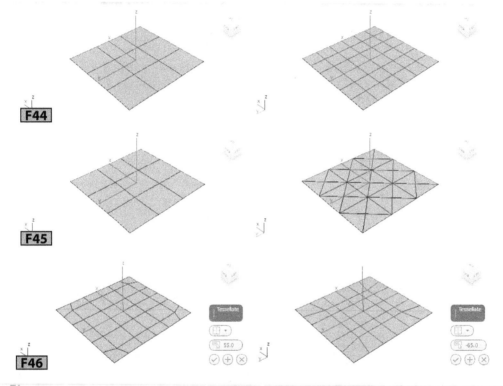

Make Planar

Makes all selected sub-objects to be coplanar. The sub-objects are forced to be coplanar along the average surface normal of the selection [see Figure F47]. If you are at the **Object** level, all vertices of the object will be forced to be coplanar. The **X**, **Y**, and **Z** buttons let you to align the plane with the local coordinate system of the object. For example, if you click **Z**, the selection will be aligned according to the local **XY** axis [see Figure F48].

View Align

It aligns all vertices of the object to the plane of the active viewport. It affects vertices only.

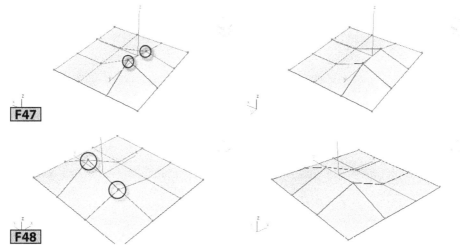

F47

F48

Grid Align

It aligns all vertices to the construction plane of the current view. Also, it moves them to that plane. If a perspective or camera viewport is active, this command aligns vertices to the home grid [see Figure F49] otherwise the current construction plane is the active grid. For example, if you make the **Front** viewport active before clicking **Grid Align**, the **XZ** plane will be used for aligning process. If you are using a grid object, the current plane will be the active grid object.

F49

Relax

It relaxes [normalizes mesh spacing] the current selection by moving each vertex towards the average location of its neighboring vertices [see Figure F50]. If you are at the **Object** level, 3ds Max applies smoothing to whole mesh otherwise the **Relax** function is applied to current sub-object selection.

F50

The setting for the **Relax** command can be accessed by clicking **Settings** on the right of **Relax**. The **Relax** caddy control appears. Table 6 summarizes the **Relax** caddy control.

Table 6: The **Relax** caddy control	
Control	**Description**
Amount	Determines how far the vertex moves each iteration relax function. It defines a percentage of the distance from the original location to the average location of the neighbors.
Iterations	Determines how many times you want to repeat the **Relax** operation.
Hold Boundary Points	When on [default], determines whether vertices at the edges of open meshes are moved or not.
Hold Outer Points	When on, 3ds Max preserves the original position of the vertices that are farthest away from the center of the object. Figure F51 shows a mesh when **Hold Outer Points** is off.

[+] [Perspective] [Standard] [Edged Faces]

F51

Hide Selected, Unhide All, Hide Unselected

These controls are available at **Vertex**, **Polygon**, and **Element** sub-object levels. Table 7 summarizes the functions of these controls.

Table 7: The sub-object visibility	
Control	**Description**
Hide Selected	Hides the selected sub-objects.
Unhide All	Unhides the hidden sub-objects.
Hide Unselected	Hides unselected sub-objects.

Copy, Paste

These controls allow you to copy and paste named selection sets from one object to another. These commands use sub-object IDs, therefore, if there is some difference between the source and target meshes, on pasting, the selection may comprises of different sub-object selected. To understand the working of these two controls, create two **Teapot** primitives and then convert them to **Editable Poly**. Make the **Polygon** mode active and select some polygons on the source object. Type the name for the selection set in the **Named Selection Sets** drop-down. Click **Copy** to open the **Copy Names Selection** dialog, select name and then click **OK** to copy the selection set. Now, activate the **Polygon** selection level for the second teapot and click **Paste**. The polygons will be highlighted.

MM2-18 Unit MM2: Working with Polygons

Delete Isolated Vertices

It is on by default. As a result, when you delete a selection of contiguous sub-objects, the isolated vertices are deleted. If off, deleting sub-object selection leaves the vertices intact.

Full Interactivity

Allows you to toggle feedback on and off for dialogs and caddies as well as for the **Quick Slice** and **Cut** controls. When on, 3ds Max updates the viewports in real-time as you use mouse in the viewport or change values numerically using keyboard.

Vertex Level

Edges and **Polygons** make a poly object. Vertices are the basic building blocks for edges and polygons. You can manipulate vertices at the **Vertex** sub-object level. The controls available for modifying the geometry at the **Vertex** level are found in the **Edit Vertices** and **Vertex Properties** rollout.

Edit Vertices Rollout

Let's discuss the controls available in this rollout.

Remove: Remove lets you delete selected vertices. The polygons that are using these vertices are combined [see the middle image of Figure F52]. The keyboard shortcut for the **Remove** function is **Backspace**.

Caution: Using Delete
*If you use the **Delete** key instead of **Backspace**, 3ds Max can create holes in the poly mesh [see the image at the right of Figure F52].*

F52

Break: Creates a new vertex for each connected polygon to the original selection that allows you to move the corners of polygons [see Figure F53].

F53

Extrude: You can use this control to extrude the vertices along a normal. 3ds Max creates new polygons that forms the sides of the extrusion [see Figure F54]. The numbers of polygons in the extrusion will be equal to the number of polygons that were associated with the selected vertex. To extrude a vertex, select it and then click **Extrude**. Drag the selected vertex vertically to set the extent of the extrusion. Drag horizontally to set the size of the base. If you have selected multiple vertices, all are affected in the same way by the **Extrude** function. RMB click to end the **Extrude** operation.

Clicking **Settings** on the right of **Extrude** opens the **Extrude** caddy control. Table 8 summarizes the **Extrude** caddy controls.

Table 8 summarizes the **Extrude** caddy control.

Table 8: The **Extrude** caddy control	
Control	**Description**
Height	Determines the extent of the extrusion in scene units.
Width	Determines the size of the base of the extrusion.

Weld: This control lets you combine the contiguous selected vertices that fall within a threshold specified using the **Weld** caddy control. To weld vertices, make a selection and then click **Settings** on the right of **Weld** to open the **Weld** caddy control. Set **Weld Threshold** and then click **OK** to weld the vertices [see Figure F55].

Chamfer: This control allows you to chamfer the vertices. To chamfer a vertex, select it and click **Chamfer**. Now, drag the vertex in a viewport to apply chamfering. If you have selected multiple vertices, all vertices will be chamfered identically [see middle image in Figure F56]. Clicking **Settings** on the right of **Chamfer** opens the **Chamfer** caddy control.

Table 9 summarizes the **Chamfer** caddy control.

Table 9: The **Chamfer** caddy control	
Control	**Description**
Vertex Chamfer Amount	Determines the extent of chamfer.
Open Chamfer	When on, you can create open space around the chamfered vertices [see right image in Figure F56]

Target Weld: This allows you to select a vertex and then weld it to a contiguous target vertex. This tool works on those vertices that are connected with a single edge. Also, this control does not allow to cross newly created edges.

To weld a vertex, select it and click **Target Weld**. When you hover the mouse pointer over the vertex, the shape of the mouse pointer changes to a plus shape. Click and drag on the vertex, a rubber band line gets attached to the mouse pointer. Now, position the mouse pointer on the neighboring vertex and when shape of the mouse changes to a plus sign, click to weld the vertices [see Figure F57].

Remove Isolated Vertices: It deletes all vertices that do not belong to any polygon of the selected object.

Remove Unused Map Verts: If there are some unused map vertices that are appearing in the **Unwrap UVW** editor but cannot be used for mapping, click this control to remove them.

Weight: You can use this control to assign weight to the selected vertices. This weight is used by the **NURMS** subdivision function and the **MeshSmooth** modifier. The vertices with larger weights pulls the smoothened result towards them.

Crease: It sets the crease value for the selected vertices. This value is used by the **OpenSubdiv** and **CreaseSet** modifiers. On increasing the crease weight, 3ds Max pulls the smoothened result toward the vertices and creates a sharp point.

Vertex Properties Rollout

The controls in this rollout are only available for the **Editable Poly** object. They are unavailable for the **Edit Poly** modifier.

Edit Vertex Colors Group: The controls in this group allow you to set the color and illumination color of the selected vertices. Click the **Color** swatch to change their color. **Illumination** allows you to change the illumination color of the vertices without changing the color of the vertices. The **Alpha** control lets you set the alpha values for the vertices. These values are used when you export the data containing full RGBA set for the color values.

Select Vertices By Group: You can turn on **Color** or **Illumination** from this group to determine whether to select vertices by using the vertex color or vertex illumination values. You can also specify a custom color for selecting vertices by using the color swatch available in this group. On clicking **Select**, 3ds Max selects the vertices depending on the selection control that you had turned on. The **Range** control allows you to specify a range for the color match.

Edge Level

Edge connects two vertices. This section covers the controls available at the **Edge** sub-object level. These controls are available in the **Edit Edges** rollout.

Insert Vertex

It allows you to subdivide the edges. To insert a vertex, click **Insert Vertex** and then click on an edge [see Figure F58]. You can continue adding vertices as long as the command is active. RMB click to exit the command.

F58

Remove: Removes the selected edges and combines the polygon [see Figure F59]. The keyboard shortcut is **Backspace**. When you remove edges, the vertices remain intact [see left image in Figure F60]. To remove the corresponding vertices, press and hold **Ctrl** when you click **Remove** [see right image in Figure F60].

F59

F60

Split

It divides the mesh along the selected edges [see Figure F61].

F61

Extrude

This control allows you to extrude the edges manually or using the precise values. The precise values can be entered using the **Extrude** caddy control. The controls in the **Extrude** caddy control are similar to that of the **Extrude** caddy at **Vertex** level, refer to Table 8.

To extrude an edge, select it and then click **Extrude**. Drag the selected edge vertically to set the extent of the extrusion. Drag horizontally to set the size of the base [see Figure F62]. If you have selected multiple edges, all are affected in the same way by the **Extrude** function. RMB click to end the extrude operation.

F62

Weld, Target Weld

Refer to the **Vertex Level** section for understanding the functioning of these controls. You need to select edge instead of vertex when dealing with edge welding.

Chamfer

This control allows you to chamfer an edge creating two or more edges for each chamfered edge. 3ds Max provides two types of chamfering: **Standard Chamfer** and **Quad Chamfer**. For **Standard Chamfer**, refer to the **Vertex Level** section. The **Quad Chamfer** type is discussed next.

Quad Chamfer

When you use the **Standard Chamfer** type, 3ds Max generates **quadrilaterals** and **triangles** [see middle image in Figure F63]. The **Quad Chamfer** type generates **quadrilaterals only** [see right image in Figure F63]. The area providing support to the chamfered region might contain triangles.

F63

When you click on **Settings** on the right of **Chamfer**, the **Chamfer** caddy control appears. Table 10 summarizes the **Chamfer** caddy control.

Table 10: The **Chamfer** caddy control	
Control	**Description**
Edge Chamfer Amount	Determines the amount of chamfer in scene units.
Connect Edge Segments	Adds number of polygons over the region of chamfer.
Edge Tension	Determines the angle between the new polygons. At the value of **1** all polygons will be coplanar. Figure F64 shows the chamfered edges with **Edge Tension** set to **0**, **0.5**, and **1**, respectively.
Open Chamfer	Deletes the faces created after the chamfer operation.

Invert Open	This option is available for **Quad Chamfer** only. Also, **Open Chamfer** should be on. When **Invert Open** is on, 3ds Max deletes all faces except those created by the chamfering operation.
Smooth	When on, it applies smoothing groups after chamfering. Also, it enables the **Smooth Type** and **Smooth Threshold** functions.
Smooth Type	There are two types of smoothing methods available. **Smooth Entire Object** applies smoothing groups to entire object. **Smooth Chamfers** only applies smoothing groups to newly created polygons.
Smooth Threshold	If angle between the normals of two adjacent polygons is less than the value specified for the **Smooth Threshold** control, the two polygons are placed in the same smoothing group.

F64

Bridge

You can use the **Bridge** control to bridge the border edges to create a polygon bridge between them. Keep in mind that **Bridge** only connects the borders edges. To create bridge between the edges, select two or more border edges, and then click **Bridge**. A bridge will be created using the existing **Bridge** settings [see Figure F65]. To set **Bridge** settings, click **Settings** on the right of **Bridge**; the **Bridge** caddy control appears. Table 11 summarizes the **Bridge** caddy control;.

F65

Table 11: The **Bridge** caddy control	
Control	**Description**
Segments	Specifies the number of polygons along the length of the bridge.
Smooth	Sets the maximum angle for smoothing to occur.
Bridge Adjacent	Controls the minimum angle between the adjacent edges across which bridging can occur. The edges that are at less than this angle will not be bridged.
Reverse Triangulation	When you are bridging two borders each of which contains different numbers of edges, you can use this control to define the method of triangulation. Figure F66 shows the bridge when **Reverse Triangulation** is **On** and **Off**, respectively.
Use Edge Selection	It allows you to choose between two methods. Either you can use the existing selection or you can choose the edges using caddy control. When you choose **Use Specific Edges**, the **Pick Edge 1**, and **Pick Edge 2** controls become available.

Pick Edge 1, Pick Edge 2	Click **Pick Edge 1** and then click a border edge in a viewport. Select the other border edge using **Pick Edge 2**, the bridge will be created between the two border edges.

F66

Connect

Allows you to refine selected edges by creating new edges between the selected edges. To create new edges, select the edges of the active object that you want to connect and then click **Connect** [see Figure F67].

Caution: Connecting edges

You can connect edges on the same polygon. The **Connect** *command will stop the new edges to cross. For example, if you select all edges of a polygon face and apply this function, only neighboring edges are connected. The new edges will not cross each other [see Figure F68].*

F67

F68

Clicking on the **Settings** on the right of **Connect** opens the **Connect** caddy control that allows you to change settings for the **Connect** command and also preview the changes before committing them [see Figure F69].

F69

Table 12 summarizes the **Connect** caddy control.

Table 12: The **Connect** caddy control	
Control	**Description**
Segments	Defines the number of new edges between each adjacent pair of selected edges.
Pinch	The relative spacing between the new and connecting edges.
Slide	The relative positioning of the new edges.

Create Shape from Selection

This control allows you to create a shape (spline) from the selected edges. The pivot of the shape will be created at the geometric center of the poly object. To create a shape, select the edges of the active object and then click **Create Shape from Selection** to open the **Create Shape** dialog. Type the new name in the **Curve Name** field and then choose the **Shape Type**. Next, click **OK** to create the shape [see Figure F70].

Edit Tri

This control gives you ability to modify the triangulation for the polygons. To turn on triangulation, click **Edit Tri**. The hidden edges appear on the object [see left image in Figure F71]. Now, to change the triangulation for a polygon, click a vertex; a rubber band line appears attached to the mouse pointer. Now, click on an adjacent vertex to create a new triangulation [see the right image in Figure F71].

Turn

It allows you to modify polygon triangulation by clicking on the diagonals. To change triangulation, click **Turn**. The current triangulation appear on the object. Click on the diagonals to change the triangulation.

Border Level

A border can be described as the edge [boundary] of a hole. As discussed earlier, if you create a cylinder and delete its caps, the adjacent row of edges form a border. You can manipulate borders using the controls available in the **Edit Borders** rollout. Most of the controls are similar to the edge and vertex controls. Select border edges and experiment with these controls. One additional control appears in the **Edit Borders** rollout called **Cap**. It caps an entire border loop with a polygon. You can use it to fill holes in an object.

A polygon is formed by connecting three or more edges. Polygons form a surface that you can render. At **Polygon** sub-object level, you can select polygons and then apply various polygon modeling functions to them. At **Element** sub-object level, you can edit groups of contiguous polygons.

Tip: Highlighting polygons
*When you select a polygon, it is highlighted in red color in the viewport. You can toggle this feature on and off by pressing the **F2** key.*

You can edit polygons and elements using the controls available in the **Edit Polygons** and **Edit Elements** rollouts, respectively.

Edit Polygons Rollout
Let's first explore the tools available in the **Edit Polygons** rollout.

Insert Vertex
Allows you to subdivide a polygon manually. It also works at the **Element** sub-object level. To subdivide the polygon, click **Insert Vertex** and then click on a polygon to subdivide it. You can continue subdividing the polygons as the command remains active until you RMB click [see Figure F72].

F72

Extrude
Extruding is a process in which polygons move along a normal and new polygons are created. This command lets you extrude the polygons. To extrude the polygons, select them in a viewport and then click **Extrude**. Position the mouse pointer on the polygons. The shape of the cursor changes to the **Extrude** cursor. Drag the cursor vertically to specify the extent of extrusion and horizontally to set the base [see Figure F73].

F73

On clicking **Settings** on the right of **Extrude**, the **Extrude** caddy control appears that allows you to specify settings for extrusion.

Table 13 summarizes the **Extrude** caddy control.

Table 13: The **Extrude** caddy control	
Control	**Description**
Extrusion Type	This drop-down provides three methods for extrusion: **Group**, **Local Normal**, and **By Polygon**. On selecting **Group**, 3ds Max extrudes polygons along the average normal of each contiguous group of polygons [see left image in Figure F74]. When **Normal** is selected, the extrusion takes place along each normal of the selected polygon [see middle image in Figure F74]. On selecting **By Polygon**, each 3ds Max extrudes each polygon individually [see the right image in Figure F74].
Extrusion Height	Determines the amount of extrusion in scene units.

F74

Outline

This command lets you increase or decrease the outside edge of each group of contiguous polygons. It does not scale, it just change the size of the outside edge of the selected polygons. To change the size of the outside edge of polygons, select a group of contiguous of polygons and then click **Outline**. Now, position the mouse pointer on the selected polygons and drag the pointer to outline the polygons [see Figure F75]. Notice in Figure F75 that the inner polygons are not affected by the **Outline** operation. If you want to manually specify the outline amount, then click **Settings** on the right of the **Outline** to open the **Outline** caddy control and specify the value using the **Amount** control.

F75

Bevel

It allows you to perform bevel function on group of contiguous selected polygons. To bevel the polygons, select them in a viewport and then click **Bevel**. Position the mouse pointer on the polygons. The shape of the cursor changes to the **Bevel** cursor. Drag the cursor vertically to define the height and horizontally to define the outline amount [see Figure F76].

F76

On clicking **Settings** on the right of **Bevel**, the **Bevel** caddy control appears that allows you to specify settings for extrusion.

Table 14 summarizes the **Bevel** caddy control.

Table 14: The **Bevel** caddy control	
Control	**Description**
Bevel Type	This drop-down provides three methods for beveling: **Group, Local Normal**, and **By Polygon**. On selecting **Group**, 3ds Max bevels polygons along the average normal of each contiguous group of polygons. When **Normal** is selected, the beveling takes place along each normal of the selected polygon. On selecting **By Polygon**, each 3ds Max bevels each polygon individually.
Height	Determines the amount of extrusion in scene units.
Outline Amount	Lets you make the outer border of the selection bigger or smaller.

Inset

This command performs a bevel with no height. To inset polygons, select them and then click **Inset**, position the cursor over the polygons and the drag to define the **Inset** amount [see Figure F77].

F77

On clicking **Settings** on the right of **Inset**, the **Inset** caddy control appears that allows you to specify settings for extrusion.

Table 15 summarizes the **Inset** caddy control.

Table 15: The **Inset** caddy control	
Controls	**Description**
Inset Type	This drop-down provides two methods for insetting: **Group**, and **By Polygon**. On selecting **Group**, 3ds Max insets polygons across each selection of multiple, contiguous polygons. On selecting **By Polygon**, 3ds Max insets each polygon individually.
Inset Amount	Determines the extent of inset in scene units.

Bridge

You have seen how we have applied **Bridge** function on the edges. It works similarly at the **Polygon** sub-object level. Here, you have to select polygons instead of edges [see Figure F78]. Figure F78 shows an external bridge [right] as well as internal bridge [left].

F78

To specify settings for the **Bridge** function, click **Settings** on the right of **Bridge** to open the **Bridge** caddy control. Table 16 summarizes the **Bridge** caddy controls.

Table 16: The **Bridge** caddy control	
Controls	**Description**
Segments	Determines the number of polygons along the length of the bridge.
Taper	Allows you to taper the bridge length towards its center. Negative values make bridge center smaller whereas the positive values makes center bigger.
Bias	Defines the location of the maximum taper amount.
Smooth	Sets the angle for smoothing.
Twist 1, Twist 2	Allow you to twist each end of the bridge.
Use Specific Borders, Use Border Selection	It allows you to choose between two methods. Either you can use the existing selection or you can choose the polygons using caddy control. When you choose **Use Specific Borders**, the **Pick Polygon 1**, **Pick Polygon 2** controls become available.
Pick Polygon 1, Pick Polygon 2	Click **Pick Polygon 1** and then click a polygon or border edge in a viewport. Select the other border edge using **Pick Polygon 2**, the bridge will be created between the two border edges.

Flip

Allows you to reverse the direction of normals on the selected polygons.

Hinge From Edge

This command allows you to perform a hinge operation in the viewport. Make a polygon selection in a viewport and then click **Hinge From Edge**. Now, drag on an edge to hinge the selection [see Figure F79]. On clicking **Settings** on the right of **Hinge From Edge**, the **Hinge From Edge** caddy control appears that allows you to specify settings for extrusion.

F79

Table 17 summarizes the **Hinge From Edge** caddy control.

Table 17: The Hinge From Edge caddy control	
Controls	**Description**
Angle	Sets the rotation angle around the hinge [see Figure F80].
Segments	Specifies the number of polygons along the extruded side.
Pick Hinge	Click it and then click on an edge to specify the hinge edge.

F80

Extrude Along Spline

Allows you to extrude a selection along a spline. To extrude, create a spline and then select the polygons that you want to extrude. Click **Extrude Along Spline** and then click the spline in a viewport to extrude the polygons [see Figure F81].

F81

On clicking **Settings** on the right of **Extrude Along Spline**, the **Extrude Along Spline** caddy control appears that allows you to specify settings for extrusion.

Table 18 summarizes the **Extrude Along Spline** caddy controls.

Table 18: The **Extrude Along Spline** caddy control

Control	Description
Segments	Determines the number of polygons along the extrusion [see Figure F82].
Taper Amount	Sets the taper amount for the extrusion.
Taper Curve	Defines the rate at which tapering occurs.
Twist	Applies a twist along the length of taper.
Extrude Along Spline Align	Aligns the extrusion along the face normal [see Figure F83].
Rotation	Sets the rotation of extrusion.
Pick Spline	Allows you to pick a spline along which the extrusion will occur.

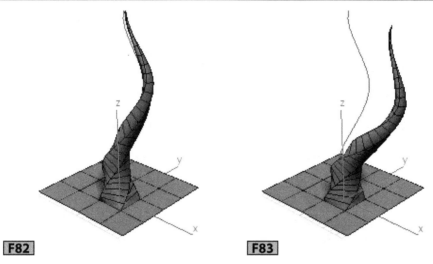

F82   F83

Edit Triangulation Turn

Refer to the **Edge Level** section for understanding the functioning of these controls.

Retriangulate

When clicked, 3ds Max automatically performs best triangulation on the selected polygon[s].

Edit Elements Rollout

Refer to **Edit Polygons** rollout for the controls available in this rollout.

Hands-on Exercises

From the **Application** menu, choose **Manage | Set Project Folder** to open the **Browse for Folder** dialog. Navigate to the **3dsmax2017projects** directory that you have created and then click **Make New Folder**. Create the new folder with the name **unit-mm2** and click **OK** to create the project directory.

Exercise 1: Creating a Serving Bowl

In this exercise, you will create model of a bowl [see Figure E1]. Table E1 summarizes the exercise:

E1

Table E1: Creating A Serving Bowl	
In this exercise, you will learn how to:	• Convert a parametric primitive to an **Editable Poly** object. • Use polygon and edge selection techniques. • Remove sub-objects from an object. • Chamfer, extrude, and inset faces. • Use the **Taper** modifier's gizmo. • Use the **TurboSmooth** modifier.
Skill level	Beginner
Time to complete	20 Minutes
Topics in the section:	• Specifying the Units for the Exercise • Creating the Bowl
Project folder	**unit-mm2**
Units	**Metric - Centimeters**
Final exercise file	**umm2-hoe1-end.max**

Specifying the Units for the Exercise

From **Customize** menu choose **Units Setup**. In the **Units Setup** dialog that opens, turn on **Metric** from the **Display Unit Scale** group. Next, select **Centimeters** from the drop-down located below **Metric**, if already not selected. Click **OK** to accept the change. RMB click on any snap toggle button on the **Main** toolbar. In the **Grid and Snap Settings** dialog that opens, choose the **Home Grid** panel and then set **Grid Spacing** to **5**, **Major Lines every Nth Grid Line** to **5**, and **Perspective View Grid Extent** to **10**. Close the **Grid and Snap Settings** dialog.

Creating the Bowl

On the **Create** panel, click **Geometry** and then on the **Object Type** rollout, click **Cylinder**. Create a cylinder in the **Top** viewport. Go to **Modify** panel and then on the **Parameters** rollout, set **Radius** to **25.591**, **Height** to **13**, **Sides** to **36**, and **Height Segments** to **2**.

Set the **Transform Type-In** boxes in the **Status Bar** to **0** to place the cylinder at the origin [see Figure E2]. Now, rename the cylinder as **bowlGeo**. RMB click on **bowlGeo**. In the **transform** quadrant of the **Quad** menu that appears, choose **Convert To: Convert to Editable Poly**. Click **Polygon** 🔲 in the **Modify** panel | **Selection** rollout and then select the top polygon of **bowlGeo**. Press **Delete** to remove the polygon.

Click **Select and Uniform Scale** 🔳 on the **Main** toolbar. Select the bottom set of vertices and uniformly scale them down about **70%** [see Figure E3]. You can use the **Scale Transform Type-In** dialog to precisely enter the scale value.

E2   E3

Click **Select Object** on the **Main** Toolbar. Select the bottom polygon of **bowlGeo** and then click **Settings** on the right of **Extrude** in the **Modify** panel | **Edit Polygons** rollout. In the **Extude's** caddy, set **Height** to **1** and click **OK** [see Figure E4]. Click **Settings** on the right of **Inset** in the **Modify** panel | **Edit Polygons** rollout. In the **Inset's** caddy, set **Amount** to **2** and click **Apply and Continue**. Now, set **Amount** to **7** and click **OK** [see Figure E5].

E4   E5

In the **Modify** panel | **Selection** rollout, **Ctrl+click Vertex**. Click **Settings** on the right of **Weld** in the **Edit Vertices** rollout. In the **Weld's** caddy, set **Weld Threshold** to **4** and click **OK**. Now, click on **Editable Poly** in the modifier stack list to exit the sub-object level. From the **Modifier List | OBJECT-SPACE MODIFIERS section**, choose **Shell**. In the **Parameters** rollout, set **Outer Amount** to **0.5**. From the **Modifier List | OBJECT-SPACE MODIFIERS** section, choose **Edit Poly**.

Click **Edge** ◁ in the **Modify** panel | **Selection** rollout. Select the edges [see Figure E6] and click **Loop** from the **Selection** rollout. Click **Settings** on the right of **Chamfer** in the **Edit Edges** rollout. In the **Chamfer's** caddy, set **Amount** to **0.1** [see Figure E7] and click **OK**.

E6   E7

Similarly, chamfer the edges at the bottom of **bowlGeo** (see Figure E8). Now, click **Edit Poly** in the stack display to activate the **Object** level.

From the **Modifier List | OBJECT-SPACE MODIFIERS** section, choose **Taper**. In the modifier stack display, expand **Taper** and click on **Gizmo** sub-object. Click **Select and Uniform Scale** on the **Main** toolbar and then scale down the gizmo [see Figure E9]. Exit **Taper's** sub-object level.

In the **Parameters** rollout, set **Amount** to **0.26** and **Curve** to **-0.93**. Also, set **Primary** to **X** and **Effect** to **Z** [see Figure E10].

What just happened?

*I have applied the **Taper** modifier to change the shape of the bowl. This modifier produces a tapered contour by scaling the ends of the geometry. The **Taper's** gizmo allows you to manipulate the result. **Amount** controls the extent of scaling. The controls in the **Primary** group define the central axis for taper. **Effect** determines the direction of taper.*

From the **Modifier List | OBJECT-SPACE MODIFIERS section**, choose **TurboSmooth**. In the **Modify** panel | **TurboSmooth** rollout set **Iterations** to **2**.

What just happened?

*The **TurboSmooth** modifier smoothen the geometry in the scene by subdividing the geometry. I have applied it to **bowlGeo** because I want to get rid of the hard outer edges. **Iterations** defines the number of times geometry is subdivided.*

Exercise 2: Creating a Kitchen Cabinet

In this exercise, you will create model of a kitchen cabinet [see Figure E1].

E1

The following table the exercise:

Table E2: Creating a Kitchen Cabinet	
In this exercise, you will learn how to:	• Convert a parametric primitive to an editable poly object • Use polygon and edge selection techniques • Remove sub-objects from an object • Chamfer edges • Extrude and inset faces
Skill level	Beginner
Time to complete	20 Minutes
Topics in the section:	• Specifying the Units for the Exercise • Creating the Kitchen Cabinet

Project folder	unit-mm2
Units	Metric - Centimeters
Final exercise file	umm2-hoe2-end.max

Specifying the Units for the Exercise

From **Customize** menu choose **Units Setup**. In the **Units Setup** dialog that opens, turn on **Metric** from the **Display Unit Scale** group. Next, select **Centimeters** from the drop-down located below **Metric**, if already not selected. Click **OK** to accept the change. RMB click on any snap toggle button on the **Main** toolbar. In the **Grid and Snap Settings** dialog that opens, choose the **Home Grid** panel and then set **Grid Spacing** to **5**, **Major Lines every Nth Grid Line** to **5**, and **Perspective View Grid Extent** to **10**. Close the **Grid and Snap Settings** dialog.

Creating the Cabinet

On the **Create** panel, click **Geometry** and then on the **Object Type** rollout, click **Box**. Create a box in the **Top** viewport. Go to **Modify** panel and then on the **Parameters** rollout, set **Length** to **38**, **Width** to **45**, and **Height** to **76**. Set the **Transform Type-In** boxes in the **Status Bar** to **0** to place the box at the origin [see Figure E2].

Convert the **Box001** to the **Editable Poly** object. Select the top and bottom polygons of the box [see Figure E3] and then click **Detach** from the **Modify** panel | **Edit Geometry** rollout. Click **OK** in the **Detach** dialog to create a new object from the selected polygons with the name **Object001**.

E2   E3

Select **Object001** from the **Scene Explorer** and activate **Polygon** ▦ sub-object level. Now, select top and bottom polygons of **Object001**. Click **Settings** on the right of **Extrude** in the **Modify panel** | **Edit Polygons** rollout. In the **Extude's** caddy, set **Height** to **5** and click **OK** [see Figure E4]. Select the polygon, as shown in Figure E5 and then move it by **3** units in the positive **X** direction [see Figure E6].

Select the top polygon and then click **Settings** on the right of **Extrude** in the **Modify** panel | **Edit Polygons** rollout. In the **Extude's** caddy, set **Height** to **5** and click **OK** [see Figure E7]. Similarly extrude the front polygon by **3** units [refer Figure E8].

E4   E5   E6

Select **Box001** from the **Scene Explorer** and then activate the **Edge** sub-object level. Select the edges, as shown in Figure E9.

E7   E8   E9

Click **Connect** in the **Modify** panel | **Edit Edges** rollout to connect the selected edges [see Figure E10]. Select the polygons as shown in Figure E11 and then click **Settings** on the right of **Inset** in the **Modify** panel | **Edit Polygons** rollout.

E10   E11

In the **Inset's** caddy, set **Inset Type** to **By Polygon**, and **Amount** to **2** and then click **OK** [see Figure E12]. Click **Settings** on the right of **Extrude** in the **Modify panel** | **Edit Polygons** rollout. In the **Extude's** caddy, set **Extrusion Type** to **By Polygon** and **Height** to **1.5** and click **OK** [see Figure E13].

Select **Box001** from the **Scene Explorer** and then on the **Modify** panel | **Edit Geometry** rollout, click **Attach**. Click on **Object001** in a viewport to attach the two objects. Now, rename the resulting mesh as **cabinetGeo**.

Activate the **Edge** sub-object and then select the outside edges. Click **Settings** on the right of **Chamfer** in the **Modify** panel | **Edit Edges** rollout. In the **Chamfer's** caddy, set **Chamfer Type** to **Quad Chamfer**, Edge **Chamfer Amount** to **0.1**, and **Connect Edge Segments** to **1**. Click **OK** [see Figure E14].

E12   E13   E14

Exercise 3: Creating a Book

In this exercise, you will create model of a book [see Figure E1].

E1

Table E3 summarizes the exercise:

Table E3: Creating model of a book	
In this exercise, you will learn how to:	• Convert a parametric primitive to an editable object • Use polygon and edge selection techniques • Add segments to the objects • Chamfer edges • Extrude faces
Skill level	Beginner
Time to complete	20 Minutes
Topics in the section:	• Specifying the Units for the Exercise • Creating the Book

Project folder	unit-mm2
Units	US Standard – Decimal Inches
Final exercise file	umm1-hoe3-end.max

Specifying the Units for the Exercise

From **Customize** menu choose **Units Setup**. In the **Units Setup** dialog that opens, select **US Standard** from the **Display Unit Scale** group. Next, select **Decimal Inches** from the drop-down located below **US Standard** and then click **OK** to accept the change. RMB click on any snap toggle button on the **Main** toolbar. In the **Grid and Snap Settings** dialog that opens, choose the **Home Grid** panel and then set **Grid Spacing** to **5**, **Major Lines every Nth Grid Line** to **5**, and **Perspective View Grid Extent** to **5**. Close the **Grid and Snap Settings** dialog.

Creating the Book

On the **Create** panel, click **Geometry** and then on the **Object Type** rollout, click **Box**. Create a box in the **Top** viewport. Go to **Modify** panel, and in the **Parameters** rollout, set **Length** to **7.44**, **Width** to **9.69**, and **Height** to **2**. Set the **Transform Type-In** boxes in the **Status Bar** to **0** to place the box at the origin. Now, rename the box as **bookGeo**.

RMB click on **bookGeo**. In the **transform** quadrant of the **Quad** menu that appears, choose **Convert To: Convert to Editable Poly**. Click **Edge** in the **Modify** panel | **Selection** rollout and then select the edge shown in Figure E2. Click **Ring** to select the edge ring [see Figure E3].

E2   E3

Click **Settings** on the right of **Connect** in the **Edit Edges** rollout. In the **Connect's** caddy, set **Slide** to **95** [see Figure E4] and then click **OK** to connect the selected edges. Similarly, add four edge loops [**Segments: 4, Slide: 0**] to the part of the book that will make up the pages [see Figure E5].

Click **Polygon** in the **Modify** panel | **Selection** rollout and then select the polygons shown in Figure E6. Click **Settings** on the right of **Inset** in the **Edit Polygons** rollout. In the **Inset's** caddy, set **Amount** to **0.08** [see Figure E7] and then click **OK** to inset the polygons.

E4   E5

E6   E7

Click **Settings** on the right of **Extrude** in the **Edit Polygons** rollout. In the **Extrude's** caddy, set **Group** to **Local Normal** and **Height** to **-0.129** [see Figure E8] and then click **OK** to extrude the polygons. Click **Edge** in the **Modify** panel | **Selection** rollout and then select all outer edges of the cover shown in Figure E9.

E8   E9

Click **Settings** on the right of **Chamfer** in the **Edit Edges** rollout. In the **Chamfer's** caddy, set **Edge Chamfer Amount** to **0.01** and **Connect Edge Segments** to **2** [see Figure E10] and then click **OK** to chamfer the edges. Click **Vertex** in the **Modify** panel | **Selection** rollout and then select the vertices shown in Figure E11.

Click **Select and Move** on the **Main** toolbar and then adjust the vertices in the **Left** viewport to modify the shape of the book [see Figure E12].

E10

E11

[+] [Top] [Standard] [Wireframe]

[+] [Perspective] [Standard] [Clay + Edged Faces]

[+] [Front] [Standard] [Wireframe]

[+] [Left] [Standard] [Wireframe]

E12

Practical Test

Complete the following test:

Create the kitchen cabinet model [see Figure P1] using the **Box** primitive. Use dimensions of your choice.

P1

Summary

The unit covered the following topics:

- Working with the polygon modeling tools
- Using the polygon modeling techniques
- Selecting polygon sub-object
- Transforming sub-objects
- Soft selecting sub-objects

This page intentionally left blank

Unit MM3: Graphite Modeling Tools

In the previous unit, I covered everything you need to know about modeling with polygons. You created geometric primitives and converted them into editable poly objects and then used the tools and commands available in the **Command Panel** to create the models. 3ds Max provides another workflow for creating and editing polygons based on the **Ribbon** interface. If you have worked with any other Autodesk product such as products from the **Revit** family, you might be aware of the **Ribbon** interface. In this unit, I describe the tools available in the **Modeling** tab of the **Ribbon** interface and how you can use them to improve your modeling workflow.

In this unit, I will cover the following:

- Working with the **Graphite Modeling Tools**
- Selecting sub-objects
- Creating models using the tools available in the **Ribbon**

The Ribbon

The **Graphite Modeling Tools** are available in the **Ribbon**. These tools offer vide variety of features for editing polygons. The **Ribbon** comprises all standard **Editable Poly** tools and some additional tools for creating, selecting, and editing geometries. By default, **Ribbon** sits on top of the viewports in the collapsed state [see Figure F1].

To expand **Ribbon**, either double-click on the empty gray area of the **Ribbon** or click **Show Full Ribbon** [marked with an arrow in Figure F1]. The **Ribbon** with the **Modeling** tab active will be displayed [see Figure F2].

Tip: Toggling display of Ribbon
*If **Ribbon** is not visible, click **Toggle Ribbon** button on the **Main** toolbar or choose **Show UI | Show Ribbon** from the **Customize** menu.*

Each tab in **Ribbon** comprises various panels such as the **Polygon Modeling** panel in the **Modeling** tab [marked with an arrow in Figure F2]. The display of panel in the tab is context sensitive. To view other panels in the tab, create a primitive in a viewport and then covert it to **Editable Poly**.

When you click on the arrow on the right of the panel's name, the panel expands revealing the tools and commands available in that panel. Figure F4 shows the expanded **Polygon Modeling** panel. Click on **Polygon Modeling** to collapse the panel [marked with arrow in Figure F4].

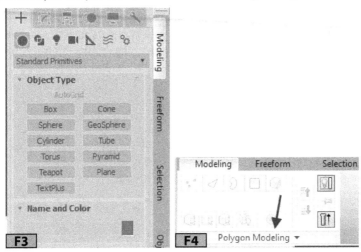

Table 1 summarizes the tabs available in the **Ribbon**.

Table 1: The tabs available in the **Ribbon**	
Tab	**Description**
Modeling	The tools in this tab are mainly used for polygon modeling. These tools are organized in different panels for easy access.
Freeform	This tab contains tools for creating and modifying geometry by painting on the surface of a geometry. You can also specify settings for paint brushes from this tab.
Selection	The special tools in this tab allow you to make sub-object selection in a unique way. For example, select sub-objects from a concave or convex area, and select sub-objects that face the viewport.
Object Paint	The tools available in this tab allow you to paint objects freehand anywhere in the scene.
Populate	This tab provides tools for adding animated pedestrians and idlers in the scene.

*3ds Max provides extended tooltip for the tools available in the **Ribbon**. Position the mouse pointer on a tool; 3ds Max displays a smaller tooltip. If you place the mouse pointer on a tool for little longer, 3ds Max expands the tooltip and sometimes you will also see an illustration in the tooltip. Figure F5 shows an expanded tooltip when mouse pointer was placed on the **Ring** tool.*

Modeling Tab

The **Modeling** tab contains the tools that you will use with the polygon models. These tools are organized in separate panels for easy access. Most of the tools in this tab are clones of the polygon editing tools found in the **Command Panel**. The best way to understand these tools is to practice them. You will use these tools in the hands-on exercises of this unit.

Freeform Tab

The **Freeform** tab [see Figure F6] provides tools for creating and modifying geometry by painting on the surface of a geometry. This tab contains three panels: **PolyDraw**, **Paint Deform**, and **Defaults**. These panels are discussed next.

PolyDraw Panel

The tools in this panel allow you to quickly sketch or edit a mesh in the main grid. You can also sketch on the surface of another object or on the object itself. This panel also provides tools for molding one object to the shape of another object. Before we explore the tools, let's understand the **Conform Options** panel which is always displayed when a conform brush tool is active.

Conform Options Panel

The options in this panel [see Figure F7] let you specify the settings for modifying tool's effects. When any conform brush tool other than the **Conform Brush** is active, the panel is named **Transform Conform Options**. Also, an additional toggle appears with the name **Offset Relative**.

F7

Here's the quick rundown to the options available in the **Conform Options** panel.

Full Strength: Defines the size of the center area represented by a white circle in the brush [see Figure F8]. The **Strength %** setting [see Figure F7] is fully applied in this area. To adjust the brush size interactively, **Shift+drag**.

Falloff: **Falloff** is represented by the bigger black circle [see Figure F8]. The **Strength** in this circle decreases from full strength to zero. To adjust the brush size interactively, **Ctrl+drag**.

Conform: It defines the rate at which the **Conform** brush deforms the painted object. Higher the values you specify for this option, instant will be the conforming effect.

Mirror: When **Mirror** is active, the tool's effect is applied equally to both sides [see Figure F9] across the mirror axis defined by the **Mirror Axis** attribute.

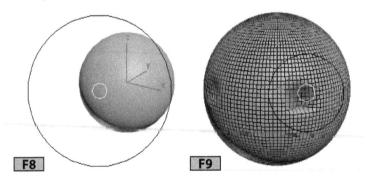

F8   F9

View/ Vertex Normal: These two options [see Figure F10] control the direction in which the **Conform** brush moves the vertices. **View** pushes vertices away from the screen therefore it is dependent on the view angle of the scene. **Vertex Normal** pushes the vertices along their own normal toward the target.

Offset Relative: This brush is only available when you use one of the transform conform brushes. When on, it helps you in retaining the original shape of the object.

F10

MM3-4   Unit MM3: Graphite Modeling Tools

Strength %: This option defines the overall rate at which a brush deforms an object. To interactive change the value for this option, **Shift+Alt+drag**.

Use Selected Verts: When on, the deform tools only affect the selected vertices. When off, it affects all vertices of the object.

Ignore Backfacing: When on, the tools affects vertices facing you.

Mirror Axis X/Y/Z: Allow you to choose the axis across which the conform action will be mirrored.

Freeze Axis X/Y/Z: When any **Freeze Axis** button is active, the tool is prevented from moving vertices on the corresponding axis of the object.

Freeze Selected Edges X/Y/Z: When any **Freeze Selected Edges** button is active, the tool is prevented from moving edges on the corresponding axis of the object. The un-selected edges move freely.

PolyDraw Panel - Drag and Conform Tools

The tools in this panel [see Figure F11] produce different effects depending on which combination keys [**Ctrl, Alt**, and **Shift**] you press. Although, **PolyDraw** tools do not require you to select any sub-object level, however, it is recommended that you use these tools at the **Vertex** sub-object level for better results.

Drag: You can use the **Drag** tool to move sub-objects on the surface or grid. Table 2 summarizes the functions available with this tool.

Table 2: Functions of the **Drag** tool	
Function	**Description**
Normal	Without any modifier keys this tool move vertices by dragging them.
Shift	Moves edges.
Ctrl+Drag	Moves polygons.
Shift+Ctrl+Drag	Moves edge loops.
Shift+Ctrl+Alt+Drag	Moves elements.

You can also use this tool to move the sub-objects in screen space [perpendicular to the current view selection]. Table 3 shows these functions.

Table 3: Functions of the **Drag** tool in the screen space

Function	Description
Alt+Drag	Moves vertices.
Alt+Shift+Drag	Moves edges.
Alt+Ctrl+Drag	Moves polygons.

Conform Brush: The **Conform** brushes move the conform object's vertices towards the target. You can use these brushes in variety of modeling scenarios such as painting a road on a hilly terrain, or painting a mask on the face of a character.

To conform an object to the target object. Select the object that you want to conform. Activate the **Vertex** sub-object level for better control. Select **Draw On: Surface** from the **Draw On** drop-down ⟨🖌 Surface ▾⟩ on the **PolyDraw** panel. Click **Pick** and then click the target object in a viewport. The name of the object appears on the **Pick** ⟨ Pick ⟩ button. Click **Conform**, adjust brush size and strength and then drag the object toward the target using the **Conform** brush. The selected object takes shape of the target object. In Figure F12, I have conformed a **Plane** primitive to a **Sphere** primitive.

F12

Apart from the basic **Conform** brush that is described above, 3ds Max also provides four transformed based variants: **Move Conform Brush** 🖌, **Rotate Conform Brush** 🖌, **Scale Conform Brush** 🖌, and **Relax Conform Brush** 🖌. The **Relax Conform Brush** applies a relax effect to vertices within a spherical volume.

PolyDraw Panel - Add Geometry and Optimize Tools

Step Build: This tool works at the **Object** level as well as the sub-objects level. You can use this tool to build a surface vertex by vertex or polygon by polygon. Table 4 summarizes the functions of this tool.

Table 4: Functions of the **Step Build** tool

Function	Description
Normal	Click to place vertices on the grid or surface.
Shift+Drag	Drag over the floating vertices to fill the gaps with quad polygons.
Ctrl+Click	Click on a polygon to delete it.
Alt+Click	Click on a vertex to remove it.

MM3-6 Unit MM3: Graphite Modeling Tools

Ctrl+Alt+Click	Click on an edge to remove it.
Ctrl+Shift+Click	Click to place and select vertices. You can also select the existing vertices.
Shift+Alt	Move the mouse pointer [do not drag] over the vertices to select them.
Ctrl+Shift+Alt	Drag mouse pointer to move a vertex on a grid or surface.

Caution: Vertex Ticks

*When the **Step Build** tool is active, vertex ticks are not always visible in the viewport. If you don't see the ticks at levels other than the **Vertex** level, change the display of the object to **By Object** in the object's display properties.*

Extend Tool: You can use this tool with the open edges that are on the border of the surface that have only one polygon attached. Table 5 summarizes the functions of this tool.

Table 5: Functions of the **Extend** tool

Function	Description
Normal	Drag a border vertex to create a polygon.
Shift+Drag	Drag a border edge to create a polygon.
Ctrl+Shift+Drag	Drag an edge to extend its entire loop.
Ctrl+Alt+Drag	Drag between two edges to create a polygon.
Ctrl+Click	Click to delete a polygon and associated isolated vertices.
Ctrl+Shift+Alt+Drag	Drag a vertex to move it on the surface or grid.
Alt+Drag (Screen Space)	Drag a border to create a polygon.
Alt+Shift+ Drag (Screen Space)	Drag a border edge to create a polygon.

Optimize Tool: This tool is used to remove the details from the model by drawing on it. Table 6 shows the functions of this tool.

Table 6: Functions of the **Optimize** tool

Function	Description
Normal	Click on the edges to collapse. It merges two vertices into one.
Shift+Drag	Drag from one vertex to another to weld them.
Ctrl+Drag	Drag between the vertices to connect them.
Alt+Click	Click to remove a vertex.
Shift+Ctrl+Click	Click to remove an edge loop.
Shift+Alt+Click	Click to remove a ring.
Ctrl+Alt+Click	Click on an edge to remove it.
Shift+Ctrl+Alt+Drag	Drag on a vertex to move it.

Draw On: The options in this drop-down allow you to choose the entity type on which you want to draw. The **Grid** ⊞ option creates geometry on the grid of the active viewport. This option works well with the orthographic view, however, you can also use it in the **Perspective** viewport. The **Surface** ⊘ option allows you to draw on another object that you specify. The **Selection** ⊘ option lets you create geometry on the selected object.

Pick: This button lets you pick an object to draw on. To pick object, choose **Surface** from the **Draw On** drop-down and then click **Pick**. Now, click on the object to draw on.

Offset: It specifies the distance that **PolyDraw** uses for creating the geometry.

PolyDraw Panel - Create Geometry Tools

⊘ **Shapes:** You can use this tool to draw polygons on a surface or grid. Click **Solve Surface** after creating the polygon to generate a workable mesh. The **Solve Surface** option will be displayed when you expand the **PolyDraw** panel [see Figure F13].

When **Shapes** is active, you can delete a polygon by clicking on it with the **Ctrl** held down. To move a polygon, drag the mouse pointer with **Ctrl+Shift+Alt** held down.

⊕ **Topology:** This tool is used to create quad polygons by drawing lines in a viewport. As you draw the quads using this tool, 3ds Max fills them with a polygon. To draw the mesh, pick **Topology** and then draw lines in a viewport. When you are done with the lines, **RMB** click to complete the operation [see Figure F14].

The drop-down associated with **Topology** contains an option, **Auto Weld**. When **Auto Weld** is on, 3ds Max automatically attaches the mesh to the selected object and weld their border vertices. If **Auto Weld** is off, **Topology** always creates a new mesh. The **Minimum Distance** control available in the expanded **PolyDraw** panel defines the resolution of the lines. The default value for this control is **10** which works well in most of the cases. When **Topology** is active, you can **Shift+Drag** to continue a line from the closest endpoint. To delete a line, click on it with **Ctrl** held down.

⌐⌐ **Splines:** This tool draws a spline on a surface or grid. The splines created using this tool are renderable. Select the desired option from the **Draw On** drop-down and then draw to create splines. All splines are combined into single [separate] object. When **Splines** is active, you can delete a spline by clicking on it with the **Ctrl** held down. You can also move a spline to the closest splines by dragging it with **Ctrl+Shift+Alt** held down.

Strips: This tool can be used to quickly layout the topology foundation for a mesh object. It paints strips of polygons that follow the mouse drag direction [see Figure F15]. If you press **Shift** before starting the painting, 3ds Max paints from the closest existing edge. If you want to create polygon between two open edges, press **Alt** and then drag between the two open edges.

F15

Surface: This tool paints a surface onto an object or grid. The size of the surface polygons are controlled by the **Minimum Distance** setting available in the expanded **PolyDraw** panel. The drop-down associated with **Surface** has an option, **Quads**. When **Quads** is on, the surface is made up of quads. When off, 3ds Max create surface with triangles. To start the surface from an existing border edge, hold **Shift** before you start the drawing. It ensures that overlapping polygons are not created. To delete a polygon, click on it with the **Shift** held down; the associated isolated vertices are also deleted.

Branches: This tool creates multi-segmented extrusions from polygons [see Figure F16]. This tool works only on the selected object and **Draw On** settings does not affect it. The extent of tapering of the branches is controlled by the **Branch Taper** setting available in the expanded **PolyDraw** panel. To create branches, drag the mouse pointer on the selected object, 3ds Max creates branches from the polygons closest to the mouse pointer. Press **Shift** to draw branches from all the selected polygons. If you are at the **Polygon** level, click with **Ctrl** held down to select a polygon. You can also select/de-select additional polygons with **Shilft+Alt** held down.

F16

Paint Deform Panel

The tools in this panel [see Figure F17] give you ability to deform mesh geometry interactively in the viewport. These tools works similarly for at the **Object** level as well at the sub-object level and are independent of any sub-object selection. To exit any tool, either click the its button or RMB click in a viewport. Let's explore various deformation tools available in 3ds Max.

Shift/ Shift Rotate/ Shift Scale

These tools are used to move, rotate, or scale objects in the screen space [see Figure F18]. These tools are like using the standard transformation tools with soft selection. However, with these tools no initial selection is required. You can revert to previous state by using the **Revert** tool. However, this tool only works if you have used any other deform tool such as **Push/Pull**.

Push/Pull

This tool drags the vertices outward [see the left image in Figure F19]. To move vertices inward, drag with the **Alt** held down [see the right image in Figure F19]. When this tool is active you can use:

- **Ctrl** to revert to the previous saved state.
- **Shift** to relax the mesh.
- **Ctrl+Shift** to resize the brush
- **Shift+Alt** to change the strength of the brush.

Note: The Paint Options panel
*When you use any deform tool except **Shift** tools, the floating **Paint Options** panel appears [see Figure F20]. You can use the settings from this panel to control the behavior of the deform tools.*

Relax/Soften

This tool allows you to soften the corners [see Figure F21]. With other brushes, you can soften a geometry with **Shift** held down.

F21

Smudge

The **Smudge** tool is used to move the vertices [see Figure F22]. It is somewhat similar to the **Shift** tool however it updates the effect continuously. Also, it does not use falloff.

Flatten

This tool lets you flatten the concave and convex areas.

Pinch/Spread

You can use this tool to move vertices together or spread them apart. To spread, drag with the **Alt** held down.

Noise

You can use this tool to add convex noise to a surface [see Figure F23]. To create concave noise, drag with **Alt** held down.

Exaggerate

This tool makes the features of the surface more pronounced by moving the convex areas outward and concave areas inward.

F22   **F23**

Constrain to Spline

Apart from the **Shift** tools, all other tools can use a spline as a path for mesh deformation. Create a spline and place it near the surface you want to deform [see left image in Figure F24]. Click **Pick** available below **Constrain to Spline** and then click on the spline in a viewport.

Make sure **Constrain to Spline** is active then pick a deform tool such as **Noise**. Now, when you paint on the object, the deform gizmo can only be moved along the spline. Drag the mouse pointer to create the deformation [see right image in Figure F24].

Paint Deform Panel

You can use this panel to save and load brush settings. The **Load All Brush Settings** option opens a dialog that you can use to load brush settings from an existing file. The **Save All Brush Settings** option opens a dialog that you can use to store brush settings to a file. The **Set Current Settings as Default** option saves the current brush settings as default.

Selection Tab

The **Selection** tab provides a wide array of tools that allow you to make sub-object selection such as you can select convex and concave areas, you can select the sub-object that face the camera, and so forth. Let's explore the various panels available in the **Selection** tab.

Select Panel

The tools in this panel lets you select the sub-object based on the certain topologies. Table 7 summarizes the tools available in this panel.

Table 7: The tools available in the **Select** panel		
Tool	**Icon**	**Description**
Tops		This tool selects the top of the extruded polygon. The selection depends on the active sub-object level. When the **Vertex**, **Edge**, or **Polygon** sub-object level is active, the vertices, edge outlines, or tops of the extruded polygons are selected. Figure F25 shows the top of the extruded polygons selected.
Open		This tool selects all open sub-objects [see Figure F26]. The final result depends on the active sub-object.
Hard		This tool is available at the **Edge** sub-object level. It selects all edges in a model whose faces do not share the same smoothing groups.
Non-Quads		This tool selects all non-quadrilateral polygons. This tool is available at **Polygon** sub-object level.
Patterns		This tool allows you to grow the current selection based on the pattern you select from the **Pattern** drop-down. The **Pattern 1** through **8** options provide different selection pattern. Make a selection in the viewport and then experiment with various patterns. **Growlines** grows the selection with gaps of unselected lines [see Figure F27]. **Checker** grows selection in from of a checker board pattern [see Figure F28]. **Dots** grows the selection such that all sub-objects have gap between them [see Figure F29]. **One Ring** grows a single polygon ring around the initial selection [see Figure F30].

By Vertex	-	When you click a vertex using this tool, all sub-objects that use the clicked vertex are selected.
By Angle	-	When on and if you select a polygon, the neighboring polygons are also selected based on the value you set in the spinner available on the right of **By Angle**.
By Material ID	-	It opens the **Material ID** dialog that you can use to set the material IDs. Also, you can select by ID and material name using this dialog.
By Smoothing Group	-	It displays a dialog that shows the current smoothing groups. To select polygon associated with a group, click the corresponding smoothing group.

F30

Stored Selection Panel

The options in this panel let you quickly and easily store and retrieve selections. You can also apply some basic operations between the stored selections. Table 8 summarizes the tools available in this panel.

Tool	Icon	Description
Table 8: The tools available in the **Stored Selection** panel		
Copy Store 1/ Copy Store 2		You can use these two buffers to place the current sub-object selection. When a buffer contains a selection, the associated button turns blue.
Paint Store 1/ Paint Store 2		These two tools restores the stored selection, clearing the existing selection. If you want to retain the current selection, click on these buttons with the **Shift** held down.
Add 1+2		It adds the two buffers and applies the selection at the current sub-object level.
Subtract 1-2		It selects non-overlapping area of **Store 1** and also clears both buffers.
Intersect		Selects the overlapping area of **Store 1** and **Store 2**.
Clear		Clears the stored selection.

Sets Panel

The tools in this panel gives you ability to copy and paste the named selection sets between objects. To use these tools, create named selection sets and then use the **Copy** and **Paste** tools from this panel to copy/paste selection from buffer.

By Surface Panel

The **Concave** /**Convex** tools allow you to select sub objects in the concave or convex area of the mesh [see Figure F31]. The spinner located next to the drop-down allows you to specify the degree of concavity or convexity.

F31

By Normal Panel

The tools in this panel lets you select sub-objects based on their normal directions on the world axes. To make a selection, choose an axis and then set the value for the **Angle** control. You can invert the selection by clicking **Invert**. The selection shown in Figure F32 is created by setting **Angle** to **87** and choosing the **Z** axis.

F32

By Perspective Panel

The tools in this panel let you select sub-objects based on the extent they point toward the active view. To make a selection, define an angle using the **Angle** control and then click **Select** [see left image in Figure F33]. If you click **Outline**, 3ds Max selects the outermost sub-objects [see the right image in Figure F33].

F33

By Random Panel

The tools in this panel select sub-objects at random number or percentage. Also, you can grow or shrink the current selection randomly. To make a selection, click **Number** # or **Percent** % to enable random selection by number or percentage and then click **Select** to make the selection from the current settings. The **Select Within Current Selection** option in the **Select** drop-down selects random sub-objects within the current selection [see Figure F34]. **Random Grow** and **Random Shrink** grows or shrinks the selection randomly.

F34

By Half Panel

These tools let you select the half of the mesh on the specified axis based on the area or volume. To select, choose an axis and then click **Select**. To toggle the selection, click **Invert Axis**.

By Pivot Distance Panel

You can use this tool to select the sub-objects based on their distance from the pivot. The **% Pivot** control defines the distance. In Figure F35, the selection is defined by setting the **% Pivot** control to **99.2%.**

F35

By View Panel

This feature allows you to select and grow sub-objects selection based on the current view. You can specify the distance using the **Grow From Perspective View** control.

By Symmetry Panel

You can use this feature to mirror the current sub-object selection on the specified local axis. This feature works on a symmetrical model. The center of the object is defined by the location of the pivot of the object.

By Color Panel

The options in this panel let you select vertices by color or illumination value. These options are available at only **Vertex** sub-object level. To select vertices, choose **Color** or **Illumination** from the drop-down. Then, use the color swatch to specify a color. Next, click **Select** ▷ to select the vertices.

By Numeric Panel

This feature allows you to select vertices by the number of connected edges or number of sides you specify. Figure F36 shows the panel at the **Vertex** and **Polygon** levels, respectively. The selection shown in Figure F37 shows the selection made by specifying number of **Sides** to **4** at the **Polygon** level.

F36

F37

Object Paint Tab

The tools available in this tab [see Figure F38] allow you to paint objects freehand anywhere in the scene or on the target objects. You can paint multiple objects in a specific order or randomly. The objects that you add by painting are not combined with other objects. You can use the **Fill** tool to fill an edge selection with the objects.

To understand the concept, create few primitives in the viewport and then create a teapot [see the left image in Figure F39]. Ensure teapot is selected in a viewport and then click **Paint With Selected Object(s)** from the **Paint Objects** panel. Make sure **Scene** is selected from the **Paint On** drop-down. Set **Spacing** to **15** and then freehand paint on the objects in the scene [see the right image in Figure F39]. RMB click to exit the paint mode.

Caution: Exiting the paint mode
You can adjust stroke after painting, therefore, do not RMB click to exit the paint mode until you are satisfied with the result.

You can use the features in the **Object Paint** tab to make creative scenes. You can also use them to populate the scenes with, for example, characters or trees. I would recommend that you practice these tools and then integrate these in your workflow to create creative artwork.

Hands-on Exercises

From the **Application** menu, choose **Manage | Set Project Folder** to open the **Browse for Folder** dialog. Navigate to the **3dsmaxprojects2017** directory that you have created and then click **Make New Folder**. Create the new folder with the name **unit-mm3** and click **OK** to create the project directory.

Exercise 1: Creating a Desk

In this exercise, you will model a desk [see Figure E1].

Table E1 summarizes the exercise:

Table E1: Creating a model of a desk		
In this exercise, you will learn how to:	•	Convert a parametric primitive to a editable object
	•	Use the tools in the Polygon Modeling Ribbon
	•	Use polygon and edge selection techniques
	•	Add segments to the object
	•	Chamfer edges
	•	Inset and Extrude faces
	•	Attach, Detach, and Bridge polygons
	•	Use the **Quick Slice** feature
	•	Use **NURMS** smoothing
Skill level	Intermediate	
Time to complete	1 Hour	
Topics in the section:	•	Specifying the Units for the Exercise
	•	Creating the Desk
Project folder	**unit-mm3**	
Units	**Metric - Centimeters**	
Final exercise file	**umm3-hoe1-end.max**	

Specifying the Units for the Exercise

From **Customize** menu choose **Units Setup**. In the **Units Setup** dialog that opens, select the **US Standard** option from the **Display Unit Scale** group. Next, select **Centimeters** from the drop-down located below the **Metric** option, if already not selected. Click **OK** to accept the change.

RMB click on any snap toggle button on the main toolbar. In the **Grid and Snap Settings** dialog that opens, choose the **Home Grid** tab and then set **Grid Spacing** to **10**, **Major Lines every Nth Grid Line** to **10**, and **Perspective View Grid Extent** to **5**. Close the **Grid and Snap Settings** dialog.

Creating the Desk

On the **Create** panel, activate **Geometry**, then on the **Object Type** rollout, click **Box**. Create a box in the **Top** viewport. On the **Modify** panel | **Parameters** rollout, set **Length** to **60**, **Width** to **150**, and **Height** to **2.5**. Click **Select and Move** on the **Main** toolbar. Set the **Transform Type-In** boxes to **0** on the **Status Bar** to place the box at the origin. Create another box in the **Top** viewport. In the **Modify** panel | **Parameters** rollout, set **Length** to **60**, **Width** to **40**, and **Height** to **62**. Align the two boxes [see Figure E2]. Create copy the box that you have just created and then align it [see Figure E3].

Now, you will start using the tools and options available in the **Graphite Modeling Tools** ribbon to start shaping the desk. By default, the ribbon is minimized below the **Main** toolbar [see Figure E4].

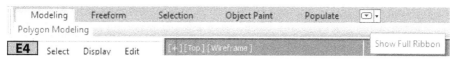

Click **Show Full Ribbon** to display the full **Ribbon** [see Figure E4]. You will see that the tools in the **Polygon Modeling** panel are inactive because no polygon model exists in the scene [all objects are primitives at this stage]. To expand the **Polygon Modeling** panel and view all tools and options available in it, click **Polygon Modeling**. This expands the panel and displays the tools available in it [see Figure E5].

Select the top box. On the **Ribbon | Polygon Modeling** panel, click **Convert to Poly** [see Figure E6]. On the **Ribbon | Geometry (All)** panel, **Shift** click on **Attach**. In the **Attach List** dialog that appears, select **Box002** and **Box003** using **Ctrl** and then click **Attach** to attach the selected boxes to the top box. Rename the unified geometry as **deskGeo**.

Tip: Opening settings of a tool
If you want to open settings for any tool available in the Ribbon, Shift click on the tool.

The **Attach** tool lets you make other objects in the scene part of the selected object. To attach other object, click **Attach** and then select the objects one by one in the viewports. To exit, RMB click in the active viewport, or click the **Attach** tool again. Shift clicking on **Attach** opens the **Attach List** dialog that allows you to select objects from a list.

Note: How materials of the objects are combined
*When you attach objects to a poly object, the materials of the objects are combined. If the objects being attached have no material, they inherit the material of the poly object. If the poly object that you are attaching to doesn't have a material, it inherits material of the objects being attached. In case, when both objects have materials applied, the resulting material is a new **Muti/sub-object** material that includes the input material.*

On the **Ribbon | Polygon Modeling** panel, click **Edge**. Select the edge as shown in Figure E7 and then on the **Ribbon | Modify Selection** panel, click **Ring**. On the **Ribbon | Loops** panel, click **Connect**. An edge loop appears.

Select the edge shown in Figure E8 and then connect them as done before [see Figure E9]. Hold **Ctrl** and double-click on the edge loop that you created earlier to select it [see Figure E10]. On the **Ribbon | Edges** panel, **Shift** click on **Chamfer**. In the **Chamfer's** caddy, set **Edge Chamfer Amount** to **0.2** and click **OK** [see Figure E11].

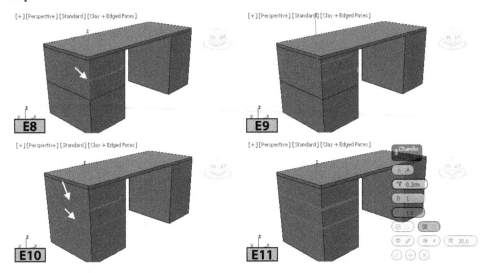

On the **Ribbon | Polygon Modeling** panel, click **Polygon**. Select the polygons [see Figure E12]. Click **Select and Move** on the **Main** toolbar. In the **Perspective** viewport, press **Shift** and move the selected polygon slightly [about 1.2 units] outward in the negative Y direction. Release **Shift**. In the **Clone Part of Mesh** dialog that appears, type **drawerGeo** in the text box next to **Clone To Object** and click **OK**.

Ensure the **drawerGeo** is selected. From the **Modifier List | Object-Space Modifiers** section, choose **Shell**. On the **Parameters** rollout, set **Outer Amount** to **1.5**. Align the **drawerGeo** with the **deskGeo** [see Figure E13]. Similarly, detach the polygon shown in Figure E14.

Name it as **drawerGeo1**, apply the **Shell** modifier and then align it with **deskGeo** [see Figure E15]. Hide the drawer geometries from the scene using the **Scene Explorer**. Select **deskGeo** and activate the **Front** viewport.

On the **Ribbon | Polygon Modeling** panel, click **Edge**. On the **Ribbon | Geometry (All)** panel, click **Slice Plane**. This will display a slice plane gizmo in the viewport and opens the **Slice Mode** panel. Adjust the position of the plane as shown in Figure E16 and then click **Slice** on **Slice Mode** panel to subdivide the geometry [see Figure E17].

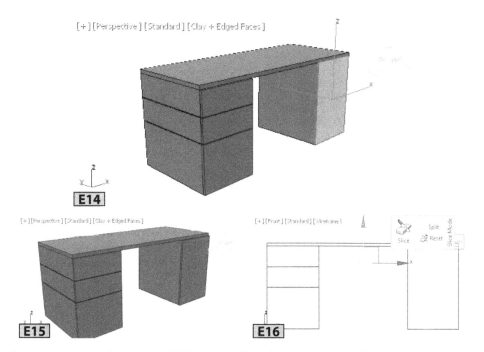

E15

E16

Similarly, add two more slices maintaining a gap of 2 units between them [see Figure E18]. On the **Ribbon | Polygon Modeling** panel, click **Polygon**. Select the polygons, refer to Figure E19. On the **Ribbon | Polygons** panel, **Shift** click **Extrude**. In the **Extrude's** caddy, set **Height** to **4** and click **OK** [see Figure E19].

E17

E18

Select the polygons shown in Figure E20. On the **Ribbon | Polygons** panel, click **Bridge** to create a bridge between the selected polygons [see Figure E21].

E19

E20

On the **Ribbon | Geometry (All)** panel, click on **Detach**. In the **Detach** dialog that appears, set **Detach as** to **sliderGeo** and click **OK**. Select **sliderGeo** and move it slightly toward the negative Y axis. On the **Ribbon**

| **Polygon Modeling** panel, click **Border** and then select the border edges of **sliderGeo** [see Figure E22]. On the **Ribbon | Geometry (All)** panel, click on **Cap Poly** to cap the boder edge. Repeat the process for the other side.

What just happened?

*The **Detach** tool separates the selected sub-objects and associated polygons as new object or element[s]. When you click **Detach**, the **Detach** dialog appears. Type the name of the new object in the **Detach as** textbox and click **OK** to create the new object with the specified name. The selection is removed from the original object. You can turn on **Detach To Element** to make the detached sub-object selection part of the original object but it becomes a new element. Turn on **Detach as Clone** to detach the selection as copy of the original selection; the selection remains intact with the original object.*

Select **deskGeo** and then select the front polygon shown in Figure E23. Move it slightly toward the negative Y axis.

On the **Ribbon | Polygon Modeling** panel, click **Edge**. On the **Ribbon | Edit** panel, click **Swift Loop** to make it active. Press **Ctrl+Shift** and then click on the edges on the drawers that you have created using **Slice Plane**. This will remove the edges [see Figure E24].

The **SwiftLoop** tool allows you to interactively place edges. As you move the cursor over the object surface, a real-tme preview is shown indicating that where the loop will be created when you click. Following are some different features of this tool:

- **Ctrl** click to select an edge loop and activate the **Edge** sub-object level automatically.
- **Alt** drag a selected edge to slide the edge loop between its bounding loops.
- **Ctrl+Alt** drag is a same as the **Alt** drag. However, it also straighten out the edge loop, if necessary.
- **Ctrl+Shift** click on a edge loop to remove it.
- **Shift** click to insert a new loop and adjust it to the flow of the surrounding surface.

Ensure the **drawerGeo** and **drawerGeo1** are visible in the scene. On the **Ribbon | Edit** panel, click **Swift Loop** to turn it off. On the **Create** panel, activate **Geometry**, then on the **Extended Primitives | Object Type** rollout, click **ChamferCyl**. Create a cylinder in the **Top** viewport. On the **Modify** panel | **Parameters** rollout, set **Height** to **6**, **Radius** to **1.5**, and **Fillet** to **0.074**. Now, set **Height Segs** to **2**, **Fillet Segs** to **3**, and **Sides** to **18**. Align it with **drawerGeo** [see Figure E25].

Select the cylinder. On the **Ribbon | Polygon Modeling** panel, click **Convert to Poly**. On the **Ribbon | Polygon Modeling** panel, click **Edge**. Select the edge shown in Figure E26. On the **Ribbon | Modify Selection** panel, click **Loop**. On the **Ribbon | Edges** panel, **Shift** click on **Chamfer**. In the **Chamfer's** caddy, set **Edge Chamfer Amount** to **0.05** and click **OK** [see Figure E27].

On the **Ribbon | Polygon Modeling** panel, **Ctrl** click **Polygon**. On the **Ribbon | Polgon Modeling** panel, click **Shrink** to select the polygons created using the chamfer edge operation [see Figure E28]. On the **Ribbon | Polygons** panel, **Shift** click **Inset**. In the **Inset's** caddy, set **Amount** to **0.02** and click **OK** [see Figure E29].

On the **Ribbon | Polygons** panel, **Shift** click **Extrude**. In the **Extrude's** caddy, set **Extrusion Type** to **Local Normal** and **Height** to **-0.03**. Next, click **OK**. On the **Ribbon | Edit** panel, click **Swift Loop** to make it active. Insert edge loops as shown in Figure E30. These edges will help in holding the shape of the groove when you will apply **NURMS** smoothing to the knob. Turn off **Switch Loop**. On the **Ribbon | Edit** panel, click **Use NURMS** to smooth the object [see Figure E31]. Create two more copies of knob and align them [see Figure E32].

[+] [Perspective] [Standard] [Clay + Edged Faces]

What just happened?

NURMS stands for Non-Uniform Rational Mesh Smooth. This tool features smoothing to the objects using NURMS subdivision; the same method used by the MeshSmooth and TurboSmooth modifiers. When you click Use NURMS, the Use NURMS panel appears. The Iterations spinner in this panel specifies the number of iterations used to smooth the poly object.

Caution: Calculation Time

Specify the number of iterations carefully. It increases the number of vertices and polygons in an object. As a result, the calculation time can increase as much as four times for each iteration. The value in the Smoothness spinner controls how sharp a corner must be before polygons ae added to smooth it.

On the **Create** panel, activate **Geometry**, then on the **Extended Primitives | Object Type** rollout, click **ChamferBox**. Create a box in the **Top** viewport. On the **Modify** panel | **Parameters** rollout, set **Length** to **2**, **Width** to **26.4**, **Height** to **1.5**, and **Fillet** to **0.05**. Set **Width Segs** to **12**. From the **Modifier List | Object-Space Modifiers** section, choose **Bend**. On the **Parameters** rollout, set **Angle** to **152** and **Bend Axis** to **X**. Now, align the handle with the **drawerGeo1** [see Figure E33].

From the **Modifier List | Object-Space Modifiers** section, choose **Taper**. On the **Modify** panel | modifier stack display, expand **Taper** and click **Gizmo**. Click **Select and Uniform Scale** on the **Main** toolbar. Change the size of gizmo along the **x-axis** [see Figure E34]. On the **Parameters** rollout, set **Amount** to **-1.1** and **Effect** to **Y**. From the **Modifier List | Object-Space Modifiers** section, choose **TurboSmooth** to smooth the handle [see Figure E35].

Convert **drawerGeo** and **drawerGeo1** to **Editable Poly**. Select **drawerGeo** and then on the **Ribbon | Polygon Modeling** panel, click **Edge**. Press **Ctrl+A** to select all the edges of **drawerGeo**. On the **Ribbon | Edges** panel, **Shift** click **Chamfer**. In the **Chamfer's** caddy, set **Edge Chamfer Amount** to **0.06** and click **OK**. Similarly, chamfer all edges of **drawerGeo1**, **sliderGeo**, and **deskGeo**.

On the **Create** panel, activate **Geometry**, then on the **Extended Primitives | Object Type** rollout, click **ChamferBox**. Create a box in the **Top** viewport. On the **Modify** panel | **Parameters** rollout, set **Length** to **4**, **Width** to **4**, **Height** to **8**, and **Fillet** to **0.353**. Set **Fillet Segs** to **2**. Ensure the **Length Segs**, **Width Segs**, and **Height Segs** are set to **1**. Rename the box as **legGeo**. Align **legGeo** as shown in Figure E36. Create seven more copies of **legGeo** and align them as shown in Figure E37.

Exercise 2: Creating a USB Drive-I

In this exercise, you will model a USB connector [see Figure E1]. Table E2 summarizes the exercise:

Table E2: Creating a USB drive	
In this exercise, you will learn how to:	• Use the tools from the **Ribbon** • Use the **ShiftLoop** tool
Skill level	Intermediate
Time to complete	40 Minutes
Topics in the section:	• Specifying the Units for the Exercise • Creating the USB Connector
Project folder	**unit-mm3**
Units	**Metric - Millimeters**
Final exercise file	**umm3-hoe2-end.max**

Specifying the Units for the Exercise

From **Customize** menu choose **Units Setup**. In the **Units Setup** dialog that opens, select the **Metric** option from the **Display Unit Scale** group. Next, select **Millimeters** from the drop-down located below the **Metric** option, if already not selected. Click **OK** to accept the change. RMB click on any snap toggle button on the main toolbar. In the **Grid and Snap Settings** dialog that opens, choose the **Home Grid** tab and then set **Grid Spacing** to **3**, **Major Lines every Nth Grid Line** to **5**, and **Perspective View Grid Extent** to **3**. Close the **Grid and Snap Settings** dialog.

Creating the USB Connector

Create a box in the **Top** viewport. On the **Modify** panel | **Parameters** rollout, set **Length** to **15**, **Width** to **30**, **Height** to **5**, and **Width Segments** to **1**. Rename the cylinder as **ucGeo**. Click **Select and Move** on the **Main** toolbar. Set the **Transform Type-In** boxes to **0** on the **status bar** to place the cylinder at the **origin**. On the **Ribbon** | **Polygon Modeling** panel, click **Convert to Poly**. Activate **Edge** sub-object level and then on the **Ribbon** | **Edit** panel, click **SwiftLoop**. Create two loops. Slide the loops toward right using **Alt** [see Figure E2]. Deactivate **SwiftLoop**.

Activate **Vertex** sub-object level and then adjust the shape of the connector using **Select and Move** and **Select and Uniform Scale** [see Figure E3]. Activate **Polygon** sub-object level and then select the front polygon. On the **Ribbon** | **Polygons** panel, **Shift** click **Inset**. In the **Inset's** caddy, set **Amount** to **0.5** and then click **OK** [see Figure E4].

On the **Ribbon** | **Polygons** panel, **Shift** click **Extrude**. In the **Extrude's** caddy, set **Amount** to **-8** and then click **OK** [see Figure E5]. Activate **Edge** sub-object level and then select the edge shown in Figure E6. On the **Ribbon** | **Modify Selection** panel, click **Ring**. On the **Ribbon** | **Loops** panel, **Shift** click **Connect**. In the **Connect's** caddy, set **Segments** to **2** and **Pinch** to **62** [see Figure E7]. Click **OK**. Similarly, create two more edge loops [see Figure E8].

Activate **Polygon** sub-object level and then select the polygon shown in Figure E9. On the **Ribbon | Polygons** panel, **Shift** click **Inset**. In the **Inset's** caddy, set **Amount** to **0.5** and **then** click **OK**. On the **Ribbon | Polygons** panel, **Shift** click **Extrude**. In the **Extrude's** caddy, set **Amount** to **-0.3** and **then** click **OK** [see Figure E10].

Activate **Edge** sub-object level and then select the edge ring shown in Figure E11. In the **Ribbon | Loops** panel, **Shift** click **Connect**. In the **Connect's** caddy, set **Segments** to **14** and **Pinch** to **-59**. Click **OK** [see Figure E12].

Activate **Polygon** sub-object level and then select every other polygon loop using the **Ctrl** and **Shift** [see Figure E13].

Now, in the **Top** viewport, remove the polygons from the selection using **Alt** [see Figure E14].

On the **Ribbon | Polygons** panel, **Shift** click **Inset**. In the **Inset's** caddy, set **Amount** to **0.1** and then click **OK**. On the **Ribbon | Polygons** panel, **Shift** click **Extrude**. In the **Extrude's** caddy, set **Extrusion Type** to **Local Normal** and **Amount** to **-0.2** and **then** click **OK** [see Figure E15]. Activate **Edge** sub-object level and then on the **Ribbon | Edit** panel, click **SwiftLoop**. Create edge loops around the sharp edges of the **ucGeo** [see Figures E16 and E17].

Now, insert an edge loop shown in Figure E18. On the **Ribbon | Edges** panel, **Shift** click **Chamfer**. In the **Chamfer's** caddy, set **Edge Chamfer Amount** to **0.05** and **Connect Edge Segments** to **1**. Click **OK**. Select the polygons created using the chamfer operation. On the **Ribbon | Polygons** panel, **Shift** click **Extrude**. In the **Extrude's** caddy, set **Amount** to **-0.04** and then click **OK** [see Figure E19].

Create more edges using the **SwiftLoop** tool [see Figure E20A]. Apply a **TurboSmooth** modifier to **usGeo** to smooth the geometry [see Figure E20B].

E17 E18 E19 E20A E20B

Create a box in the **Top** viewport. On the **Modify** panel | **Parameters** rollout, set **Length** to **14**, **Width** to **20**, **Height** to **4**, and **Width Segments** to **1**. Raname the cylinder as **cGeo**. On the **Ribbon | Polygon Modeling** panel, click **Convert to Poly**. Activate **Polygon** sub-object level and then select the front polygon. On the **Ribbon | Polygons** panel, **Shift** click **Inset**. In the **Inset's** caddy, set **Amount** to **0.5** and then click **OK** [see Figure E21]. On the **Ribbon | Polygons** panel, **Shift** click **Extrude**. In the **Extrude's** caddy, set **Amount** to **-6** and then click **OK** [see Figure E22].

E21 E22

Activate **Edge** sub-object level and then select the ring shown in Figure E23. In the **Ribbon | Loops** panel, **Shift** click **Connect**. In the **Connect's** caddy, set **Segments** to **2** and **Pinch** to **-85**. Click **OK**. Select the newly created polygons and on the **Ribbon | Polygons** panel, **Shift** click **Extrude**. In the **Extrude's** caddy, set **Amount** to **-0.2**, type to **Local Normal** and **then** click **OK** [see Figure E24]. Activate **Edge** sub-object level. Insert edge loops using **SwiftLoop** as shown in Figure E25. Activate **Polygon** sub-object level. Select the polygons shown in Figure E26 and delete them using **Delete**.

Activate **Edge** sub-object level and select the outer edges shown in Figure E27. On the **Ribbon | Edges** panel, **Shift** click **Chamfer**. In the **Chamfer's** caddy, set **Edge Chamfer Amount** to **0.06** and **Connect Edge Segments** to **3**. Click **OK**. Select the edges that make up the holes and then on the **Ribbon | Edges** panel, **Shift** click **Extrude**. In the **Extrude's** caddy, set **Height** to **-0.1** and **Width** to **0** and then click **OK**. Place the metal connector inside its case. Now, create a new box primitive and then place inside the metal connector as shown in Figure E28.

Create a cylinder in the **Top** viewport. On the **Modify** panel | **Parameters** rollout, set **Radius** to **2**, **Height** to **4.3**, and **Height Segments** to **5**. Align it with the USB drive, refer to Figure E29. On the **Ribbon | Polygon Modeling** panel, click **Convert to Poly.** Activate **Polygon** sub-object level and then select the polygons shown in Figure E29.

MM3-30   Unit MM3: Graphite Modeling Tools

On the **Ribbon | Polygons** panel, **Shift** click **Inset**. In the **Inset's** caddy, set **Amount** to **0.2** and **then** click **OK**. On the **Ribbon | Polygons** panel, **Shift** click **Extrude**. In the **Extrude's** caddy, set **Amount** to **-0.5** and **then** click **OK** [see Figure E30]. If you find that the metal connector is large in size, you can adjust the shape by moving the verticies [see Figure 31].

E30   E31

Exercise 3: Creating a USB Drive-II

In this exercise, you will model a USB drive [see Figure E1].

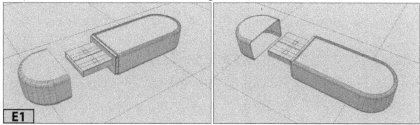

E1

Table E3 summarizes the exercise:

Table E3: Creating model of a USB drive	
In this exercise, you will learn how to:	• Use the tools from the **Ribbon**
Skill level	Intermediate
Time to complete	1 Hour
Topics in the section:	• Specifying the Units for the Exercise • Creating the USB Drive
Project folder	**unit-mm3**
Units	**Metric - Millimeters**
Final exercise file	**umm3-hoe3-end.max**

Specifying the Units for the Exercise

From **Customize** menu choose **Units Setup**. In the **Units Setup** dialog that opens, select the **Metric** option from the **Display Unit Scale** group. Next, select **Millimeters** from the drop-down located below the **Metric** option, if already not selected. Click **OK** to accept the change. RMB click on any snap toggle button on the main toolbar. In the **Grid and Snap Settings** dialog that opens, choose the **Home Grid** tab and then set **Grid Spacing** to **3**, **Major Lines every Nth Grid Line** to **3**, and **Perspective View Grid Extent** to **3**. Close the **Grid and Snap Settings** dialog.

Creating the USB Drive

Create a cylinder in the **Top** viewport. On the **Modify** panel | **Parameters** rollout, set **Radius** to **7.5**, **Height** to **7**, **Height Segments** to **1**, and **Sides** to **32**. Rename the cylinder as **usbGeo**. Click **Select and Move** on the **main toolbar**. Set the **Transform Type-In** boxes to **0** on the **Status Bar** to place the cylinder at the **origin**. On the **Ribbon | Polygon Modeling** panel, click **Convert to Poly**. Activate **Vertex** sub-object level and then select the vertices in the **Front** viewport [see Figure E2].

In the **Top** viewport, move the selected vertices towards right along the x-axis about **25** units [see Figure E3].

On the **Ribbon | Geometry (All)** panel, click **Slice Plane**. This will display a slice plane gizmo in the viewport and opens the **Slice Mode** panel. Adjust the position of the plane as shown in Figure E4 and then click **Slice** on **Slice Mode** panel to subdivide the geometry. On the **Ribbon | Geometry (All)** panel, click **Slice Plane** to deactivate the slice plane feature.

Activate **Edge** sub-object level and then in the **Front** viewport, drag a selection window to select the edges [see Figure E5]. Press **Ctrl+I** to invert the selection. **Remove** the edges from the selection that you created using **Slice Plane**. On the **Ribbon | Edges** panel, **Shift** click **Chamfer**.

In the **Chamfer's** caddy, set **Edge Chamfer Amount** to **0.8** and **Connect Edge Segments** to **7** [see Figure E6]. Click **OK**.

Activate **Polygon** sub-object level and then select polygons [see Figure E7].

E5   E6

E7

On the **Ribbon | Geometry (All)** panel, click **Detach**. In the **Detach** dialog that appears, type **capGeo** in the **Detach as** text box and then click **OK**. Move the cap slightly towards left and then apply a **Shell** modifier to it. On the **Parameters** rollout, set **Outer Amount** to **0.4**. Activate **Border** sub-object level for **usbGeo** and then make the border selection [see Figure E8]. On the **Ribbon | Geometry (All)** panel, click **Cap Poly** to create a polygon.

Activate **Polygon** sub-object level and then select the newly created polygon. On the **Ribbon | Polygons** panel, click **Shift** click **Inset**. In the **Inset's** caddy, set **Amount** to **0.5** and then click **OK**. On the **Ribbon | Polygons** panel, click **Shift** click **Extrude**. In the **Extrude's** caddy, set **Amount** to **0.8** and **then** click **OK**. Activate **Edge** sub-object level and then select the edge loops shown in Figure E9. On the **Ribbon | Edges** panel, **Shift** click **Chamfer**. In the **Chamfer's** caddy, set **Edge Chamfer Amount** to **0.1** and **Connect Edge Segments** to **4.** Click **OK**.

E8   E9

Activate **Polygon** sub-object level and then select the top polygon of the **usbGeo**. On the **Ribbon | Polygons** panel, click **Shift** click **Inset**. In the **Inset's** caddy, set **Amount** to **0.3** and **then** click **OK** [see Figure E10]. On the **Ribbon | Polygons** panel, click **Shift** click **Extrude**. In the **Extrude's** caddy, set **Amount** to **-0.4** and **then** click **OK** [see Figure E11].

Activate **Edge** sub-object level and then select the loop shown in Figure E12. On the **Ribbon | Edges** panel, **Shift** click **Chamfer**. In the **Chamfer's** caddy, set **Edge Chamfer Amount** to **0.4** and **Connect Edge Segments** to **4.** Click **OK** [see Figure E13]. Now, create the USB connector as done in the previous exercise.

Summary
The unit covered the following topics:

- Working with the **Graphite Modeling Tools**
- Selecting sub-objects
- Creating models using the tools available in the **Ribbon**

Unit MM4: Working with Shapes

A shape in 3ds Max is an object consists of one or more lines. These lines which can be 2D or 3D, are used to create components for other objects. 3ds Max provides two types of shape objects **Splines** and **NURBS** curves. Most of the default shapes in 3ds Max are splines.

3ds Max provides twelve basic spline objects, five extended spline objects, and two types of NURBS curves. You can use these objects in the following ways:

- Generate planar and 3d surfaces
- Paths and shapes for the loft components
- Generate extrusions
- Generate revolved surfaces
- Define motion path for animations

Apart from what mentioned above, you can also render the shape as is. When rendering is enabled for the shapes, 3ds Max renders them using a circular or rectangular cross section.

You can convert a basic spline or an extended spline to an editable spline object. This object offers a variety of controls to create less regular and complex shapes. It allows you to edit the shape at the sub-object level. However, when you convert a spline to an **Editable Spline** object, you cannot adjust the creation parameters. The editable spline object will be discussed later in this unit.

Spline and Extended Splines Primitives

You can access the shape creation tools from the **Create** ➕ panel. Go to the **Create** panel and then click **Shapes** ⬡. A drop-down appears below the **Shapes** button with three entries: **Splines**, **NURBS Curves**, and **Extended Splines** [see Figure F1]. Table 1 summarizes the available tools:

Table 1: The shapes tools available in 3ds Max	
Splines	**Line, Rectangle, Circle, Ellipse, Arc, Donut, NGon, Star, Text, Helix, Egg**, and **Section**
NURBS Curves	**Point Curve** and **CV Curve**
Extended Splines	**WRectangle, Channel, Angle, Tee**, and **Wide Flange**

You can also access these tools from the **Create** menu. If you are using the enhanced menu system, you can access shapes from the **Objects** menu.

Spline Primitives

In this section, I will explain the basic spline primitives. Let's start with the **Line** spline.

Note: AutoGrid

This option allows you to automatically create object on the surface of other objects. It creates a temporary construction plane on the face that you click. The orientation of the plane is dependent on the normals of the face.

Line Spline

A **Line** spline is a free-form spline that is made up of multiple segments. To create a line, go to the **Create** panel, click **Shapes**, and then click **Line** button on the **Object Type** rollout. Notice that various rollouts appear in the **Create** panel. Choose the creation method from the **Creation Method** rollout. Click or drag in the viewport to create the first vertex [If you click, a **Corner** vertex is created otherwise a **Bezier** vertex will be created]. Now, click or drag to create additional points. To finish the creation method, do one of the following: either right click to create an open spline [see Figure F2] or click on the first vertex and then choose **Yes** from the **Spline** dialog that appears [see Figure F3].

F2   F3

Tip: Constraining new points

*Press and hold **Shift** while creating splines to constrain new points to **90** degrees angle increments. Ensure that you are using the default initial type settings.*

Tip: Constraining new points to a custom angle increment

*You can also constrain new points to a custom angle increment value. Choose **Grids And Snaps | Grid And Snap Settings** from the **Tools** menu. In the **Grid and Snap Settings** dialog that appears, choose the **Options** panel and then set a value for the **Angle** spinner. Close the dialog. Now, press and hold **Ctrl** while creating new points to constrain them to the value specified for the **Angle** spinner.*

Tip: Punning and orbiting while creating splines

*If a spline requires two or more steps for its creation [such as **Line** or **Donut** spline], you can pan and orbit the viewport between the creation steps.*

Note: Editable Spline object

*3ds Max automatically converts a **Line** spline to an editable spline object because it has no dimensions parameters.*

Now, let's take a look at the various aspects/parameters associated with the **Line** spline. Many of them are common to most of the spline objects.

Combining Shapes While Creating Them

3ds Max allows you to combine shapes to create compound shapes. You can use this feature to create complex shapes. To create a compound shape, on the **Create** panel, turn off the switch preceding the **Start**

New Shape button and then begin creating shapes. Each spline that you create, added to the compound spline. You can check whether all splines are part of a compound shape or not. Go to the **Modify** 🗗 panel and then click **Editable Spline** in the modifier stack. You will notice that all splines are selected in the viewport [see Figure F4].

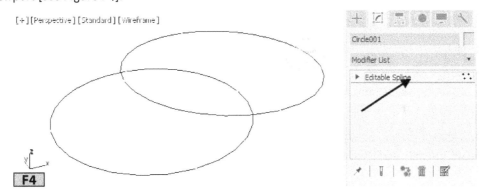

Caution: Parametric nature of splines
You cannot change creation parameters of a compound shape. For example, if you first create a circle, and then add a rectangle to create a compound shapes, you cannot switch back and change the creation parameters of the circle.

Creation Method Rollout
The controls in this rollout allow you to specify what type of vertex that will be created when you click or drag vertices in the viewport. The creation method options for the **Line** spline are different from other spline primitives.

Table 2 summarizes the controls available in the **Creation Method** rollout.

Table 2: Controls in the **Creation Method** rollout of the **Line** spline	
[Group]/Control	**Description**
[Initial Type Group]	The controls in this group set the type of vertex created when you click [not drag] a vertex location.
Corner	**Corner** creates sharp points and spline created is linear to either side of the point.
Smooth	**Smooth** creates a smooth curve through the vertex that you can adjust manually. The curvature of the spline segment is controlled by the spacing of the vertices. Figure F5 shows the splines created using the **Corner** [left image] and **Smooth** [right image] initial type options.
[Drag Type Group]	The controls in this group define the type of vertex created when you drag a vertex location.
Corner, Smooth	The **Corner** and **Smooth** controls work as discussed above.
Bezier	The **Bezier** control produces a smooth adjustable curve. The amount of curvature and direction of the curve are controlled by dragging the mouse at each vertex. You can manually change the smoothness or curvature by manipulating the vertex handles [refer third image in Figure F6].

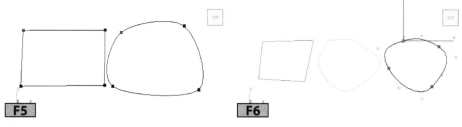

F5   F6

Keyboard Entry Rollout

You can use the **Keyboard Entry** rollout to precisely place vertices of a spline. To add a vertex, enter its coordinates in the **X**, **Y**, and **Z** spinners and then click **Add Point** to add a new point.

The subsequent points you insert will be added to the existing line until you click **Close** or **Finish**. **Close** closes the shape whereas **Finish** completes the line without closing it.

Rendering Rollout

The options in this rollout let you toggle the shape renderability in the viewports as well as in the rendered output. You can also generate the mapping coordinates and convert the mesh to an editable mesh or editable poly object.

Table 3 summarizes the controls available in the **Rendering** rollout.

Table 3: Controls in the **Rendering** rollout of the **Line** spline	
Control	**Description**
Enable In Renderer	Turn on the **Enable In Renderer** to render the shape as 3D mesh using the **Radial** or **Rectangular** parameters set for the renderer. When on, **Renderer** gets selected in this rollout. Now, you have two options for controlling the size of the mesh: **Radial** and **Rectangular**. **Radial** renders the shape with a circular cross section whereas **Rectangular** displays the mesh of the spline as a rectangle. Figure F7 shows the spline shape with the circular cross section on rendering [**Thickness=2, Sides=12**]. Figure F8 shows the mesh with the rectangular cross section [**Length=6, Width=2**].
Enable In Viewport, Use Viewport Settings	Turn on **Enable In Viewport** to display the shape in the viewport as 3D mesh with circular or rectangular cross section [see Figures F9 and F10]. Turn on **Use Viewport Settings** to display the mesh using the **Viewport** settings. When on, **Viewport** is activated and then you can use the **Viewport** settings to control the appearance of mesh of the spline in the viewport.
Generate Mapping Coords	Turn on **Generate Mapping Coords** to apply mapping coordinates to the spline mesh. 3ds Max generates coordinates in **U** and **V** directions. The **U** coordinate wraps around the spline whereas the **V** coordinate is mapped along the length of the spline.
Real-World Map Size	The **Real-World Map Size** switch will only be available if you turn on **Generate Mapping Coords**. This control allows you to specify the actual width and height of a 2D texture map in the **Material Editor**.

Auto Smooth	**Auto Smooth** is turned on by default. The spline is automatically smoothed using the threshold value defined by the **Threshold** spinner available below **Auto Smooth**. This value is an angle measured in degrees.

Radial and Rectangular Options: Now, let's have a look at the various controls available for radial and rectangular cross sections. Table 4 summarizes these controls.

Table 4: Various controls available for radial and rectangular cross sections

Control	Description
Thickness	Controls the diameter of the rendered spline mesh. Figure F11 shows the splines rendered with **Thickness** value set to **0.5** and **1**, respectively.
Sides	Controls the number of sides [or facets] of the mesh. Figure F12 shows the splines rendered with the **Sides** value set to **4** and **62**, respectively.
Angle	It controls the orientation of the rendered cross section. Figure F13 shows the splines rendered with the **Angle** value set to **0** and **60**, respectively.
Length	Controls the size of the cross section along the local Y-axis.
Width	Controls the size of the cross section along the local X-axis.
Aspect	It controls the aspect ratio of width to length. If the **Lock** button next to the spinner is active, adjusting length or width automatically adjusts the other to maintain the aspect ratio.

Interpolation Rollout

The controls on this rollout allow you to adjust the smoothness of a curve. Each spline segment is made up of divisions called steps. Higher the number of steps, smoother the curve will be. By default, **Optimize** is turned on. When on, 3ds Max removes the steps that are not necessary. When **Adaptive** is on, the **Steps** control becomes inactive. It sets the number of steps for each spline to produce smooth looking result. Figure F14 shows the wireframe view of the spline mesh created using the **Optimize** and **Adaptive** splines.

Note: Adaptive

*When **Adaptive** is on, the straight segments get zero steps.*

F14

Creation Method Rollout

Many spline shapes in 3ds Max allow you to use a creation method. You have already worked on the **Line** spline's creation methods. The **Text** and **Star** splines do not have a **Creation Method** rollout. Most of the spline primitives have **Edge** and **Center** creation methods. If the **Edge** method is selected, the first click defines a point on the side or at a corner of the shape and then you drag a diameter or drag to a diagonal point. In the **Center** method, the first click defines the center of the shape and then you drag a corner point or radius.

Rectangle Spline

It creates square or rectangular splines [see Figure F15]. If you want to create a square spline, press and hold **Ctrl** while dragging in a viewport. To create a rectangular spline, first select a creation method and then drag the mouse pointer in a viewport to create a rectangle.

Table 5 summarizes the controls available in the **Parameters** rollout of the **Rectangular** spline:

Table 5: Controls in the **Parameters** rollout of the **Rectangular** spline	
Control	**Description**
Length, Width	The **Length** and **Width** controls specify the size of the rectangle along the **Y** and **X** axes, respectively.
Corner Radius	The **Corner Radius** control allows you to create rounded corners.

Circle Spline

It allows you to create close circular splines made up of four vertices [see Figure F16]. To create a circular spline, first select the creation method and then drag the mouse pointer in a viewport to draw a circle. Table 6 summarizes the controls available in the **Parameters** rollout of the **Circle** spline:

Table 6: Controls in the **Parameters** rollout of the **Circle** spline	
Control	Description
Radius	The **Radius** control specifies the center to edge distance of the circle.

F15   F16

Ellipse Spline

You can use it to create circular or elliptical splines [see Figure F17]. If you want to create a circular spline, press and hold **Ctrl** while dragging in the viewport. To create an elliptical spline, first select the creation method and then drag the mouse pointer in the viewport to draw the ellipse.

Table 7 summarizes the controls available in the **Parameters** rollout of the **Ellipse** spline:

Table 7: Controls in the **Parameters** rollout of the **Ellipse** spline	
Control	Description
Length, Width	The **Length** and **Width** controls specify the size of the ellipse along the local **Y** and **Z** axes, respectively.
Outline, Thickness	The **Outline** control lets you create an elliptical outline, see middle image in Figure F17. The **Thickness** control lets you specify the thickness of the ellipse.

Arc Spline

You can use the **Arc** spline to create open and closed partial circles made up of four vertices [see Figure F18].

F17   F18

Creation Method Rollout

The **Arc** spline provides two methods for creating arcs: **End-End-Middle** and **Center-End-End**. To create an arc using the **End-End-Middle** method, make sure **End-End-Middle** is selected in the **Creation Method** rollout and then drag in the viewport to define the two ends of the arc. Now, release the mouse button. Move the mouse pointer up or down to specify the third point between the two end points.

To create an arc using the **Center-End-End** method, make sure **Center-End-End** is selected in the **Creation Method** rollout and then click to set the radial center of the arc. Drag the mouse pointer and click to specify the start point of the arc. Now, move the mouse and click to specify the other end of the arc.

Table 8 summarizes the controls available in the **Parameters** rollout of the **Arc** spline:

Table 8: Controls in the **Parameters** rollout of the **Arc** spline	
Control	**Description**
Radius	**Radius** specifies the radius of the arc.
From, To	**From** specifies the location of the start point which is measured as angle from the local positive Y-axis. **To** specifies the location of the end point which is measured as angle from the local positive X-axis.
Pie Slice	When **Pie Slice** is on, it creates straight segments from the endpoints to the radial center which results in closed spline [see Figure F19].
Reverse	When **Reverse** is on, the direction of the **Arc** spline is reversed.

Donut Spline

It creates the donut like shape of two concentric circles [see Figure F20]. To create a **Donut** spline, first select a creation method. Drag the mouse pointer and then release the mouse button to define the first circle of the donut. Move the mouse pointer and then click to define the second concentric donut circle.

F19   F20

Table 9 summarizes the controls available in the **Parameters** rollout of the **Donut** spline:

Table 9: Controls in the **Parameters** rollout of the **Donut** spline	
Controls	**Description**
Radius 1, Radius 2	The **Radius 1** and **Radius 2** controls specify the radius of the first and second circle, respectively.

NGon Spline

It creates flat sided splines with N number of sides and vertices [see Figure F21]. To create an **NGon** spline, select a creation method and then drag the mouse pointer in a viewport. Release the mouse button to create the spline.

Table 10 summarizes the controls available in the **Parameters** rollout of the **NGon** spline:

Table 10: Controls in the **Parameters** rollout of the **NGon** spline	
Control	**Description**
Radius, Inscribed, Circumscribed	The **Radius** control specifies the distance from the radial center to the edge of the NGon. If **Inscribed** is on [default], the distance is measured from the radial center to the corners. If **Circumscribed** is on, the distance is from the radial center to the side centers.

Sides	Sides specifies the number of sides which range from **3** to **100**.
Corner Radius	**Corner Radius** controls rounding applied to the corners of the NGon.
Circular	When **Circular** is on, 3ds Max creates a circular NGon which is equivalent to a circular spline but it may contain more than four vertices. The **Circle** spline creates a circular spline object with four control vertices.

Star Spline

It creates closed star-shaped splines with any number of points [see Figure F22]. To create a **Star** spline, drag the mouse pointer and then release the mouse button to define the first radius. Move the mouse pointer and then click to define the second radius. The second radius can be less, equal, or greater than the first radius depending on how you moved the mouse pointer.

F21   F22

Table 11 summarizes the controls available in the **Parameters** rollout of the **Star** spline:

Table 11: Controls in the **Parameters** rollout of the **Star** spline	
Control	**Description**
Radius 1, Radius 2	The **Radius 1** and **Radius 2** controls specify the first set of vertices [created with the first drag] and second set of vertices, respectively.
Points	**Points** controls the number of points on the star. **Distortion** control allows you to produce a sawtooth effect. This effect is generated by rotating the **Radius 2** vertices about the center of the star.
Fillet Radius 1, Fillet Radius 2	**Fillet Radius 1** and **Fillet Radius 2** controls let you smooth the first and second set of vertices, respectively. The rounding is created by producing two **Bezier** vertices per point.

Text Spline

It creates splines in the shape of the text [see Figure F23]. The text can be created using any **Windows** font [both **TrueType** and **OpenType**] installed on your system as well using the **Type 1 PostScript** font installed in the **Fonts** folder of the 3ds Max installation folder.

To create text, enter the text in the **Text** text box and then either click in a viewport to place the text or drag the mouse pointer to place the text in a viewport and then release the mouse button.

Table 12 summarizes the controls available in the **Parameters** rollout of the **Text** spline:

Table 12: Controls in the **Parameters** rollout of the **Text** spline	
Control	**Description**
Text Controls	From this rollout, you can choose the font, font size, alignment, kerning [distance between letters], and leading [distance between lines] for the text that you enter in the **Text** text box. The **Text** text box does not support word-wrap however you can paste multiple lines from the clipboard.

Helix Spline

It creates spiral like shapes [see Figure F24]. To create a **Helix** spline, click and drag the mouse pointer to set the starting point as well as its starting radius [**Center Creation** method] or diameter [**Edge Creation** method]. Now, move the mouse pointer vertically and then click to define the height. Move the mouse pointer and then click to define the end radius.

F23   F24

Table 13 summarizes the controls available in the **Parameters** rollout of the **Helix** spline:

Table 13: Controls in the **Parameters** rollout of the **Helix** spline	
Control	**Description**
Radius 1, Radius 2	The **Radius 1** and **Radius 2** controls specify the radius of helix start and end, respectively. **Height** controls the height of the helix.
Turns	Turns specifies the number of turns in the helix.
Bias	**Bias** forces the turns in the helix to accumulate at the one end of the helix. Figure F25 shows the rendered helix with **Bias** set to **-1, 0.2**, and **1**, respectively.
CC and CCW	**CC** and **CCW** specify whether helix should turn clockwise or counterclockwise.

Egg Spline

It creates an egg shaped spline [see Figure F26]. To create an **Egg** spline, drag the mouse pointer vertically to define the initial dimension of the egg. Now, drag horizontally to change the orientation [angle] of the egg. Release the mouse button to compete the creation process.

F25   F26

Table 14 summarizes the controls available in the **Parameters** rollout of the **Egg** spline:

Table 14: Controls in the **Parameters** rollout of the **Egg** spline	
Controls	**Description**
Length, Width	The **Length** and **Width** controls specify the length and width of the egg along its long and short axes, respectively.
Outline, Thickness	When **Outline** is on, **Thickness** sets the distance between the main shape of the egg and its outline.
Angle	**Angle** specifies the angle of rotation around shape's local Z axis. When **Angle** is equal to **0**, the narrow end of the egg is at the top.

Section Spline

The **Section** spline is a special type of spline that lets you generate splines based on a cross-sectional slice through a geometry objects. To create a **Section** shape, click **Section** from the **Object Type** rollout and then drag a section plane in the viewport. Now, place and orient the plane in the viewport using transformation tools [see Figure F27]. Notice a yellow line is displayed where the section intersects the mesh. Now, on the **Section Parameters** rollout of the **Command Panel**, click **Create Shape**. In the **Name Section Shape** dialog that appears, type the name for the spline and then click **OK**. Now, select the shape in the **Scene Explorer** and then move it away using the **Move Tool** [see Figure F28].

F27   F28

Table 15 summarizes the controls available in the **Section Parameters** rollout of the **Section** spline.

Table 15: Controls in the **Section Parameters** rollout of the **Section** spline	
[Group]/Control	**Description**
Create Shape	When you click this button, a shape is created based on the currently displayed intersection lines. The shape generated is an editable spline.
[Update]	The controls in this group specify when the intersection line is updated.
When Section Moves	It updates the intersection line when you move or resize the section shape.
When Section Selected	It updates the intersection line when you select the section shape. Click **Update Section** to update the intersection.
Manually	It updates the intersection line only when you click **Update Section**.
[Section Events]	These controls let you specify the extents of the cross section.

Infinite	When on, the selected plane is infinite in all directions [see Figure F29].
Section Boundary	When on, the cross section is generated only for objects that are within or touched by the boundary of the section shape [see Figure F30].
Off	No cross section is displayed or generated.
Color Swatch	You can use it to change the display color of the intersection.

Section Size Rollout

The **Length** and **Width** controls in the **Section Size** rollout control the size of the section rectangle.

Extended Spline Primitives

In this section, I will explain the extended spline primitives. Let's start with the **WRectangle** spline.

WRectangle Spline

The **WRectangle** spline [walled rectangle] lets you create a closed shape from two concentric rectangles. Each rectangle is made up of four vertices [see Figure F31]. To create a **WRectangle** spline, drag the mouse pointer in a viewport and then release the mouse button to define the outer rectangle. Move the mouse pointer and then click to define the inner rectangle.

Table 16 summarizes the controls available in the **Parameters** rollout of the **WRectangle** spline.

Table 16: Controls in the **Parameters** rollout of the **WRectangle** spline	
Control	**Description**
Length, Width	These controls define the length and width of the **WRectangle** section.
Thickness	Controls the thickness of the **WRectangle** section.
Sync Corner Fillets	When on, the value specified for **Corner Radius 1** is used for both the interior and exterior corners.
Corner Radius 1	When **Sync Corner Fillets** is off, it controls the radius of the exterior corners.
Corner Radius 2	This control is only available when **Sync Corner Fillets** is off. It controls the radius of the interior corners.

Channel Spline

It creates a closed C shaped spline [see Figure F32]. To create a **Channel** spline, drag the mouse pointer in a viewport and then release the mouse button to define the outer perimeter. Move the mouse pointer and then click to define the thickness of the walls of the channel.

Table 17 summarizes the controls available in the **Parameters** rollout of the **Channel** spline.

Table 17: Controls in the Parameters rollout of the Channel spline	
Control	**Description**
Length, Width	These controls define the length and width of the channel section.
Thickness	Controls the thickness of the channel section.
Sync Corner Fillets	When on, the value specified for **Corner Radius 1** is used for both the interior and exterior corners.
Corner Radius 1	When **Sync Corner Fillets** is off, it controls the radius of the exterior corners.
Corner Radius 2	This control is only available when **Sync Corner Fillets** is off. It controls the radius of the interior corners.

Angle Spline

It creates a closed L shaped spline [see Figure F33]. To create an **Angle** spline, drag the mouse pointer in a viewport and then release the mouse button to define the initial size of the angle. Move the mouse pointer and then click to define the thickness of the walls of the angle. Table 18 summarizes the controls available in the **Parameters** rollout of the **WRectangle** spline.

F32   F33

Table 18: Controls in the Parameters rollout of the Angle spline	
Control	**Description**
Length, Width	These controls define the height and width of the vertical leg and horizontal legs, respectively.
Thickness	Controls the thickness of the legs of the angle.
Sync Corner Fillets	When on, the value specified for **Corner Radius 1** controls the radius for both the vertical and horizontal legs.
Corner Radius 1	When **Sync Corner Fillets** is off, it controls the exterior radius between the vertical and horizontal legs of the spline.

Corner Radius 2	This control is only available when **Sync Corner Fillets** is off. It controls the interior radius between the vertical and horizontal legs of the spline.
Edge Radii	Controls the interior radius at the outermost edges of the vertical and horizontal legs.

Tee Spline

It creates a closed T shaped spline [see Figure F34]. To create a **Tee** spline, drag the mouse pointer in a viewport and then release the mouse button to define the initial size of the tee.

Move the mouse pointer and then click to define the thickness of the walls of the tee.

Table 19 summarizes the controls available in the **Parameters** rollout of the **Tee** spline.

Table 19: Controls in the **Parameters** rollout of the **Tee** spline	
Control	**Description**
Length, Width	These controls define the height and width of the vertical web and flange crossing, respectively.
Thickness	Controls the thickness of the web and flange.
Corner Radius	Controls the radius of the two interior corners between the vertical web and horizontal flange.

Wide Flange Spline

It creates a closed I shaped spline [see Figure F35]. To create a **Wide Flange** spline, drag the mouse pointer in a viewport and then release the mouse button to define the initial size of the wide flange. Move the mouse pointer and then click to define the thickness of the walls of the wide flange.

F34   F35

Table 20 summarizes the controls available in the **Parameters** rollout of the **Wide Flange** spline.

Table 20: Controls in the **Parameters** rollout of the **Wide Flange** spline	
Controls	**Description**
Length, Width	These controls define the height and width of the vertical web and horizontal flange crossing, respectively.
Thickness	Controls the thickness of the wide flenges.
Corner Radius	Controls the radius of the two interior corners between the vertical web and horizontal flanges.

Editing Splines

You can convert a spline object to an editable spline object. The editable spline object allows you to create complex shapes using the three sub-object levels that this object provides: **Vertex**, **Spline**, and **Segment**.

The vertices define points and curve tangents. The segments connects vertices. The splines are made up of one or more connected segments.

You can convert a spline object to the editable spline object by using one of the following methods:

1. Select a spline in a viewport and then go to the **Modify** panel. Next, RMB click on the spline entry in the stack display and then choose **Convert To: Editable Spline** from the pop up menu displayed [see Figure F36].
2. Select a spline in a viewport and then RMB click. Choose **Transform** [in lower right quadrant] | **Convert To:** | **Convert to Editable Spline** [see Figure F37].
3. Select a spline in a viewport and then apply the **Edit Spline** modifier to it.
4. Import a **.shp** file to the scene.
5. Merge a shape from a 3ds Max file.

Note: Edit Spline modifier
*You can use the **Edit Spline** modifier to convert a spline to the editable spline object. However, when you convert a spline to the editable spline object, you lose the creation parameters of the spline.*

Note: Line spline
*By default, the **Line** spline to an editable spline object because it has no dimensions parameters. Therefore, you don't need to convert a **Line** spline to the editable spline object.*

Note: Compound shapes
A compound shape made up of two or more splines is automatically an editable spline object.

Selecting Sub-objects

You can select sub-objects using one of the following ways:

1. Expand the spline object's hierarchy from the stack display and then choose a sub-object level [see Figure F38].
2. Click a selection button from the **Selection** rollout [see Figure F38].
3. RMB click on a spline object in a viewport and then choose the sub-object level from the upper left quadrant of the **Quad** menu displayed [see Figure F39].
4. Choose a selection or transform tool and then click on the sub-objects in a viewport using the standard selection techniques.

Note: Cloning sub-objects
*You can clone the sub-objects by first selecting them and then press and hold **Shift** while transforming them.*

Note: Adding and removing from the selection
*To select a segment, vertex, or spline, click it. To add to the sub-object selection, press and hold **Ctrl** and click. You can also drag a selection region to select a group of sub-objects. To subtract from the sub-object selection, press and hold **Alt** and click. You can also drag a selection region to deselect a group of sub-objects.*

Vertex Level

Vertices define points and curve tangents for a spline object. To select a vertex type, select vertex or vertices and then RMB click. Now, choose the required level from the upper left quadrant of the **Quad** menu [see Figure F40].

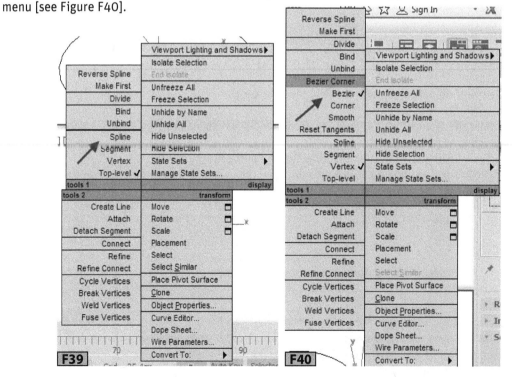

Table 21 shows the list of vertex types available in 3ds Max.

Table 21: The vertex types	
Type	**Description**
Corner	Creates non-adjustable vertices that generates sharp corners [see Figure F41].
Bezier	Creates adjustable vertices with locked continuous tangent handles that produces a smooth curve. The curvature is determined by the direction and magnitude of the tangent handles [see Figure F42]. You can adjust the tangent handles using the **Select and Move** and **Select and Rotate** tools.
Bezier Corner	Creates adjustable vertices with discontinuous tangent handles that produces a sharp corner [see Figure F43]. The curvature is determined by the direction and magnitude of the tangent handles. You can adjust the tangent handles using the **Select and Move** and **Select and Rotate** tools.
Smooth	Creates non-adjustable vertices that generates smooth continuous curves. The curvature is determined by the spacing between the adjacent vertices [see Figure F44].

Tip: Resetting tangents
*To reset the tangent position, RMB click on the vertex or vertices and then choose **Reset Tangents** from the upper left quadrant of the **Quad** menu.*

Tip: Vertex types in the Quad menu
*If you are at **Vertex** sub-object level, the vertex types are always displayed in the **Quad** menu. The mouse pointer doesn't have to be exactly over the vertices.*

Geometry Rollout
Now, let's explore the options available for editing the editable spline object at sub-object level. These options are listed in the **Geometry** rollout.

New Vertex Type Group
The controls in this group lets you choose the type of tangency for vertices that are created when you clone segments or splines using the **Shift** key.

Create Line

Create Line adds more lines to the existing selected spline. The lines are separate splines but are part of the selected spline. To add another spline to the selected spline, select the existing spline and then create the new spline in the same way as you create the line spline.

Break

Break allows you to split a spline at the selected vertex or vertices. To split a spline, select on or more vertices and then click **Break**. Two overlapping vertices will be created at the break point. Use the **Select and Move** tool to separate the vertices [see Figure F45].

F45

Attach

Attach attaches another spline object from the scene to the selected spline to create a compound shape. To attach a spline, select the spline and then click **Attach**. Now, hover the mouse pointer on the target spline. When the shape of the mouse pointer changes, click on the target spline to attach it to the selected spline.

When you attach shapes, the materials assigned to the two objects are combined. Here's how:

- If the target object does not have a material assigned, it inherits the material from the selected object.
- If the selected object does not have a material assigned, it inherits the material from the target object.
- If both objects have materials, the **Attach Options** dialog appears [see Figure F46]. Select the desired options from the dialog and then click **OK**. The resulting material will be a **Multi-Subobject** material.

Attach Multiple

Attach Multiple lets you attach multiple shapes to a selected spline in a single operation. To understand this feature, select a spline object and then click **Attach Multiple**. Now, select the shapes in the **Attach Multiple** dialog that appears [see Figure F47] and click **OK** to attach the selected shapes.

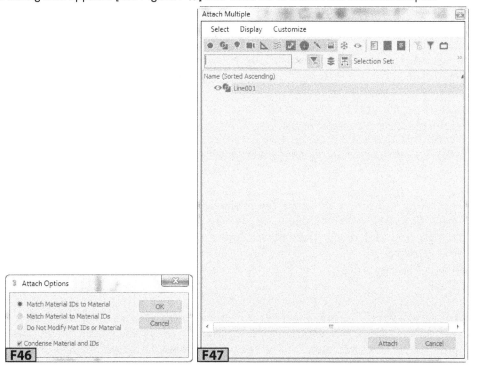

F46

F47

Note: Reorienting attached splines

*When **Reorient** is on, the attached splines are reoriented so that the local coordinate system of the attached splines is aligned with the selected spline.*

Cross Section

Cross Section allows you to create a spline cage out of cross sectional shapes. To create spline cage, make sure that all splines are attached. Click **Cross Section** and then click on the first spline, then second, and so forth. RMB click to complete the process and create a cage [see Figure F48].

F48

Tip: Keeping vertices together

*If you want to edit the spline cage, turn on **Area Selection** in the **Selection** rollout before selecting the vertices otherwise you would not be able to keep their position together. In Figure F49, the vertex shown in the right is selected after turning on **Area Selection** from the **Selection** rollout.*

Refine

Refine adds vertices to the spline object without changing the curvature of the spline. To add vertices, click **Refine** and then hover the mouse pointer on the segments in a viewport. The shape of the mouse pointer changes on the eligible segments. Now, click to add a vertex. When you are done, click **Refine** again or press RMB.

If you click on an existing vertex, 3ds Max displays a dialog asking if you want to refine the vertex or connect to the vertex. If you choose **Connect Only,** a new vertex will not be created instead the clicked vertex will be connected to the existing vertex.

Caution: Connecting vertices
*You must turn on **Connect** before clicking **Refine**.*

The type of vertex created during the **Refine** operation is dependent on the bordering vertices of the segment:

- If bordering vertices are smooth, a vertex of **Smooth** type is created.
- If bordering vertices are of **Corner** type, a vertex of **Corner** type is created.
- If either of the bordering vertices are of a **Corner** or **Bezier Corner** type, a vertex of **Bezier Corner** type is created.
- If the bordering vertices do not fit in the above mentioned criterion, a vertex of Bezier type is created.

Connect: It creates a new spline sub-object by connecting the two vertices.

To understand functioning of **Connect**, create two straight lines in a viewport and attach them [see Figure F50]. Select **Vertex** sub-object level. Turn on **Connect**. Notice that there are some options that get activated in the **Refine** group. Now, click **Refine** and then click on the first segment. Now, click on the second segment [see Figure F51], RMB click to create to connect two vertices [see Figure F52].

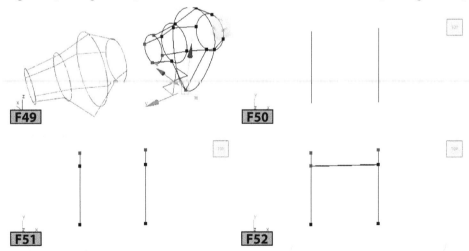

F49   F50   F51   F52

When **Linear** is on, the **Refine** operation creates straight lines using the vertices of **Corner** type. When off, the created vertices are of **Smooth** type. **Closed** allows you to create closed splines by connecting the first and last vertices [see Figure F53, the numbers show clicking order].

When **Bind first** is on, it sets the first vertex created to be bound to the center of the selected segment [see Figure F54]. **Bind last** sets the last vertex created to be bound to the center of the selected segment.

Note: Bound vertices

*Binding vertices helps in connecting splines when building a spline network for use with the **Surface** modifier. To distinguish the bound vertices from the standard vertices, 3ds Max makes them black. You cannot transform a bound vertex directly. However, you can move it by shifting the connected vertices. You can also change the type of the bound vertices from the upper left quadrant of the **Quad** menu.*

Automatic Welding

When on, the end vertices are welded together automatically, if the end vertices fall within a distance specified using **Threshold**.

Note: Automatic welding

This feature is available at the object as well as at all the sub-object levels.

Weld

Weld welds two end vertices or two adjacent vertices into a single vertex. To weld vertices, move the vertices close to each other and click **Weld**. If the vertices fall within a threshold defined by the control next to **Weld**, the selected vertices are welded to a single vertex [see Figure F55].

Connect

Connect connects two end vertices. To connect the vertices, click **Connect** and then drag the mouse pointer from one end vertex to another end vertex.

Insert

Insert lets you add one or more vertices creating additional segments in a spline. Click **Insert** and then click on the spline to attach the mouse pointer to the spline. Now, click to place the vertex. You can continue creating vertices. RMB click to end the operation. A single click create a corner vertex whereas dragging the mouse pointer creates a Bezier vertex.

Make First

It allows you to define which vertex in a spline is the first vertex. The first vertex in a spline is indicated by a small box around it. To make a vertex first vertex, select the vertex and then click **Make First**. If you are editing an open spline, the first vertex should be end point that is already not a first vertex. On closed spline, you can make any vertex first vertex.

The first vertex has special significance in many operations in 3ds Max. I will discuss the first vertex usages in the later units. Table 22 summarizes the importance of first vertex:

Table 22: First vertex use	
Use	**Description**
Loft Path	Indicates the start of the path [Level 0].
Loft Shape	Controls the initial skin alignment.
Path Constraint	Indicates the start of the path [indicates 0% on the location of the path].
Trajectory	Indicates the first position key.

Fuse

Fuse lets you move all selected vertices to their average center. To fuse the vertices, select them and then click **Fuse** to move the vertices to same location [see Figure F56]. Note that the **Fuse** operation does not weld the vertices, it simply moves them to same location.

F56

Cycle

Cycle allows you to select a specific vertex from the group of coincident vertices [vertices that shares the same location]. To select a specific vertex, select one or more vertices that share the same location, and then click **Cycle** repeatedly until you select the vertex you are looking for.

CrossInsert

CrossInsert adds vertices at the intersection of two splines that are part of the same spline object. To add vertex, click **CrossInsert** and then click at the intersection of the two splines. If the distance between the splines is within the threshold defined by the control next to **CrossInsert**, the vertices are added to both splines [see Figure F57].

F57

Fillet

Fillet lets you create the rounded corners by adding new control vertices. You can create rounded corners by dragging the mouse pointer in a viewport or by entering precise values in the control on the right of **Fillet**. To fillet the vertices, click **Fillet** and then drag the vertices in a viewport to add rounded corners. As you drag with **Fillet**, the control on its right shows the fillet amount [see Figure F58]. You can continue dragging to add fillet to other vertices. To finish the operation, RMB click.

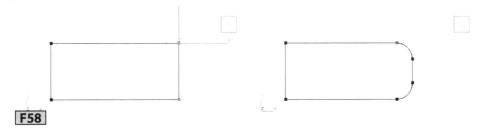

F58

Chamfer

Chamfer chops off the selected vertices by creating segments connecting new vertices [see Figure F59]. Like **Fillet** you can chamfer edges interactively or by entering precise values.

F59

Tangent

The controls available in this group let you copy paste vertex handles from one vertex to another. To copy tangent, select a vertex and then click **Copy**. Click on the tangent to copy tangent to the clipboard. Now, select another vertex, click **Paste**, and then click on the tangent of the vertex to paste the tangent [see Figure F60]. When **Paste Length** is on, the length of the handle is also copied.

F60

Hide

It allows you to hide the selected vertices and connected segments.

Unhide All

Unhide All allows you to unhide all hidden objects.

Bind

Bind lets you create bound vertices. To create a bound vertex, click **Bind** and then drag from any end vertex to any segment expect the one connected to the vertex, a dashed line connects the vertex and the current mouse position. When the mouse is over an eligible segment, the pointer changes to the **Connect** symbol. When you release the mouse button, the vertex jumps to the center of the segment and bound to it.

Unbind

Unbind lets you disconnect the bind vertices.

Delete

Allows you to delete the selected vertices as well as one attached segment per deleted vertex.

Show selected segs

Lets you display the selected segments in red color at the **Vertex** sub-object level [see Figure F61]. When off, the segments displayed in red only at **Segment** sub-object level.

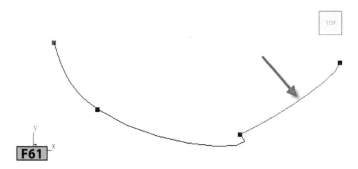

F61

Segment Level

A segment is a part of spline between two vertices of the spline. You can select one or more segments by activating the **Segment** sub-object level. Once selected, you can transform them using the transformation tools.

Most of the controls available for segments are similar to those discussed in the **Vertex Level** section. The other controls available at the segment sub-object level are discussed next.

Geometry Rollout

Divide

Divide subdivides the selected segment(s) by adding a number of vertices that are specified by using the control available on the right of this spinner. To subdivide a segment, select segment or segments of the spline. Now, specify the number of vertices and then click **Divide** [see Figure F62]. The distance between the vertices is dependent on the curvature of the segment.

F62

Delete

Deletes the selected segments from the spline [see Figure F63].

F63

Detach

It lets you detach/copy selected segments from the spline. To detach segment or segments, select them and then click **Detach**. In the **Detach** dialog that appears, type name in the **Detach as** text box and then click **OK**. The segment will be detached from the spline and new shape will be created [see Figure F64].

F64

There are some other controls that can be used with the detach operation. Table 23 summarizes these options.

Control	Description
Table 23: The **Detach** options	
Same Shp	When on, **Reorient** gets deactivated. The detached segment remains part of the same spline. If **Copy** is also on, the detached segment is copied at the same location.
Reorient	When on, the detached segment copies the transformation values of the spline's creation local coordinate system.
Copy	Copies the selected segment without detaching it from the spline.

Surface Properties Layout

The controls in this section allow you to apply different material IDs to spline segments. The material appears on the renderable shapes. To assign material ID to a segment or segments, select them and then enter the **ID** in the **Set ID** spinner. **Select ID** lets you select the segments corresponding to the material ID set in the spinner on the right of **Select ID**. The drop-down below **Select ID** shows the name of the sub-materials, if you have applied **Multi-Subobject** material to the object. If you have applied a material other than the **Multi-Sub-object** material, this drop-down will be inactive.

When **Clear Selection** is on, selecting a new ID or material name deselects the previously selected segments or splines.

Changing Segment Properties

You can switch the between the **Curve** or **Line type** for the selected segments. To change the type, select segments and then RMB click. Now, choose **Line** or **Curve** from the upper left quadrant of the **Quad** menu [see Figure F65]. Figure F66 shows a segment converted from the **Curve** type to **Line** type.

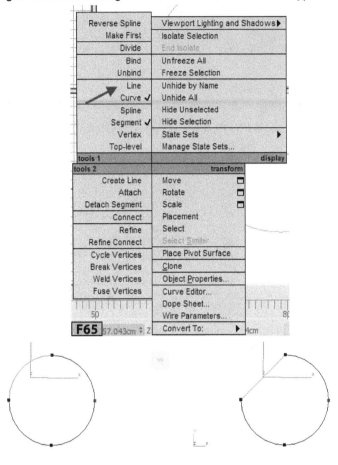

F65

F66

The **Spline** sub-object level allows you to select single spline or multiple splines in a single object. Once selected, you can transform them using the transformation tools. Most of the controls available for segments are similar to those discussed in the **Vertex Level** and **Segment Level** sections. The other controls available at the segment sub-object level are discussed next.

Geometry Rollout
Connect Copy Group

Connect Copy works when you make a clone of the spline using **Shift**. You must turn on **Connect Copy** before the cloning operation. When on, 3ds Max creates a new spline sub-object that connects the vertices of the original and cloned objects [see Figure F67]. **Threshold** defines the distance that the soft selection uses during the **Connect Copy** operation.

F67

Outline

Outline makes a copy of the spline. The copy offsets in all directions specified by the spinner on the right of **Outline**. You can also create an outline interactively by using the mouse. To create an outline, select one or more splines and then click **Outline**. Now, drag a spline to create outline [see Figure F68].

F68

Caution: Selecting splines

If there is one spline is in the scene, it is automatically selected for the outlining process. However, if you are using spinner to add outline, you must select it first.

Note: Open spline

If you are outlining an open spline, the outlining process creates a single closed spline [see Figure F69].

F69

When **Center** is on, the original spline and its outline moves away from an invisible center line by the distance specified by dragging operation or by the value specified for the spinner on the right of **Outline**.

Boolean

Boolean combines two splines. It alters the first spline you select and deletes the other one. There are three types of **Boolean** operations available. Table 24 summarizes those operations:

Table 24: The boolean operations	
Operation	**Description**
Union	Combines two overlapping splines into a single spline. The overlapping portion is removed.

Subtraction	Subtracts the overlapping portion of the second spline from the first spline.
Intersection	Leaves the overlapping portions of the two splines.

To boolean splines, make sure both splines are part of a single spline object [use **Attach** to attach them]. Select a spline and then click **Union**, **Subtraction**, or **Intersection**. Now, click **Boolean**. Hover the mouse pointer on the second spline and then click when shape of the cursor changes to complete the operation [see Figure F70].

F70

Mirror
Mirror allows you to mirror splines horizontally, vertically, and diagonally. To mirror a spline, ensure it is selected and then click **Mirror Horizontally**, **Mirror Vertically**, or **Mirror Both**. Next, click **Mirror** to complete the operation [see Figure F71].

F71

If **Copy** is on, 3ds Max creates a mirror copy of the spline [see Figure F72].

F72

When **About Pivot** is on, 3ds Max mirrors the spline along its geometric center otherwise mirrors along the spline object's pivot point [see Figure F73].

F73

Trim
Trim allows you to clear the overlapping segments in a shape. The two splines must overlap each other and they should be part of the same spline object. To trim a spline, select the spline that will be used to trim the target spline. Click **Trim** and hover the cursor over the spline that you want to trim and then click when the shape of the cursor changes [see Figure F74].

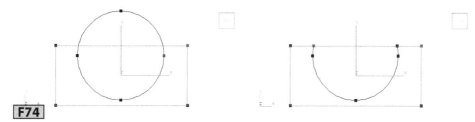

F74

Extend

Extend allows you to extend an open spline. To extend spline, you need a segment that can extend to an intersecting segment of the spline. **Extend** does not work if intersection is not possible. To understand **Extend** feature, create a circle and a line [see the left image in Figure F75]. Convert the circle to an editable spline object and then attach is with the line. Select the **Spline** sub-object mode, click **Extend**. Now, click on the each end of the line to extend it to the circle [see the right image in Figure F75].

F75

Explode

Explode breaks the segment of the selected spline and convert segments into separate splines or objects. There are two options available for the explode operation: **Splines** and **Objects**. If you choose **Objects**, the **Explode** dialog appears. Type a name in the **Object Name** text box and click **OK**. Each successive object will use a name appended with an incremented three-digit number. For example, if you type name as **myShape** and click **OK**. The name of other objects will be: **myShape001**, **myShape002**, **myShape003**, and so forth.

Note: Explode and Detach
***Explode** is **Detach** on steroids.*

Changing the Spline Type

You can change the spline type from **Curve** to **Line** and visa-versa. To change type, select the spline and RMB click. Choose **Line** or **Curve** from the upper left quadrant of the **Quad** menu. Right image in Figure F76 shows the spline object converted from **Curve** type into **Line** type.

F76

*You can use the **Shape Check** utility to check self-intersecting splines and NURBS curves. The self-intersecting shapes may produce unpredicted results when used in loft, extrude, and lathed operations. To check intersection point, go to the **Utilities** panel and then click on **More** to open **Utilities** dialog. Select **Shape Check** from the **Utilities** list and click **OK**. The **Shape Check** rollout appears in the **Utilities** panel. Click **Pick Object** and then click the spline or NURBS curve in a viewport. The red squares appear on the intersection points [see Figure F77].*

F77

Hands-on Exercises

From the **Application** menu, choose **Manage | Set Project Folder** to open the **Browse for Folder** dialog. Navigate to the folder where you want to save the files and then click **Make New Folder**. Create the new folder with the name **unit-mm4** and click **OK** to create the project directory.

Exercise 1: Creating a Glass Model

In this exercise, you will model a glass using the **Line** primitive and **Lathe** modifier [see Figure E1].

E1

Table E1 summarizes the exercise:

Table E1: Creating model of a glass	
In this exercise, you will learn how to:	• Create a line using **Line** spline • Create surface using the **Lathe** modifier • Fillet vertices
Skill level	Beginner
Time to complete	15 Minutes
Topics in the section:	• Specifying the Units for the Exercise • Creating the Glass
Project folder	**unit-mm4**
Units	**Generic Units**
Final exercise file	**umm4-hoe1-end.max**

Specifying the Units for the Exercise

From **Customize** menu choose **Units Setup**. In the **Units Setup** dialog that opens, select the **Generic Units** option from the **Display Unit Scale** group.

Creating the Glass

Go to the **Create** ➕ panel, click **Shapes** , then click **Line**. In the **Front** viewport, create a shape [see Figure E2]. In the **Modify** panel | **Selection** rollout, click **Vertex** . Select the vertices shown in Figure E3 and then RMB click. Choose **Bezier** from the **tool 1** quadrant of the **Quad** menu.

Note: Object level

*When you first access the **Modify** panel with an editable spline selected, you are at the **Object** level.*

Click **Select and Move** ✛ from the **Main** toolbar. Adjust the shape of the curve by moving the vertices and tangents [see Figure E4]. In the **Modify** panel | **Geometry** rollout, click **Fillet**. Click and drag over the vertices [see Figure E5] to apply fillet to them [see Figure E6].

From the **Modifier List** | **Object-Space Modifiers** section, choose **Lathe**. In the **Modify** panel | **Parameters** rollout, click **Min** in the **Align** group. Set **Segments** to **22** [see Figure E7]. Now, check **Weld Core**.

Exercise 2: Creating a Glass Table

In this exercise, you will model a glass table using the **Rectangle** spline, **ChamferCyl** primitive, and **Extrude** modifier [see Figure E1]

E1

Table E2 summarizes the exercise:

Table E2: Creating model of a glass table	
In this exercise, you will learn how to:	• Create a rectangle using **Rectangle** spline • Extrude spline using the **Extrude** modifier
Skill level	Beginner
Time to complete	15 Minutes
Topics in the section:	• Specifying the Units for the Exercise • Creating the Glass Table
Project folder	**unit-mm4**
Units	**Generic Units**
Final exercise file	**umm4-hoe2-end.max**

Specifying the Units for the Exercise

From **Customize** menu choose **Units Setup**. In the **Units Setup** dialog that opens, select the **Generic Units** option from the **Display Unit Scale** group.

Creating the Glass Table

Go to the **Create** panel, click **Shapes**, then click **Rectangle**. In the **Front** viewport, create a shape. Click **Select and Move** on the **Main** toolbar. Set the **Transform Type-In** boxes to **0** on the **status bar** to place the rectangle at the origin. On the **Modify** panel | **Parameters** rollout, set **Length** to **55**, set **Width** to **149**, and **Corner Radius** to **16** [see Figure E2].

RMB click on the rectangle and then choose **Convert To: | Convert to Editable Spline** from the **transform** quadrant of the **Quad** menu. On the **Modify** panel | **Selection** rollout, click **Spline**. Click on the rectangle in a viewport to select the **Spline** sub-object [see Figure E3]. On the **Modify** panel | **Geometry** rollout, set **Outline's** spinner to **-8** to create an outline [see Figure E4].

[+][Front][Standard][Wireframe]   [+][Front][Standard][Wireframe]

E2   E3

Apply a **Extrude** modifier to the rectangle. On the **Parameters** rollout, set **Amount** to **-100** to extrude the shape [see Figure E5]. In the **Front** viewport, **Shift** drag the spline and then create two instances of it using the **Clone Options** dialog's options [see Figure E6].

[+][Front][Standard][Wireframe]   [+][Perspective][Standard][Default Shading]

E4   E5

Go to the **Create** panel, click **Geometry** | **Extended Primitives**, then click the **ChamferCyl** button. In the **Top** viewport, create a cylinder. On the **Modify** panel | **Parameters** rollout, set **Radius** to **6**, **Height** to **16**, **Fillet** to **0.8**, and **Fillet Segs** to **0**. Now, align the cylinder with the table [see Figure E7]. Create three more copies of the cylinder and align them [see Figure E8].

[+][Front][Standard][Wireframe]   [+][Perspective][Standard][Default Shading]

E6   E7

[+][Perspective][Standard][Default Shading]

E8

In this exercise, you will model a corkscrew using the **Helix** Spline and **Loft** compound object [see Figure E1].

Table E3 summarizes the exercise:

Table E3: Creating model of a corkscrew	
In this exercise, you will learn how to:	• Use the **Helix** spline • Create surfaces using the **Loft** compound object
Skill level	Beginner
Time to complete	15 Minutes
Topics in the section:	• Specifying the Units for the Exercise • Creating the Corkscrew
Project folder	**unit-mm4**
Units	**Generic Units**
Final exercise file	**umm4-hoe3-end.max**

Specifying the Units for the Exercise

From **Customize** menu choose **Units Setup**. In the **Units Setup** dialog that opens, select the **Generic Units** option from the **Display Unit Scale** group.

Creating the Corkscrew

Go to the **Create** panel, click **Shapes**, then click **Helix**. In the **Top** viewport, create a shape. On the **Modify** panel | **Parameters** rollout, set **Radius 1** to **8**, **Radius 2** to **8**, **Height** to **120**, and **Turns** to **5.5**. In the **Front** viewport, rotate it by **-90** degrees around Z-axis [see Figure E2.

RMB click on the helix and then choose **Convert To:** | **Convert to Editable Spline** from the **transform** quadrant of the **Quad** menu. On the **Modify** panel | **Selection** rollout, click **Vertex** and then move the **start yellow vertex** toward left about **60** units in the **Front** viewport [see Figure E3].

E2

E3

[+] [Top] [Standard] [Wireframe]   [+] [Front] [Standard] [Wireframe]

Apply a **Normalize Spl.** modifier to the helix. On the **Modify** panel | **Parameters** rollout, set **Seg Length** to **5**. RMB click on the helix and then choose **Convert To: | Convert to Editable Spline** from the **transform** quadrant of the **Quad** menu. Go to the **Create** panel, click **Shapes**, then click **Circle**. In the **Left** viewport, create a circle. On the **Modify** panel | **Parameters** rollout, set **Radius** to **2.5**. Select helix in a viewport. Go to the **Create** panel, click **Geometry | Compound Objects**, then click **Loft**. On the **Creation Method** rollout, click **Get Shape** and then click circle in a viewport to loft the circle along the helix [see Figure E4].

What just happened?
*You might have noticed that there were tons of vertices on the helix when I converted it to an editable spline. To reduce the number of vertices, I have applied the **Normalize Spl.** modifier to the helix spline. This modifier add news control points at regular intervals.*

[+] [Perspective] [Standard] [Default Shading]

E4

On the **Modify** panel | **Skin Parameters** rollout | **Options** group, set **Shape Steps** to **1** and **Path Steps** to **2**. On the **Modify** panel | **Deformations** rollout, click **Scale**. In the **Scale Deformation** dialog that opens, click **Insert Corner Point** and then add a point below the **80** mark [see Figure E5]. Now, click **Move Control Point** and move the end point downward [see Figure E6] to scale the end area of the corkscrew [see Figure E7]. Go to the **Create** panel, click **Geometry | Extended Primitives,** then click the **ChamferCyl** button. In the **Top** viewport, create a cylinder.

E5   E6

On the **Modify** panel | **Parameters** rollout, set **Radius** to **9.3, Height** to **6.5, Fillet** to **0.41, Sides** to **32,** and **Fillet Segs** to **3.** Now, align the cylinder with the corkscrew [see Figure E8].

E7   E8

Exercise 4: Creating a Model of a Glass and Liquid

In this exercise, you will model a glass and liquid [see Figure E1].

E1

Table E4 summarizes the exercise:

Table E4: Creating Model of a Glass and Liquid	
In this exercise, you will learn how to:	• Create profiles using splines • Use the **Lathe** modifier
Skill level	Intermediate
Time to complete	1 Hour

Topics in the section:	• Specifying the Units for the Exercise
	• Setting the Blueprint
	• Creating the Glass
	• Creating the Liquid
Project folder	**unit-mm4**
Units	**Generic Units**
Final exercise file	**umm4-hoe4-end.max**

Specifying the Units for the Exercise

From **Customize** menu choose **Units Setup**. In the **Units Setup** dialog that opens, select the **Generic Units** option from the **Display Unit Scale** group.

Setting the Blueprint

Go to the **Create** panel, click **Geometry**, then click **Plane**. In the **Front** viewport, create a plane. On the **Modify** panel | **Parameters** rollout, set **Length** to **100** and **Width** to **75**. Click **Material Editor** from the **Main** toolbar. Create a standard material using the **Material Editor** and apply it to the plane. Use the **glassRef.png** for the **Diffuse** map. You need to turn on the **Show Shaded Material in the Viewport** switch for the material to display the image on the plane in the viewport. Ensure in the **Coordinates** rollout, **Use Real-World Scale** is off and **U Tiling** and **V Tiling** are set to **1**. Make sure the **Front** viewport is active and then press **G** to turn off the grid. Also, change display mode to **Default Shading** [see Figure E2]. RMB click on the plane and then choose **Object Properties** from the **Quad** menu. Turn on the **Freeze** switch from the **Interactivity** area and turn off the **Show Frozen in Gray** switch from the **Display Properties** area.

Creating The Glass

Go to the **Create** panel, click **Shapes**, then click **Line**. In the **Front** viewport, create a shape [see Figure E3]. In the **Modify** panel | **Selection** rollout, click **Vertex**. On the **Modify** panel | **Geometry** rollout, click **Fillet**. Click and drag over the vertices to get the shape [see Figure E4]. Make sure the **X** coordinate value for the selected vertices shown in Figure E5 is same. Hide the **plane**.

Make sure the profile of the curve is selected and then apply a **Lathe** modifier to it. In the **Modify** panel | **Parameters** rollout, click **Min** in the **Align** group. Set **Segments** to **32**. Now, turn on **Weld Core** [see Figure E6]. Hide the plane and then rename the geometry as **glassGeo**.

Creating The Liquid

Select **glassGeo** and then on the **Ribbon | Polygon Modeling** panel, click **Convert to Poly.** Activate **Edge** sub-object level and then on the **Ribbon | Edit** panel, click **SwiftLoop.** Insert an edge loop as shown in Figure E7. Click **SwiftLoop** again to deactivate it. Activate **Polygon** sub-object level and then select the inner polygons shown in Figure E8.

Shift drag the selected polygons to the right [see Figure E9]. In the **Clone Part of Mesh** dialog that opens, select **Clone to Object** and then type **liquidGeo** as the name of the clone, and then click **OK**. Select **liquidGeo** and then activate **Border** sub-object level. Now, select the border [see Figure E10].

On the **Ribbon | Geometry (All)** panel, click **CapPoly**. Now, activate **Polygon** sub-object level and then select the cap polygon. On the **Ribbon | Polygons** panel, **Shift** click **Inset** . In the **Inset's** caddy, set **Amount** to **5** and **then** click **OK** [see Figure E11].

On the **Ribbon | Polygon Modeling** panel, **Ctrl** click **Vertex**. On the **Ribbon | Vertices** panel, **Shift** click **Weld**. In the **Weld's** caddy, set **Weld Threshold** to **15** and **then** click **OK** [see Figure E12] to weld the vertices.

Activate **Edge** sub-object level and then select the edge loop shown in Figure E13. On the **Ribbon | Edges** panel, **Shift** click **Chamfer**. In the **Chamfer's** caddy, set **Edge Chamfer Amount** to **0.09** and **Connect Edge**

Segments to **2** [see Figure E14]. Click **OK**. Select **glassGeo** and then apply the **Normal** modifier to it. Align the **glassGeo** and **liquidGeo** using the **Align** tool.

Exercise 5: Creating a Jug

In this exercise, we are going to create model of a jug using spline and polygon modeling techniques [see Figure E1].

The following table summarizes the exercise.

Table E5: Creating Model of a Jug	
In this exercise, you will:	• Set units to **Centimeters** • Use the **Line** primitive to create path for **Loft** feature • Use the **NGon** primitive to create shapes for the **Loft** feature • Create handle of the jug by extruding polygons along a spline • Refine the model by adding segments to it
Topics in this section:	• Getting Ready • Creating Shape of the Jug Using Line and NGon Spline Primitive • Creating the Handle of the Jug Using Extrude Along Spline Feature • Refining the Model
Skill Level	Intermediate
Project Folder	**unit-mm4**
Final Exercise File	**umm4-hoe5-end.max**
Time to Complete	30 Minutes

Getting Ready

Start 3ds Max and then reset it. From **Customize** menu choose **Units Setup**. In the **Units Setup** dialog that opens, select **Metric** from the **Display Unit Scale** group. Next, select **Centimeters** from the drop-down located below **Metric**, if already not selected. Click **OK** to accept the change.

Creating Shape of the Jug Using Line and NGon Spline Primitive

Activate the **Front** viewport. Go to the **Create** panel, click **Shapes**, and then ensure that **Shapes** is selected in the drop-down below the **Shapes** button. On the **Object Type** rollout, click **Line**. Expand the **Keyboard Entry** rollout, and then click **Add Point** to add a point at the origin. Now, set **Y** to **30** and then click **Add Point**. This action creates a line in the **Front** viewport [see Figure E2]. This line will serve as path for the **Loft** tool. Click **Select Object** on the **Main** toolbar to deactivate the line tool.

On the **Object Type** rollout, click **NGon** and then create an **NGon** in the **Front** viewport. On the **Modify** panel | **Parameters** rollout, set **Radius** to **7**, and **Sides** to **26**. Turn on the **Circular** switch. Create four more copies of the **NGon**. The total number of **NGons** will be **5** [see Figure E3]. Change the radius of the three rightmost **NGons** to **4** [see Figure E4].

The last **NGon** will be the spout of the jug. Select it and then covert it to **Editable Spline** object. Activate the **Vertex** sub-object level and then select the top four vertices as shown in Figure E5.

RMB click on the vertices and then choose **Corner** from the **tool1** quadrant of the **Quad** menu. Now, select the middle two vertices and move them using the **Move** tool [see Figure E6]. Ensure the vertices are still selected and them RMB click. On the **tool1** quadrant of the **Quad** menu, choose **Smooth** to make the shape of the spout [see Figure E7]. Deactivate the **Vertex** sub-object level.

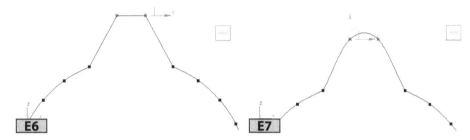

Select the **Line** in the **Front** viewport. Go to the **Create** panel, click **Geometry**, and then ensure that **Compound Objects** is selected in the drop-down below the **Geometry** button. On the **Object Type** rollout, click **Loft**. On the **Path Parameters** rollout, ensure **Path** to set to **0** and click **Get Shape** button on the **Creation Method** rollout. Now, click on the **NGon** on the right of the line. Set **Path** to **1** and then click **Get Shape**. Now, click on the second **NGon** in the **Front** viewport. Similarly, pick the other three **NGons** with **Path** value set to **82**, **85**, and **100**, respectively. This action creates the shape of the jug in the viewport [see Figure E8].

On the **Modify** panel, turn off the **End Cap** switch from the **Skin Parameters | Capping** group. On the **Options** group, set **Shape Steps** to **0** and **Path Steps** to **3**. Turn on the **Linear Interpolation** switch. Now, delete all spline objects from the scene. Add a **Shell** modifier to the stack and then set **Outer Amount** to **0.559** in the **Modify** panel | **Parameters** rollout [see Figure E9].

Creating the Handle of the Jug Using Extrude Along Spline Feature

Convert model to an **Editable Poly** object. Now, select the edges as shown in Figure E10. On the **Ribbon |** **Loops** panel, click **Connect** with the **Shift** held down, the **Connect Edges** caddy appears in the viewport. Set **Segments** to **4** [see Figure E11] and click **OK**. In the **Right** viewport, create a shape as shown in Figure E12. Now, select the polygons as shown in Figure E13.

On the **Ribbon | Polygon** panel, click **Extrude on Spline** with the **Shift** held down, the **Extrude Along Spline** caddy appears. Click **Pick Spline** and then click on the path in a viewport to extrude the selected polygon along the spline. In the **Extrude Along Spline** caddy, set the values as shown in Figure E14 and then click **OK**. Now, refine the model, refer to Figure E15 through E18 and then apply the **Turbosmooth** modifier to the jug.

E17

E18

Practical Test

Complete the following test:

Test 1: Creating the Candle Stand

Create the candle stand model [see Figure P1] using the **Line** primitive.

P1

Summary
The unit covered the following topics:

- Generate planar and 3d surfaces
- Paths and shapes for the loft components
- Generate extrusions
- Generate revolved surfaces
- Define motion path for animations

Unit MM5: Modifiers

Modifiers in 3ds Max allow to sculpt or edit the objects without changing its base structure. For example, if you apply a **Taper** modifier to a cylinder, you will still able to change its parametric properties such as **Radius** and **Height**. Modifiers can change the geometry of the objects as well as their properties. In other words, modifiers add more parameters to the objects.

In this unit, I will describe the following:

- Using modifiers
- Stack display
- Object-space modifiers vs World-space modifiers
- How transform affects modifiers

Following are some points that you should remember about modifiers:

- When you apply modifiers to the objects, they are stored in a stack and displayed as a stack in the **Modify** panel. You can change the order of the modifiers in the stack to change the effect of the modifier. You can also collapse the stack to make the changes permanent.
- You can apply any number of modifiers to an object.
- When you delete a modifier, its effect on the object also vanishes.
- You can copy modifiers from one object to another.
- The order of the modifier in the stack determines the final effect. Each modifier in the stack affects the modifiers that are applied after it.
- You can apply modifiers to sub-object levels.
- You can toggle the effect of the modifiers from the stack display.

Object Space Modifiers Vs World Space Modifiers

Some modifiers that 3ds Max offers operate in the world-space. These modifiers use the world-space coordinates and are applied to the object after all object-space modifiers and transforms have been applied. You can apply the world-space modifiers like any other object-space modifier. A world-space modifier is indicated by either an asterisk of the text **WSM**.

On the other hand, the object-space modifiers affect the geometry of the object in local space. They use object's local coordinate system. The local coordinate system relates specifically to the selected object. Each object has its own local center and coordinate system. The local center and the coordinate system define the object's local space. Unlike the world coordinate system, the directions of the object's axes [X, Y, and Z] depends on the current transform of the object.

Transform

Transform [move, rotate, and scale] are the most basic manipulations of the 3d objects. Unlike most of the modifiers, transforms are independent of internal structure of an object. The transformation values are stored in a matrix called **Transformation Matrix**. This matrix is applied to the entire object. The matrix is applied after all object-space modifiers have been applied but before the word-space modifiers.

Data Flow

Once you create an object and apply a modifier to it, 3ds Max evaluates the flow as per the table given below:

Table 1: The Data Flow

Order	Category	Modifiers/Transform/Properties	Illustration
1	Creation Parameters	Cylinder	
2	Object Modifiers	Bend, Taper	
3	Transforms	Rotate, Position, and Scale	
4	Space Warps	Ripple	
5	Object Properties	Checker Material	

Using Modifiers

You can access modifiers from the **Modifiers** menu, the **Modifier List** from the **Modify** panel, and from the applicable **Modifier Set** menu. To keep all modifiers organized, 3ds Max has grouped them in the **Modifier** menu. The following table summarizes the options available in the **Modifier** menu.

Table 2: The **Modifier** menu overview

Menu Item	Sub-menu Items
Selection Modifier	FFD Select, Mesh Select, Patch Select, Poly Select, Select By Channel, Spline Select, and Volume Select

Patch/Spline Editing	Cross Section, Delete Patch, Delete Spline, Edit Patch, Edit Spline, Fillet/Chamfer, Lathe, Normalize Spline, Renderable Spline Modifier, Surface, Sweep, and Trim/Extend
Mesh Editing	Cap Holes, Chamfer, Delete Mesh, Edit Mesh, Edit Normals, Edit Poly, Extrude, Face Extrude, MultiRes, Normal Modifier, Optimize, ProOptimizer, Quadify Mesh, Smooth, STL Check, Symmetry, Tessellate, Vertex Paint, and Vertex Weld
Conversion	Turn to Mesh, Turn to Patch, and Turn to Poly
Animation	Attribute Holder, Flex, Linked XForm, Melt, Morpher, Patch Deform, Patch Deform (WSM), Path Deform, Path Deform (WSM), Skin, Skin Morph, Skin Wrap, Skin Wrap Patch, SpineIK Control, Surf Deform, and Surf Deform (WSM)
Cloth	Cloth, Garment Maker, and Welder
Hair and Fur	Hair and Fur (WSM)
UV Coordinates	Camera Map, Camera Map (WSM), MapScaler (WSM), Projection, Unwrap UVW, UVW Wrap, UVW Mapping Add, UVW Mapping Clear, UVW and XForm
Cache Tools	Point Cache, and Point Cache (WSM)
Subdivision Surfaces	Crease, CreaseSet, HSDS Modifier, MeshSmooth, OpenSubdiv, and TurboSmooth
Free Form Deformers	FFD 2x2x2, FFD 3x3x3, FFD 4x4x4, FFD Box, and FFD Cylinder
Parametric Deformers	Affect Region, Bend, Displace, Lattice, Mirror, Noise, Physique, Push, Preserve, Relax, Ripple, Shell, Slice, Skew, Stretch, Spherify, Squeeze, Twist, Taper, Substitute, XForm, and Wave
Surface	Disp Approx, Displace Mesh (WSM), Material, and Material By Element
NURBS Editing	Displace Approx, Surf Deform, and Surface Select
Radiosity	Subdivide, and Subdivide (WSM)
Cameras	Camera Correction

Using the Modify Panel

To apply a modifier to an object, select the object in the scene and then go to the **Modify** panel. The name of the selected object appears on the top of the **Modify** panel. Apply a modifier to the object by using one of the following methods:

- Choose a modifier from the **Modifier List** available in the **Modify** panel. You can either use mouse to click on the **Modifier** or use the keyboard. For example, if you are looking for the **Mirror** modifier, type **mi**, the modifiers whose name starts with **mi** [in this case the **Mirror** modifier only] appear in the **Modifier List**. Now, you can click on the **Modifier** or press **Enter** to apply it.
- Choose a modifier from the **Modifiers** menu.
- If the **Modifier** buttons are available in the on the **Modify** panel, click one of the buttons.

Tip: Dragging a modifier to an object

*To drag a modifier form one object to another object in the scene, select an object that already has a modifier. To copy a modifier without instancing it, drag the modifier name from the stack display to the target object in the scene. If you want to create an instance, **Ctrl+drag** the modifier's name.*

Tip: Modifier Instances

*When you create an instance of a modifier, its name appears in italics in the **Modify** panel indicating that the modifier is instanced.*

Using the Configure Modifier Sets Dialog

When you click on the **Configure Modifier Sets** button in the **Modify** panel [below modifier stack], a menu is displayed. Choose **Show Buttons** from the menu to display the modifier buttons below the **Modifier List**. The buttons associated with the currently selected set will be displayed in the **Modify** panel. You can select various sets from the menu. Figure F1 shows the buttons associated with the **Selection Modifiers** set.

When you choose the **Configure Modifier Sets** option from the menu, the **Configure Modifier Sets** dialog appears [see Figure F2]. This dialog lets you create custom modifier and button sets for the **Modify** panel. To create a new set, set the number of desired buttons using **Total Buttons**, and then drag a modifier from the modifier list to a button.

You can also add a modifier by first highlighting the button and then double-clicking a modifier in the **Modifier List**. When you assign a modifier by double-clicking on its name, the highlight moves to the next button in the **Modifiers** group. Now, enter the name of the new set in the **Sets** edit field and then click **Save** to save the set. Click **OK** from the **Configure Modifier Sets** dialog to exit it. Similarly, you can modify an existing set.

Using the Modifier Stack

The modifier stack [also referred to as just stack] is a list of modifiers that you apply to an object. The stack is evaluated from bottom to top. The first entry in the stack [from bottom] is always the object. The object-space modifiers appear above the object type. The world-space modifiers and space warps bound to the object are placed at the top.

You can use the stack in one of the following ways:

- Find a particular object and adjust its parameters using rollouts.
- Change the order of modifiers.
- Deactivate the effect of modifier in the stack, viewport, or both.
- Select components [such as **Gizmo** or **Center**] of a modifier.
- Delete modifiers.

The buttons at the bottom of the stack allow you to manage the stack. Table 3 summarizes the functioning of the buttons.

Table 3: The buttons found below the modifier stack		
Name	**Icon**	**Description**
Pin Stack		It locks the stack and all controls in the **Modify** panel to the selected object stack.
Show End Result		When active, it shows the effect of the entire stack on the selected object. When inactive, shows the result up to the currently highlighted modifier.
Make Unique		It makes an instanced object unique.
Remove Modifier		It deletes the current modifier from the stack.
Configure Modifier Sets		When this button is clicked, a menu is displayed that lets you configure the modifier button sets.

Tip: Copying and pasting modifiers
You can copy and paste modifiers between the object. RMB click on a modifier, a popup menu appears. You can use the ***Cut****,* ***Copy****,* ***Paste****, and* ***Paste Instanced*** *options from the menu to edit the stack.*

Caution: World-space modifiers
While copy pasting the modifiers, ensure that you select the world-space and object-space modifiers separately. The ***Cut****,* ***Copy****, and* ***Paste*** *options are disabled in the menu if you select both types of modifiers.*

Caution: Word-space modifiers
Caution: Word-space modifiers
If you paste a word-space modifier in a section of object-space modifiers, the paste occurs at the top of the world-space section.

Collapsing the Stack

You can collapse the modifier stack of an editable object to merge the cumulative effect of the collapsed modifiers. You might collapse the modifier stack in one of the following situations:

- You have finished the model and you want to keep it as is.
- You want to discard animation tracks.
- You want to save the memory by simplifying the model.

In most of the cases, collapsing the entire modifier stack or part of the stack saves memory. However, some modifiers such as **Bevel** when collapsed increases the file size as well as the memory used.

Caution: Parametric nature of the objects
Once you collapse the modifier stack, you lose access to the parametric creation parameters of the object.

Tip: Preserving the original copy
*Before you collapse a stack, choose **Save As | Save Selected** from the **Application** menu to preserve a copy of the original parametric object.*

3ds Max provides two options to collapse the stack: **Collapse To** and **Collapse All**. You can access these options by RMB clicking on the stack. The **Collapse To** option collapses the stack up to and including the chosen modifier to an editable object. You can still adjust the modifiers above the chosen modifier. The resultant object type depends on the uppermost modifier and type of geometry it outputs. For example, if the uppermost modifier is **Edit Poly**, the resultant object will be an **Editable Poly** object. If no such modifier exists in the stack, the resultant object is an editable mesh. The **Collapse All** option collapses the entire stack. It does not affect any world-space bindings.

Exploring Modifiers

As already discussed, 3ds Max offers two types of modifiers: **Word-Space Modifiers** and **Object-Space modifiers**. Let's explore these modifiers

Hair and Fur Modifier (World Space)

This modifier is the engine of the **Hair and Fur** feature in 3ds Max. You can apply this modifier to either a mesh object or a spline object. If you apply it to splines, the hair grows between the splines. When you select an object on which you have applied this modifier, hair is displayed in the viewports. You cannot select the fur itself in the viewports, however, you can select hair guides using the **Guides** sub-object level.

Note: Hair in the viewports
*The hair only renders in the **Perspective** or **Camera** viewports. If you try to render an orthographic viewport, 3ds Max presents a warning that says that the hair will not appear in the render.*

Camera Map Modifier (World Space)

This modifier is similar to the **Camera Map** modifier. It is used to apply the **UVW** mapping coordinates to the object based on a specified camera. It causes the object to blend with the background if you apply same map to the object as you apply to the scene environment. To apply a **Camera Map** modifier, create a scene with a camera and one or more objects. Ensure that the object that you want to map is visible to the camera in the scene. Apply the **Camera Map** modifier and then click **Pick Camera** from the **Camera Mapping** rollout and click on the camera in a viewport. Now, you need to apply a map to the background. Press **8** to open the **Environment & Effects** dialog. Assign a map using the **Environment map** button. Now, open the **Material Editor** and drag the map from the **Environment and Effects** dialog to the **Material Editor**, choose **Instance** from the dialog that appears and then click **OK**. Set the tiling in the **Coordinates** rollout, if required.

Apply a material to the object in the scene and then assign the map you just created to the **Diffiuse** component of the material [see Figure F3]. To create the render shown in Figure F3, I have applied a **Checker** map to both the environment and the object. Notice that the **Checker** map on the object matches the background but the shading effect of the material makes the object visible. To blend the object completely in the background, set the **Specular Level** and **Glossiness** of the material to **0**. Also, turn off the self-illumination color and set the **Self Illumination** to **100**. Now, take a render using the camera that you have assigned to the modifier [see Figure F4].

Displace Mesh Modifier (World Space)

This modifier allows you to see the effect of the **Displacement** mapping on editable mesh objects in the viewports. Also, you can see the effect of the **Displacement** mapping if you have applied a **Disp Approx** modifier to an object. This is useful when you want to visualize the effect of **Displacement** mapping in the viewports especially when you have animated the **Displacement** map or when you want to create an editable mesh from the displace geometry in the scene.

To understand the functioning of this modifier, create a **Plane** primitive with **Length**, **Width**, **Length Segs**, and **Width Segs** values set to **150**, **150**, **50**, and **50**, respectively. Apply the **Displacement Approx** modifier to the plane. Open the **Material Editor** and apply the **Standard** material to the plane. Connect the **Noise** map with the **Displacement** slot of the material. Now, add the **Displace Mesh (WSM)** modifier to the stack. The effect of the **Displacement** map appears in the viewport [see Figure F5].

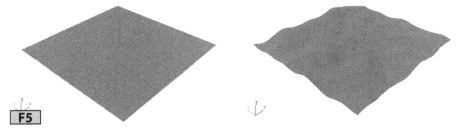

Note: The Displacement Approx modifier
If you are applying displacement to an editable mesh object, you don't need to apply this modifier in order to see the displacement effect in the viewport.

If you have changed parameters of the map [the **Noise** map in this case], click **Update** on the **Displacement Approx** rollout to update the mesh in the viewports. When **Subdivision Displacement** is on, this modifier uses the settings that you specify on the **Subdivision Method** group of the rollout. You can also use the presets available in the **Subdivision Presets** group of the rollout. If **Subdivision Displacement** is off, this modifier applies the map by moving the vertices just as the **Displace** modifier does.

Displace NURBS Modifier (World Space)

This modifier is same as the **Displace Mesh** modifier, however, it is used with the **NURBS** objects. If a **Displacement** map is applied to a **NURBS** object, the mesh shows the effect of the **Displacement** in the viewports when you add this modifier to the stack.

MapScalar Modifier (Word Space)

This modifier is used to maintain the scale of a map that is applied to the object. In other words, it lets you resize the geometry without changing the scale of the map. Create a box and set its **Length**, **Width**, and **Height** to **70**. Create a **Standard** material with a **Checker** map connected to its **Diffuse** slot. Apply the material to the box. Add the **MapScalar** modifier to the stack. In the **Parameters** rollout of the modifier, set scale and offset values using the **Scale**, **U Offset**, and **V Offset** controls. Now, resize the box using the **Scale** tool. You will notice that the scale of the map does not change regardless of how the geometry is scaled [see Figure F6].

F6

Note: The Scale control
*If the **Use Real-World Texture Coordinates** switch is on in the **General** panel of the **Preferences** dialog, the value **1** is displayed for the **Scale** control. If switch is off, the value **100** is displayed for the **Scale** control.*

Patch Deform Modifier (World Space)

This modifier allows you to deform an object based on the contours of a patch object.

Point Cache Modifier (World Space)

This modifier allows you to store the modifier and sub-object animation to a disk file in your HDD. This file records changes in the vertex positions. When animation is played back, this file is used instead of the modifier keyframes. This modifier is useful when computation for vertex animation slows down the system and playback. This modifier is also useful in cloth animations.

Subdivide Modifier (World Space)

This modifier is similar to the object-space **Subdivide** modifier. However, in the world-space version, the size limit is on for the mesh after it is transformed into world space coordinates.

Surface Mapper Modifier (World Space)

This modifier takes a map assigned to the **NURBS** surface and then projects it onto the modified objects. It is useful in applying a single map to a group of surface sub-objects within the same **NURBS** model. Create a **Point Surf** NURBS object and a teapot in the scene [see the left image in Figure F7]. Create a **Standard** material and connect a **Checker** map to the **Diffuse** component of the material. Apply the material to both the **NURBS** object and teapot. Select the **Teapot** in a viewport and then add the **Surface Mapper** modifier to the stack of the **Teapot**. In the **Parameters** rollout of the **Modify** panel, click **Pick NURBS Surface** and then click on the **NURBS** object in a viewport. The **NURBS** object projects the map onto the **Teapot** [see the right image in Figure F7].

F7

SurfDeform Modifier (World Space)

The functioning of this modifier is same as of the **PathDeform (WSM)** modifier, except that it uses a **NURBS Point** or **CV** surface instead of a curve.

Affect Region Modifier

This modifier is a surface modeling tool. It work well with at the **Vertex** sub-object level. You can use it to create a bubble or indentation in the surface. When you add this modifier to stack, it assigns an arrow like gizmo to the object that you can use in the viewport to alter the geometry. The controls in the **Parameters** rollout allow you to numerically control the shape of the deformation [see Figure F8].

F8

Attribute Holder Modifier

This modifier allows you to hold custom attributes for the objects in the **Modify** panel. It is an empty modifier to which you can add the custom attributes. It is a stripped down version of the **Parameter Collector** dialog that can collect only the custom attributes and appears on the **Modify** panel instead of a floating dialog.

Create a **Cylinder** primitive in the scene with the **Radius** and **Height** parameters set to **10** and **100**, respectively. Add the **Bend** modifier to the stack followed by the **Attribute Holder** modifier. Ensure that the **Attribute Holder** modifier is highlighted in the stack. Choose **Parameter Editor** from the **Animation** menu to open the **Parameter Editor** dialog. Alternatively, press **Alt+1**.

In this dialog, set **Add to Type** to **Selected Object's Current Modifier**, **Parameter Type** to **Float**, **UI Type** to **Slider**, and **Name** to **Cylinder Height** [see Figure F9]. Click **Add** from the **Attribute** Rollout, the **Cylinder Height** control appears in the **Modify Panel | Custom Attributes** rollout [see Figure F10]. Click **Add** on the **Attribute** rollout of the **Parameter Editor** dialog. Set **Add to Type** to **Selected Object's Current Modifier**, **Parameter Type** to **Integer**, **UI Type** to **Spinner**, and **Name** to **Cylinder H Segments**. In the **Integer UI Options** rollout, set **Range | From** and **Range | To** to **1** and **60**, respectively. Similarly, add two more float spinners with the name **Bend Angle**, and **Bend Direction**, respectively [see Figure F11]. Close the **Parameter Editor** dialog.

Press **Alt+5** to open the **Parameter Wiring** dialog. On the left pane of the dialog, choose **Objects | Cylinder001 | Modified Object | Cylinder (Object) | Height**. On the right pane, choose **Objects | Cylinder001 | Modified Object | Attribute Holder | Custom_Attributes | Cylinder Height**. Now, click **Two-way connection** followed by **Connect** to create a connection between the selected attributes [see Figure F12]. The label on the **Connect** button changes to **Update**. Similarly, connect the **Cylinder (Object) | Height Segments**, **Bend | Angle**, and **Bend | Direction** controls from the left pane to **Cylinder H Segs**, **Bend Angle**, and **Bend Direction**, respectively, controls of the right pane [see Figure F13]. Close the **Parameter** Wiring dialog.

Now, experiment with the controls available in the **Modify** panel | **Custom Attributes** rollout of the **Attribute Holder** modifier [see Figure 14].

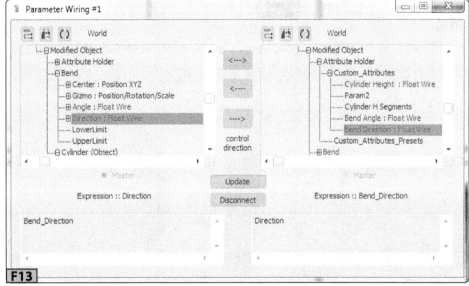

Bend Modifier

You can use this modifier to create a uniform 360 bend on a geometry about a single axis. You can limit bend to a section of the geometry as well as you can control the bend angle and direction.

To bend an object, add the **Bend** modifier to the stack. In the **Parameters** rollout of the modifier, set **Angle** and **Direction** in the **Bend** group to specify the angle to bend from the vertical plane and direction of the bend relative to the horizontal plane, respectively. Specify the axis to be bent from the **Bend Axis** group. To limit the bend effect to a particular area of the object, turn on the **Limit Effect** switch and then specify the limit using the **Upper Limit** and **Lower Limit** controls [see Figure F15].

F14

F15

This modifier offers two sub-objects. You can change the effect of the modifier using the **Gizmo** sub-object by transforming or animating it [see Figure F16]. You can translate or animate the **Center** sub-object to change the shape of the **Gizmo** resulting in the change of the bend effect [see Figure F17].

F16

F17

This modifier allows you to extrude spline shapes into 3D objects and then applies a flat or round bevel on the edges. You can control the beveling from the **Bevel Values** rollout of the modifier. Create a **Text** spline and then add a **Bevel** modifier to the stack. Adjust the parameters on the **Parameters** and **Bevel Values** rollouts of the modifier [see Figure F18].

F18

Keep Lines From Crossing
Separation: 2.54cm

Bevel Values

Start Outline: 0.0cm

Level 1:
  Height: 25.4cm
  Outline: -0.508cm
☑ Level 2:
  Height: 15.24cm
  Outline: 0.508cm
☐ Level 3:

Bevel Profile Modifier

This modifier is another version of the **Bevel** modifier but it extrudes a shape using a path or profile [beveling profile]. Create a shape and profile curve and then apply the **Bevel Profile** modifier to the shape's stack.

Create a **Text** object and a **Helix** object. Select the **Text** object and add **Bevel Profile** to the stack. In the **Modify** panel | **Parameters** rollout | **Bevel Profile** group, click **Pick Profile** and then click the **Helix** object in a viewport to create bevel [see Figure F19].

F19

Camera Map Modifier

This modifier is the object-space version of the **Camera Map (WSM)** modifier. It assigns the planar mapping coordinates based on the current frame and specified camera. This behavior is different from the **Camera Map (WSM)** modifier which updates the coordinates at every frame.

Cap Holes Modifier

This modifier build faces on the holes in a mesh. This modifier works well with the planar holes, however, it does a reasonable job when applied to non-planar holes [see Figure F20].

Cross Section Modifier

This modifier creates a skin across multiple various shaped splines by connecting the vertices of the 3D splines. The result is another spline object to which you can apply the **Surface** modifier to create a patch surface. These two modifiers sometimes also referred to as **Surface Tools**.

F20

Create an **Arc** object in the scene and convert it to **Editable** spline. Now, create three more copies of the Arc object and change their shape using the **Scale** tool [see the left image in Figure F21]. Attach all splines to form a single spline object. Add the **Cross Section** modifier to form a combined spline [see the middle image in Figure F21]. Now, add the **Surface** modifier to the stack to create skin [see the right image in Figure F21].

F21

Now, to change the shape, edit the combined spline at sub-objects level. The output of the **Surface** modifier is a patch surface. Therefore, you can add the **Edit Patch** modifier to the stack and edit the surface using the patch edit controls.

Delete Mesh Modifier

This modifier allows you to parametrically delete sub-object selection based on faces, vertices, edges, and objects. Create a **Teapot** object and then add the **Poly Select** modifier to the stack. Select the polygons as shown in the left image of Figure F22. Add a **Delete Mesh** modifier to delete the selected faces [see the right image in Figure F22].

F22

Delete Patch Modifier

It provides parametric deletion based on the patch sub-object selection. The possible choices are vertices, edges, patches, and elements.

Delete Spline Modifier

It provides parametric deletion based on the **Spline** sub-object selection. The possible choices are vertices, segments, and splines. Create a **Line** object. Add the **Spline Select** modifier to the stack and then select a segment. Now, add the **Delete Spline** modifier to the stack to delete the selected segment [see Figure F23].

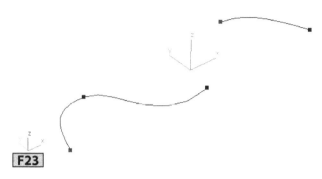

F23

Displace Approx Modifier

See the **Displace Mesh Modifier (World Space)**.

Displace Modifier

This modifier pushes the object's geometry to reshape it using a map or bitmap texture. This modifier allows you to apply the effect using two methods:

- Apply the effect directly onto the object using the **Strength** and **Decay** values.
- Apply the effect using the grayscale values of a bitmap image.

You can use this modifier to simulate magnetic push like effect by animating its gizmos. The four gizmos provided by this modifier are: **Planar**, **Cylindrical**, **Spherical**, and **Shrink Wrap**. These gizmos are used to distribute the force specified by the **Strength** and **Decay** values.

Create a **Plane** primitive with **30** length and width segments. Add a **Displace** modifier to the stack and then set **Strength** to **-100** and **Decay** to **-0.66** in the **Parameters** rollout of the modifier. Choose **Spherical** from the **Map** group of the rollout and then select **Gizmo** sub-object from the stack. Now, use the **Move** tool to see the effect of this modifier [see the left image in Figure F24]. You can also use a bitmap or map to produce this effect. Click **None** associated with the **Map** control in the **Image** group to open the **Material/Map Browser**. Double-click on **Noise** to select this map. Select **Planar** from the **Map** group, the effect of the modifier is displayed in the viewport [see the right image in Figure F24].

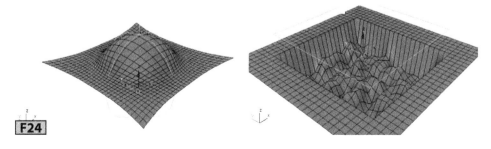

F24

To change the parameters of the **Noise** map, drag the **Map** button to the **Material Editor**. Choose **Instance** from the dialog box displayed. Now, double-click on the map node to view its properties. Change the properties as per need.

Edit Mesh Modifier

The **Edit Mesh** modifier has all the capabilities of the **Editable Mesh** object except that you cannot animate sub-objects.

Edit Normal Modifier

You can use this modifier to procedurally and interactively change the vertex normals of an object. This modifier is specifically used when you intend to output the meshes for the game engines and 3D rendering engines that support specified normals. The orientation of the vertex normals affects how light is reflected by the neighboring surfaces. By default in 3ds Max, rules of real-world physics are followed in which the angle of reflection is equal to the angle of incidence. However, using this modifier, you can set the angle of reflection as required.

Edit Patch Modifier

The **Edit Patch** modifier has all the capabilities of the **Editable Patch** object except that you cannot animate sub-objects.

Edit Poly Modifier

The **Edit Poly** modifier has all the capabilities of the **Editable Poly** object except **Vertex Color** information, **Subdivision Surface** rollout, **Weight** and **Crease** settings, and **Subdivision Displacement** rollout. This modifier lets you animate sub-object transforms and parameters.

Edit Spline Modifier

The **Edit Spline** modifier has all the capabilities of the **Editable Spline** object. The **Rendering** and **Interpolation** rollouts are not available for this modifier. Also, you cannot create direct vertex animation using this modifier.

Extrude Modifier

This modifier allows you to add depth to a shape object. It also makes the shape object parametric. Create a **Rectangle** shape object and covert it to editable spline. Create an outline and apply **Extrude** modifier to the spline object. In the **Parameters** rollout, specify a value for the **Amount** control to set the depth of extrusion [see Figure F25]. Specify a value for the **Segments** control to set the segments that will be created for the extruded object.

You can use the **Cap Start** and **Cap End** controls to generate a flat surface over the start and end of the extruded object [see Figure F25]. The controls in the **Output** group let you choose the output mesh type when stack is collapsed. The available options are **Patch**, **Mesh**, and **NURBS**.

Face Extrude Modifier

This modifier extrudes the faces along their normals [see Figure F26]. There are many differences between the **Face Extrude** function and the **Face Extrude** modifier. The one big difference is that all parameters of this modifier are animatable.

F25   **F26**

FFD Modifiers

FFD stands for **Free-Form** deformation. You can use these modifiers in a variety of ways. You can use it to create bulge in a mesh, animate dancing cars, and so forth. When you apply a **FFD** modifier such as **FFD 2x2x2**, **FFD 3x3x3**, or **FFD 4x4x4**, it surrounds the selected geometry with a lattice. You can transform the lattice and use its control points to adjust the shape of the geometry [see Figure F27].

F27

Each modifier provides a different lattice resolution [**2x2x2**, **3x3x3**, and **4x4x4**]. For example, a **4x4x4** resolution produces a lattice with four control points across each of its dimensions resulting in **12** points in each side of the lattice.

There are three sub-objects available with this modifier. At **Control Points** sub-object level, you can select the control points of the lattice and then change the shape of the underlying geometry by transforming them. At the **Lattice** sub-object level, you can transform the lattice box separately from the geometry. At **Set Volume** level, the color of the lattice control points turns green. You can select and manipulate the points without affecting the underlying geometry. You should use this level to set the initial state of the lattice.

Note: The FFD(box) and FFD(cyl) modifiers
*You can use the **FFD(box)** and **FFD(cyl)** modifiers to create box-shaped or cylinder-shaped FFD lattices. These modifiers are also available as space warps.*

Fillet/Chamfer Modifier

This modifier lets you fillet or chamfer corner vertices between linear segments of the shape objects. This modifier rounds corners where the segments meet by adding new control vertices. It also bevels the corners. This modifier works on the splines at the sub-object level. It does not work between two independent shape objects.

Create a **Star** shape object in the scene and add the **Fillet/Chamfer** modifier to the stack. Now, at the **Vertex** sub-object level of the modifier, select the vertices that you want to affect and then specify the desired settings in the **Edit Vertex** rollout to generate different shapes [see Figure F28].

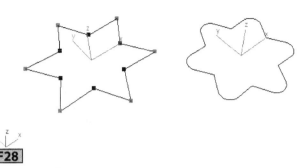

F28

Flex Modifier

This modifier creates virtual springs between vertices of an object thus simulating a soft body dynamics behavior. You can control the stiffness and stretching of the springs. You can also control the sway of the springs that is how much the spring angle changes in relation with the movement of the springs. This modifier works with NURBS, patches, polygon and mesh objects, shapes, FFD space warps, and any plug-in-based object types that can be deformed.

HSDS Modifier

HSDS stands for **Hierarchical SubDivision Surfaces**. This modifier implements the Hierarchical SubDivision Surfaces. You can use this modifier to as a finishing tool for subdivision surfaces.

Lathe Modifier

You can use the **Lathe** modifier to rotate a shape or NURBS curve about a specified axis. Create a **Shape** object [see the left image in Figure F29] and add the **Lathe** modifier to the stack. In the **Parameters** rollout of the modifier, ensure that **Degrees** is set to **360** to create a full 360 degrees lathe. Specify the segments for the lathe object using the **Segments** control. Click **Y** in the direction group to set the **Y** axis as the axis of revolution relative to the pivot point of the object. Click **Min** from the **Align** group to align the axis of revolution to the minimum extent of the shape. The right image in Figure F29 shows the full lathe object.

F29

You can turn on the **Weld Core** switch to weld vertices that lie on the axis of revolution. This modifiers also presents the **Axis** sub-object. At this level, you can transform and animate the axis of revolution.

Lattice Modifier

This modifier allows you to create renderable structure from a geometry. It can be thought of an alternative method to create wireframe effect. It gives you options to create joints, struts, or both. Figure F30 shows a sphere with joints, struts, and both join and struts, respectively.

F30

Linked XForm Modifier

This modifier links the transform of any object or sub-object selection to another object. The other object is called the control object. The transforms of the control object are passed onto the object or sub-object selection.

Create a **Sphere** and a **Cone** primitive in the scene. **Cone** will be the control object. Now, select sphere and add **Linked XForm** modifier to the stack. In the **Parameters** rollout, click **Pick Control Object** and then click on cone in a viewport. Now, when you transform the cone, the sphere will also receive the transforms.

Delete the modifier from the stack and convert sphere to **Editable Poly**. At **Vertex** sub-object level, select some vertices [see left image in Figure F31]. Link **Cone** to vertices as discussed above. Now, when you move the cone, the selected vertices will also receive the transform.

F31

MapScalar Modifier

See the **MapScalar Modifier (Word Space)** modifier.

Material Modifier

This modifier allows you to animate, or change the assignment of the existing material IDs on an object.

MaterialByElement Modifier

This modifier allows you to apply different material IDs to objects containing multiple elements. You can apply IDs at random or you can use a formula. Select **Random Distribution** from the **Parameters** rollout to assign the material IDs to different elements at random. The **ID Count** control lets you assign the minimum number of materials IDs to be assigned. Select **List Frequency** to define a percentage of each [up to eight] of the material IDs.

Melt Modifier

This modifier allows you to create realistic melting effect on all types of objects, including editable patches and NURBS object. It also works on the sub-object selections passed up the stack. Create a cylinder with enough sub-divisions and then apply the **Melt** modifier to it. In the **Melt** group of the **Parameters** rollout, specify the strength of the melt using the **Amount** control. The **% of Melt** control in the **Spread** group lets you specify the spread of the melt [see Figure F32]. The controls in the **Solidity** group determine the center of the melted object. There are several presets available in this group that you can use to specify the solidity of the object. If you want to specify a custom solidity, select **Custom** from this group.

F32

This modifier has two sub-objects, **Gizmo** and **Center**. You can transform and animate these two sub-objects to change the effect of the melt.

Mesh Select Modifier

This modifier provides a superset of the selection functions available in the **Edit Mesh** modifier. It allows you to pass the sub-object selection up the stack to other subsequent modifier.

MeshSmooth Modifier

This modifier allows you to smooth the geometry by subdividing it. You can use this modifier to produce a **Non-Uniform Rational MeshSmooth** object, **NURMS** in short. A **NURMS** objects is similar to the **NURBS** object in which you set different weights for vertices [see Figure F33]. You can farther alter the geometry by modifying the edge weight.

F33

You can choose the desired method from the **Subdivision Method** drop-down of the **Subdivision Method** rollout. The available methods are: **NURMS**, **Classic**, and **Quad** Output. The **Iteration** control in the **Subdivision Amount** rollout lets you specify the number of times you want to subdivide the mesh.

MM5-20 Unit MM5: Modifiers

Mirror Modifier

This modifier allows you to parametrically mirror an object or a sub-object selection [see Figure F34]. Apply this modifier to the stack and then select the axis or axis pair from the **Mirror Axis** group of the **Parameters** rollout. If you want to create a copy of the object, select the **Copy** switch and then specify the offset distance using the **Offset** control.

Tip: Modeling a character
*When you have created one side of a character and you want to mirror the other side, use the **Symmetry** modifier instead of the **Mirror** modifier as the **Symmetry** modifier allows you to weld the seam which results in a better looking model.*

Morpher Modifier

You can use this modifier to change the shape of the mesh, patch, or **NURBS** model. Morphing is generally used for lip-sync and facial expressions. This modifier also allows you to morph splines and world-space **FFDs**. Also, you can morph from one shape to another using this modifier.

MultiRes Modifier

This modifier reduces the number of polygons in a mesh to improve the rendering time [see Figure F35]. You can also reduce the number of vertices and polygons using the **Optimize** modifier. However, this modifier has certain advantages over the **Optimize** modifier such as it is faster and lets you specify exact percentage for reduction. You can also specify the vertex count for reductions.

To reduce the polygons, apply this modifier to the stack. In the **Generation Parameters** group of the **MultiRes Parameters** rollout, click **Generate** to initialize the modifier. In the **Resolution** group, specify a value for the **Vert Percent** or **Vert Count** to reduce the polygons.

Noise Modifier

This modifier alters the position of the vertices of an object along any combination of three axes [see Figure F36]. You can use it to create random variations in the shape of the object. You can also animate the change in shape of the mesh. Add the modifier to the stack and then in the **Strength** group of the **Parameters** rollout, set the strength using the **X**, **Y**, and **Z** controls. Turn on the **Fractal** switch from the **Noise** group to produce a fractal like effect [see Figure F37]. When you turn on this switch, the **Roughness** and **Iterations** controls appear in the rollout. You can use these controls to determine the extent of the fractal variation and number of iteration used by the modifier, respectively.

Normal Modifier

This modifier allows you to unify or flip the normals of an object without first converting it to an **Edit Mesh** modifier. Turn on the **Unify Normals** switch in the **Parameters** rollout to unify the normals so that they all point in the same direction, usually outward. Turn on the **Flip Normals** switch to reverse the direction of all surface normals.

F36　　F37

Normalize Spline Modifier

You can use this modifier to add new control points at regular interval in a spline [see Figure F38]. This is useful in normalizing the spline that you will use with the motion paths. The **Set Length** control in the **Parameters** rollout lets you set the length of the spline segments. 3ds Max uses this control to set the vertices at the regular intervals. The **Accuracy** control lets you define the precision of the normalization. The range for this control is 1 to 20.

Optimize Modifier

See the **MultiRes Modifier**.

Patch Select Modifier

This modifier provides a superset of selection functions available in the **Edit Patch** modifier.

Patch Deform Modifier (Object Space)

See the **PatchDeform Modifier (World Space)** modifier.

PathDeform Modifier (Object Space)

See the **PathDeform Modifier (World Space)** modifier.

Point Cache Modifier (Object Space)

See the **Point Cache Modifier (World Space)** modifier.

Poly Select Modifier

This modifier provides a superset of selection functions available in the **Edit Poly** modifier.

Preserve Modifier

When you push and pull vertices to model a surface, the edges of the mesh get stretched that results in an irregular geometry. This modifier allows you to retain [as much as possible] the original length of the edge thus producing a cleaner mesh.

Projection Modifier

This modifier is generally used for producing normal bumps maps. Apply this modifier to the low-resolution object and then pick a high resolution object as the source of the projected normals.

Projection Holder Modifier

This modifier appears when the **Project Mapping** feature of the **Projection** modifier is used. It contains data generated by the **Project Mapping** feature such as **UVW** mapping data.

ProOptimizer Modifier

This modifier allows you to interactively reduce the number of vertices in a model while preserving the original appearance/features of the model such as material, mapping, and vertex color information. When this modifier is used, the memory requirement for a model are reduced. You can optimize a model using one of the following two methods:

- You can use the **ProOptimizer** modifier to interactively optimize the model.
- You can use the **Batch ProOptimizer** utility to optimize multiple scenes at one go. When you use this utility, you can optimize the meshes before you import them to save the time.

Push Modifier

This modifier allows you to push the selected vertices inward or outward along the average vertex normals to create an inflation like effect [see Figure F39].

Quadify Mesh Modifier

You can use this modifier to convert object structure to quadrilateral polygons using the relative size that you specify. This modifier helps you to create mesh with rounded model with help of the **Smooth** modifier.

Relax Modifier

This modifier allows you to reduce the surface tension by moving the vertices closer to or away from their neighbors. This results in smooth object, however, the model appears little smaller than the un-relaxed model.

Note: Neighboring Vertex
A neighboring vertex is the vertex that shares a visible edge with the current vertex.

Renderable Spline Modifier

This modifier makes a spline object renderable without needing to convert it to an **Editable Spline** object. It also allows you to apply same rending properties to multiple splines. This modifier is useful when you link an AutoCAD drawing.

Ripple Modifier

You can use this modifier to create a ripple effect on the geometry [see Figure F40]. You can use its **Gizmo** sub-object to change the ripple effect.

Select By Channel Modifier

This modifier is used with the **Channel Info** utility. When you save a vertex selection into a subcomponent using the **Channel Info** utility, you can use this modifier to quickly access the selection.

Shell Modifier

This modifier allows you to give thickness to an object by creating extra set of faces on the opposite direction of the existing faces [see Figure F41]. You can specify the offset distances using the **Inner Amount** and **Outer Amount** controls available in the **Parameters** rollout.

Skew Modifier

This modifier can be used to create a uniform offset in an object's geometry [see Figure F42]. You can control and direction of the skew on any of three axes. You can also limit the skew effect by turning on the **Limit Effect** switch and then using the **Upper Limit** and **Lower Limit** controls.

Skin Modifier

This modifier is a skeleton deformation tool that allows you to deform one object with another object. You can deform the **Mesh**, **Patch**, and **NURBS** objects using the bones, splines, and other objects.

Skin Morph Modifier

This modifier allows you to use a bone's rotation to drive the deformation of the mesh object. This modifier is used with other modifiers such as **Skin** and **Physique**.

Skin Wrap Modifier

You can use this modifier to deform an object with another object. Although, you can use this modifier in a variety of ways but its primary use is to animate a high-resolution object mesh with help of a low-resolution mesh.

MM5-24 Unit MM5: Modifiers

Skin Wrap Patch Modifier

This modifier allows you to deform a mesh object with help of a patch object. Each point on the patch object influences a surrounding volume of points on the mesh object.

Slice Modifier

You can use this modifier to slice though selected objects or sub-objects using a cutting plane. Its functioning is similar to the **Slice** function of the **Editable Mesh** object. However, it does not require to be an **Editable Poly** or **Editable Mesh** object. You can also animate the position and rotation of the slicing plane.

Smooth Modifier

You can smooth a faceted geometry using this modifier. It eliminates the faceting by grouping the faces into smoothing groups. It smoothens the faces based on the angle of adjacent faces.

Spherify Modifier

This modifier distorts an object into a spherical shape [see Figure F43]. The end result is dependent on the topology of the object.

F43

Spline IK Control Modifier

The basic use of this modifier is to prepare a spline or **NURBS** curve for use with the **Spline IK Solver**. When this modifier is applied to a spline object, you can transform its vertices without needing to access the **Vertex** sub-object level. It places knots [control points] at each vertex and then you can manipulate the knots to change the shape of the spline.

Spline Select Modifier

This modifier is a superset of the selection functions found in the **Edit Spline** modifier. It passes a sub-object selection up the stack to other modifiers.

Squeeze Modifier

The modifier lets you create a squeezing [create bulge] effect on the objects [see Figure F44]. The vertices closest to the object's pivot point move inward. The squeeze operation is applied around the **Squeeze** gizmo's local Z axis.

STL Check Modifier

This modifier checks if the object is correct for exporting to an **STL** file format. **STL** [**stereolithography**] files are used by the specialized machines to create prototype models based on the supplied **STL** file. The **STL** file must have a complete and closed surface.

Stretch Modifier

The **Stretch Modifier** allows you to create traditional squash and stretch effects that are used in animations [see Figure F45]. This modifier applies a scale effect along a specified axis and opposite scale along the two remaining minor axes.

F44 **F45**

Subdivide Modifier (Object Space)

See the **Subdivide Modifier (World Space)** modifier.

Substitute Modifier

This modifier allows you to replace one or more objects with other objects in a viewport or at render time. The substitute object can be instanced in the current scene or can be referenced from an external file. This modifier is useful for the designers who use 2D shapes in their AutoCAD drawings. When they link the AutoCAD drawing to 3ds Max, they want to see how the object will look like in their design. This modifier allows them to achieve that objective.

Surface Modifier

See the **Cross Section Modifier**.

Surface Select Modifier

This modifier allows you to add a **NURBS** sub-object selection in the stack. Then, you can modify the selected sub-objects. It can select any kind of NURBS sub-objects except imports.

SurfDeform Modifier (Object Space)

See the **SurfDeform Modifier (World Space)** modifier.

Sweep Modifier

You can use this modifier to extrude a cross section along an underlying spline or **NURBS** curve path. It provides a number of pre-made cross sections such as angles, channels, wide flenges, and so forth [see Figure F46]. You can also use a custom spline or NURBS curve as custom sections.

Symmetry Modifier

See the **Mirror** modifier.

Taper Modifier

This modifier creates tapered contours by scaling both ends of an object's geometry [see Figure F47]. It scales up one end and scales down the other end. You can also limit the taper effect.

Tessellate Modifier

This modifier is used to subdivide the faces of a mesh [see Figure F48]. It is useful in smoothing the curved surface and creating additional geometry for other modifiers to act on. The **Tension** control in the **Parameters** rollout allows you to add convexity or concavity to the subdivided surface.

MM5-26 Unit MM5: Modifiers

F46

F47

F48

Trim/Extend Modifier

This modifier is used to clean up the overlapping or open splines in a multi-spline shape. To trim you need the intersecting splines. If the section intersects at both ends, the entire section will be deleted by this modifier up to the two intersections. To extend, you need an open spline.

TurboSmooth Modifier

This modifier is like the **MeshSmooth** modifier with the following differences:

- **TurboSmooth** is faster and memory efficient than the **MeshSmooth** modifier.
- **TurboSmooth** uses a single subdivision method, NURMS. It has no sub-object levels and outputs a triangle-mesh object.

Turn To gPoly Modifier

This modifier converts geometry to the hardware mesh format used internally by 3ds Max. This internal hardware format allows 3ds Max to speed up the performance when the mesh is edited.

Turn To Mesh Modifier/ Turn To Patch Modifier/ Turn To Poly Modifier

These modifiers allow you to apply the object conversions in the modifier stack. When you apply general purpose modifiers, these modifiers give you ability to explicitly control the output type of the object before hand.

Twist Modifier

This modifier creates a twisting effect on the surface of an object [see Figure F49]. You can control the angle of twist as well as you limit the effect of the **Twist** modifier. When you add this modifier to the stack, its gizmo is placed at the pivot point of the object and the gizmo lines up with the local axis of the object.

UVW Mapping Modifiers

These modifiers are used to control the texture mapping. You can use them to manage UV coordinates and to apply materials to the objects.

Vertex Weld Modifier

This modifier works similar to the **Weld** feature in an **Editable Poly** and similar objects. You can use this modifier to combine the vertices that lies within a specified distance from each other.

Vertex Paint Modifier

This modifier allows you to paint vertex colors onto an object. The amount of color that 3ds Max applies to the vertex depends on the distance of the vertex from the position of the cursor on the face. You can also paint vertex alpha and illumination values as well.

Volume Select Modifier

This modifier lets you make a sub-object selection of vertices or faces. You can use a cylinder-shaped or sphere shaped gizmo, or an object in the scene to define the volume of the selection area to which you can then apply other modifiers.

Wave Modifier

This modifiers creates a wave like effect [see Figure F50]. You can use the standard **Gizmo** and **Center** sub-objects to change the wave effect. This modifier is similar to the **Wave** space warp which is useful when you want to create a wave effect on the large number of objects.

F49   F50

XForm Modifier

This modifier is used to apply transformations to the objects. You can use it to animate the transformations of a sub-object selection. Also, you can transform an object at any point in the stack.

Hands-on Exercises

From the **Application** menu, choose **Manage | Set Project Folder** to open the **Browse for Folder** dialog. Navigate to the **3dsmax2017projects** directory that you have created and then click **Make New Folder**. Create the new folder with the name **unit-mm5** and click **OK** to create the project directory.

In this exercise, you will model a building using various modifiers [see Figures E1 through E4].

Table E1 summarizes the exercise:

Table E1: Creating Model of a Building	
In this exercise, you will learn how to:	• Use the **Twist**, **Taper**, **Lattice**, and **Blend** modifiers to change the shape of the geometry • Use polygon and edge selection techniques • Use the **Edit Poly** modifier • Chamfer edges
Skill level	Intermediate
Time to complete	45 Minutes
Topics in the section:	• Specifying the Units for the Exercise • Creating the Tower • Creating the Mullions • Creating the Outer Shell
Project folder	**unit-mm5**
Units	**Metric - Meters**
Final exercise file	**umm5-hoe1-end.max**

Specifying the Units for the Exercise

From **Customize** menu choose **Units Setup**. In the **Units Setup** dialog that opens, select the **Metric** option from the **Display Unit Scale** group. Next, select **Meters** from the drop-down located below the **Metric** option, if already not selected. Click **OK** to accept the change.

RMB click on any snap toggle button on the main toolbar. In the **Grid and Snap Settings** dialog that opens, choose the **Home Grid** tab and then set **Grid Spacing** to **10**, **Major Lines every Nth Grid Line** to **10**, and **Perspective View Grid Extent** to **7**. Close the **Grid and Snap Settings** dialog.

Creating the Tower

On the **Create** panel, click **Geometry**, and then on the **Object Type** rollout, click **Box**. In the **Perspective** viewport, drag out a box of any size. Go to **Modify** panel, and on the **Parameters** rollout, set **Length** to **80**, **Width** to **80**, and **Height** to **400**. Also, set **Length Segs** to **8**, **Width Segs** to **8**, and **Height Segs** to **50** [see Figure E5].

Change the name of the object to **Tower**. Now, you will apply various modifiers to create distinct building shape. From the **Object-Space Modifiers** section of the **Modifier List**, select **Taper**. In the **Taper** group of the **Parameters** rollout, set **Amount** to **0.35** and curve to **2.04**. The building bulges out [see Figure E6].

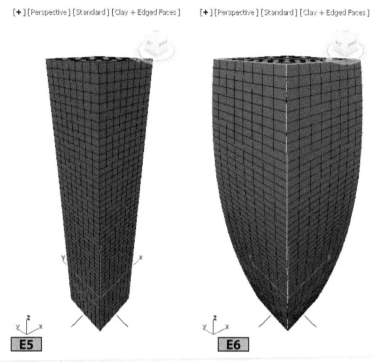

[+][Perspective][Standard][Clay + Edged Faces]   [+][Perspective][Standard][Clay + Edged Faces]

E5   E6

From the **Object-Space Modifiers** section of the **Modifier List**, select **Bend**. In the **Bend** group of the **Parameters** rollout, set **Angle** to **27.5** and **Bend Axis** to **Y**. The building bends along the Y axis [see Figure E7]. From the **Object-Space Modifiers** section of the **Modifier List**, select **Twist**. In the **Twist** group of the **Parameters** rollout, set **Angle** to **45.5** and **Bias** to **93.5**. The building twists along the Z axis [see Figure E8].

Creating the Mullions

Select **Tower** in the **Scene Explorer** and then RMB click on it. From the **Quad** menu that opens, choose **Clone** to open the **Clone Options** dialog. Select **Reference** from the **Object** group. Next, type **Mullions** in the **Name** text box and the click **OK**.

In the **Scene Explorer**, click **Tower's** bulb icon to hide it. Go to **Modify** panel and from the **Object-Space Modifiers** section of the **Modifier List**, select **Edit Poly**. In the **Selection** rollout, click **Polygon** and then select the center polygons [see Figure E9]. Click **Grow** thrice to select all top polygons of the building [see Figure E10].

E7

E8

E9

E10

Delete the selected polygons by pressing **Delete**. Similarly, delete the bottom polygons. From the **Object-Space Modifiers** section of the **Modifier List**, select **Lattice**. In the **Struts** group of the **Parameters** rollout, set **Radius** to **0.5**, and **Sides** to **5**. Al, turn on **Smooth**.

Creating the Outer Shell

In the **Scene Explorer**, click the **Mullions's** bulb icon to hide it. Select **Tower** and create a clone with the name **Shell**. Make sure to select **Reference** from the **Object group** in the **Clone Options** dialog.

Make sure **Tower** and **Mullions** are not visible in the scene and **Shell** is visible in the scene. Select the **top** and **bottom** polygons of **Shell** and delete them as done earlier. Also, turn off the **Twist**, **Bend**, and **Taper** modifiers.

In the **Selection** rollout, make sure the **Ignore Backfacing** switch is on. In the **Front** viewport, select polygons [see Figure E11]. Press **Delete** to remove the selected polygons. Similarly, remove polygons from the other remaining two sides. Use a different pattern for these sides [see Figure E12].

E11   E12

In the **Selection** rollout, click **Edge** and then select the four corner edges [see Figure E13]. Now, click **Loop** to select the loops. In the **Edit Edges** rollout, click **Chamfer's** settings box to open the **Chamfer** caddy controls. Set **Amount** to **1.636** and **Segments** to **5** [see Figure E14].

E13   E14

Click **OK**. From the **Object-Space Modifiers** section of the **Modifier List**, select **Shell**. In the **Parameters** rollout, set **Outer Amount** to **2.0** [see Figure E15]. Now turn on the **Shell's Twist**, **Taper**, and **Bend** Modifiers. Turn on the **Tower** and **Mullions** from the **Scene Explorer**. Assign colors of your choice to **Tower**, **Shell**, and **Mullions** [see Figure E16]. Now, create different version of the building [see Figure E17].

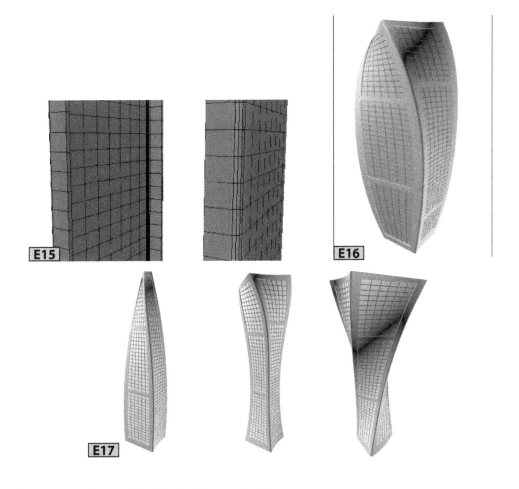

E15

E16

E17

Exercise 2: Creating a Model of a Paper Basket

In this exercise, you will model a melted waste paper basket using various modifiers [see Figure E1].

E1

Table E2 summarizes the exercise:

Table E2: Creating model of a paper basket	
In this exercise, you will learn how to:	• Use the **Twist, Taper,** and **Shell** modifiers
	• Use polygon and edge selection techniques
	• Use the **Edit Poly** modifier
	• Inset faces

Skill level	Beginner
Time to complete	35 Minutes
Topics in the section:	• Specifying the Units for the Exercise • Creating the Basket
Project folder	**unit-mm5**
Units	**Metric - Centimeters**
Final exercise file	**umm5-hoe2-end.max**

Specifying the Units for the Exercise

From **Customize** menu choose **Units Setup**. In the **Units Setup** dialog that opens, select the **Metric** option from the **Display Unit Scale** group. Next, select **Centimeters** from the drop-down located below the **Metric** option, if already not selected. Click **OK** to accept the change. RMB click on any snap toggle button on the main toolbar. In the **Grid and Snap Settings** dialog that opens, choose the **Home Grid** tab and then set **Grid Spacing** to **5**, **Major Lines every Nth Grid Line** to **10**, and **Perspective View Grid Extent** to **8**. Close the **Grid and Snap Settings** dialog.

Creating the Basket

On the **Create** panel, click **Geometry**, and then on the **Object Type** rollout, click **Cylinder**. In the **Perspective** viewport, drag out a cylinder of any size. Go to **Modify** panel, and on the **Parameters** rollout, set **Radius** to **14.5** and **Height** to **30**. Also, set **Height Segments** to **12** and **Sides** to **40** [see Figure E2].

From the **Object-Space Modifiers** section of the **Modifier List**, select **Edit Poly**. In the **Selection** rollout, click **Vertex** and then select **top row of vertices** of the cylinder in the **Front** viewport. RMB click on the **Select and Move** button on the **Main** toolbar.

In the **Offset:Screen** group of the Move **Transform Type-In** dialog that opens, set **Y** to **5** and then press **Enter** to move the vertices by **5** units in the **Y** direction [see Figure E3].Select all the vertices except the bottom row and move them by **6** units in the **Y** direction [see Figure E4].

In the **Selection** rollout, click **Polygon** and then select all the middle polygons [see Figure E5]. In the **Edit Polygons** rollout, click **Inset's Settings** button. In the **Inset's** caddy control, select **By Polygon** from **Group**. Now, set amount to **0.3** and click **OK** to inset the selected polygons. Delete the polygons. Select the top cap polygon and delete it as well [see Figure E6]. From the **Object-Space Modifiers** section of the **Modifier List**, select **Shell**. In the **Parameters** layout, set **Outer Amount** to **0.5**.

[+][Front][Standard][Wireframe]

[+][Front][Standard][Wireframe]

E4

E5

[+][Perspective][Standard][Clay + Edged Faces]

E6

From the **Object-Space Modifiers** section of the **Modifier List**, select **Taper**. In the **Parameters** layout, set **Amount** to **0.44** and **Curve** to **-0.7**. From the **Object-Space Modifiers** section of the **Modifier List**, select **Twist**. In the **Parameters** layout, set **Angle** to **66.5**.

Summary

The unit covered the following topics:

- Using modifiers
- Stack display
- Object-space modifiers vs World-space modifiers
- How transform affects modifiers

Unit MBME1 - Hands-on Exercises

Before starting the exercises of this unit, let's first create the project folder. From the **Application** menu, choose **Manage | Set Project Folder** to open the **Browse for Folder** dialog. Navigate to the **3dsmax2017projects** directory that you have created and then click **Make New Folder**. Create the new folder with the name **unit-mbme1** and click **OK** to create the project directory.

Exercises
Exercise 1 - Creating a Chair
In this exercises, you will create model of a chair, as shown in Figure E1.

E1

The following table summarizes the exercise:

Table E1 - Creating a Chair	
Skill level	Intermediate
Time to complete	40 Minutes
Topics in the section	• Getting Started • Creating the Frame of the Chair • Creating Seats of the Chair
Project Folder	3dsmax2017projects/unit-mbme1
Units	Decimal Inches
Final exercise file	umbme1-hoe1-end.max

Getting Ready
Start a new scene in 3ds Max and set units to **Decimal Inches**. Ensure that the project folder is set to **3dsmax2017projects/unit-mbme1**.

Creating Frame of the Chair

Go to the **Create** panel, click **Shapes** and then click **Line**. Expand the **Keyboard Entry** rollout and then set **X, Y**, and **Z** to **9.886, -10.75**, and **0.086**, respectively. Click **Add Point** to create the 1st point. Similarly create other points using the values given in Table E1.1. After entering the values shown in the table, click **Finish**; the line appears in the viewports [see Figure E2].

Table E1.1 - Coordinates for creating points			
Point	**X**	**Y**	**Z**
1st	9.886"	-10.75"	0.086"
2nd	-9.836"	-10.75"	0.086"
3rd	-9.836"	-10.75"	14.834"
4th	6.285"	-10.75"	14.834"
5th	9.886"	-10.75"	27.011"

In the **Modify** panel | **Rendering** rollout, turn on the **Enable In Renderer** and **Enable In Viewport** switches. Now, set **Thickness** to **0.9** and **Sides** to **14**. Make sure **Line001** is selected and then create a copy of the line by **Shift** dragging it about **21** units along the **Y** axis [see Figure E3].

Select **Line001** and then in the **Modify** panel | **Geometry** rollout, click **Attach**. Now, click **Line002** in the viewport to attach the two lines. Turn on **Vertex** snapping from the **Main** toolbar. Activate the **Vertex** sub-object level and then click **Create Line** from the **Geometry** rollout. Drag from one vertex to another to create a line [see Figure E4]. Click on **Create Line** to deactivate it. Also, turn off snapping.

Select the vertices [see Figure E5] and then click **Weld** from the **Geometry** rollout to weld the vertices. Repeat the process for the vertices locate at the other end of the line. Now, select the vertices shown in Figure E6. In the **Geometry** rollout, type **1.5** in the field located next to **Fillet** control and then press **Enter** to fillet the vertices [see Figure E7].

On the **Create** panel, click **Geometry** and then on the **Object Type** rollout, click **Tube**. Create a tube in the viewport. Go to **Modify** panel and then on the **Parameters** rollout, set **Radius 1** to **0.641**, **Radius 2** to **0.429**, and **Height** to **2.133**. Also, set **Sides** to **32**. Align the tube with the frame [see Figure E8]. Create a copy of the tube and then align it with the other side of the frame.

Creating Seats of the Chair

On the **Create** panel, click **Geometry** and then on the **Object Type** rollout, click **Box**. Create a box in the **Top** viewport. Go to **Modify** panel and then on the **Parameters** rollout, set **Length** to **24.283**, **Width** to **14.152**, and **Height** to **2.988**. Set **Length Segs**, **Width Segs**, and **Height Segs** to **4**, **4**, and **3**, respectively. Align the box, as shown in Figure E9. From the **Modifier List | OBJECT-SPACE MODIFIERS** section, choose **Turbosmooth**. In the **Parameters** rollout, set **Iterations** to **2**.

Now, we'll create piping for the seat. Convert the object to editable poly. Activate the **Edge** mode and select the edge loops [see Figure E10]. On the **Modify** panel | **Edit Edges** rollout, click **Create Shape From Selection** to open the **Create Shape** dialog. Click **OK** to close the dialog and create the shape.

Select **Shape001** and then in **Modify** panel | **Rendering** rollout, set **Thickness** to **0.2** [see Figure E11]. Select **Box001** and then in **Modify** panel | **Edit Geometry** rollout, click **Attach**. Click on **Shape001** to combine the two objects.

From the **Modifier List | OBJECT-SPACE MODIFIERS** section, choose **FFD 3x3x3**. Activate the **Control Points** sub-object level and select the middle control points. Move the points downwards to create a bend in the seat [see Figure E12]. Convert the stack to the editable poly. Now, create a copy of the seat and then rotate/scale to create the back support [see Figure E13].

Tip: Aligning back seat
*To easily align [rotate] the back support with the frame, move the pivot point at the bottom of the back support. Also, use the **Local** coordinate system.*

Exercise 2 - Creating a Lamp

In this exercise, you will create a model of a lamp [see Figure E1].

The following table summarizes the exercise:

Table E2 - Creating a Lamp	
Skill level	Intermediate
Time to complete	40 Minutes
Topics in the section	* Getting Started * Creating the Lamp
Project Folder	3dsmax2017projects/unit-mbme1
Units	Generic
Final exercise file	umbme1-hoe2-end.max

Getting Ready

Start a new scene in 3ds Max and set units to **Generic**. Ensure that the project folder is set to **3dsmax2017projects/unit-mbme1**.

Creating the Lamp

On the **Create** panel, click **Geometry** and then on the **Extended Primitives | Object Type** rollout, click **Hedra**. Create a hydra in the viewport. Go to **Modify** panel and then on the **Parameters** rollout | **Family** group, select **Dodec/Icos**. In the **Family Parameters** group, set **P** and **Q** to **0.32** and **0.35**, respectively. Set **Radius** to **40** [see Figure E2]. Convert hedra to editable poly. Activate the **Polygon** mode and select the polygon shown in Figure E3.

On the **Ribbon | Modeling** tab | **Modify Selection** panel, click **Similar** [see Figure E4] to select the polygon similar to the selected polygon [see Figure E5]. Press **Delete** to delete the selected polygons. Press **Ctrl+A** to select all polygons. Click **Settings** on the right of **Extrude** in the **Modify** panel | **Edit Polygons** rollout. In the **Extude's** caddy, set extrude **Type** to **By Polygon** and **Height** to **10** and click **Apply and Continue**. Now, click **OK** [see Figure E6]. On the **Modify** panel | **Selection** rollout, click **Grow**. Press **Ctrl+I** to invert the selection and then press **Delete** to delete the polygons [see Figure E7].

Activate the Edge mode and then select the edges, as shown in Figure E8. On the **Ribbon | Modeling** tab | **Modify Selection** panel, click **Similar**. Click **Settings** on the right of **Chamfer** in the **Modify** panel | **Edit Edges** rollout. In the **Chamfer's** caddy, set **Chamfer Type** to **Quad Chamfer**, **Edge Chamfer Amount** to **0.294**, and **Connect Edge Segments** to **1**. Click **OK**.

Select the Element mode and click on the hedra in the viewport. On the **Ribbon** | **Modeling** tab | **Subdivision** panel, click **Tessellate** [see Figure E9]. Activate the **Edge** mode and then select the edges shown in Figure E10. On the **Ribbon** | **Modeling** tab | **Modify Selection** panel, click **Similar**. On the **Modify** panel | **Edit Edges** rollout, click **Create Shape From Selection** to open the **Create Shape** dialog. Click **OK** to create the shape [see Figure E11].

Select **Shape001**. On the **Modify** panel | **Rendering** rollout, turn on the **Enable In Renderer** and **Enable In Viewport** switches. Now, set **Thickness** to **0.9** and **Sides** to **14**. Select **Hedra001** and then on the **Modifier List** | **OBJECT-SPACE MODIFIERS** section, choose **Turbosmooth**. In the **Parameters** rollout, set **Iterations** to **2** [see Figure E12]. Select **Shape001** and **Hedra001**. Group them with the name **Lamp**.

Now, create the stand for the lamp and align it with the stand.

Exercise 3 - Creating a Waste Bin

In this exercise, you will create a model of a waste bin [see Figure E1].

E1

The following table summarizes the exercise:

Table E3 - Creating a Waste Bin	
Skill level	Intermediate
Time to complete	50 Minutes
Topics in the section	* Getting Started * Creating the Waste Bin
Project Folder	3dsmax2017projects/unit-mbme1
Units	Decimal Inches
Final exercise file	umbme1-hoe3-end.max

Getting Ready

Start a new scene in 3ds Max and set units to **Decimal Inches**. Ensure that the project folder is set to **3dsmax2017projects/unit-mbme1**.

Creating the Waste Bin

On the **Create** panel, click **Geometry** and then on the **Object Type** rollout, click **Cylinder**. Create a cylinder in the **Top** viewport. Go to **Modify** panel and then on the **Parameters** rollout, set **Radius** to **15**, **Height** to **45**, **Sides** to **50**, and **Height Segments** to **30**. Convert cylinder to the editable poly object. Activate the **Polygon** mode, select the top polygon and then delete it [see Figure E2].

Select the top and bottom polygon loops [see Figure E3] and then click **Settings** on the right of **Extrude** in the **Modify** panel | **Edit Polygons** rollout. In the **Extude's** caddy, set **Extrude Type** to **Local Normal** and **Height** to **1.2** and click **OK**. Ensure the newly created polygons are still selected and then click **Settings** on the right of **Bevel** in the **Modify** panel | **Edit Polygons** rollout. In the **Bevel's** caddy, set **Bevel Type** to **Local Normal**, **Height** to **0.6**, **Outline** to **-0.9333**. Click **OK** [see Figure E4].

Select every alternate column of polygons using **Shift**, see Figure E5. Now using the **Alt** key, remove polygons form the selection [see Figure E6]. Click **Settings** on the right of **Extrude** in the **Modify** panel | **Edit Polygons** rollout. In the **Extude's** caddy, set **Extrude Type** to **Local Normal** and **Height** to **-0.5** and click **OK**. From the **Modifier List | OBJECT-SPACE MODIFIERS** section, choose **Shell** [see Figure E7]. Now, we'll create lid for the waste bin.

On the **Create** panel, click **Geometry** and then on the **Object Type** rollout, click **Cylinder**. Create a cylinder in the **Top** viewport. Go to **Modify** panel and then on the **Parameters** rollout, set **Radius** to **17**, **Height** to **2**, **Sides** to **50**, and **Height Segments** to **1**. Convert cylinder to the editable poly object. Activate the **Polygon** mode, convert cylinder to editable poly, select the bottom polygon [see Figure E8], and then click **Settings** on the right of **Inset** in the **Modify** panel | **Edit Polygons** rollout. In the **Inset's** caddy, set **Amount** to **1** and click **OK** [see Figure E8]. Click **Settings** on the right of **Extrude** in the **Modify** panel | **Edit Polygons** rollout. In the **Extude's** caddy, set **Extrude Type** to **Local Normal** and **Height** to **-1** and click **OK** [see Figure E9]. Now, align the lid with the bin.

Select the outer edges of lid and then chamfer them [refer to Figure E10] for chamfer settings. Select the top polygon of the lid and then click **Settings** on the right of **Inset** in the **Modify** panel | **Edit Polygons** rollout. In the **Inset's** caddy, set **Amount** to 9 and click **OK.** Make sure the polygon is still selected and then move it slightly upwards [see Figure E11]. Let's now create handle for the lid.

On the **Create** panel, click **Geometry** and then on the **Object Type** rollout, click **Torus**. Create a torus in the **Top** viewport. Go to **Modify** panel and then on the **Parameters** rollout, set **Radius 1** to **4.64**, **Radius 2** to **0.84**, **Segments** to **50**, and **Sides** to **18**. Also, turn on the **Slice On** switch and then set **Slice From** and **Slice To** to **90**, and **270**, respectively. Now, align the torus at the center of the lid [see Figure E12].

Exercise 4 - Creating the Apple Logo
In this exercise, you will create 3D Apple logo [see Figure E1].

The following table summarizes the exercise:

Table E4 - Creating the Apple Logo	
Skill level	Basic
Time to complete	30 Minutes
Topics in the section	* Getting Started * Creating the Logo
Project Folder	3dsmax2017projects/unit-mbme1
Units	Generic
Final exercise file	umbme1-hoe4-end.max

Getting Ready

Start a new scene in 3ds Max and set units to **Generic**. Ensure that the project folder is set to **3dsmax2017projects/unit-mbme1**.

Go to the **Create** panel, click **Geometry**, and then click **Plane**. In the **Front** viewport, create a plane. On the **Modify** panel | **Parameters** rollout, set **Length** to **180** and **Width** to **150**. Set **Length Segs** and **Width Segs** to **2** each.

Click **Material Editor** from the **Main** toolbar. Create a standard material using the **Material Editor** and apply it to the plane. Use the **apple-logo.jpg** for the **Diffuse** map. You need to turn on the **Show Shaded Material in the Viewport** switch for the material to display the image on the plane in the viewport. Ensure in the **Coordinates** rollout, **Use Real-World Scale** is off and **U Tiling** and **V Tiling** are set to **1**. Make sure the **Front** viewport is active and then press **G** to turn off the grid. Also, set the shading to **Default Shading** in the **Front** viewport. RMB click on the plane and then choose **Object Properties** from the **Quad** menu to open the **Object Properties** dialog. On the **Interactivity** section of the dialog, turn on the **Freeze** switch and on the **Display Properties** section, clear the **Show Frozen in Gray** switch [see Figure E2].

What just happened?

Here, we've froze the object. Once you freeze the object, you won't be able to accidentally select or move it and it would be easy for you to trace the logo using splines.

Creating the Logo

Go to the **Create** panel, click **Shapes**, and then click **Line**. In the **Front** viewport, create a shape [see Figure E3]. Ensure line is selected and then activate the **Vertex** mode from the **Modify** panel. Now, adjust the shape of the line according to the background image [see Figure E4].

[+][Front][Standard][Default Shading]   [+][Front][Standard][Edged Faces]

E2   E3

Activate the **Spline** level and select the spline in the viewport. Now, in the **Modify** panel | **Geometry** rollout, turn on the **Copy** switch and then click **Mirror**. Press **S** to turn on the **Snap** toggle and then snap the copied spline with the original spline [see Figure E5]. Weld the vertices that you just snapped [see Figure E6]. Go to the **Create** panel, click **Shapes**, and then click **Line**. Select **Edge** from the **Creation Method** rollout. Create a circle [see Figure E7].

Convert circle to editable spline. Now, attach the two shapes. Activate the **Spline** level from the **Modify** panel and then select the spline that makes the main shape of the logo. On the **Geometry** rollout, click **Subtraction** button corresponding to the **Boolean** control and then click **Boolean**. Now, click on the circle in the viewport to trim the shape [see Figure E8]. Similarly, create two circles for the upper part of the logo [see Figure E9]. Convert them to editable spline, attach them, and then apply the **Intersection Boolean** operation [see Figure E10]. Attach the shapes. Now to make the unified spline smooth, on the **Modify** panel | **Interpolation** rollout, set **Steps** to **32**. Hide the plane object using the **Scene Explorer**.

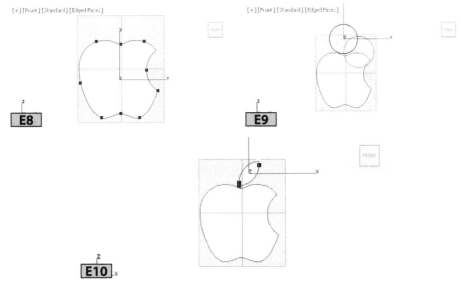

From the **Modifier List | OBJECT-SPACE MODIFIERS** section, choose **Bevel**. In the **Bevel Values** rollout, set **Start Outline** to **-0.5**, **Level 1 Height** to **0.5**, **Level 1 Outline** to **0.5**, **Level 2 Height** to **5**, **Level 2 Outline** to **0**, **Level 3 Height** to **0.5**, and **Level 3 Outline** to **-0.5**. On the **Parameters** rollout | **Surface** section, set **Segments** to **2**.

Exercise 5 - Creating a Bottle

In this exercise, you will create a bottle using the **Loft** compound object [see Figure E1].

E1

The following table summarizes the exercise:

Table E5 - Creating the Bottle	
Skill level	Intermediate
Time to complete	45 Minutes
Topics in the section	* Getting Started * Creating the Bottle
Project Folder	3dsmax2017projects/unit-mbme1
Units	Generic
Final exercise file	umbme1-hoe5-end.max

Getting Ready

Start a new scene in 3ds Max and set units to **Generic**. Ensure that the project folder is set to **3dsmax2017projects/unit-mbme1**.

Go to the **Create** panel, click **Geometry**, and then click **Plane**. In the **Front** viewport, create a plane. On the **Modify** panel | **Parameters** rollout, set **Length** to 180 and **Width** to 150. Set **Length Segs** and **Width Segs** to 2 each.

Click **Material Editor** from the **Main** toolbar. Create a standard material using the **Material Editor** and apply it to the plane. Use the **whiskey.jpg** for the **Diffuse** map. You need to turn on the **Show Shaded Material in the Viewport** switch for the material to display the image on the plane in the viewport. Ensure in the **Coordinates** rollout, **Use Real-World Scale** is off and **U Tiling** and **V Tiling** are set to 1. Make sure the **Front** viewport is active and then press **G** to turn off the grid. Also, set the shading to **Default Shading** in the **Front** viewport. RMB click on the plane and then choose **Object Properties** from the **Quad** menu to open the **Object Properties** dialog. On the **Interactivity** section of the dialog, turn on the **Freeze** switch and on the **Display Properties** section, clear the **Show Frozen in Gray** switch [see Figure E2].

Creating the Bottle

Go to the **Create** panel, click **Shapes**, and then click **Line**. In the **Front** viewport, create a shape [see Figure E3] that is aligned with the vertical center of the bottle. You can create line anywhere in the scene but placing it at the center of the bottle will help you in the modeling process. Go to the **Create** panel, click **Geometry**, and then click **Rectangle**. Create a rectangle in the viewport. On the **Modify** panel | **Parameters** rollout, set **Length** to 40, **Width** to 40, and **Corner Radius** to 8. Go to the **Create** panel, click **Geometry**, and then click **Circle**. Create a circle in the viewport. On the **Modify** panel | **Parameters** rollout, set **Radius** to 7.5 [see Figure E4].

Ensure the line is selected in and then click **Loft** on **Create** panel | **Geometry** | **Compound Objects** | **Object Type** rollout. Click **Get Shape** on the **Creation Method** rollout and then click the rectangle in the viewport to create the lofted object. On the **Path Parameters** rollout, set **Path** to 100. Click **Get Shape** on the **Creation Method** rollout and then click the circle in the viewport to create the basic shape of the bottle [see Figure E5].

RMB click on the lofted objects and choose **Object Properties** from the **Quad** menu to open the **Object Properties** dialog. In the **Display Properties** of the dialog, turn on the **See-Through** switch. Click **OK** to close the dialog box.

What just happened?

Notice in Figure E5, the image is obscured by the lofted object. Here, I have enabled the x-ray mode for the object so that we can see through it.

Enable the **Shape** sub-object level of the **Loft** object from the **Modify** panel and then select the rectangle shape on the loft object. Create a copy of the shape using **Shift+Drag** operation. Now, uniformly scale the copied rectangle so that it fits in the profile of the bottle [see Figure E6]. Repeat the process until you get a rough shape using the copies of rectangle and circle [see Figure E7].

E6   E7

Now, hide the plane geometry and turn off the x-ray mode [see Figure E8] from the **Object Properties** dialog. Make sure bottle is selected and then on **Modify** panel | **Skin Parameters** rollout, turn of the **Cap End** switch. From the **Modifier List** | **OBJECT-SPACE MODIFIERS** section, choose **Shell**. In the **Parameters** rollout, set **Outer Amount** to **0** and **Inner Amount** to **1**.

E8

If you render the geometry, you would see that facets are appearing on the bottle. Let's fix it. From the **Modifier List** | **OBJECT-SPACE MODIFIERS** section, choose **Smooth**. In the **Parameters** rollout, turn on the **Auto Smooth** switch to smooth the geometry.

What just happened?

*Here, I've applied the **Smooth** modifier to eliminate the facets on geometry by grouping faces into smoothing groups. Faces in the same smoothing group appear as a smooth surface when you render the geometry.*

In this exercise, you will create a chair using the spline and polygon modeling techniques [see Figure E1].

E1

The following table summarizes the exercise:

Table E6 - Creating the Chair	
Skill level	Intermediate
Time to complete	45 Minutes
Topics in the section	* Getting Started * Creating the Chair
Project Folder	3dsmax2017projects/unit-mbme1
Units	Decimal Inches
Final exercise file	umbme1-hoe6-end.max

Getting Ready

Start a new scene in 3ds Max and set units to **Decimal Inches**. Ensure that the project folder is set to **3dsmax2017projects/unit-mbme1**.

We'll first create a box that will work like a template that will help us in the modeling process. On the **Create** panel, click **Geometry** and then on the **Object Type** rollout, click **Box**. Create a box in the **Top** viewport. Go to **Modify** panel and then on the **Parameters** rollout, set **Length** to **20**, **Width** to **20**, and **Height** to **30**. Set **Length Segs**, **Width Segs**, and **Height Segs** to **1**, **4**, and **2**, respectively. Set the **Transform Type-In** boxes in the **Status Bar** to **0** to place the box at the origin [see Figure E2].

Creating the Chair

Activate the Front viewport and enable snapping [Vertex] by pressing S. Go to the **Create** panel, click **Shapes**, and then click **Rectangle**. In the **Front** viewport, create a shape [see Figure E3]. Convert rectangle to editable spline. Activate the **Vertex** level and then press **Ctrl+A** to select all vertices. RMB click and then choose **Corner** from **Quad** menu | **tool1** quadrant. Now, move the top vertices as shown in Figure E4.

[+] [Perspective] [Standard] [Edged Faces]   [+] [Front] [Standard] [Wireframe]

E2   E3

Press **Ctrl+A** to select all vertices and then on the **Modify** panel | **Geometry** rollout, enter **2** [type 2 and then press **Enter**] in the **Fillet** field to fillet all the vertices [see Figure E5]. In the **Modify** panel | **Rendering** rollout, turn on the **Enable In Renderer** and **Enable In Viewport** switches. Now, set **Thickness** to **1.5**. Turn off snapping.

On the **Create** panel, click **Geometry** and then on the **Extended Primitives** | **Object Type** rollout, click **Chamfer Box**. Create a box in the **Top** viewport. Go to **Modify** panel and then on the **Parameters** rollout, set **Length** to **1.25**, **Width** to **4.02**, and **Height** to **1.62**. Set **Length Segs**, **Width Segs**, **Height Segs** and **Fillet Segs** to **1, 1, 1,** and **3** respectively. Align it with the base of the chair [see Figure E6]. Create a copy of the box and then align, as shown in Figure E7.

Select the line and the two chamfer boxes. Click **Mirror** on the **Main** toolbar. In the **Mirror** dialog that appears, set the values shown in Figure E8 and click **OK** to accept the value and create copy of the selected geometry [see Figure E8]. Hide **Box001**.

On the **Create** panel, click **Geometry** and then on the **Object Type** rollout, click **Plane**. Create a plane in the **Top** viewport. On the **Modify** panel | **Parameters** rollout, set **Length**, **Width**, **Length Segs**, and **Width Segs** to **23, 20, 1,** and **1**, respectively. Align it with the base [see Figure E9].

Active the **Edge** mode and select the back edge [refer to Figure E10]. Now, extrude the edge upward by **15** units [see Figure E10]. Similarly, extrude the front edge [see Figure E11]. Now, select the middle edge. Click **Settings** on the right of **Chamfer** in the **Modify** panel | **Edit Edges** rollout. In the **Chamfer's** caddy, set **Chamfer Type** to **Standard Chamfer**, **Edge Chamfer Amount** to **1.5**, and **Connect Edge Segments** to **4**. Click **OK** [see Figure E12]. Select the edge ring shown in Figure E13.

Click **Settings** on the right of **Chamfer** in the **Modify** panel | **Edit Edges** rollout. In the **Connect's** caddy, set **Segments** to **2**, **Pinch** to **88**, and then click **OK** [see Figure E14]. Similarly, create more edges using the **Connect's** caddy [see Figure E15].

Activate the **Vertex** mode and then select the vertices shown in Figure E16. From the **Modifier List** | **OBJECT-SPACE MODIFIERS** section, choose **FFD 3x3x3**. Activate the **Control Points** sub-object level and select the middle control points. Move the points downwards to create a bend in the seat [see Figure E17]. Convert the stack to the editable poly. Similarly, create bend in the back support [see Figure E18]. Collapse the stack.

E16   E17

From the **Modifier List | OBJECT-SPACE MODIFIERS** section, choose **Shell**. In the **Parameters** rollout, set **Outer Amount** to **0.678**. Collapse the stack to editable poly. Activate the **Edge** mode and then create loops using the **Swift Loop** tool [see Figure E19]. From the **Modifier List | OBJECT-SPACE MODIFIERS** section, choose **Turbosmooth**.

E18   E19

Press **Ctrl+A** to select all geometry in the scene and then choose **Group** from the **Group** menu. Name the group as **Chair**. Set the **Status Bar | Transform Type-In** X, Y, and Z boxes to **70**, **0**, and **15**, respectively. Choose **Use Transform Coordinate Center** from the **Main** toolbar. Choose **Array** from the **Tools** menu to open the **Array** dialog. Set the values as shown in Figure E20 and click **OK** to make copies of the **Chair** group [see Figure E21]. Choose **Use Pivot Point Center** from the **Main** toolbar.

E20

E21

Now, create a table using the techniques described above.

Exercise 7 - Creating a Flask

In this exercise, you will create a flask using the spline and polygon modeling techniques [see Figure E1].

E1

The following table summarizes the exercise:

Table E7 - Creating the Chair	
Skill level	Intermediate
Time to complete	60 Minutes
Topics in the section	* Getting Started * Creating the Flask
Project Folder	3dsmax2017projects/unit-mbme1
Units	Generic
Final exercise file	umbme1-hoe7-end.max

Getting Ready

Start a new scene in 3ds Max and set units to **Generic**. Ensure that the project folder is set to **3dsmax2017projects/unit-mbme1**.

Creating the Flask

First, create the main body of the flask using the **Loft** compound object, as done in Exercise 5. Set the **Radius** of the top-most circle as **12** and bottom-most circle as **18** units.

On the **Create** panel, click **Geometry** and then on the **Object Type** rollout, click **Tube**. Create a tube in the viewport. Go to **Modify** panel and then on the **Parameters** rollout, set **Radius 1** to **13**, **Radius 2** to **12**, and **Height** to **12**. Also, set **Sides** to **24**. Align the tube with the rest of the flask [see Figure E2].

Make sure tube is selected and then RMB click on it. From the **Quad** menu | **display** quadrant, choose **Isolate Selection**. Convert tube to editable poly and activate the **Vertex** mode. In the Top viewport select the vertices [see Figure E3] and then in Front viewport, remove the bottom vertices from the selection [see Figure E3]. We don't want to move the bottom vertices in order to seamlessly align the spout and the main body. Move the vertices in the Top viewport towards left [see Figure E4]. Remove the second row of vertices [from bottom] from the selection and move rest of the vertices in the Top viewport. Repeat the process row by row [see Figure E5]. You can further refine the shape by moving vertices and polygons.

On the **Modify** panel | **Edit Geometry** rollout, click **Collapse**. Now, select the center vertex. Click **Settings** on the right of **Chamfer** in the **Modify** panel | **Edit Vertices** rollout. In the **Chamfer's** caddy, set **Vertex Chamfer Amount** to **3.5** and then click **OK**. Now, select the center polygon and inset it by **0.4** units, see Figure E8. Select the newly created polygons [see Figure E9] and then extrude them by **8** units [see Figure E10]. Align the end vertices of the extrusion using the **Select and Scale** tool along the **Z** axis. Now, create few edges loops as shown in Figure E11 by connecting edges.

Select top and bottom outer edges of the tube. Click **Settings** on the right of **Chamfer** in the **Modify** panel | **Edit Edges** rollout. In the **Chamfer's** caddy, set **Chamfer Type** to **Standard Chamfer**, **Edge Chamfer Amount** to **0.054**, and **Connect Edge Segments** to **2**. Click **OK** [see Figure E6]. Make a polygon selection shown in Figure E7.

E8

E9

E10

E11

From the **Modifier List | OBJECT-SPACE MODIFIERS** section, choose **Turbosmooth**. Make sure tube is selected and then RMB click on it. From the **Quad** menu | **display** quadrant, choose **End Isolate** [see Figure E12]. Create a cylinder and align it [see Figure E13].

E12

E13

Create a tube and apply the **Taper** and **Bend** modifiers to it [see Figure E14]. Now, create a cap using the Geosphere [see Figure E15].

E14

E15

Exercise 8 - Creating an Exterior Scene

In this exercise, you will model an exterior scene using various modeling techniques [see Figure E1.

E1

The following table summarizes the exercise:

Table E8 - Creating the Chair	
Skill level	Intermediate
Time to complete	60 Minutes
Topics in the section	* Getting Started * Creating the Scene
Project Folder	3dsmax2017projects/unit-mbme1
Units	Meters
Final exercise file	umbme1-hoe7-end.max

Getting Ready

Start a new scene in 3ds Max and set units to **Meters**. Ensure that the project folder is set to **3dsmax2017projects/unit-mbme1**.

Creating the Scene

On the **Create** panel, click **Geometry** and then on the **Object Type** rollout, click **Box**. Create a box in the viewport. Go to **Modify** panel and then on the **Parameters** rollout, set **Length** to **20**, **Width** to **60**, and **Height** to **8**. Create another box and then set its **Length** to **14**, **Width** to **52**, and **Height** to **8**. Also, set **Length Segs, Width Segs, and Height Segs** to **4, 14, and 1**, respectively. Now, align the boxes [see Figure E2].

Select the **Box001** in a viewport and then convert it to **Editable Poly**. Activate the **Edge** mode and then connect the edges [see Figure E3]. Activate the **Polygon** mode and then inset the front two faces [see Figure E4]. Now, extrude the faces by **-5** units [see Figure E5]. Create a box and then set its **Length** to **4.61**, **Width** to **0.602**, and **Height** to **6.827**. Also, set **Length Segs**, **Width Segs**, and **Height Segs** to **1, 1, and 1**, respectively. Now, align the box [see Figure E6]. Create instances of the box using **Shift** dragging [see Figure E7].

Select **Box002** and convert it to **Editable Poly**. Select the polygon shown in Figure E8. Now, inset the polygons by **0.22** units [see Figure E9]. Now, extrude the polygons by **-0.25** units. Make sure the polygons are still selected and then enter **glassSelection** in the **Named Selection Sets** field on the **Main** toolbar.

Create a **Plane** primitive and then set its **Length** and **Width** to **600**, and **800**, respectively. Align the plane as shown in Figure E10. Create a box with **Lngth** to **36**, **Width** to **71**, and **Height** to **0.2**. Align it as shown in Figure E11.

Create a **Rectangle** spline in the viewport and then set its **Length**, **Width**, and **Corner Radius** to **12**, **48**, and **4**, respectively. Apply the **Extrude** modifier to it and then set **Amount** to **0.4**. Align the rectangle, as shown in Figure E12. Now, create a light pole using the spline and polygon modeling techniques. Create an instance of the pole and align [see Figure E13]. Create doors for the building [see Figure E14]. Now, create a logo using the **TextPlus** primitive [see Figure E15].

This page intentionally left blank

Unit MT1-Material Editors

A material editor is a dialog that allows you to create, and edit materials as well as to assign them to the objects in the scene. A material in 3ds Max defines how light is reflected and transmitted by the objects in a scene.

In the unit, I will describe the following:

- **Compact Material Editor**
- **Slate Material Editor**

3ds Max offers two material editors, **Compact Material Editor** and **Slate Material Editor**. These editors offer a variety of the functions and features that allow you to design realistic looking surfaces in 3ds Max. To open an editor, choose **Compact** 🔳 or **Slate** ⚡ option from the **Material Editor** flyout on the **Main** toolbar. You can also open an editor by choosing **Compact Material Editor** or **Slate Material Editor** from the **Rendering** menu | **Material Editor** sub-menu | **Compact Material Editor/Slate Material Editor**. If you are using the enhanced menu system, these options are in the **Material** menu | **Create/Edit Materials** sub-menu.

Compact Material Editor

This was the only material editor available prior to the 2011 release of 3ds Max. It is comparatively a small dialog [see Figure F1] than the **Slate Material Editor** and allows you to quickly preview the material. If you are assigning materials that have already been designed, this material editor is the preferred choice.

Note: Additional Features
*The **Compact Material Editor** has some options such as **Video Color Check** and **Custom Sample Objects** that are not available in the **Slate Material Editor**.*

The **Compact Material Editor's** interface consists of menu bar at the top [see Figure F1], sample slots below the menu bar, and toolbars at the bottom and right of the sample slots. Now onward, I will refer to these toolbars as horizontal and vertical toolbars, respectively. The interface also contains many rollouts. The content on these rollouts depends on the active material slot and the type of material it hosts.

Note: Switching Editors
*If you want to switch to **Slate Material Editor**, choose **Slate Material Editor** from the editor's **Modes** menu.*

Sample Slots

The sample slots allow you to preview material and maps. By default, six sample slots appear in the editor. You can increase the number of slots by choosing **Cycle 3x2, 5x3, 6x4 Sample Slots** from the editor's **Options** menu. This option cycles through the 3x2, 5x3, and 6x4 slots arrangement. To make a sample slot active, click on the sample slot. The active sample slot appears with a white border around it.

The Compact Material Editor allows you to edit up to 24 material at a time. However, the scene might contain an unlimited numbers of materials. When you finish a material and apply it to the objects in the scene. You can use the slot occupied by that material to design the next material.

By default, material appears on a sphere geometry in a sample slot. You can change the sphere to cylinder or cube by choosing the desired option from the **Sample Type** flyout. This flyout is the first entry in the editor's vertical toolbar. To view a magnified version of the sample slot in a floating window, double-click on it. You can resize the window to change the magnification level of the sample slot.

Hot and Cool Materials

A sample slot is considered to be hot if it is assigned to one or more surfaces in the scene. When you use the editor to adjust properties of a hot material the changes are reflected in the viewport at the same time. The corners of a sample slot indicates whether the material is hot or not. Here are the possibilities:

No triangle: The material is not used in the scene.
Outlined white triangle: The material is hot and the changes you make to it will change the material displayed in the scene.
Solid white triangle: The material is not only hot but it is also applied to the currently selected object in the scene.

Notice the three sample slots in Figure F2 that shows three possibilities: a hot material applied to the currently selected, a hot material is applied to the scene but not on the currently selected object, and a cool material which is active but not assigned to scene, respectively. If you want to make a hot material cool, click **Make Material Copy** from the horizontal toolbar. You can have the same material with the same name in multiple slots but only one slot can be hot. However, you can have more than one hot sample slot as long as each sample slot has a different material.

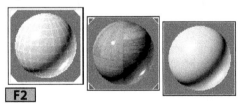

F2

Note: Dragging a material
If you drag a material to copy it from one sample slot to another, the destination slot will be cool whereas the original slot remains hot.

When you RMB click on a sample slot, a popup menu appears. Table 1 summarizes the options available in this menu.

Table 1: Sample slot RMB click menu	
Option	Description
Drag/Copy	This is on by default. When on, dragging a sample slot copies the material from one sample slot to another.
Drag/Rotate	When you select this option, dragging the sample slot rotates the sample geometry in the slot. This is useful in visualizing the map in the slot.
Reset Rotation	Resets the sample slot's rotation.
Render Map	Opens the **Render Map** dialog that allows you to render the current map. You can create an **AVI** file if the map is animated.
Options	Opens the material editor's options.
Magnify	Generates a magnified view of the current sample slot.
Select By Material	Selects objects based on the material in the sample slot.
Highlight Assets in the ATS dialog	This option is typically used for the bitmap textures. It opens the **Asset Tracking** dialog with the assets highlighted.
Sample Windows Options	You can use these options to change the number of slots displayed in the material editor.

Managing Materials with the Compact Material Editor

By default, the **Standard** material is displayed when you select a sample slot. If you want to use the **Standard** material, you can choose the desired shading model from the drop-down available in the **Shader Basic Parameters** rollout of the editor and then assign colors or maps to the various components of the material. For example, if you want to assign a map to the **Diffuse** component of the material, click on the button located at the right of the **Diffuse** color swatch to open the **Material/Map Browser** which is a modeless dialog. From the browser, select the map from the **Maps | General/Scanline/Environment** rollout and then click **OK**.

Tip: Material Map Browser
You can also double-click on a map to select it and close the browser.

For example, if you want to apply a checker map, double-click on the **Checker** map from the **Maps | General** rollout of the browser. Once you select the map, 3ds Max shows rollouts in the editor that you can use to edit the properties of the map. To go back to the parent level, click **Go To Parent** from the horizontal toolbar.

You can also copy map from one component to another component. For example, you have applied a map to the **Diffuse** component of the material and you want to copy it to **Opacity** component. Drag the **Diffuse's** button onto the **Opacity's** button, the **Copy (Instance) Map** dialog appears. Select the desired option from the **Method** group and then click **OK** to create an instance, a copy, or just to swap the materials from one slot to another.

Note: Other materials
*If you want to use any other material than the **Standard** material, click on **Type** button [currently labelled as **Standard**] to open the **Material/Map Browser**. Double-click on the desired material from the **Materials | General/Scanline** rollout; the **Replace Material** dialog appears with options to discard the old material or keep the old material as a sub-material. Choose the desired option and click **OK**. The label **Standard** on the button will be replaced by the type of the new material. For example, if you have chosen **Blend**, the **Standard** label will be replaced by the **Blend** label.*

By default, 3ds Max gives a name to each material. This appears name below the horizontal toolbar. If you want to change the name, edit the name in the field. The name field only displays 16 characters but the material name can be longer than 16 characters.

If the material you want to change is present in the scene but is not displayed in any of the sample slots, you can get it directly from the scene. To do this, select the object in the scene and click a sample slot to make it active. From the horizontal toolbar, click **Get Material** 🔘 to open the **Material/Map Browser**. Find the scene material in the **Scene Materials** rollout and then double-click on the name of the material. You can also drag the material name to the sample slot. When you get a material from the scene, it is initially a hot material.

To apply a material to the objects in the scene, drag the sample slot that contains the material to the object[s] in the scene. If there is only one object selected in the scene, the material is immediately applied to that object. If there are more than one objects in the scene, 3ds Max prompts you to choose whether to apply the material to the single object or to the whole selection. You can also apply material to the selection by clicking **Assign Material To Selection** 🔳 on the horizontal toolbar. Once you apply material to objects in the scene, click **Show Shaded Material in Viewport** 🔳 on the horizontal toolbar to view the material on the objects in the scene.

Tip: Hot material
When you apply a material to an object, the material becomes a hot material.

Tip: Removing material from an object
*To remove a material from an object, select the object and then execute the following command from the **MAXScript Listener**: $.material=undefined.*

Note: Selecting objects that have the same material applied
*From the vertical toolbar, click **Select By Material** 🔘 . This button will not be available unless the active sample slot contains a material that is applied to the objects in the scene. The **Select Objects** dialog appears. Those objects onto which the material has been applied appear highlighted in the dialog. Click **Select** to select the objects in the scene.*

You can also save a material to the library. A material library helps you in organizing materials. You can use a material from a library in another scene, if required. To save a material to the library, on the horizontal toolbar, click **Put To Library** 🔳 , the **Put To Library** dialog appears. In this dialog, change the name of the material or leave as is. Click **OK** to save the material. The material is saved in the currently opened library. If no library is open, a new library is created. You can save this library as a file using the **Material/Map Browser** controls.

To get a material from the library, click **Get Material** 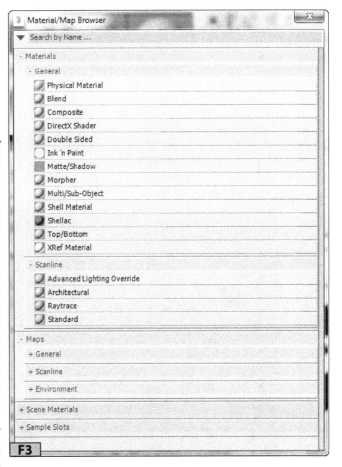 to open the **Material/Map Browser**. Now, open a library group. In the list of the materials in the library, double-click on the name of the material that you intend to use. The material you choose from the library replaces the material in the active sample slot.

Material/Map Browser

The **Material/Map Browser** [see Figure F3] allows you to choose a material, map, or mental ray shader. When you click the **Type** button or any button on the **Compact Material Editor**, a modal version of the **Material/Map Browser** opens.

Note: Slate Material Editor
*In the **Slate Material Editor**, the **Material/ Map Browser** appears as a panel and always visible.*

At the top-left corner of the browser, the **Material/Map Browser Options** button ▼ is available. When you click this button, a menu is displayed from where you can set various options for the **Material/Map Browser**. The **Search by Name** field on the right of the button allows you to filter the maps and materials in the browser. For example, if you type **grad** in the field and press **Enter**, the maps and materials will be displayed below the field whose names start with the characters **grad** [see Figure F4].

The main part of the browser is the list of materials and maps arranged in the rollouts [groups]. You can collapse or expand these groups.

Note: Creating custom groups
*You can also create custom groups in the browser. To create a group, open the **Material/Map Browser Options*** ▼
*menu and then choose **New Group**. The **Create New Group** dialog appears. In this dialog, type the name of the group*
*and click **OK**. Now, you can drag the materials or maps from other groups and drop on the new group.*

Caution: Materials and maps in the Material/Map Browser
*By default, the **Material/Map Browser** only displays those maps and materials that are compatible with the active*
renderer.

Note: Material/Map Browser's contextual menu
When you RMB click on the header of a rollout, a popup menu appears [see
Figure F5]. This menu shows the general options related to that particular group.

Material Explorer

The **Material Explorer** [see Figure F6] allows you to browse and manage
all materials in a scene. You can open the explorer from the **Rendering**
menu. If you are using the enhanced menu system, you can open it from
the **Materials** menu | **Tools (Material Set)** sub-menu. You can also open
it as an extended viewport. To do this, choose **Material Explorer** from the **Point-Of-View (POV) Viewport**
label menu | **Extended Viewports**.

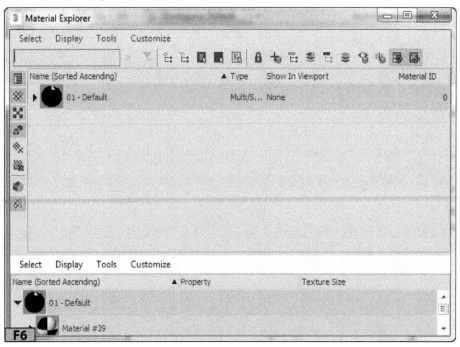

The **Compact Material Editor** lets you set the properties of the materials but there is limitations on
number of materials it can display at a time. However, with the **Material Explorer**, you can browse all
the materials in the scene. You can also see the objects onto which the materials are applied, you can
change the material assignment, and manage materials in other ways.

Slate Material Editor

The **Slate Material Editor** is little complex than the **Compact Material Editor**. In this editor, the entities are displayed in form of nodes that you can wire together to create material trees. If you are working on a large scene with lots of materials, this editor is the preferred choice. The powerful search function provided by this editor, lets you find materials in a complex scene easily.

I mostly used the **Slate Material Editor** as its interface [see Figure F7] is more intuitive when it comes to designing materials. I have marked various components of the interface with numbers in Figure F7. Table 2 summarizes the **Slate Material Editor's** interface.

Table 2: The **Slate Material Editor's** interface overview	
Number	**Description**
1	Menu bar
2	Toolbar
3	Material/Map Browser
4	Status
5	Active View
6	View navigation
7	Parameter Editor
8	Navigator

There are three main visual elements of the **Slate Material Editor**: **Material/Map Browser**, **Active View**, and **Parameter Editor**. The **Active View** is the area where you create material trees and make connections between nodes using wires. The **Parameter Editor** is the area where you adjust settings of maps and materials.

You can float the components of the editor such as **Material/Map Browser**, or **Parameter Editor** [except view]. For example, to float the **Material/Map Browser**, double-click on its title. To dock it back to the editor, again double-click on its title.

Note: Preview window

By default, each material preview window opens as a floating window. When you dock a material preview window, it docks to the upper left area of the editor.

When you add materials or maps in the **Slate Material Editor**, they appear as nodes [see left image in Figure F8] in the active view.

You can then connect these nodes using wires to make material trees. A node has several components, here's is a quick rundown.

- The title bar of the node shows name of the material or map, material or map type, and a small preview icon of the material or map.
- Below the title bar the component of the material or map appear. By default, 3ds Max shows only those components that you can map.
- On the left side of each component a circular slot [marked as 1 in the right image of Figure F8] is available for input. You can use these sockets to wire maps to the node.
- On the right of the node, a circular slot [marked as 2 in the right image of Figure F8] that is used for the socket.

You can collapse a node to hide its slots. To do this, click on the minus sign [marked as 1 in Figure F9] available on the upper right corner of the node. To resize a node horizontally, drag the diagonal lines available on the bottom-right of the node [marked as 2 in Figure F9].

When you resize a node horizontally, it's easier to read the name of the slots. To change the preview icon size, double-click on the preview. To reduce the preview, double-click again. When a node's parameters are displayed in the **Parameter Editor**, 3ds Max shows a dashed border around the node in the active view [see Figure F10].

To create a new material, drag the material from the **Material/Map Browser** to the active view, 3ds Max places a node for the material in the active view. It is a good habit to change the name of the material immediately. It will make your life easier if you are working on a complex scene with tons of materials. To rename a material, RMB click on it and choose **Rename**. In the **Rename** dialog, change the name of the material and click **OK**. To change the properties of the material, double-click the node in the active view and then change the properties from the **Parameter Editor**.

Tip: Renaming materials
The name of a material can contain special characters, numbers, and spaces.

To get a material from the scene, click **Pick Material From Object** from the toolbar. Now, click on the object in a viewport to get the material. To apply a material to objects in the scene, drag the output socket of the node and then drop the wire on an object in the scene. As you drag the mouse in a viewport, a tooltip appears below the mouse pointer showing the name of the object. You can apply the material even if the object is not selected. If there is only one object selected in the scene, the material is immediately applied to that object. If there are more than one objects in the scene, 3ds Max prompts you to choose whether to apply the material to the single object or to the whole selection. You can also apply material to the selection by clicking **Assign Material To Selection** on the toolbar.

To make a copy of the existing material, drag the material from the **Material/Map Browser | Scene Materials** group (or any library) to the active View. The **Instance (Copy)** dialog appears. Select **Instance** or **Copy** from this dialog and click **OK**. To duplicate a node in the active view, select the node[s] that you want to duplicate and then drag the nodes with the **Shift** held down.

To select the objects onto which you have applied the same material, in the active view, select the node and then click **Select By Material** from the toolbar. 3ds Max opens the **Select Objects** dialog with the objects highlighted. Click **Select** to select the highlighted objects.

Selecting, Moving, and Laying Out Nodes

To select a node, ensure the **Select Tool** [hotkey **S**] is active, and then click on the node. To select multiple nodes, click on the nodes with the **Ctrl** held down. If you want to remove nodes from the selection, click on the nodes with **Alt** held down. To select all nodes, press **Ctrl+A**. To invert the selection, press **Ctrl+I**. To select none of the nodes, press **Ctrl+D**. To select children, press **Ctrl+C**. To select a node tree, press **Ctrl+T**. These functions are also accessible from the **Select** menu of the editor.

Note: Selected node
When a node is selected in the view, a white border appears around it. Also, the background including the title bar is darker. When node is not selected, the border appears gray and background is lighter.

Tip: Deselecting nodes
*To deselect nodes, click on the blank area of the view using the **Select Tool**.*

To move a node, drag it in the active view. To create clone of a node, drag it with the **Shift** held down. If you drag a node with **Ctrl+Shift** held down, 3ds Max clones the node and all its children. These methods also work on multiple selections.

If you want to move a node and its children, click **Move Children** from the toolbar and drag a node. You can toggle this feature temporarily without clicking **Move Children** by moving the node with **Ctrl+Alt** held down. This feature can be accessed from the editor's **Options** menu. You can click the **Hide Unused** option from the toolbar to hide the unused ports on the selected material.

The layout buttons on the toolbar allow you to arrange nodes in the active view. The **Layout All - Vertical** and **Layout All - Horizontal** buttons on the toolbar allow you to arrange nodes in an automatic layout along the vertical or horizontal axis in the active view. These options are also available in the editor's **View** menu. The **Layout Children** button allows you to automatically layout the children of the selected node.

If you turn on the **Show Shaded Material In Viewport** from the toolbar for a material, a red diagonal shape appears on the node in the active view [see the left image in Figure F11]. The **Navigator** also shows a red diagonal shape to indicate this [see the middle image in Figure F11]. This shape also appears in the **Scene Materials** rollout of the **Material/Map Browser** [see the right image in Figure F11].

Previewing Materials

The **Preview** window [see Figure F12] of the editor allows you to visualize how material or map will appear in the scene. The main part of the window is a rendering of the material or map. You can resize this window like you resize any other window in 3ds max that is, by dragging its corners. Making a window larger helps you in visualizing the material, however, larger previews take longer to render. To open this window, RMB click on a node and then choose **Open Preview Window** from the popup menu.

To close a window, click **X** on the upper-right corner of the window. By default, a sphere is displayed as a sample geometry in the scene. If you want to change this geometry, choose **Cylinder** or **Box** from **RMB click** menu | **Preview Object Type** sub-menu. You can open any number of **Preview** windows in the editor. However, the drop-down available at the bottom of the **Preview** window allows you to switch the previews in a single window.

Caution: Preview window
*When open a new scene, the **Preview** window remains open, however, it may not correspond to any material. I recommend that you close all **Preview** windows before creating a new scene. The previews are not saved with the scene.*

When the **Auto** switch is on in the **Preview** window, 3ds Max automatically renders the preview again when you make any changes to the properties of a material or map. When this switch is off, the **Update** button becomes active. The render will be displayed only when you click **Update**. The **Show End Result** toggle available on the right of **Update** allows you to control when the **Preview** window displays a map. When off ![icon], the **Preview** window shows the map itself. When on, the **Preview** window shows the end result that is, the final result of the node.

Wiring Nodes

As you already know, wires are used to connect material or map components. To understand the wiring process, from the **Material/Map Browser | Materials** rollout | **General** rollout, drag **Standard** to the active view to create a **Standard** material node. Similarly, drag **Checker** from the **Material/Map Browser | Maps** rollout | **General** rollout to the active view to create a **Checker** node [see left image in Figure F13]. Click-drag the **Standard** material's **Diffuse Color** socket, a wire appears. Now, drop the wire on the output socket of the **Checker** node to make a connection [see the right image in Figure F13]. You can also connect in reverse. You can connect the output socket of the **Checker** node to the **Diffuse Color** slot of the **Standard** material.

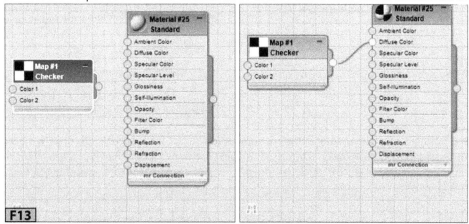

F13

Now, drag and the **Standard** material's **Bump** socket to the blank area, a popup menu appears [see the left image in Figure F14], choose **Standard | Noise** from the menu to insert a **Noise** node and make connection between the **Noise** node and **Bump** socket of the **Standard** material [see the right image in Figure F14].

F14

You can also connect a map directly to a socket without first dragging to the active view. To do this, drag the **Falloff** map from the **Material/Map Browser | Maps** rollout | **General** rollout to the **Reflection** socket of the **Standard** material. When the socket turns green, release the mouse to make the connection [see Figure

F15]. Another way to connect a node to a socket is that to double-click on a socket to open the **Material/Map Browser**. Now, select the desired map or material from the browser. You can also drag a wire on the title bar of a node. A popup menu appears [see Figure F16] that allows you to select component to wire.

To delete a connection [wire], select the wire and then press **Delete**. The selected wire appears in white color. You can also drag away a wire from a socket where it has been connected to terminate the connection. To replace one map with another, drag from the new map's output socket to the output socket of the original map.

To insert a node into a connection, drag the node from the **Material/Map Browser** and then drop it on the wire. You can also drag from one of the node's input sockets to the wire to insert the node. If a node is lying on the active view and you want to insert it, drop the node on the wire with **Ctrl** held down. To disconnect an inserted node, drag the node and then press **Alt** while dragging.

When you RMB click on a wire, a popup menu appears [see Figure F17]. Choose **Change Material/Map Type** to open the **Material/Map Browser** and then choose a different type for the material or map. This option always affects the child node. The **Make Node Unique** option makes the child unique if the child node is instanced. The **Make Branch Unique** makes the child unique, as well as duplicates children of the child if the child node is instanced.

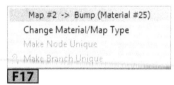

Views

The active view is the main area of the **Slate Material Editor** where all action takes place. The navigating the active view is similar to the navigating a scene in 3ds Max. To pan the view, drag with the MMB. If you drag with the MMB and **Ctrl+Alt** held down, 3ds max zooms the view. You can also zoom by scrolling the wheel. The navigational tools are also available at the bottom-right corner of the editor's interface.

Table 3 summarized these controls.

Table 3: The **Slate Material Editor** navigational controls		
Control	**Hotkey[s]**	**Menu**
Zoom percentage drop-down list	-	
Pan Tool	Ctrl+P	View	Pan Tool
Zoom Tool	Alt+Z	View	Zoom Tool
Zoom Region Tool	Ctrl+W	View	Zoom Region Tool
Zoom Extents	Ctrl+Alt+Z	View	Zoom Extents
Zoom Extents Selected	Z	Zoom Extents Selected
Pan to Selected	Alt+P	View	Pan to Selected

If you are working on a complex scene, you might face difficulties locating nodes in the active view. You can use the search function of the editor to locate the nodes in the scene. Make a habit of renaming the nodes as you create them so that you can find the nodes using their names. To search a node, click the **Search For Nodes** button available on the bottom-left corner of the active view, 3ds Max expands the search tool. Type the name of the node in the search field and press **Enter** to locate the node and zoom on the node in the active view.

By default, the **Navigator** window appears on the upper-right corner of the **Slate Material Editor**. This window is most useful when you have lots of material trees displayed in the active view. This window shows a map of the active view. The red rectangle in the navigator shows the border of the active view. If you drag the rectangle, 3ds max changes the focus of the view.

Named Views

If you are working on a complex scene, you can create named views to organize materials in a scene. You can create any number of views in the editor and then make one of them the active view. When you open the editor in a new scene, a single view is displayed with the name **View1**. To manage views, RMB click on one of the tab and then choose the desired options from the popup menu displayed [see Figure F18].

To cycle through the tabs, use the **Ctrl+Tab** hotkeys. You can also select a view from the drop-down available above the **Navigator**. To move a tree from one view to another, RMB click on the node and then choose **Move Tree to View** | **Name of the View** from the popup menu.

Summary

The unit covered the following topics:

- **Compact Material Editor**
- **Slate Material Editor**

Unit MT2 - General/Scanline Materials and Maps

The **General/Scanline Materials** materials are are non-photometric materials. Do not use these materials if you plan to create physically accurate lighting models. However, these materials are suitable for games, films, and animation. In this unit, we are going to look at the standard materials and maps.

In this unit, I'll describe the following:

- General/Scanline materials
- General maps

General/Scanline Materials

Let's explore the **Scanline** materials.

Standard Material

A surface having a single color reflects many other colors such as ambient, diffuse, and specular. The **Standard** materials use a four-color model to simulate the reflected colors from a surface. However, there may be variations depending on the shader you use. The **Ambient** color appears where surface is lit (the surface in the shadow) by the ambient light only. The **Diffuse** color appears on the surface when the lights falls directly on it. The term **Diffuse** is used because light is reflected in various directions. The **Specular** color appears in the highlights. Highlights are reflection of light sources on the surface.

Generally, shiny surfaces have specular highlights where the viewing angle is equal to the angle of incident. Metallic surfaces show another type of highlights called glancing highlights. The glancing highlights have a high angle of incidence. Some surfaces in the real-world are highly reflective. To model such surfaces, you can use a reflection map or use raytracing. The **Filter Color** is the color transmitted through an object. The **Filter Color** will only be visible, if **Opacity** is less than **100** percent.

The three color components blend at the edge of their respective regions. The **blend** of the **Diffuse** and **Ambient** components is controlled by the shader. However, you can control the blending by using the **Standard** material's highlight controls.

To create a **Standard** material, press **M** to open the **Slate Material Editor**. On the **Material Editor | Material /Map Browser | Materials | Scanline** rollout, double-click **Standard** to add a standard material node to the active view. Figure F1 shows the **Standard** material's interface. If you double-click on the material node, its attributes appear in various rollouts on the **Parameter Editor**. The controls on these rollouts change according to the shader type chosen from the **Shader Basic Parameters** rollout [see Figure F2].

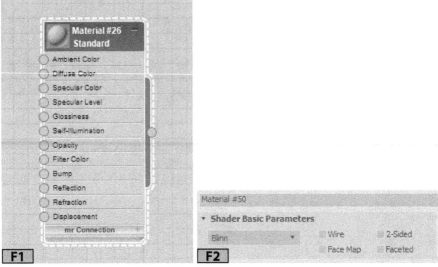

F1

F2

The controls in this rollout let you choose the type of shader to use with the **Standard** material. **Wire** lets you render the material in the wireframe mode [see Figure F3]. You can change the size of the wire using the **Size** control on the material's **Extended Parameters** rollout. Figure F4 shows the render with **Size** set to **2**. **2-Sided** allows you to make a 2-sided material. When you select this option, 3ds Max applies material to the both sides of the selected faces.

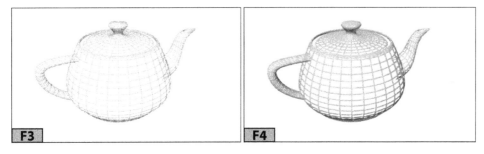

F3

F4

Note: One-sided faces

In 3ds Max, faces are one-sided. The front side is the side with the surface normals. The back side of the faces is invisible to the renderer. If you see this other side from the back, the faces will appear to be missing.

The **Face Map** control allows you to apply the material to the faces of the geometry. If material is a mapped material, it requires no mapping coordinates and automatically applied to each face. Figures F5 and F6 show the render with the **Face Map** switch is in off and on states, respectively. The **Faceted** control renders each face of the surface as if it were flat [see Figure F7].

Tip: Rendering both sides of a face

*There are two ways to render both sides of a face. Either you can turn on **Force 2-Sided** in the **Render Setup** dialog | **Common** panel | **Options** section or apply a two sided material to the faces.*

The **Shader** drop-down located at the extreme left of the rollout lets you choose a shader for the material.

F5 F6 F7

Here's is the quick rundown to the various material shaders:

Phong Shader

You can use this shader to produce realistic highlights for shiny, and regular surfaces. This shader produces strong circular highlights. This shader can accurately render bump, opacity, shininess, specular, and reflection maps. When you select the **Phong** shader, the **Phong Shader Parameters** rollout appears in the material's **Parameter Editor** [see Figure F8].

Phong Shader Parameters Rollout

The controls in this rollout, let you set the color of the material, shininess, and transparency of the material. The **Ambient**, **Diffuse**, and **Specular** controls let you set the colors for ambient, diffuse, and specular color components, respectively. To change a color component, click on the color swatch and then use the **Color Selector** to change the values of the color component. You can also copy one color component to another by dragging the source color swatch to the target color swatch. In the **Copy or Swap Colors** dialog that appears, click **Swap**, or **Copy** button. Click **Cancel** to cancel the operation. You can lock or unlock two color components using the **Lock** button [see Figure F9].

F8 F9

The buttons located on the right of color swatches can be used to apply texture maps to the respective color components. On clicking these buttons, the **Material/Map Browser** appears that allows you to select a map for the color component. If you want to apply different maps to the **Ambient** and **Diffuse** components, click on the **Lock** button located to the right of these components [see Figure F10].

F10

Self-Illumination Group: You can use the controls in this group to make the material self-illuminated. The illusion of self-illumination is created by replacing shadows with the diffuse color. There are two ways to enable self-illumination in 3ds Max. Either you can turn on the switch located in this group and use a self-illumination color or use the spinner.

Note: Self-illuminated materials
Self-illuminated materials do not show shadows cast onto them. Also, they are unaffected by the lights in the scene.

Opacity Group: You can use the controls in this group, to make a material opaque, transparent, or translucent. To change the opacity of the material, change opacity to a value less than 100%. If you want to use a map for controlling opacity, click **Opacity** map button.

Specular Highlight Group: Phong, Blinn, and **Oren-Nayar-Blinn** shaders produce circular highlights and share same highlight controls. **Blinn** and **Oren-Nayar-Blinn** shaders produce soft and round highlights than the **Phong** shader. You can use the **Specular Level** control to increase or decrease the strength of a highlight. As you change the value for this control, the **Highlight** curve and the highlight in the preview changes. The shape of this curve affects the blending between the specular and diffuse color components of the material. If the curve is steeper, there will be less blending and the edge of the specular highlight will be sharper. To increase or decrease the size of the highlight, change the value for **Glossiness**. **Soften** softens the specular highlights especially those formed by the glancing light.

Extended Parameters Rollout

The **Extender Parameters** rollout [see Figure F11] is same for all shaders except **Strauss** and **Translucent** shaders. The controls in this rollout allow you to control the transparency and reflection settings. Also, it has controls for adjusting the wireframe rendering.

Advanced Transparency Group: These controls do not appear for the **Translucent** shader. **Falloff** allows you to set the falloff and its extent. **In** increases transparency toward the inside of the object (like glass bottle) whereas **Out** increases transparency toward the outside of the object (like clouds). **Amt** lets you adjust the amount of transparency at the outside or inside extreme.

The **Type** controls let you specify how transparency is applied. The **Filter** color swatch computes a filter color that it multiplies with the color behind the transparent surface. The **Subtractive** option subtracts from the color behind the transparent surface. The **Additive** option adds to the color behind the transparent surface.

Index of Refraction allows you to set the index of refraction used by refraction map and raytracing.

Reflection Dimming group: This group does not appear for the **Strauss** shader. These controls dim the reflection in shadow. Tun on the **Apply** switch to enable reflection dimming. **Dim Level** controls the amount of dimming that takes place in shadow. **Refl. Level** affects the intensity of the reflection that is not in shadow.

SuperSampling Rollout

The **SuperSampling** rollout [see Figure F12] is used by the **Architectural, Raytrace, Standard**, and **Ink 'n Paint** materials to improve the quality of the rendered image. It performs an additional antialiasing pass on the material thus resulting in more render time. By default, a single **SuperSampling** method is applied to all materials in the scene.

Note: Super Sampling
*The **Super Sampling** method is ignored by **mental ray** as it has its own sampling algorithm.*

Maps Rollout: The **Maps** rollout [see Figure F13] is available for all materials. The controls in this rollout allow you to assign maps to various components of the material. To assign map to a component, click a map button. Now, choose the desired map option from the **Material/Map Browser** that opens.

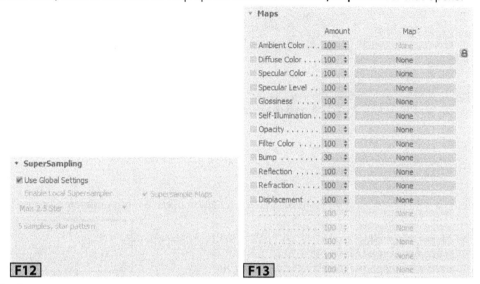

F12   **F13**

Blinn Shader

This is the default shader. It produces rounder, softer highlights than the **Phong** shader. The **Blinn** and **Phong** shaders have the same basic parameters.

Metal Shader

You can use the **Metal** shader to create realistic-looking metallic surfaces and a variety of organic-looking materials. The metal material calculates their specular color automatically. The output specular color depends on the diffuse color of the material and the color of the light.

This shader produces distinctive highlights. Like the **Phong** shader, **Specular Level** still controls intensity. However, **Glossiness** affects both the intensity and size of the specular highlights. Figure F14 shows the controls in **Metal Basic Parameters** rollout.

Oren-Nayar-Blinn Shader

This shader is a variant of the **Blinn** shader and can be used to model matte surfaces such as fabric. It has two additional controls to model a surface with the matte look: **Diffuse Level** and **Roughness**.

[Oren-Nayar-Blinn Basic Parameters rollout | Advanced Diffuse Group]: Diffuse Level controls [see Figure F15] the brightness of the diffuse component of the material. It allows you to make the material lighter or darker. **Roughness** allows you to control the rate at which the diffuse component blends into the ambient component.

F14

F15

Note: The Roughness Parameter

The **Roughness** *parameter is available only with the* **Oren-Nayar-Blinn** *and* **Multi-Level** *shaders, and with the* **Arch & Design** *and* **Physical** *materials* (**mental ray**).

Note: Diffuse Level control

The **Blinn**, **Metal**, **Phong**, *and* **Strauss** *shaders do not have the* **Diffuse Level** *control.*

Strauss Shader

This shader is a simpler version of the **Metal** shader. It can be used to model the metallic surfaces.

Strauss Basic Parameters Rollout: The **Color** control [see Figure F16] lets you specify the color of the material. The **Strauss** shader automatically calculates the ambient and specular color components. **Glossiness** controls the size and intensity of the specular highlights. On increasing the value for this control, the highlight gets smaller and the material appears shiner. The **Metalness** control adjust the

F16

metalness of the surface. The effect of this control is more prominent when you increase the **Glossiness** value. **Opacity** sets the transparency of the material.

Anisotropic Shader

You can use this shader to create surfaces with elliptical, anisotropic highlights. This shader is suitable for modeling hair, glass, or brushed metal. The **Diffuse Level** controls are similar to that of the **Oren-Nayar-Blinn** shading controls, and basic parameters controls are similar to that of the **Blinn** or **Phong** shading, except the **Specular Highlights** parameters.

Anisotropic Basic Parameters Rollout | Specular Highlight Group: The **Specular Level** [Figure F17] control sets the intensity of the specular highlights. On increasing the value for this control, the highlight goes brighter. **Glossiness** controls the size of the specular highlights. The **Anisotropy** controls the anisotropy or shape of the highlight. **Orientation** controls the orientation of the highlight. This value is measured in degrees.

Multi-Layer Shader

This shader is similar to the **Anisotropic** shader. However, it allows you to layer two sets of specular highlights. The highlights are layered that allows you to create complex highlights. Figure F18 shows the two specular layers in the **Multi-Layer Basic Parameters** rollout.

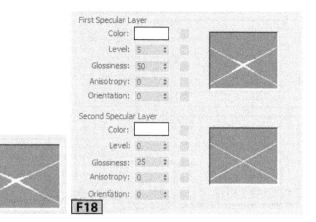

F17

F18

Translucent Shader

This shader is similar to the **Blinn** shader but allows you set the translucency of the material. A translucent object not only allows light to pass through but it also scatters light within.

Translucent Basic Parameters Rollout | Translucency Group: The **Translucent Clr** control [see Figure F19] sets the translucency color that is the color of the light scattered within the material. This color is different from the **Filter** color which

F19

is the color transmitted through transparent or semi-transparent material such as glass. The **Opacity** control sets the opacity or transparency of the material.

Note: The mental ray renderer

*The **mental ray** renderer is used in hands-on-exercises of this book.*

Raytrace Material

This material is an advanced surface-shading material. It supports the same diffuse surface shading that a **Standard** material supports.

However, it also supports fog, color density, translucency, fluorescence, and other special effects. This material is capable of creating fully raytraced reflections and refractions. Figure F20 shows the **Raytrace** material's interface.

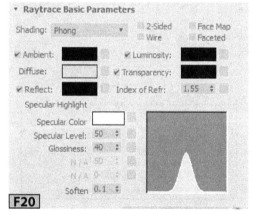

F20

Architectural Material

The properties of this material [see Figure F21] create realistic looking images when used with Photometric lights and Radiosity. Therefore, you should use this material when you are looking for high level of accuracy. If you don't need the high detail this material produces, use the Standard material or any other material.

F21 anced Lighting Override

When you create a new **Architectural** material, you can choose from a wide variety of templates that are built into this material. You can use these templates as starting point for the shading model you wish to create. You can choose template from the drop-down available in the **Templates** rollout.

Advanced Lighting Override Material

You can use this material to directly control the radiosity properties of a material. You can use this material directly. It is a always a supplement to the base material [see Figure F22]. This material has no effect on the ordinary renderings. It is used with Radiosity and Light Tracing solutions.

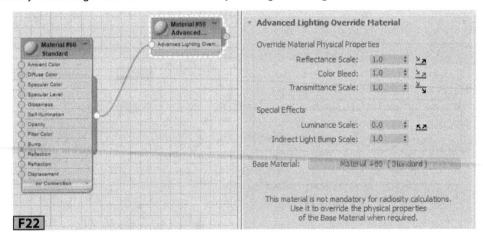

F22

This material has two primary usages:

*   Adjusting properties of a material used in a Radiosity and Light Tracing solutions.
*   Contributing energy to the Radiosity solution with self-illuminating objects.

Caution: The mental ray renderer
*The **mental ray** renderer does not support this material.*

MT2-8   Unit MT2 - General/Scanline Materials and Maps

General Materials

Let's explore the **General** materials.

Blend Material

The **Blend** material allows you to mix two materials on a single side of the surface. You can use the **Mix Amount** parameter [see Figure F23] to control the way two materials are blended together. You can also animate this control. The **Material 1** and **Material 2** controls let you assign the two materials to be blended. You can also use the corresponding switches to turn material on or off. The **Interactive** option specifies which of the materials or mask map will be displayed in the viewport by the interactive renderer.

The **Mask** control lets you assign a map as mask. The lighter and darker areas on the mask map control the degree of blending. The lighter areas displays more of the **Material 1** whereas the darker areas show more of **Material 2**. The **Mix Amount** controls the proportion of blend in degrees. A value of **0** means only **Material 1** will be visible on the surface whereas a value of **100** means **Material 2** will be visible on the surface.

When you assign a mask map for blending, you can use the mixing curve to affect the blending. You can use the controls in the **Transition Zone** group to adjust the level of the **Upper** and **Lower** limits.

Note: Interactive renderer and Blend material
Only one map can be displayed in the viewports when using the interactive renderer.

Note: Blend Material and Noise Map
*The **Mix Amount** control is not available when you use mask to blend the material. Using a **Noise** map as mixing map can produce naturally looking surfaces.*

Double Sided Material

The **Double Sided** material lets you assign two different materials to the front and back surface of an object. The **Facing Material** and **Back Material** controls [see Figure F24] allow you to specify the material for the front and back faces, respectively. The **Translucency** control allows you to blend the two materials. There will be no blending of the materials if **Translucency** is set to **0**. At a value of **100**, the outer material will be visible on the inner faces and inner material will be visible on the outer faces.

Composite Material

This material can be used to composite up to ten materials. The materials are composited from top to bottom. The maps can be combined using additive opacity, subtractive opacity, or using an amount value. The **Base Material** control [see Figure F25] allows you to set the base material. The default base material is the **Standard** material.

The **Mat.1** to **Mat.9** controls are used to specify the material that you want to composite. Each material control has an array of buttons called **ASM** buttons. These buttons control how the material is composited. The **A** button allows you to use the additive opacity.

The colors in the materials are summed based on the opacity. The **S** button allows you to use the subtractive opacity. The **M** button is used to mix the materials using a value. You can enter the value in the spinner located next to the **M** button. When the **M** button is active, amount ranges from **0** to **100**. When amount is **0**, no compositing happens and the material below is not visible. If the amount is **100**, the material below is visible.

Tip: Composite Material v Composite Map
*If you want to achieve a result by combining maps instead of combining materials, use the **Composite** map that provides greater control.*

Note: Overloaded compositing
*For additive and subtractive compositing, the amount can range from **0** to **200**. When the amount is greater than **100**, the compositing is overloaded. As a result, the transparent area of the material becomes more opaque.*

Morpher Material
The **Morpher** material is used with the **Morpher** modifier. For example, when a character raises his eyebrows, you can use this material to display wrinkles on his forehead. You can blend the materials the same way you morph the geometry using the channel spinners of the **Morpher** modifier.

Multi/Sub-Object Material
The **Multi/Sub-Object** material allows you to assign materials at the sub-object level. The number field [see Figure F26] shows the number of sub-materials contained in the **Multi/Sub-Object** material. You can use the **Set Number** button to set the number of sub-materials that make up the material. The **Add** button allows you to a new sub-material to the list. Use the **Delete** button to remove currently chosen sub-material from the list. The **ID**, **Name**, and **Sub-Material** controls allow you to sort the list based on the material id, name, and sub-material, respectively.

To assign materials to the sub-objects, select the object and assign the **Multi/sub-Object** material to it. Apply a **Mesh Select** modifier to the object. Activate the **Face** sub-object level. Now, select the faces to which you will assign the material. Apply a **Material Modifier** and then set the material ID value to the number of the sub-material you need to assign.

Shellac Material

Shellac material allows you to mix two materials by superimposing one over the other. The superimposed material is known as the **Shellac** material. The **Base Material** control [Figure F27] lets you choose or edit the base sub-material. The **Shellac Material** control lets you choose or edit the **Shellac** material. The **Shellac Color Blend** control adjusts the amount of color mixing. The default value for this control is **0**. Hence, the **Shellac** material has

F27

no effect on the surface. There is no upper limit for this control. Higher values overload the colors of the **Shellac** material. You can also animate this parameter.

Top/Bottom Material

This material lets you assign two different materials to the top and bottom portions of an object. You can also blend the two materials. The top faces of an object are those faces whose normals point up. The bottom faces have the normals down. You can control the boundary between the top and bottom using the controls available in the **Coordinates** group [see Figure F28].

The **World** option lets you specify the direction according to the world coordinates of the scene. If you rotate the object, the boundary between the top and bottom faces

F28

remains in place. The **Local** option allows you to control the direction using the local coordinate system.

You can specify the top and bottom materials using the **Top** and **Bottom** controls, respectively. The **Swap** button allows you to swap the material. You can blend the edge between the top and bottom materials using the **Blend** control. The value for this control ranges from **0** to **1**. If you set **Blend** to **0**, there will be a sharp line between the top and bottom materials. At **100**, the two materials tint each other.

The **Position** control allows you to specify the location where the division between the two materials will occur. The value for this control ranges from **0** to **1**. If you set **Position** to **0**, only top material will be displayed. At **100**, only bottom material will be displayed.

Matte/Shadow Material

The **Matte Shadow** material is used to make whole objects or any set of faces into matte objects. The matte objects reveal the background color or the environment map. A matte object is invisible but it blocks any geometry behind it however it does not block the background. The matte objects can also receive shadows. The shadows cast on the matte object are applied to the alpha channel. To properly generate shadows on a matte object, turn off **Opaque Alpha** and then turn on **Affect Alpha**.

Ink 'n Paint Material

The **Ink 'n Paint** material is used to create cartoons effects. This material produces shading with inked borders.

DirectX Shader Material

It is a special material that allows you to shade objects in the viewport using DirectX (Direct3D) shaders. When you use this material, materials in the viewport more accurately represent how they will look on some other software or hardware device.

Tip: Quicksilver hardware renderer
*You can use the **Quicksilver hardware renderer** to render **DirectX Shader** materials.*

XRef Material

This material lets you use a material applied to an object in another 3ds Max scene file. This material is typically used with the XRef objects. You can also use the **Override Material** rollout to assign a local material to the XRef'd object.

Physical Material

Physical material allows you to model shading effects of the real-world materials with ease. This material is the layered material that gives you ability to efficiently use the physically-based workflows. This material is compatible with **ART** and **mental ray** renderers.

General/Scanline Maps

Maps allow you to improve the appearance of the materials. They also help you to enhance the realism of the materials. You can use maps in a variety of ways, you can use them to create environments, to create image planes for modeling, to create projections from light, and so forth. You can use the **Material/Map Browser** to load a map or create a map of a particular type. A map can be used to design different elements of a material such as reflection, refraction, bump, and so forth.

Maps and Mapping Coordinates

When you apply a map to any object, the object must have mapping coordinates applied. These coordinates are specified in terms of UVW axes local to the object. Most of the objects in 3ds Max have the **Generate Mapping Coordinates** option. When on, 3ds Max generates default mapping coordinates.

UVW Mapping Coordinate Channels

Each object in 3ds Max can have **99** UVW mapping coordinates. The default mapping is always assigned the number **1**. The **UVW Map** modifier can send coordinates to any of these **99** channels.

3ds Max gives you ability to generate the mapping coordinates in different ways:

- The **Generate Mapping Coords** option is available for most of the primitives. This option provides a projection appropriate to the shape of the object type.
- Apply the **Unwrap UVW** modifier. This modifier comes with some useful tools that you can use to edit mapping coordinates.
- Apply the **UVW Map** modifier. This modifier allows you to set a projection type from several projection types it provides.

Here's the quick rundown to the projection types:

- **Box projection:** It places a duplicate of the map image on each of the six sides of a box.

- **Cylindrical projection:** This wraps the image around the sides of the object. The duplicate images are also projected onto the end caps.

- **Spherical projection:** This projection type wraps the map image around a sphere and gather the image at the top and bottom.

- **Shrink-wrap projection:** This type is like the spherical projection but creates one singularity instead of two.

- Use special mapping coordinates. For example, the **Loft** object provides built-in mapping coordinates.
- Use a **Surface Mapper** modifier. This modifier uses a map assigned to a NURBS surface and projects it onto the object(s).

Here's quick rundown to the cases when you can apply a map and you don't need mapping coordinates:

- Reflection, Refraction, and Environment maps.
- 3D Procedural maps: **Noise** and **Marble**.
- Face-mapped materials.

Tip: UVW Remove utility
*The **UVW Remove** utility removes mapping coordinates or materials from the currently selected objects. The path to the utility is as follows: **Utilities** panel | **Utilities** rollout | **More** button | **Utilities** dialog | **UVW Remove**. You can also remove material from objects using the **UVW Remove** utility.*

Real-World Mapping
The real-world mapping is an alternative mapping method that you can use in 3ds Max. This type of mapping considers the correct scaling of the texture mapped materials applied to the geometry in the scene.

Note: Autodesk Materials
Autodesk materials require you to use the real-world mapping.

In order to apply the real-world mapping correctly, two requirements must be met. First, the correct style of UV texture coordinates must be assigned to the geometry. In other words, the size of the UV space should correspond to the size of the geometry. To address this issue, the **Real-World Map Size** switch is added to the many rollouts in 3ds Max [see Figure F29].

The second requirement is available in the **Coordinates** rollout of the **Material Edito**, the **Use Real-World Scale** switch. When this switch is on, **U/V** changes to **Width/Height** and **Tiling** changes to **Size** [see Figure F30].

Parameters [F29]

Length: 31.612
Width: 55.732
Height: 35.369

Length Segs: 1
Width Segs: 1
Height Segs: 1

☑ Generate Mapping Coords.
☐ Real-World Map Size

Coordinates [F30]

● Texture ○ Environ Mapping: Explicit Map Channel ▾

☐ Show Map on Back   Map Channel: 99
☑ Use Real-World Scale

	Offset	Size	Mirror Tile	Angle
Width:	0.0	1.0	☐ ☑	U: 0.0
Height:	0.0	1.0	☐ ☑	V: 0.0
				W: 0.0

● UV ○ VW ○ WU

Blur: 1.0   Blur offset: 0.0   Rotate

Note: Real-world Mapping
The real-world mapping is off in 3ds Max, by default.

Tip: Real-World Map Size check box
*You can turn on **Real-World Map Size** by default from the **Preferences** dialog by using the **Use Real-World Texture Coordinates** switch. This option is available in the **Texture Coordinates** section of the **General** panel.*

Output Rollout

The options in this rollout [see Figure F31] are responsible for setting the internal parameters of a map. These options can be used to determine the rendered appearance of the map. Most of the controls on this rollout are for the color output.

Output [F31]

☐ Invert   Output Amount: 1.0
☐ Clamp   RGB Offset: 0.0
☐ Alpha from RGB Intensity   RGB Level: 1.0
☐ Enable Color Map   Bump Amount: 1.0

Color Map :
○ RGB ● Mono   Copy CurvePoints

Note: Output Rollout
*These controls do not affect the bump maps except the **Invert** toggle, which reverses the direction of the bumps and bump amount.*

MT2-14   Unit MT2 - General/Scanline Materials and Maps

2D Maps

The 2D maps are two-dimensional images that are mapped to the surface of the geometric objects. You can also use them to create environment maps. The **Bitmap** is the simplest type 2D maps. 3ds Max also allows you to create 2D maps procedurally.

Coordinates Rollout

The **Coordinates** rollout shown in Figure F30 allows you to adjust coordinate parameters to move a map relative to the surface of the object. This rollout also allows you to set tiling and mirroring of the texture pattern. The repetition of the texture pattern on the surface of an object is known as tiling. The mirroring is a form of tiling in which 3ds Max repeats the map and then flips the repeated map.

In this rollout, there are two options that you can use to control the mapping type. These options are **Texture** and **Environ**. The **Texture** type applies texture as a map to the surface. The **Environ** type uses map as an environment map. For both of these options, you can select the types of coordinates from the **Mapping** drop-down.

Here's the list of options available in the **Mapping** drop-down:

- **Explicit Map Channel:** It uses any map channel from **1** to **99**. When you select this option, **Map Channel** becomes active.
- **Vertex Color Channel:** This option uses assigned vertex colors as a channel.
- **Planar from Object XYZ:** This option uses planar mapping based on the object's local coordinates.
- **Planar from World XYZ:** This option uses planar mapping based on the scene's world coordinates.
- **Spherical Environment/Cylindrical Environment/Shrink-wrap Environment:** These options project the map into the scene as if it were mapped to an invisible object in the background.
- **Screen:** This option projects a map as a flat backdrop in the scene.

Noise Rollout

You can add a random noise to the appearance of the material using the parameters available in this rollout [see Figure F32]. These parameters modify the mapping of pixels by applying a fractal noise function.

Bitmap

This map is the simplest type of map available in 3ds Max. This map is useful for creating many type of materials from wood to skin. If you want to create an animated material, you can use an animation or video file with this map. When you select this map, the **Select Bitmap Image File** dialog opens. Navigate to the location where the bitmap file is stored and then click **Open** to select the file.

Tip: Bitmap and Windows Explorer
*You can also create a bitmap node by dragging a supported bitmap file from **Windows Explorer** to the **Slate Material Editor**.*

Tip: Viewport Canvas
*The **Viewport Canvas** feature allows you create a bitmap on the fly by painting directly onto the surface of the object. To open the canvas, choose **Viewport Canvas** from the **Tools** menu.*

Checker Map

This map is a procedural texture that applies a two-color checkerboard pattern [see Figure F33]. The default colors used to produce the pattern are black and white. You can also change these colors with map and it's true for all color components of the other maps.

Camera Map Per Pixel Map

This map allows you to project a map from the direction of a particular camera. It is useful when you are working on a matte painting. Figure F34 shows the **Marble** map projected on the teapot using the camera [see Figure F35]. Figure F36 shows the node network.

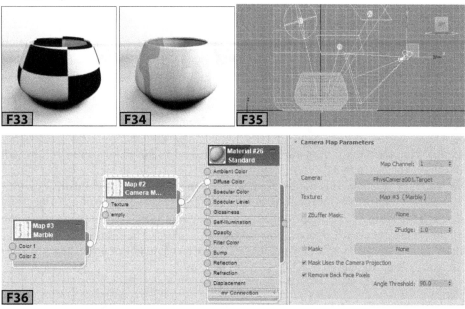

Note: Two maps with the sane name
If a map with the same name exists in two places, only one map is loaded to save the loading time. If you have two maps with different contents but with the same name, only the first map encountered by 3ds Max appears in the scene.

Tip: Swapping Colors
*You can swap colors by dragging one color swatch over another and then choosing **Swap** from the popup menu.*

Warning: Camera Map Per Pixel Map
This map cannot be used with the animated objects or animated textures.

Gradient Map

This map type allows you to create a gradient that shades from one color to another. Figure F37 shows the shift from one color to another. The red, green, and blue colors are used for the gradient. Figure F38 shows the result when the fractal noise is applied to the gradient. Figure F39 shows the node network.

Gradient Ramp Map

This map is similar to the **Gradient** map. Like the **Gradient** map, it shades from one color to another, however, you can use any number of colors [see Figure F40]. Also, you have additional controls to create a complex customized ramp. Figure F41 shows the node network used to produce the result shown in Figure F40.

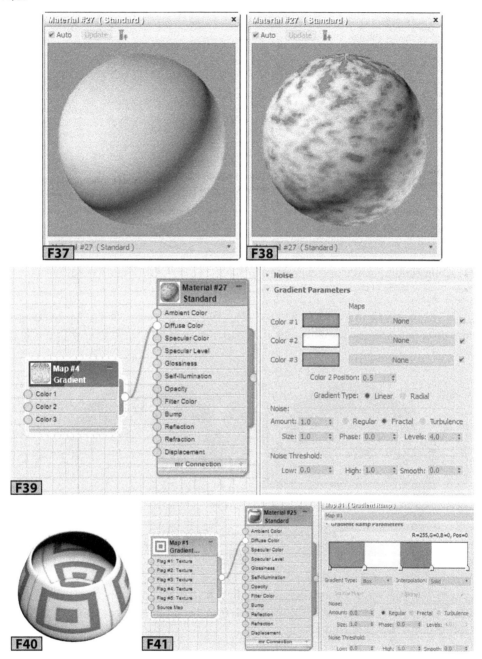

Normal Bump Map

This map allows you to connect a texture-baked normal map to a material. Figure F42 shows the bump on the surface created using the **Normal Bump** map. Figure F43 shows the node network.

F42

F43

Substance Map

This map is used with the **Substance** parametric textures. These textures are resolution-independent 2D textures and use less memory. Therefore, they are useful for exporting to the game engines via the **Algorithmic Substance Air** middleware.

Swirl Map

This map is 2D procedural map that can be used to simulate swirls [see Figure F44].

Tiles Map

You can use this map to create a brick or stacked tiling of colors or maps. A number of commonly used architectural brick patterns are available with this map. Figure F45 shows render with the **English Bond** type applied.

F44   F45

Vector Map

Using this map, you can apply a vector-based graphics, including animation as textures. You can also use **AutoCAD Pattern** (PAT) files, **Adobe Illustrator** (AI) files, **Portable Document** (PDF) files, and **Scalable Vector Graphics** (SVG) files [see Figure 46].

Vector Displacement Map

This map allows you to displace the meshes in three directions whereas the traditional method permits displacement only along the surface normals.

3D Maps

3D maps are patterns generated by 3ds Max in 3D space. Let's have a look at various 3D maps.

Cellular Map

You can use this map to generate a variety of visual effects such as mosaic tiling, pebbled surfaces, and even ocean surfaces [see Figure F47].

Dent Map

This map generated a procedural map using a fractal noise algorithm. The effect that this produces depends on the map type chosen.

Falloff Map

The **Falloff** map generates a value from white to black based on the angular falloff of the face normals. Figure F48 shows the **Falloff** map applied to the geometry with the **Falloff** type set to **Fresnel**.

Marble Map

You can use this map to create a marble texture with the colored veins against [see Figure F49] a color background.

Noise Map

This map allows to create a noise map that creates the random perturbation of a surface based on the interaction of two colors or materials. Figure F50 shows the **Noise** map with the **Noise Type** set to **Fractal**.

Particle Age Map

This map is used with the particle systems. This map changes the color of the particles based on their age.

Particle MBlur Map

This map can be used to alter the opacity of the leading and trailing ends of particles based on their rate of motion.

Perlin Marble Map

This map is like the **Marble** map. However, it generates a marble pattern using the **Perlin Turbulence** algorithm.

Smoke Map

You can use this map [see Figure F51] to create animated opacity maps to simulate the effects of smoke in a beam of light, or other cloudy, flowing effects.

Speckle Map

This map [see Figure F52] can be used to create granite-like and other patterned surfaces.

Splat Map

This map can be used to create patterns similar to the spattered paint [see Figure F53].

Stucco Map

You can use this map [see Figure F54] as a bump to create the effect like a stuccoed surface.

Waves Map

You can use this map as both bump or diffuse map [see Figure F55]. This map is used to create watery or wavy effects.

Wood Map

This map creates a wavy grain like wood pattern [see Figure F56]. You can control the direction, thickness, and complexity of the grain.

Compositor Maps

These maps are specifically designed for compositing colors and maps. Let's have a look at these maps.

Composite Map

You can use this map to layer other maps atop each other using the alpha channel and other methods.

Mask Map

This map can be used to view one material through another on the surface.

Mix Map

With this map, you can combine two colors or materials on a single side of the surface. You can also animate the **Mix Amount** parameter to control how two maps are blended together over time.

RGB Multiply Map

This map combines two maps by multiplying their RGB values. This map is generally used as a **Bump** map.

Color Modifiers Maps

These maps change the color of the pixels in a material. Let's have a look:

Color Correction Map

This map is allows you to modify color of a map using various tools. This map uses a stack-based method.

Output Map

You can use this map to apply output settings to the procedural maps such as **Checker** or **Marble**. These maps don't have the output settings.

RGB Tint Map

This map adjusts the three color channels in an image.

Vertex Color Map

In 3ds Max, you can assign vertex colors using the **VertexPaint** modifier, the **Assign Vertex Colors** utility, or the vertex controls for an editable mesh, editable patch, or editable poly. This map makes any vertex coloring applied to an object available for rendering.

Reflection and Refraction Maps

These maps are used to create reflections and refractions. Here's is a quick rundown.

Flat Mirror Map

This map produces a material that reflects surroundings when it is applied to the co-planer faces. It is assigned to the **Reflection** map of the material.

Raytrace Map

This map allows you to create fully raytraced reflections and refractions. The reflections/refractions generated by this map are more accurate than the **Reflect/Refract** map.

Reflect/Refract Map

You can use this map to create a reflective or refractive surface. To create reflection, assign this map type to the reflection map. To create refraction, apply it to the **Refraction** map.

Thin Wall Refraction Map

This map can be used to simulate a surface as if it part of a surface through a plate of glass.

Other Maps

In 2017 version of 3ds Max, Autodesk has introduced some new maps. Here's is a quick rundown.

Shape Map

You can use this map to create resolution independent graphical textures that you can animate. This map uses splines to apply textures to the selected object. The results can be fully animated. You can set outlines, fill colors as well as the map boundaries. You can change the shape of the spline even after applying it to the object in the scene. Also, all adjustment to the shape can be keyframed as a result you can animate the textures. The functioning of this map is demonstrated in an hands-on exercise later in the unit.

Text Map

Like splines, you can also create textures using text. You can create creative textures using the **Text** map and all adjustments can be animated. The functioning of this map is demonstrated in an hands-on exercise later in the unit.

TextureObjMask

This texture map allows you to control the textures using a primitive control object [plane, box, or sphere]. You can use the box or sphere primitive to control inside/outside color. The plan primitive allows you to control above/below color. The functioning of this map is demonstrated in an hands-on exercise later in the unit.

Color Map

This map allows you to create solid color swatches and bitmaps. You can easily create and instance solid color swatches that allows you to maintain consistency and accuracy of color choices. You can also use a bitmap as an input and adjust gamma and gain.

Combustion

You can use this map to interactively create maps using Autodesk Combustion and 3ds Max simultaneously. When you paint a map in combustion the material automatically updated in 3ds Max [material editor and shaded viewports].

Caution: Combustion

This map works only if Autodesk Combustion is installed on your system. 3ds Max is only available for Windows, as a result, you can not use this map on a Macintosh system.

Map Output Selector

This map is used with the multi-output map such as Substance. It tells 3ds Max which output to use. This map is automatically inserted when you assign an output of multi-output Substance map to input of a material.

MultiTile

This texture allows you to implement support for UDIM, Z-Brush, and Mudbox compaitble multi-tile textures. ZBrush is the default value.

Hands-on Exercises

From the **Application** menu, choose **Manage | Set Project Folder** to open the **Browse for Folder** dialog. Navigate to the folder where you want to save the files and then click **Make New Folder**. Create the new folder with the name **unit-mt2** and click **OK** to create the project directory.

Exercise 1: Creating the Gold Material

In this exercise, we are going to create the gold material.

The following table summarizes the exercise.

Table E1: Creating the gold material	
Topics in this section:	• Getting Ready • Creating the Gold Material
Skill Level	Beginner
Project Folder	**unit-mt2**
Start File	**umt2-hoe1-1to13-start.max**
Final Exercise File	**umt2-hoe1-end.max**
Time to Complete	10 Minutes

Getting Ready

Open the **umt2-hoe1-1to13-start.max** file in 3ds Max.

Creating the Gold Material

Press M to open the **Slate Material Editor**. On the **Material/Map Browser | Materials | General** rollout, drag the **Standard** material to the active view. Rename the material as **goldMat**. Apply the material to **geo1, geo2**, and **geo3**. Save the scene as **umt2-hoe1-end.max**. On the **Parameter Editor | goldMat | Shader Basic Parameters** rollout, choose **Multi-Layer** from the drop-down. On the **Multi-Layer Basic Parameters** rollout, set **Diffuse** to **RGB [148, 70, 0]** and then set **Diffuse Level** to **25**. Take a test render [see Figure E1].

Now, we will add specularity and reflection to add the detail. On the **First Specular Layer** section, set **Color** to **RGB [247, 227, 10]**. Set **Level** to **114**, **Glossiness** to **32**, **Anisotropy** to **82**, and **Orientation** to **90**. On the **Second Specular Layer** section, set **Color** to **RGB [192, 77, 8]**. Set **Level** to **114**, **Glossiness** to **32**, **Anisotropy** to **82**, and **Orientation** to **90**. On the **Maps** rollout, click **Reflection** map button. On the **Material/Map Browser** that appears, double-click **Falloff**.

On the **Parameter Editor | Falloff | Falloff Parameters** rollout, click the **Swap Color/Maps** button. Also, set **Falloff Type** to **Fresnel**. Click white swatch map button and then on the **Material/Map Browser** that appears, double-click **Raytrace** in the **General** rollout. On the **Parameter Editor | Raytrace | Raytracer Parameters** rollout, select **Reflection** from the **Trace Mode** section. Take a test render [see Figure E2].

On the **Falloff | Mix Curve** rollout, RMB click on the first point and then choose **Bezier-Corner** from the contextual menu [see Figure E3]. Similarly, convert second point to **Bezier-Corner** and change the shape of the curve as shown in Figure E4. Now, take a render to view the final result [see Figure E5].

E1

E2

Mix Curve

E3

Corner
Bezier-Smooth
✓ Bezier-Corner

Mix Curve

E4

E5

Exercise 2: Creating the Copper Material

In this exercise, we are going to create the copper material.

The following table summarizes the exercise.

Table E2: Creating the copper material	
Topics in this section:	• Getting Ready • Creating the Copper Material
Skill Level	Beginner
Project Folder	**unit-mt2**

Start File	**umt2-hoe1-end.max**
Final Exercise File	**umt2-hoe2-end.max**
Time to Complete	10 Minutes

Getting Ready

Make sure the **umt2-hoe1-end.max** file that you created in Hands-on Exercise 1 is open in 3ds Max.

Creating the Copper Material

Press M to open the **Slate Material Editor**, if not already open. Create a copy of the **goldMat** node by shift dragging it [see Figure E1].

Rename the node as **copperMat** and then apply it to **geo1**, **geo2**, and **geo3**. Save the scene as **umt2-hoe2-end.max**.

On the **Multi-Layer Basic Parameters** rollout, set **Diffuse** to RGB **[88, 28, 9]**. On the **First Specular Layer section**, set **Color** to RGB **[177, 75, 44]**.

On the **Second Specular Layer section**, set **Color** to RGB **[255, 123, 82]**. Take the render [see Figure E2].

Exercise 3: Creating the Brass Material

In this exercise, we are going to create the brass material.

The following table summarizes the exercise.

Table E3: Creating the brass material		
Topics in this section:	<ul><li>Getting Ready</li><li>Creating the Brass Material</li></ul>	
Skill Level	Beginner	
Project Folder	**unit-mt2**	
Start File	**umt2-hoe2-end.max**	
Final Exercise File	**umt2-hoe3-end.max**	
Time to Complete	10 Minutes	

Getting Ready

Make sure the **umt2-hoe2-end.max** file that you created in Hands-on Exercise 2 is open in 3ds Max.

Creating the Brass Material

Press M to open the **Slate Material Editor**, if not already open. Create a copy of the **copperMat** node by **Shift** dragging it. Rename the node as **brassMat** and then apply it to **geo1**, **geo2**, and **geo3**.

On the **Multi-Layer Basic Parameters** rollout, set **Diffuse** to **RGB [49, 38, 14]**. On the **First Specular Layer** section, set **Color** to **RGB [212, 154, 30]**. On the **Second Specular Layer** section, set **Color** to **RGB [174, 98, 61]**. Take the render [see Figure E1] and then save the file with the name **umt2-hoe3-end.max**.

E1

Exercise 4: Creating the Chrome Material

In this exercise, we are going to create the chrome material.

The following table summarizes the exercise.

Table E4: Creating the chrome material	
Topics in this section:	• Getting Ready • Creating the Chrome Material
Skill Level	Beginner
Project Folder	**unit-mt2**
Start File	**umt2-hoe1-1to13-start.max**
Final Exercise File	**umt2-hoes4-end.max**
Time to Complete	10 Minutes

Getting Ready

Make sure the **hoes1-1to13-start.max** is open in 3ds Max.

Creating the Chrome Material

Load **umt2-hoe1-1to13-start.max** in 3ds Max. Press **M** to open the **Slate Material Editor**. On the **Material/Map/Browser | Materials | General** rollout, drag the **Standard** material to the active view. Rename the material as **chromeMat**. Apply the material to **geo1**, **geo2**, and **geo3**. Save the scene as **umt2-hoes4-end.max**.

On the **Parameter Editor | chromeMat | Blinn Basic Parameters** rollout, click the **Diffuse** color swatch. On the **Color Selector : Diffuse Color** dialog, set **Value** to **12** and click **OK**. On the **Specular Highlights** section, set **Specular Level** to **150** and **Glossiness** to **80**.

E1

On the **Maps** rollout, set **Reflection** to **90** and then click the **Reflection** map button. On the **Material Map Browser** that appears, double-click **Raytrace**. On the **Raytrace** map | **Raytracer Parameters** | **Background** section, click **None**. On the **Material/Map Browser** that appears, double-click **Bitmap**. In the **Select Bitmap Image File** dialog that appears, select **refMap.jpeg**. Render the scene [see Figure E1].

Exercise 5: Creating the Brushed Aluminum Material

In this exercise, we are going to create the brushed aluminum material using Photoshop and 3ds Max. The following table summarizes the exercise.

Table E5: Creating the brushed aluminum material	
Topics in this section:	• Getting Ready • Creating the Brushed Aluminum Material
Skill Level	Beginner
Project Folder	**unit-mt2**
Start File	**umt2-hoe1-1to13-start.max**
Final Exercise File	**umt2-hoe5-end.max**
Time to Complete	15 Minutes

Getting Ready

Make sure the **umt2-hoe1-1to13-start.max** is open in 3ds Max.

Creating the Brushed Aluminum Material

Start Photoshop. Create a **1000 x 1000 px** document and fill it with **50%** gray color. Choose **Noise** | **Add Noise** from the **Filter** menu and then set the parameters as shown in Figure E1 and then click **OK**. Choose **Blur** | **Motion Blur** from the **Filter** menu and then set the parameters as shown in Figure E2 and then click **OK**.

Choose **Adjustments | Brightness\Contrast** from the **Image** menu and then set the parameters as shown in Figure E3 and then click **OK**. Save the document as **scratch.jpg**.

Load **umt2-hoe1-1to13-start.max** in 3ds Max, if not already loaded. Press **M** to open the **Slate Material Editor**. On the **Material/Map Browser | Materials | General** rollout, drag the **Standard** material to the active view. Rename the material as **balMat**. Apply the material to **geo1**, **geo2**, and **geo3**.

On the **Parameter Editor | balMat | Shader Basic Parameters** rollout, choose **Oren-Nayar-Blinn** from the drop-down. On the **Parameter Editor | balMat | Oren-Nayar-Blinn Basic Parameters** rollout, click **Ambient** color swatch. On the **Color Selector : Ambient Color** dialog, set **Value** to **84** and click **OK**. Unlock the **Ambient** and **Diffuse** components of the material.

Click the **Diffuse** map button and then on the **Material/Map Browser** that appears, double-click **Mix**. On the **Parameter Editor | Mix map**, set **Color 1** to **127** and assign **scratch.jpg** to **Color 2** using the **Bitmap** map. Set **Mix** Amount to **72%**. On the **balMat | Oren-Nayar-Blinn Basic Parameters** rollout | **Advanced Diffuse** section, set **Diffuse Level** to **81**, and **Roughness** to **80**. Now, take a test render [see Figure E4].

On the **Parameter Editor | balMat | Oren-Nayar-Blinn Basic Parameters** rollout | **Specular Highlight** section, set **Specular Level** to **156**, **Glossiness** to **13**, and **Soften** to **0.48**. Now, take a test render [see Figure E5]. On the **Parameter Editor | scratch.jpg | Output** rollout, set **Output Amount** to **0.6**. Take a render [see Figure E6]. Save the file as **umt2-hoe5-end.max**.

Exercise 6: Creating the Denim Fabric Material

In this exercise, we are going to create the denim fabric material using Photoshop and 3ds Max.

The following table summarizes the exercise.

Table E6: Creating the denim fabric material	
Topics in this section:	• Getting Ready • Creating the Denim Fabric Material
Skill Level	Beginner

Project Folder	unit-mt2
Start File	umt2-hoe1-1to13-start.max
Final Exercise File	umt2-hoe6-end.max
Time to Complete	15 Minutes

Getting Ready

Make sure the **umt2-hoe1-1to13-start.max** is open in 3ds Max.

Creating the Denim Fabric Material

Start Photoshop. Create a **1000 x 1000 px** document and fill it with **RGB [41, 67, 102]** color. Create a new layer and fill it with **50%** gray. Press **D** to switch to the default colors. Choose **Filter Gallery| Sketch | Halftone Pattern** from the **Filter** menu and then set the parameters as shown in Figure E1 and then click **OK**. Choose **Pixelate | Mezzotint** from the **Filter** menu and then set the parameters as shown in Figure E2 and then click **OK**.

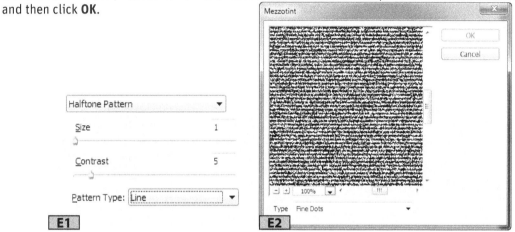

Duplicate the layer and rotate and scale the duplicate layer [see Figure E3]. Choose **Blur | Gaussian Blur** from the **Filter** menu and then apply a blur of radius **1**. Set blending mode to **Multiply**. Also, set the blending mode of the middle layer [Layer 1] to **Softlight** [Figure E4].

Save the file as **denimFebric.jpg**. Choose **Flatten Image** from the **Layer** menu to flatten the image. Now, press **Ctrl+Shift+U** to desaturate the image and then save it as **denimFebricBump.jpg**. In 3ds Max, press **M** to open the **Slate Material Editor**. On the **Material/Map Browser | Materials | Scanline** rollout, drag the **Standard** material to the active view. Rename the material as **denimMat**. Apply the material to **geo1**, **geo2**, and **geo3**.

Save the scene as **umt2-hoe6-end.max**. On the **Parameter Editor | denimMat | Shader Basic Parameters** rollout, choose **Oren-Nayar-Blinn** from the drop-down. On the **Parameter Editor | denimMat | Oren-Nayar-Blinn Basic Parameters** rollout, click **Ambient** color swatch.

On the **Color Selector : Ambient Color** dialog, set **RGB** to **50, 53**, and **57** and click **OK**. Unlock the **Ambient** and **Diffuse** components of the material. Click the **Diffuse** map button and then on the **Material Map Browser** that appears, double-click **Bitmap**. Assign **denimFebric.jpg**. On the **denimMat | Oren-Nayar-Blinn Basic Parameters** rollout | **Advanced Diffuse** section, set **Diffuse Level** to **250**, and **Roughness** to **75**. Now, take a test render [see Figure E5].

On the **Parameter Editor | denimMat | Oren-Nayar-Blinn Basic Parameters** rollout | **Specular Highlight** section, set **Specular Level** to **7**, and **Glossiness** to **10**. Take a test render [see Figure E6]. On the **Maps** rollout, ensure **Bump** is set to **30%** and then click **Bump** map button.

On the **Material/Map Browser** that appears, double-click **Bitmap**. On the **Select Bitmap Image File** dialog that appears, select **denimFebricBump.jpg**. Take a test render [see Figure E7].

Exercise 7: Creating the Blend Material
In this exercise, we are going to create a blend material.

The following table summarizes the exercise.

Table E7: Working with the blend material	
Topics in this section:	• Getting Ready • Working with the Blend Material
Skill Level	Beginner
Project Folder	**unit-mt2**
Start File	**umt2-hoe1-1to13-start.max**
Final Exercise File	**umt2-hoe7-end.max**
Time to Complete	15 Minutes

Getting Ready
Make sure the **umt2-hoe1-1to13-start.max** is open in 3ds Max.

Working with the Blend Material

Save the scene as **umt2-hoe7-end.max**. Press **M** to open the **Slate Material Editor**. On the **Material/Map Browser | Materials | General** rollout, drag the **Blend** material to the active view. Rename the materials connected to the **Blend** node as **mat1** and **mat2**. Apply the **Blend** material to **geo1**, **geo2**, and **geo3**.

Assign **ConcreteBare.jpg** to the **mat1 | Diffuse** map and **ConcreteBare1.jpg** to the **mat2 | Diffuse** map. Take a test render [see Figure E1]. Assign a **Noise** map to the **Blend** material's **Mask** control. On the **Mixing Curve** section, turn on the **Use Curve** switch and set **Upper** to **0.78** and **Lower** to **0.3**. Take a test render [see Figure E2].

On the **Parameter Editor | Noise Parameters** rollout, set **Noise Type** to **Fractal**, **High** to **0.9**, and **Size** to **15.5**. Take a test render and press **Ctrl+S** to save the file. For the sake of clarity, I have rendered [see Figure E3] a plane with **mat1** (left image), **mat2** (middle image), and **Blend** (right image) materials applied. Figure E4 shows the node network.

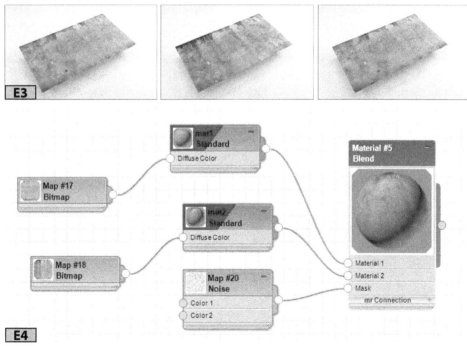

Exercise 8: Creating the Double-Sided Material

In this exercise, we are going to create a double-sided material.

The following table summarizes the exercise.

Table E8: Working with the double-sided material	
Topics in this section:	• Getting Ready • Working with the Double-Sided Material
Skill Level	Beginner
Project Folder	**unit-mt2**
Start File	**umt2-hoe1-1to13-start.max**
Final Exercise File	**umt2-hoe8-end.max**
Time to Complete	15 Minutes

Getting Ready

Make sure the **umt2-hoe1-1to13-start.max** is open in 3ds Max. Save file as **umt2-hoe8-end.max**.

Working with the Double Sided Material

Delete **geo4, geo1, geo6** from the scene and place a teapot at the center of **geo5**. Go to the **Modify** panel and then on the **Parameters** rollout | **Teapot Parts** section, turn off **Handle, Spout,** and **Lid** switches. Also, set **Segments** to **32**.

Press **M** to open the **Slate Material Editor**. On the **Material/Map Browser** | **Materials** | **General** rollout, drag the **Double Sided** material to the active view. Rename the materials connected to the **DoubleSided** node as **mat1** and **mat2**. Apply the material to the teapot.

Now, we will assign maps to the back and facing materials of the **Double Sided** material. The **Facing Material** is represented by **mat1** whereas the **Back Material** is represented by **mat2**.

Assign **ConcreteBare.jpg** to the **mat1** | **Diffuse** map. Assign a **Perlin Marble** map to the **mat2** | **Diffuse** map. Set **Translucency** to **25** in the **Double Sided** material | **Double Sided Basic Parameters** rollout. Take a test render [see Figure E1] and press **Ctrl+S** to save the file. Figure E2 shows the node network.

In this exercise, we are going to create a **Shellac** material.

The following table summarizes the exercise.

Table E9: Working with the **Shellac** material	
Topics in this section:	• Getting Ready • Working with the **Shellac** Material
Skill Level	Beginner
Project Folder	**unit-mt2**
Start File	**umt2-hoe8-end.max**
Final Exercise File	**umt2-hoe9-end.max**
Time to Complete	15 Minutes

Getting Ready

Make sure the **umt2-hoe8-end.max** is open in 3ds Max. Save it as **umt2-hoe9-end.max**. Turn on the **Lid** for the teapot.

Working with the Shellac Material

Press **M** to open the **Slate Material Editor**. On the **Material/Map Browser | Materials | General** rollout, drag the **Shellac** material to the active view.

Rename the materials connected to the **Base Material** and **Shellac Mat** ports of the **Shellac** node as **mat1** and **mat2**, respectively. Apply the material to the teapot.

Assign the **Swirl** map to the **mat1 | Diffuse** map and **Wood** map to the **mat2 | Diffuse** map. Set **Shellac Color Blend** to **86** in the **Shellac Basic Parameters** rollout. Take a test render [see Figure E1].

E1

In this exercise, we're going to create a microscopic material [see Figure E1]. The following material(s) and map(s) are used in this exercise: **Standard, Mix, Falloff**, and **Noise**.

The following table summarizes the exercise.

Table E10: Creating the microscopic material	
Topics in this section:	• Getting Ready • Creating the Microscopic Material
Skill Level	Beginner
Project Folder	**unit-mt2**

Start File	umt2-hoe10-start.max
Final Exercise File	umt2-hoe10-end.max
Time to Complete	15 Minutes

Getting Ready
Make sure the **umt2-hoe10-start.max** is open in 3ds Max.

Creating the Microscopic Material
Press **M** to open the **Slate Material Editor** and then create a new **Standard** material and assign it to the **sphGeo** in the scene. Rename the material as **msMat**. Connect a **Falloff** map to the **msMat's Diffuse** port. On the **Parameter Editor | Falloff** map | **Falloff Parameters** rollout | **Front:Side** section, set first color swatch to **RGB [20, 20, 20]** and second color swatch to white. Set **Falloff Type** to **Perpendicular/Parallel**. Ensure **Falloff Direction** is set to **Viewing Direction (Camera Z-Axis)** [see Figure E2]. Also, set the **Mix Curve** to as shown in Figure E3.

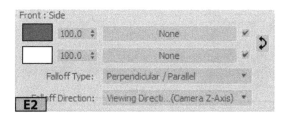

Now, you will create two **Noise** maps and mix them using the **Mix** map. Connect a **Mix** map to the **msMat's Bump** port. On the **Parameter Editor | Mix** map | **Mix Parameters** rollout, set **Mix Amount** to **37.8**. On the **Slate Material Editor**, connect two **Noise** maps, one each to the **Color 1** and **Color 2** ports. For the **Color 1 | Noise** map use the settings shown in Figure E4. Figure E5 shows the **Noise** map settings connected to **Color 2**. Figure E6 shows the node network.

Now, render the scene. Notice that the output is little bit on the darker side. To address this, on the **Parameter Editor | Falloff** map | **Falloff Parameters** rollout | **Front:Side** section, set first color swatch to **RGB [80, 80, 80]**. Render the scene [see Figure E1].

Exercise 11: Creating Material for a Volleyball

Here, we are going to apply texture to a volleyball [see Figure E1]. Right image in Figure E1 shows the reference whereas the left image shows the rendered output. The following material(s) and map(s) are used in this exercise: **Multi/Sub-Object**, **Standard**, and **Noise**.

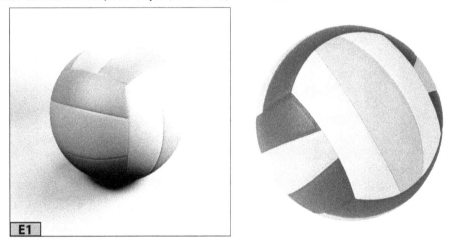

The following table summarizes the exercise.

Table E11: Creating material for a volleyball	
Topics in this section:	• Getting Ready • Creating Material for a Volleyball
Skill Level	Beginner
Project Folder	**unit-mt2**
Start File	**umt2-hoe11-start.max**
Final Exercise File	**umt2-hoe11-end.max**
Time to Complete	15 Minutes

Getting Ready

Make sure the **umt2-hoe11-start.max** is open in 3ds Max. Save the file as **umt2-hoe11-end.max**.

Creating Material for a Volleyball

Select the **VolleyBallGeo** in any viewport and then go to the **Modify** panel. On the **Selection** rollout, click **Element** and then select the elements that make the yellow part of the volleyball [see Figure E2]. See the right image in Figure E1 for reference.

On the **Modify panel | Polygon: Material IDs** rollout, set **ID** to **1** [see Figure E3]. Similarly, select the blue and white elements and assign them ID **2** and **3**, respectively. Press **M** to open the **Slate Material Editor** and then create a new **Multi/Sub-object** material and assign it to the **VolleyBallGeo** in the scene. Rename the material as **vbMat**. On the **Parameter Editor | vbMat | Multi/Sub-Object Parameters** rollout, click **Set Number** and then set **Number of Materials** to **3** in the dialog that appears. Next, click **OK**. In the **Slate Material Editor**, connect a **Standard** material to the port **1** of the **vbMat**. On the **Parameter Editor | Blinn Basic Parameter** rollout, set the **Diffuse** component to **RGB [242, 140, 8]**. On the **Specular Highlights** section, set **Specular Level** to **71** and **Glossiness** to **28**.

Connect a **Noise** map to the **Bump** port of the **Standard** material. Set **Bump** to **2%**. On the **Parameter Editor | Noise map | Noise Parameters** rollout, set **Noise Type** to **Turbulence**, **Levels** to **9**, and **Size** to **0.5**. On the **Slate Material Editor**, select the **Standard** material and **Noise** map. Now, create a copy of the selected nodes using **SHIFT**. Connect the new Standard material to the port **2** of the **vbMat**. Similarly, create another copy and connect it to port **3**. Figure E4 shows the node network. Set **Diffuse** components of the material connected to the port **2** and **3** to **RGB [11, 91, 229]** and **RGB [236, 236, 230]**, respectively. Now, press F9 to take a render.

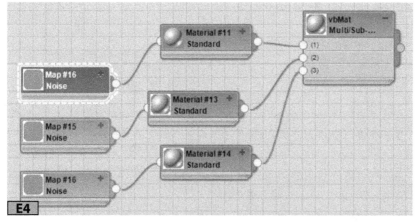

Here, we are going to apply texture to a water tunnel [see Figure E1]. The following material(s) and map(s) are used in this exercise: **Raytrace**, **Standard**, **Mix**, and **Noise**.

E1

The following table summarizes the exercise.

Table E12: Creating material for a water tunnel	
Topics in this section:	• Getting Ready • Creating Material for a Water Tunnel
Skill Level	Beginner
Project Folder	**unit-mt2**
Start File	**umt2-hoes12-start.max**
Final Exercise File	**umt2-hoes12-end.max**
Time to Complete	15 Minutes

Getting Ready

Make sure the **umt2-hoes12-start.max** is open in 3ds Max.

Creating Material for a Water Tunnel

Press **M** to open the **Slate Material Editor** and then create a new **Raytrace** material and assign it to the **waterGeo** in the scene. Rename the material as **waterMat**. On the **Parameter Editor | Raytrace Basic Parameter** rollout, set **Diffuse** to black. Set **Transparency** to **RGB (146, 175, 223)**. Set **Reflect** to **RGB [178, 178, 178]**. On the **Specular Highlight** section, set **Specular Level** to **161** and **Glossiness** to **29**. Connect a **Noise** map to the **Bump** port of the **waterMat**. Use the default values for the **Noise** map. Press **F9** to render the scene [Figure E2].

On the **Slate Material Editor**, create a new **Standard** material and assign it to the **caveGeo** in the scene. Rename the material as **caveMat**. Connect a **Mix** map to the **Diffuse** port of the **caveMat**. Connect a **Noise** map to the **Color 1** port of the **Mix** map. On the **Noise Parameters** rollout, set **Noise Type** to **Turbulence**, **Levels** to **10**, **Size** to **31.7**. Set **Color 1** to **RGB [132, 77, 6]** and **Color 2** to **RGB [154, 100, 79]**. Connect a **Noise** map to the **Color 2** port of the **Mix** map. On the **Noise Parameters** rollout, set **Noise Type** to **Turbulence**, **Levels** to **10**, **Size** to **72**. Set **Color 1** to **RGB [212, 84, 45]** and **Color 2** to **RGB [181, 99, 54]**.

On the **Parameter Editor | Mix Parameters** rollout, set **Mix Amount** to **40**. On the **Mixing curve** section, turn on the **Use Curve** switch and then set **Upper** to **0.6** and **Lower** to **0.53**. Take a test render [Figure E3].

Connect a **Mix** map to the **Displacement** port of the **caveMat**. Set **Displacement** to **25%**. Connect a **Noise** map to the **Color 1** port of the **Mix** map. On the **Noise Parameters** rollout, set **Noise Type** to **Turbulence**, **Levels** to **8.4**, **Size** to **21.2**. Connect a **Noise** map to the **Color 2** port of the **Mix** map. On the **Noise Parameters** rollout, set **Noise Type** to **Turbulence**, **Levels** to **10**, **Size** to **81.5**. On the **Parameter Editor | Mix Parameters** rollout, set **Mix Amount** to **18.4**. Take a test render [Figure E4].

Similarly, create a material for the **floorGeo**. If you want to see the values I have used, open **umt2-hoe12-end.max** and check the **floorMat** material.

Exercise 13: Creating Rusted Metal Texture

Let's now create a rusted metal texture [see Figure E1]. The following material(s) and map(s) are used in this exercise: **Standard**, **Composite**, **Bitmap**, **Color Correction**, and **Noise**. The following table summarizes the exercise.

Table E13: Creating rusted metal texture	
Topics in this section:	• Getting Ready • Creating Rusted Metal Texture
Skill Level	Beginner
Project Folder	**unit-mt2**
Start File	**umt2-hoe1-1to13-start.max**
Final Exercise File	**umt2-hoe13-end.max**
Time to Complete	15 Minutes

Getting Ready

Make sure the **umt2-hoe1-1to13-start.max** is open in 3ds Max. Save the file with the name **umt2-hoe13-end.max**.

E1

Creating Rusted Metal Texture

Press **M** to open the **Slate Material Editor**. In the **Material/Map Browser | Materials | General** rollout, double-click on **Standard** to add a **Standard** material to the active view. Rename the material as **rustMat** and apply it to **geo1**, **geo2**, and **geo3**.

In the **Parameter Editor | Shader Basic Parameters** rollout, turn on the **2-Sided** switch. Connect a **Composite** map to the **rustMap's Diffuse Color** port. Now, connect **rust.jpg** to the **Composite** map's **Layer 1** port [see Figure E2].

E2

On the **Parameter Editor | Composite** map | **Composite Layers | Layer 1** rollout, click **Add a New Layer** button to add a new layer [see Figure E3]. Notice that a new port with the name **Layer 2** has been added to the **Composite** map node in the active view. Connect **rustPaint.jpg** to the **Composite** map's **Layer 2** port. On the **Parameter Editor | Composite** map | **Composite Layers | Layer 2** rollout, set **Opacity** to **10%** and blend mode to **Color Dodge** [see Figure E4].

E3   E4

Now, take a test render [see Figure E5]. Connect **scratchesMask.jpg** to the **Composite** map's **Layer 2 (Mask)** port using a **Bitmap** map. Now, check the **Invert** checkbox from the **Bitmap's Output** rollout. Take a test render [see Figure E6]. On the **Slate Material Editor's** active view, create copy of the **Bitmap** node connected to the **Composite** map's **Layer 2 (Mask)** node using **Shift**. Connect the duplicate node to the **Bump** node of **rustMat**. On the **Parameter Editor | rustMat | Maps** rollout, set bump map's strength to **10%** and then take a test render [see Figure E7].

E5   E6   E7

Exercise 14: Shading an outdoor Scene

In this exercise, we are going to apply materials and textures to an outdoor scene [see Figure E1]. The following table summarizes the exercise.

E1

Table E14: Shading an outdoor scene	
In this exercise, you will:	• Apply material to the objects • Use the **UVW Map** modifier • Apply textures to the material
Topics in this section:	• Getting Ready • Shading the Scene
Skill Level	Intermediate
Project Folder	**unit-mt2**
Start File	**umt2-hoe14-start.max**
Final Exercise File	**umt2-hoe14-end.max**
Time to Complete	30 Minutes

Getting Ready

Make sure the **umt2-hoe14-start.max** is open in 3ds Max. Save the file with the name **umt2-hoe14-end.max**.

Shading the Scene

Select **wallGeo** from the **Scene Explorer** and then press **M** to open the **Slate Material Editor**. Drag **Standard** from the **Material/Map Browser | Maps | Scanline** rollout to the **Active View**. Rename the material as **wallMat**. RMB click on the **wallMat** node and then choose **Assign Material to Selection**. Again, RMB click and then choose **Show Shaded Material in Viewport**.

In the **Active View**, drag the **Diffuse Color** socket onto the empty area and release the mouse button. Choose **General | Bitmap** from the popup menu. In the **Select Bitmap Image File** dialog that opens, select **redBrick.png** and then click **Open** to make a connection between the **Diffuse Color** socket and texture. Double-click on the **Bitmap** node and then in the **Parameter Editor | Coordinates** rollout, set **U Tiling** and **V Tiling** to **4**. Similarly, connect the **Bump** socket to the **redBrickGray.png** and set **Tiling** to **4**.

Notice in the viewport the map is displayed on the wall [see the left image in Figure E2]. Ensure **wallGeo** is selected in the **Scene Explorer** and then go to **Modify** panel and add the **UVW Map** modifier to the stack. Select the modifier's **Gizmo** and scale the texture so that the size of the bricks appear in right proportions [see the right image in Figure E2].

Select **floorGeo** from the **Scene Explorer** and then in the **Slate Material Editor**, drag **Standard** from the **Material/Map Browser | Maps | General** rollout to the **Active View**. Rename the material as **roadMat**. RMB click on the **roadMat** node and then choose **Assign Material to Selection**. Again, RMB click and then choose **Show Shaded Material in Viewport**. In the **Active View**, drag the **Diffuse Color** socket onto the empty area and release the mouse button. Choose **General | Bitmap** from the popup menu. In the **Select Bitmap Image File** dialog that opens, select **road.jpg** and then click **Open** to make a connection between the **Diffuse Color** socket and texture. Notice in the viewport, the texture appears on the **floorGeo** [see Figure E3]. Now, we need to change the direction of the yellow line. We will do so by using the **UVW Map** modifier.

Ensure **floorGeo** is selected in the **Scene Explorer** and then go to **Modify** panel and add the **UVW Map** modifier to the stack. Select the modifier's **Gizmo** and rotate it by **90** degrees by using the **Rotate** tool. You can also use the **Move** tool to position the texture on the geometry [see Figure E4].

Now, we will apply the material to billboard. We will use the **Multi/Subobject** material. The ID **1** has been assigned to the screen component of the board whereas rest of the geometry is held by ID **2**. Select **billBoardGeo** from the **Scene Explorer** and then add a **Multi/Subobject** node to the **Active View**. Rename the material as **billboardMat**. In the **Parameter Editor**, click **Set Number**. Now, in the **Set Number of Materials** dialog, set **Number of Materials** field to **2** and click **OK**. RMB click on the **billboardMat** node and then choose **Assign Material to Selection**.

Drag the **1** socket to the empty area of the view and then choose **Materials | Scanline | Standard** from the popup menu. Connect the **Standard's** materials **Diffuse Color** socket to the **honda.jpg**. Connect another **Standard** material to the **2** socket of the **billboardMat**. In the **Parameter Editor | Blinn Basic Parameters rollout | Specular Highlight** group of the **Standard** material, set **Specular Level** and **Glossiness** to **92** and **33**, respectively. Also, set **Diffuse** color to **RGB [20, 20, and 20]**. The material appears on the **billBoardGeo** in the viewport [see Figure E5]. You need to enable **Show Shaded Material in Viewport** for the two Standard materials. Create two **Standard** materials and assign dark gray and yellow colors to them. Now, apply these materials to alternate brick from the **brickGrp** group [see Figure E6].

Now, create a chrome material as done in Exercise 4. Do not assign the **refMap.jpg** to the **Raytrace** map. In the **Scene Explorer**, select **bsGeo11, bsGeo12, bsGeo15, bsGeo16, bsGeo18, bsGeo19, bsGeo20, bsGeo22, bsGeo23, bsGeo24, bsGeo26,** and **bsGeo27**. Assign chrome material to the selected objects [see Figure E7]. Also, assign chrome material to **bsGeo3**, and **bsGeo6**.

In the **Scene Explorer**, select **bsGeo04, bsGeo05, bsGeo07,** and **bsGeo08**. Drag **Standard** from the **Material/Map Browser | Maps | General** rollout to the **Active View**. Rename the material as **woodMat**. RMB click on the **woodMat** node and then choose **Assign Material to Selection**. Again, RMB click and then choose **Show Shaded Material in Viewport**. In the **Active View**, drag the **Diffuse Color** socket onto the empty area and release the mouse button. Choose **General | Wood** from the popup menu. In the **Parameter Editor | Wood | Wood Parameters** rollout, change **Color #2** to **RGB[106, 25, 0]**. The wood texture is displayed in the viewport [see Figure E8].

In the **Scene Explorer**, select **bsGeo21**, and **bsGeo25** and then drag **Standard** from the **Material/Map Browser | Maps | General** rollout to the **Active View**. Rename the material as **roofMat**. RMB click on the **roofMat** node and then choose **Assign Material to Selection**. Again, RMB click and then choose **Show Shaded Material in Viewport**. In the **Parameter Editor | roofMat | Blinn Basic Parameters** rollout, change **Diffuse** to **RGB[23, 241, 12]** and then set **Opacity** to **25**. Figure E9 shows the roof material in the viewport.

[+] [Perspective] [Standard] [Default Shading]

E9

Exercise 15: Texturing a Cardboard Box

Let's start by texturing a cardboard box [see Figure E1] using the **UV Editor**.

E1

The following Table summarizes the exercise.

Table E15: Texturing a cardboard texture	
Topics in this section:	• Getting Ready • Texturing the Cardboard Box
Skill Level	Intermediate
Project Folder	**unit-mt2**
Final Exercise File	**umt2-hoe15-end.max**
Time to Complete	20 Minutes

Getting Ready

Reset 3ds Max. Set units to **Generic Units** and then create a box with the **Length, Height**, and **Width** set to **190**.

Texturing the Cardboard Box

Ensure the box is selected in a viewport and then go to **Modify** panel. Add the **Unwrap UVW** modifier to the stack. Click **Polygon** on the **Selection** panel and then press **Ctrl+A** to select all polygons. On the **Projection** rollout, click **Box Map** and then click again to deactivate. On the **Edit UVs** rollout, click **Open UV Editor** to open the **Edit UVWs** window. Choose **Unfold Mapping** from the **Mapping** menu of the window. The **Unfold Mapping** dialog appears. Click **OK** to accept the default settings and unfold UVs [see Figure E2].

Choose **Pick Texture** from the drop-down located on the top-right corner of the window, the **Material/Map Browser** appears. In the browser, double-click on **Bitmap** from the **Maps | General** rollout. In the **Select Bitmap Image File** dialog, select **cardboard_texture.png** and click **Open**. The **cardboard_texture.png** appears in the **Edit UVWs** window [see Figure E3].

Click **Vertex** from the bottom-left corner of the window to activate the **Vertex** selection mode. All the vertices are selected. If they are not selected, press **Ctrl+A** to select them. Ensure **Move Selected Subobjects** is active from the window's toolbar and then align all UVs to the background texture [see Figure E4]. Press and hold **Shift** while dragging to constrain the movement.

Now, select a complete column of row of the vertices and align them with the background texture [see Figure E5]. You can also select vertices in a viewport. If the UVs are not in the straight line, you can use **Align Horizontally to Pivot** and **Align Vertically to Pivot** from the **Quick Transform** rollout of the window to straighten the UVs. Close the Edit UVWs window.

Press **M** to open the **Slate Material Editor**. From the **Material/Map Browser | Material** rollout | **Scanline** rollout, double-click **Standard** to add it to the **Active View** and then assign it to the box in the scene. Rename the material as **boxMat**. Connect **ardboard_texture.png** texture to the **Diffuse** slot of the material. RMB click on **boxMat** node and choose **Show Shaded Material in Viewport** from the menu to display the texture in the viewport.

E4   E5

Exercise 16: Texturing a Dice

Let's start by texturing a dice [see Figure E1] using the **UV Editor**. In this Exercise we will export the UVs template to the Photoshop and then use Photoshop to create the texture. We will then import the texture back into 3ds Max and will apply it to the dice geometry.

E1

The following Table summarizes the exercise.

Table E16: Texturing a dice	
Topics in this section:	Getting Ready Texturing a Dice
Skill Level	Intermediate
Project Folder	**unit-mt2**
Final Exercise File	**umt2-hoe16-end.max**
Time to Complete	20 Minutes

Getting Ready

Reset 3ds Max. Set units to **Generic Units** and then create a box with the **Length**, **Height**, and **Width** set to **190**.

Texturing the Dice

Ensure the box is selected in a viewport and then go to **Modify** panel. Add the **Unwrap UVW** modifier to the stack. Click **Polygon** on the **Selection** panel and then press **Ctrl+A** to select all polygons. On the **Projection** rollout, click **Box Map** and then click again to deactivate.

On the **Edit UVs** rollout, click **Open UV Editor** to open the **Edit UVWs** window. Choose **Unfold Mapping** from the **Mapping** menu of the window. The **Unfold Mapping** dialog appears. Click **OK** to accept the default settings and unfold UVs. Choose **Render UV Template** from the **Tools** menu to open the **Render UVs** dialog. Click **Render UV Template** on the dialog. The **Render Map** window appears. Click **Save Image** on the window's toolbar to open the **Save Image** dialog. Type **dice_template** in the **File name** field and choose **PNG Image File** from the **Save as** type drop-down.

Click **Save** to save the template. Click **OK** from the **PNG Configuration** dialog. Now, close all windows and dialogs, if open. Open **dice_template.png** in **Photoshop**. **Layer 0** appears in the **Layers** panel. Create a new layer below **Layer 0** and fill it with **black** [see Figure E2].

Now, using **Photoshop** tools and features create dice texture according to the dice template. I am putting simple numbers to identify the faces of the dice [see Figure E3]. You should go ahead and create a nice looking dice texture for your dice model.

Now, switch off the **black** layer and the **template** layer. Save the **Photoshop** document as **dice_texture.png**.

In 3ds Max, apply a **Standard** material to the box. Set **Diffuse color** to **red**. Connect **dice_texture.png** to the **Diffuse Color** and **Opacity** slots of the material's node, respectively. In the **dice_texture.png** map | **Bitmap Parameters** rollout, turn off the **Premultiplied Alpha** switch. Render the scene.

Exercise 17: Texturing a Dice - II

In this Exercise, we will use an alternate method to texture a dice. You will use six different maps for the six faces of the dice.

The following Table summarizes the exercise.

Table E17: Texturing a dice - II	
Topics in this section:	• Getting Ready • Texturing a Dice
Skill Level	Intermediate
Project Folder	**unit-mt2**
Final Exercise File	**umt2-hoe17-end.max**
Time to Complete	20 Minutes

Getting Ready

Reset 3ds Max. Set units to **Generic Units** and then create a box with the **Length**, **Height**, and **Width** set to **90**.

Texturing the Dice

Ensure the box is selected in a viewport and add the **UVW Map** modifier to the stack. Select **Box** in the **Mapping** group of the **Parameters** rollout. Click **Fit** on the **Alignment** group. RMB click on the box in a viewport and then choose **Convert To : Convert to Editable Poly** from the **Quad** menu.

Press **M** to open the **Slate Material Editor** and then from the **Material/Map Browser | General | Maps** rollout, drag **Standard** to the active view. Connect **side-1.jpg** to the **Diffuse** slot of the material. Similarly, add **5** more **Standard** maps and assign **side-2.jpg** to **side-6.jpg** to them. RMB click on the **Standard** material nodes and then choose **Show Shaded Material in Viewport** from the menu.

Now, add **a Multi/Sub-Object** node to the active view. In the **Parameter Editor**, click **Set Number**. Set **Number of Materials** to **6** and then click **OK**. Connect all **Standard** materials to the **Muli/Sub-Object** material. Figure E2 shows the node network. Figure E3 shows the maps in the viewport.

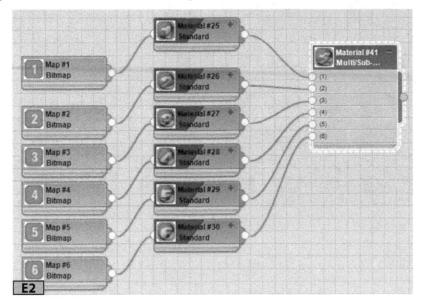

E2

Apply the **Muli/Sub-Object** material to the box in the scene. 3ds Max assigns the maps to the faces of the box. Now, if you want to change a map for a polygon, select that polygon in a viewport and then change the **ID** of the polygon from the **Polygon: Material IDs** rollout of the **Modify** panel.

You can use the **UV Editor** to change the orientation of the map. For example, if you want to change the orientation of the top face [see Figure E4], add **Unwrap UVW** modifier to the stack and then click **Polygon** from the **Selection** rollout. Select the top polygon and click **Open UV Editor** from the **Edit UVs** rollout. Press **A** to enable angel snap and then click **Rotate Selected Subobjects** from the toolbar. Now, rotate the selected polygon by **90** degrees to change the orientation of the map.

E3   E4

Exercise 18: Working with the ShapeMap

In this exercise, we will create a resolution independent map using the **ShapeMap**.

The following Table summarizes the exercise.

Table E18: Working with the ShapeMap	
Topics in this section:	• Getting Ready • Working with ShapeMap
Skill Level	Beginner
Project Folder	**unit-mt2**
Final Exercise File	**umt2-hoe18-end.max**
Time to Complete	20 Minutes

Getting Ready

Open **umt2-hoe18-start.max** in 3ds Max.

Working with the ShapeMap

Press **M** to open the **Slate Material Editor** and then from the **Material/Map Browser** | **General** | **Maps** rollout, drag **Standard** to the active view. Connect **ShapeMap** to the **Diffuse** slot of the material. Select the plane in the viewport. RMB click on the material node and then choose **Assign Material to Selection**.

Again, RMB click and then choose **Show Shaded Material in Viewport**. Notice only standard logo is displayed in the viewport at this moment [see Figure E1].

On the **Parameter Editor** | **ShapeMap** | **Shape Parameters** rollout, click **None** and then click the apple logo spline in any viewport. The shape is now displayed on the plane in the viewport [see Figure E2]. On the **Closed Shapes** section, turn on the **Render Outline** switch. On the **Outlines** section, set **Width** to **5**.

E1 E2

Set **Fill Color**, **Line Color**, **Background Color** to **RGB [141, 141, 141]**, **RGB [252, 255, 0]**, and **RGB [156, 188, 247]**, respectively. On the **Map Boundary** section, select **Manual** and then set **Width** and **Height** to **537**, and **300**, respectively.

The logo is now centered on the plane [see Figure E3]. Take a render [see Figure E4]. Now, if zoom in on an area of the logo and then render, you would notice that you will still get a high resolution output [see Figure E5].

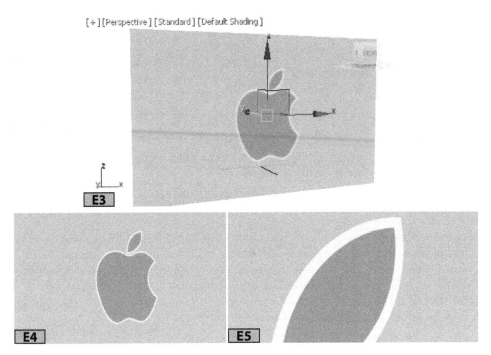

[+][Perspective][Standard][Default Shading]

E3

E4

E5

Exercise 19: Working with Text Map

In this exercise, we will create a resolution independent map using the **Text Map**.

The following Table summarizes the exercise.

Table E19: Working with Text Map	
Topics in this section:	• Getting Ready • Working with Text Map
Skill Level	Beginner
Project Folder	**unit-mt2**
Final Exercise File	**umt2-hoe19-end.max**
Time to Complete	20 Minutes

Getting Ready

Open **umt2-hoe19-start.max** in 3ds Max.

Working with the Text Map

Press **M** to open the **Slate Material Editor** and then from the **Material/Map Browser | General | Maps** rollout, drag **Standard** to the active view. Connect **Text Map** to the **Diffuse** slot of the material. Select the plane in the viewport. RMB click on the material node and then choose **Assign Material to Selection**.

Again, RMB click and then choose **Show Shaded Material in Viewport**. Notice only standard logo is displayed in the viewport at this moment [see Figure E1].

On the **Parameter Editor | Text Map | Text Parameters** rollout, click **None** and then click the **TextPlus** object in any viewport. The text is now displayed on the plane in the viewport [see Figure E2]. On the **Characters** section, turn on the **Render Outline** switch. On the **Outlines** section, set **Width** to **5**.

Set **Fill Color**, **Line Color**, **Background Color** to **RGB [141, 141, 141]**, **RGB [252, 255, 0]**, and **RGB [156, 188, 247]**, respectively. On the **Map Boundary** section, select **Manual** and then set **Width** and **Height** to **500**, and **200**, respectively.

The text is now centered on the plane [see Figure E3]. Take a render [see Figure E4]. Now, if zoom in on an area of the text and then render, you would notice that you will still get a high resolution output [see Figure E5].

In this exercise, we will create a resolution independent map using the **TextureObjMask** map.

The following Table summarizes the exercise.

Table E20: Working with TextureObjMask map	
Topics in this section:	• Getting Ready • Working with TextureObjMask Map
Skill Level	Beginner
Project Folder	**unit-mt2**
Final Exercise File	**umt2-hoe20-end.max**
Time to Complete	20 Minutes

Getting Ready

Open **umt2-hoe20-start.max** in 3ds Max.

Working with the TextureObjMask Map

Press **M** to open the **Slate Material Editor** and then drag **TextureObjMask** to the active view. On the **Parameter Editor | TextureObjMask | Parameters** rollout, click **Control Object's None** button and then click on the sphere in a viewport to make it the control object.

Now, drag the **Cellular** and **Noise** maps to the active view. Change the color as desired and then connect Cellular map to the **Texture1** [outside texture] port of the **TextureObjMask** and **Noise** map to the **Texture2** [inside texture] port [see Figure E1]. In the **Parameter Editor | TextureObjMask | Parameters** rollout, set **Transition Range** to **25**.

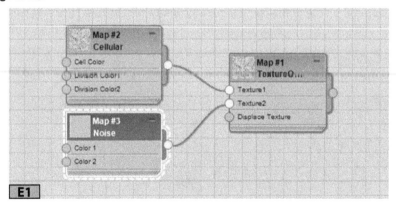

E1

Now, create a **Standard** material and connect its **Diffuse** port to the **TextureObjMask.** Select the plane in a viewport and RMB click on the material node and then choose **Assign Material to Selection**. Again, RMB click and then choose **Show Shaded Material in Viewport**. Take a test render [see Figure E2]. The sphere is obscuring the plane rendering. Create another **Standard** material and set its **Opacity** to **35**. Take a test render [see Figure E3].

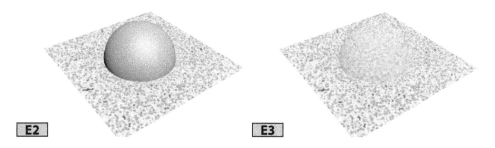

E2   E3

Summary
The unit covered the following topics:

- General/Scanline materials
- General maps

This page is intentionally left blank

Unit MT3-Physical, mental ray, and Autodesk Materials

3ds Max offers several materials that are used with the **mental ray** renderer. These materials are only visible in the **Material/Map Browser** if the active renderer is **NVIDIA mental ray** or **Quicksilver Hardware** renderer. The mental ray materials can be divided into three categories: Autodesk Materials, **Arch & Design** Material, and special-purpose mental ray materials.

In this unit, I'll describe the following:

- Autodesk Materials
- Arch & Design Material
- Physical Material

The **Physical** material is physically-based material and it is compatible with both the **ART** and **mental ray** renderers. Autodesk Materials are used to model commonly used surfaces in the construction, design, and the environment. These materials correspond to the materials found in other Autodesk products such as **Autodesk AutoCAD**, **Revit** and **Autodesk Inventor**. So, if you work between these applications, you can share surface and material information among them.

The mental ray **Arch & Design** material allows you improve rendering quality of the architectural renderings. This material is particularly useful when used to simulate glossy surfaces. The special-purpose mental ray materials are used to design special purpose materials such as car paint material, subsurface scattering material, and so forth.

Autodesk Materials

Autodesk Materials are based on the **Arch & Design** material. These materials work best when you use them with physically accurate lights such as photometric lights in a scene, modeled in the real-world units. However, the interface of the Autodesk materials is much simpler than the **Arch & Design** material, therefore, you can achieve good results in less time using Autodesk materials.

Many of the Autodesk materials use **Autodesk Bitmaps**. The **Autodesk Bitmap** is a simple bitmap type. This bitmap type always uses the real-world mapping coordinates. Therefore, if you have applied a **UVW Map** modifier to any geometry, make sure you turn on **Real-World Map Size** on the **Parameters** rollout. You can also change the default bitmap assignment.

Caution: Autodesk Bitmap compatibility
*3ds Max allows you to disconnect a bitmap, or replace it with another map. However, if you disconnect an **Autodesk Bitmap** in other application such as **Autodesk AutoCAD**, you won't be able to read the Autodesk material. If you are using other applications, make sure that you do not replace the bitmap with a map that only 3ds Max understands.*

Autodesk Ceramic

You can use this material to model the glazed ceramic material including porcelain.

Open **autoMat_begin.max**. Open the **Slate Material Editor**. On **Material/Map Browser | Materials | Autodesk**, double-click on **Autodesk Ceramic** to display the material's interface in the active view [see Figure F1]. Double-click on the material's node in the active view. In the **Material Editor | Ceramic** rollout, ensure that **Ceramic** is selected as **Type**. The **Ceramic** type produces look of earthenware.

Apply the material to teapot in the scene and take a test render [see Figure F2]. On the **Ceramic** rollout, set **Type** to **Porcelain**. Click **Color** swatch and change color to blue.

Color sets the color of the material. The other two options available for the **Color** control are **Use Map** and **Color By Object**. The **Use Map** option allows you to assign a map to color component of the material. If you set **Color** to **Color By Object**, 3ds Max uses the object's wireframe color as the material color. The **Finish** control lets you adjust the finish and reflectivity of the material.

Note: Color by object
*When you use the **Color By Object** option, the color appears on rendering but not in the viewport or material previews.*

Make sure **Finish** is set to **High Gloss / Glazed** and take a test render [see Figure 3]. Make sure **Finish** is set to **Satin** and take a test render [see Figure F4]. Make sure **Finish** is set to **Matte** and take a test render [see Figure F5]. Now, set **Finish** to **High Gloss / Glazed**.

On the **Finish Bumps** rollout, check **Enable** and make sure **Type** is set to **Wavy** and **Amount** to **0.3**. Now, take a test render [see Figure F6].

The options in the **Finish Bumps** rollout can be used to simulate the patterns that appear in glaze during firing. You can also create custom bumps by using the **Custom** option from the **Type** drop-down. **Amount** sets the strength of the pattern to apply.

On the **Finish Bumps** rollout, turn off **Enable**. On the **Relief Pattern** rollout, turn on **Enable**. Click the **Image** button. On the **Parameters** rollout, click **Source None** button. Select **patten.jpg** from the **Select Bitmap Image File** dialog and click **Open**. On the **Relief Pattern** rollout, set **Amount** to **1.2** and take a test render [see Figure F7].

F6   F7

The options in the **Relief Pattern** rollout allow you to model a pattern stamped into the clay. **Amount** controls the height of the relief pattern.

Autodesk Concrete

This material allows you to model the concrete material. Figure F8 shows its interface. The **Sealant** control of the **Concrete** rollout, controls the reflectiveness of the surface. **None** [see Figure F9] does not affect the surface finish. **Epoxy** [see Figure F10] adds a reflective coating on the surface whereas **Acrylic** [see Figure F11] adds a matte reflective coating.

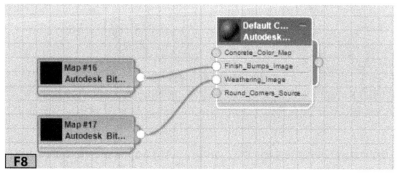

F8

The **Type** control in the **Finish Bumps** area allows you to set the texture of the concrete. **Broom Straight** which is a default type, specifies a straight broom pattern [see Figure F12]. **Broom Curved** uses a curving broom pattern [see Figure F13]. **Smooth** creates a pattern with speckled irregularities [see Figure F14].

Polished uses a completely smooth pattern [see Figure F15]. **Stamped/Custom** allows you to specify a bitmap for generating the pattern [see Figure F16].

Weathering applies a slight variation in the brightness on the surface of the concrete. The default weathering method is **Automatic** that applies weathering automatically. You can use **Custom** to specify a custom weathering pattern.

Autodesk Generic

This material provides a generic interface for creating a custom appearance. You can convert an Autodesk material to the **Autodesk Generic** material by RMB clicking on the node in the **Slate Material Editor | Active View** and then choosing **Copy as Generic** from the popup menu.

Autodesk Glazing

This material allows you to model a thin and transparent material such as glazing in windows and doors. The **Color** control in the **Glazing** rollout lets you choose the color for the sheet of glass. Figure F17 shows the teapot rendered with the **Blue Green** color applied to it.

Autodesk Harwood

This material is used the model the appearance of a wood. The **Stain** control in the **Wood** rollout allows you to choose a stain to add to the base harwood pattern. Figure F18 shows the wood material with **Brown Stain** color.

The **Finish** control lets you choose the surface finish of the harwood. The **Glossy Varnish** is the default option [see Figure F18]. The other options available are: **Semi-Gloss Varnish** [see Figure F19], **Satin Varnish** [see Figure F20], and **Unfinished** [see Figure F21].

The **Used For** control lets you adjust the appearance of the wood. **Flooring** uses an ocean shader that adds a slight warp to the large surfaces, improving the realism. When you choose **Furniture**, the surfaces are not warped. However, you can use the **Relief Pattern** map to achieve various effects.

When you check **Enable** in the **Relief Pattern** rollout, **mental ray** generates a relief pattern like bump map on the wood surface. The **Type** control lets you choose the relief pattern. When you choose **Based on wood grain**, it generates a relief pattern based on the image map used to create the wood pattern. **Custom** allows you to choose a custom map for the relief pattern. **Amount** lets you adjust the height of the relief pattern.

Autodesk Masonry/CMU

This material can be used to model masonry or concrete masonry units [**CMUs**]. Figure F22 and F23 shows the brick and CMU material.

Autodesk Metal

You can use this material to model various metallic surfaces. The **Type** control in the **Metal** rollout lets you choose the type of material you want to create. These materials define the base color and texture of the material. Figure F24 show the brass material. The **Finish** control lets you choose the surface finish for the surface. Figures F24 and F25 show the brass material with the **Polished** and **Brushed** finish, respectively.

Autodesk Metallic Paint

This material allows you to model a metallic paint surface such as paint of a car [see Figure F26].

Autodesk Mirror

This material lets you model a mirror material [see Figure F27].

Autodesk Plastic/Vinyl

This material allows you to model the surfaces that have a synthetic appearance such as plastic or vinyl [see Figures F28 and F29].

Autodesk Point Cloud Material

This is a special purpose material that is automatically applied to any point-cloud object in the scene. This material allows you to control the overall color intensity, ambient occlusion, and shadows.

Autodesk Solid Glass

This material allows you to model the appearance of the solid glass [see Figure F30].

Autodesk Stone

You can use this material to create the appearance of the stone [see Figures F31 and F32]. The **Type** control in the **Finish Bumps** rollout lets you specify the bump pattern. Available options are: **Polished Granite**, **Stone Wall**, **Glossy Marble**, and **Custom**.

Autodesk Wall Paint

This material can be used to model the appearance of a painted surface such as paint on the walls of a room [see Figures F33 and F34]. The **Application** control in the **Wall Paint** rollout lets you choose the texture method. In other words, you can control how paint is applied on the surface. **Roller** is the default method. Other two methods are **Brush** and **Spray**.

Autodesk Water

This material can be used to model appearance of a water surface [see Figure F35]. The **Type** control in the **Water** rollout lets you choose the scale and texture of the water.

The available options are **Swimming Pool**, **Generic Reflective Pool**, **Generic Stream/River**, **Generic Pond/Lake**, and **Generic Sea/Ocean**. The **Color** control lets you specify the color of the water. This option is only available for **Generic Stream/River**, **Pond/Lake**, and **Sea/Ocean**.

The following options are available for adjusting the color of the water: **Tropical**, **Algae/Green**, **Murky/Brown**, **Generic Reflecting Pool**, **Generic Stream/River**, **Generic Pond/Lake**, **Generic Sea/Ocean** and **Custom**.

Arch & Design Material

The mental ray **Arch & Design** material is a specialized material that allows you to create physically accurate renderings. It is designed to support most of the materials used in the architecture and product design renderings. This material includes self-illumination, ambient occlusion, and advanced options for reflectivity and transparency. It can also round off the sharp corners and edges as a render effect. It is especially fine-tuned for fast glossy reflections and refractions thus improving the workflow and performance.

The **Arch & Design** material has built-in description for all important controls. You can view the details in form of a tooltip. To view the tooltip, hover the cursor over a control's spinner, color swatch, checkbox, and so forth. The **Arch & Design** material attempts to be physically accurate and it outputs a high dynamic range. The visual appeal of the material depends on how colors inside the renderer are mapped to colors displayed on the screen. When you are using the **Arch & Design** material, it is recommended that you use an exposure control such as the **mr Photographic Exposure Control**. When using the **Arch & Design** material, make sure that you use atleast one of the two methods used with **mental ray** for indirect illumination: Final Gathering or Global Illumination. For best results, you can combine final gathering with global illumination. Also, it is recommended that you use physically accurate lights such as **Photometric** lights with the **Arch & Design** material.

To create an **Arch & Design** material, press **M** to open the **Slate Material Editor**. On the **Material/Map Browser | Materials | mental ray** rollout, double-click on **Arch & Design**. The material's interface is displayed in the active view [see Figure F36]. Figure F37 shows a render of teapot with the default **Arch & Design** material applied to it. We will explore the **Arch & Design** material in detail in hands-on exercises.

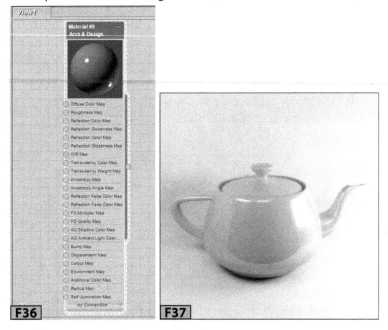

F36   F37

Physical Material

Physical material allows you to model shading effects of the real-world materials with ease. This material is the layered material that gives you ability to efficiently use the physically-based workflows. This material is compatible with **ART** and **mental ray** renderers. Do not use the legacy **Scanline** renderer with it as **Scanline** renderer shows just the approximation of the shader and does not support many crucial features.

This material is comprised of the following:

- A base layer that represents a diffuse color or colored metallic reflections. There can be an option clear-coat layer at the top. The clear-coat layer stays at the top of all layers and reduces energy based on how much energy it reflects and transparency color of the coating.
- Transparency layer
- Sub-surface scattering/translucency layer
- Emission [Self-Illumination] layer. This layer does not participate in the energy conversation and adds energy.

The energy conservation model of this material is somewhat like the **Arch & Design** material. The sum of various shading components can not exceed 100%. One exception is emission, in this case, energy is added. The energy calculation is based on the weight parameters instead of color parameters. This material ensures that the light does not amplify. When the **Metalness** parameter of the material is set to **1**, the material is opaque. It does not produce any Diffuse/Transparency/Sub-surface Scattering effects.

The Physical material comes with number of presets that you can use as a quick starting point. You can select the presets from the **Presets** rollout of the material. The **Material mode** drop-down also in the **Presets** rollout, lets you choose a mode. The two available modes are **Standard** and **Advanced**. The **Advanced** mode is the superset of the **Standard** mode with hidden parameters. In most of the cases, the parameters in the **Standard** mode are sufficient to make physically plausible materials. Some of the advanced parameters are: **Reflection Color** and **Weight**, **Diffuse Roughness**, and controls in the **Advanced Reflectance Parameters** rollout.

Hands-on Exercises

From the **Application** menu, choose **Manage | Set Project Folder** to open the **Browse for Folder** dialog. Navigate to the folder where you want to save the files and then click **Make New Folder**. Create the new folder with the name **unit-mt3** and click **OK** to create the project directory.

Exercise 1: Creating the Leather Material

Let's start by creating a leather material [see Figure E1] using the **Arch & Design** material.

The following table summarizes the exercise.

Table E1: Creating the leather material	
Topics in this section:	• Getting Ready • Creating the Leather Material
Skill Level	Intermediate

Project Folder	**unit-mt3**
Start File	**umt3-hoe1to8-start.max**
Final Exercise File	**umt3-hoe1-end.max**
Time to Complete	20 Minutes

Getting Ready

Open **umt3-hoe1to8-start.max**. Save the scene with the name **umt3-hoe1-end.max**.

Creating the Leather Material

Press **M** to open the **Slate Material Editor**. On the **Material/Map Browser | Materials | mental ray** rollout, double-click on **Arch & Design**. Apply the material to **geo1**, **geo2**, and **geo3** in the scene. On the **Parameter Editor | Templates** rollout, choose **Pearl Finish** from the drop-down. Rename the material as **brownLeatherMat**.

E1

Pearl Finish creates soft blurry reflections without affecting colors or maps. **Matte Finish** allows you to simulate an ideal **Lambertian** shading without affecting the colors or maps. **Glossy Finish** lets you simulate strong reflections without affecting colors or maps.

On the **Main material parameters** rollout, click **Color's** button. On the **Material/Map Browser | Maps | General** rollout, double-click **Bitmap**. On the **Select Bitmap Image File** dialog, choose **brownLeather.jpg**. On the **Gamma** section of the dialog, choose **Override** and set the spinner next to it to **2.2** and then click **Open**.

Tip: General Maps Rollout
*You can also assign diffuse map on the **General Maps** rollout using the **Diffuse Color** option.*

Color controls the color of the surface in direct light. **Diffuse Level** allows you to control the brightness of the diffuse color component. **Roughness** controls the blending of the diffuse component into the ambient component. The **Roughness** values ranges from **0** to **1**. At the **0** value, classical **Lambertian** shading is used. Higher values creates more powdery look.

Tip: Gamma 2.2 Setup
To know more about Gamma 2.2 setup in 3ds Max, visit the following link: http://www.risingpolygon.co/2016/05/gamma-22-setup-linear-workflow-in-3ds.html.

The **Arch & Design** material is energy conserving therefore the actual diffuse level used depends on the reflectivity and transparency. This material makes sure that diffuse+reflection+refraction is less than equal to **1**. The incoming light energy is properly distributed to diffuse, reflection, and refraction components so that it maintains the first law of thermodynamics. If you add reflectivity, the energy must be taken from somewhere, therefore the diffuse and transparency component will be reduced accordingly.

The rules for the energy are as follows:

- **Transparency** takes energy from the diffuse color. If you set transparency to **100%**, there will be no diffuse color.
- **Reflectivity** takes energy from diffuse and transparency, therefore, **100%** reflectivity means there is no diffuse color or transparency on the surface.
- **Translucency** is a type of transparency. The **Translucency Weight** parameter defines the percentage of transparency versus translucency.

On the **brownLeather.jpg | Coordinates** rollout, set **U** and **V** to **0.6** in the **Tiling** column. Also, set **Blur** to **0.2** and take a test render [see Figure E2].

On the **Parameter Editor | brownLeatherMat | Special Purpose Maps** rollout of the material, click **Bump's None** button. On the **Material/Map Browser | Maps | General** rollout, double-click **Bitmap**. On the **Select Bitmap Image File** dialog, choose **brownLeather_bump.jpg**. On the **brownLeather_bump.jpg | Coordinates** rollout, set **U** and **V** to **0.6** in the **Tiling** column. Also, set **Blur** to **0.2**. On the **Special Purpose Maps** rollout of the material, set **Bump** to **0.1** and take a test render [see Figure E3].

You can use the **Bump** map button to assign a bump map. The strength of the bump can be adjusted using the spinner located on the left of the button. If you turn on **Do not apply bumps to the diffuse shading**, bumps are applied to all components except the diffuse.

On the **Main material parameters** rollout, turn off **Fast (interpolate)** to generate more accurate glossiness.

When **Fast (interpolate)** is on, a smoothing algorithm is used that allows rays to be reused and smoothed. As a result, you get faster and smoother glossy reflections at a cost of accuracy.

When **Highlight + FG only** is turned on, actual rays are not traced in the scene. Only highlights are shown. In addition to this, soft reflections are shown that are produced by final gathering. You can use this option on surfaces that are less essential in the scene. This option works well with surfaces having weak reflections and blurred glossy reflections.

Metal material sets the color of reflection cast by the metallic materials. When **Metal material** is on, the **Color** control defines the color of reflections. The **Reflectivity** control sets the weight between the diffuse reflections and metallic reflections. When off, the **Reflection Color** control defines the color. The **Reflectivity** control plus **BRDF** settings define the intensity and color of the reflections.

Set **Glossiness** to **0.3**. **Glossiness** controls the sharpness of reflection/transparency. The values ranges from **0** [extremely diffuse or blurry transparency] to **1** [completely clear transparency].

Set **Reflectivity** to **0.2** and take a test render [see Figure E4].

Reflectivity controls the overall level of reflectivity. The reflectivity and color values, also known as specular highlight, define the level of reflections and its intensity. **Glossy Samples** specifies the number of rays [samples] **mental ray** shoots in order to calculate the glossy refraction. Higher values produce smooth result at a cost of render time.

Tip: Glossy Samples
A value of 32 is enough for most renderings. If you set **Glossy Samples** *to 1, only one ray is shot, regardless of the actual value of* **Glossiness***. It boosts the rendering performance. You can use it for your test renderings.*

On the **BRDF** rollout, make sure **Custom Reflectivity Function** is selected and then set **0 deg. refl** to **0.2** and **Curve shape** to **2**. Now, take a test render [see Figure E5].

| E4 | E5 |

BRDF stands for **Bidirectional Reflectance Distribution Function**. In the real world, the reflectivity of the surface is dependent on the view angle. **BRDF** function allows you to control the reflectivity of the surface based on the angle it is viewed. In real-world surfaces such as glass, water, and other dielectric materials with **Fresnel** effects, the angular dependency of reflection is dependent on **IOR** or index of refraction.

The **Arch & Design** material allows you to set the angular based reflectivity values using **0-degree** faces [surfaces directly facing the camera] and **90-degree** faces [surfaces 90 degrees to the camera]. **Curve Shape** controls the falloff of the BRDF curve. When you choose **By IOR [fresnel reflections]**, the reflectivity is entirely guided by the material's index of refraction.

MT3-12   Unit MT3 - Physical, mental ray, and Autodesk Materials

On the **Fast Glossy Interpolation** rollout, set **Interpolation grid density** to **1** (same as rendering) and take a test render [see Figure E6].

Warning: Interpolation

Interpolation *can cause artifacts because it is calculated on the low res grid. It can also cause oversmoothing as it blends neighbors of the low resolution grid.* **Interpolation** *works with the flat surfaces. It does not work well with wavy or highly detailed surfaces that uses the bump map.*

The controls in the **Fast Glossy Interpolation** rollout can be used to interpolate reflections and refractions thus producing smooth results and improving rendering performance. The interpolation works by pre-calculating glossy reflections in a grid across the image. The number of rays shot by **mental ray** is governed by reflection **Glossy Samples** and refraction **Glossy Samples**.

E6

Press **Ctrl+S** to save the scene with the name **umt3-hoe1-end.max**.

Exercise 2: Creating the Chrome Material

Ok, now we have some knowledge of the **Arch & Design** material. Now, let's create the chrome material [see Figure E1].

The following table summarizes the exercise.

Table E2: Creating the chrome material	
Topics in this section:	• Getting Ready • Creating the Chrome Material
Skill Level	Intermediate
Project Folder	**unit-mt3**
Start File	**umt3-hoe1to8-start.max**
Final Exercise File	**umt3-hoe2-end.max**
Time to Complete	10 Minutes

Getting Ready
Open the **umt3-hoe1to8-start.max**.

Creating the Chrome Material
Apply an **Arch & Design** material to **geo1**, **geo2**, and **geo3** in the scene. On the **Parameter Editor | Main material parameters** rollout | **Diffuse** section, set **Color** to **white**. Setting color to white will create a very highly reflective surface. On the **Reflection** group, set **Reflectivity** to **1**. Also, turn on **Metal material**. Now, take a test render.

Metal material allows you to define the reflection color using the **Diffuse color** parameter.

On the **Refraction** group, set **Color** to **Black** and set **IOR** to **25**.

The **Color** control on the **Refraction** group sets the color of the refraction. You can also use this control to create the colored glass. On the **BRDF** rollout, select **By IOR (fresnel reflections)** and take a render [see Figure E1]. Save the scene with the name **umt3-hoe2-end.max**.

E1

Exercise 3: Creating the Copper Material

Now, let's create the different copper materials [see Figures E1, E5, and E12].

The following table summarizes the exercise.

Table E3: Creating the copper material	
Topics in this section:	• Getting Ready • Creating the Copper Material
Skill Level	Intermediate
Project Folder	**unit-mt3**
Start File	**umt3-hoe1to8-start.max**
Final Exercise File	**umt3-hoe3-end.max**
Time to Complete	20 Minutes

Getting Ready

Open the **umt3-hoe1to8-start.max**. Save the scene with the name **umt3-hoe3-end.max**.

Creating the Copper Material

Let's start with the polished copper material.

Apply an **Arch & Design** material to **geo1, geo2,** and **geo3** geometry in the scene. On the **Parameter Editor | Templates** rollout, choose **Glossy Finish** from the drop-down. On the **Parameter Editor | Main material parameters** rollout | **Diffuse** group, set **Color** to the following RGB values: **0.592, 0.278,** and **0.165**. On the **Reflection** group, set **Reflectivity** to **1** and **Glossiness** to **0.9**. Also, turn on **Metal material**.

On the **Refraction** group, set **IOR** to **1.5**. On the **BRDF** rollout, choose **By IOR (fresnel reflections)** and take a render [see Figure E1].
Now, let's create the copper material with satin finish.

Apply a default **Arch & Design** material to **geo1, geo2,** and **geo3** in the scene. On the **Parameter Editor | Main material parameters** rollout | **Diffuse** group, set **Color** to the following RGB values: **0.592, 0.278,** and **0.165**. On the **Reflection** group, set **Reflectivity** to **0.8** and **Glossiness** to **0.5**. Also, turn on **Metal material**. Take a test render [see Figure E2]. You will see that the material is bright. You need to reduce the brightness of the material.

Set **Diffuse Level** to **0.3** to make the material less bright and take a test render. On the **Anisotropy** rollout, set **Anisotropy** to **0.05** to change the shape of the highlights and take a test render [see Figure E3].

E1   E2   E3

Anisotropy controls the shape of the highlight. At the value **1**, there will be no anisotropy and highlight will be round. At the value **0.01**, the highlight will be elongated. **Rotation** controls the orientation of the highlight. The values for **Rotation** ranges from **0** to **1**, **1** represents **360** degrees.

On the **Reflection** group, set **Glossy Samples** to **16** to increase the quality of the glossiness. On the **BRDF** rollout, set **0 deg. refl** to **0.9** and take a test render [see Figure E4]. Notice in the render that you need to reduce **Glossiness** value.

On the **Reflection** group, set **Glossiness** to **0.4**. On the **Fast Glossy Interpolation** rollout, set **Neighboring points to look up** to **8** and turn on **High detail distance**. Next, set distance to **1** for High detail distance. Now, take a test render [see Figure E5].

Neighboring points to look up lets you set the number of stored grid points are looked up to smooth out the reflective glossiness. The default value for this parameter is **2**. Higher values smear the glossiness. **High detail distance** allows **mental ray** to trace second set of rays to create a clearer version of the glossiness within the specified radius defined by this parameter.

Now, let's create the brushed copper material.

Apply a default **Arch & Design** material to the teapot in the scene. On the **Parameter Editor | Main material parameters** rollout | **Diffuse** group, set **Color** to the following RGB values: **0.592**, **0.278**, and **0.165**. On the **Reflection** group, set **Reflectivity** to **0.5** and **Glossiness** to **0.5** as well. Also, turn on **Metal material**. Now, take a test render [see Figure E6].

E4   E5   E6

Now, we will use the **Noise** map to create brushed metal look in the reflections.

On the **Reflection** group, click **Color** button. On the **Material/Map Browser | Maps | General** rollout, double-click **Noise**. On the **Noise Parameters** rollout, set **Noise Type** as **Fractal** and set **Size** to **1** to create tiny dots in the noise pattern [see Figure E7]. On the **Coordinates** rollout, set **Source** to **Explicit Map Channel**. Also, set **V, V,** and **W** to **0.5, 100,** and **100** in the **Tiling** column, respectively to create streaks in the noise pattern [see Figure E8].

E7   E8

On the **Noise Parameters** rollout, set **Color #1** to medium gray [**Value=122**] and take a test render [see Figure E9]. On the material's **Refraction** group, set **IOR** to **45**. On the **BRDF** rollout, select **By IOR (fresnel reflections)** and take a test render [see Figure E10]. On the **Anisotropy** rollout, set **Anisotropy** to **0.05** to change the shape of the highlights and take a test render [see Figure E11].

E9   E10   E11

Now, I will increase the reflectivity and glossiness values of the surface.

On the material's **Reflection** group, set **Reflectivity** and **Glossiness** to **0.8**. Set **Glossy Samples** to **16**. On the **Fast Glossy Interpolation** rollout, set **Interpolation grid density** to **1/4 (quarter resolution)**, **Neighboring points to look up** to **4**, and turn on **High detail distance**. Next, set distance to **2** for **High detail distance**. Now, take a render [see Figure E12]. Press **Ctrl+S** to save the scene.

Exercise 4: Creating Glass/Thin Plastic film Materials

In this exercise, we're going to create different glass and thin plastic film materials [see Figures E1, E2, E4, E6, E7, and E9]. Let's start with the clear glass material. This material is suitable for solid geometries with some thickness.

E12

The following table summarizes the exercise.

Table E4: Creating the glass/thin plastic film materials	
Topics in this section:	• Getting Ready • Creating Glass/Thin Plastic film Materials
Skill Level	Intermediate
Project Folder	**unit-mt3**
Start File	**umt3-hoe1to8-start.max**
Final Exercise File	**umt3-hoe4-end.max**
Time to Complete	20 Minutes

Getting Ready
Open the **umt3-hoe1to8-start.max**. Save the scene with the name **umt3-hoe4-end.max**.

Creating Glass/Thin Plastic film Materials
Here's the process:

Apply an **Arch & Design** material to **geo1**, **geo2**, and **geo3** in the scene. On the **Parameter Editor | Main material parameters** rollout | **Diffuse** group, set **Color** to **black**. On the **Reflection** group, set **Reflectivity** to **1**. On the **Refraction** group, set **Transparency** to **1** and **IOR** to **1.5**. On the **BRDF** rollout, choose **By IOR (fresnel reflections)** and take a render. On the **Advanced Rendering Options** rollout, set **Max Trace Depth** to **8** in the **Reflections** and **Refraction** groups. Take a test render [see Figure E1].

When the trace depth is equal to the value specified by the **Reflections** group | **Max Trace Depth** control, **mental ray** shows only highlights and emulated reflections created using **Final Gathering**. The material behaves as if **Highlights+FG** is on in the **Main material parameters** rollout | **Reflection** group.

E1

Cutoff Threshold sets a threshold level at which reflections are rejected. The default value for this control is **0.01**. At this value, rays that contribute less than **1%** to the final pixel are ignored.

Max Distance allows you to limit the reflections to a certain distance. It helps in speeding up the rendering as **mental ray** does not include distant objects to glossy reflections. **Fade to end color** lets you fade the reflections to this color. This is suitable for indoor scenes. When this option is turned off, reflections fade to the environment color which is suitable for outdoor scenes.

The optimization settings for the refraction are almost identical to those for reflections. When the trace depth is equal to the value specified by the **Refraction** group | **Max Trace Depth** control, the material refracts black.

Advanced Reflectivity Options group | **Visible area lights cause no Highlights** control, when on, the **mental ray** area lights with **Area Light Parameters** rollout | **Show Icon In Renderer on**, create no specular highlights.

When **Skip reflections on inside (except total internal reflection)** is on, **mental ray** retains total internal reflection [**TIR**]. Most of the reflections inside the transparent objects are very faint except few known as **TIR**. When this option is on, **mental ray** boosts the performance by ignoring the weak reflections but retaining **TIRs**. **Relative Intensity of Highlights** controls the intensity of specular highlights versus the intensity of true reflections.

Next, we will create tinted glass.

On the **Refraction** group, set **Color** to the following RGB values: **0.969**, **0.729**, and **0.659**. Now, take a test render [see Figure E2].

Next, you will create frosted glass.

On the **Refraction** group, set **Transparency** and **Glossiness** to **0.8** and take a test render [see Figure E3]. You will notice that you need to reduce the glossiness farther to make a believable frosted glass. If you reduce the **Glossiness** value, you need to increase samples to compensate. Set **Glossiness** and **Glossy Samples** to **0.5** and **16**, respectively, and take a test render [see Figure E4].

Now, the render is looking much better. Adding a little bit of translucency will make the effect much better so let's do it.

Turn on **Translucency** and set **Weight** to **0.2**. Change **Translucency Color** to the following RGB values: **0.969**, **0.729**, and **0.659** and then take a test render [see Figure E5].

Translucency is a special form of transparency. If you want a material to be translucent, there should exist some transparency in the material. The **Weight** parameter defines how much of the existing transparency is used as translucency. For example, if you set **Weight** to **0.3**, **30** percent of the transparency is used as translucency. It is best suited for thin walled objects such as windows panes or plastic films. **Color** controls the translucency color.

Note: Sub-surface Scattering
*You can create sub-surface scattering effects by using the glossy transparency with the translucency. However, the effect is not as good as created using the dedicated **SSS** shaders.*

On the **Diffuse** group, set **Diffuse Level** to **0.52** to reduce the brightness of the material. Press **Ctrl+S** to save the file.

Next, you will create a glass material that does not include any refraction. This glass is ideal for windows panes with single face.

Open **umt3-hoe4-start.max**. Apply an **Arch & Design** material to the plane geometry in the scene. On the **Parameter Editor | Main material parameters** rollout | **Diffuse** group, set **Color** to black. On the **Reflection** group, set **Reflectivity** to **1**. On the **Refraction** group, set **Transparency** to **1** and **IOR** to **1.5**. On the **BRDF** rollout, choose **By IOR (fresnel reflections)** and take a render.

On the **Refraction** group, set **Color** to the following RGB values: **0.737**, **0.776**, and **0.98**. On the **Advanced Rendering Options** rollout, set **Max Trace Depth** to **8** in the **Reflection** and **Refraction** groups. On the **Advanced Transparency Options** rollout, choose **Thin-walled (can use single face)** for **Glass / Translucency treat objects as**. Now, take a render [see Figure E6].

E6

When you choose **Thin-walled (can use single face)**, the object behaves as if it is made of a very thin sheet of transparent material. On the other hand, **Solid (requires two sides on every object)** tells **mental ray** that the object is made of a solid, transparent substance.

Tip: Creating Magic Walls
Back Face Culling *makes the surfaces invisible to the camera when seen from the reverse side. You can use this option to create magic walls. If you create walls of a room using planes with the normal facing inwards, you can render room from outside. The camera will see into the room, but the wall will still exists and behave normally. For example, they will cast shadows, photon will be bounced off them.*

When you turn off **Transparency propagates Alpha channel**, the transparent objects have an opaque alpha. When on, the alpha-channel information is passed on to the background. The refraction and other transparency effects propagate the alpha of the background "through" the transparent object.
The two parameters in the **Indirect Illumination Options** group are multipliers. **FG/GI multiplier** lets you adjust the material response to the indirect light. **FG Quality** is a local multiplier for the number of final gather rays shot by the material.

Next, you will create a thin blurry plastic material.

Apply the default **Arch & Design** material to the plane geometry in the scene. On the P**arameter Editor | Main material parameters** rollout | **Diffuse** group, set **Color** to white. On the **Reflection** group, set **Reflectivity** to **1**. On the **Refraction** group, set **Transparency** to **0.9**, **Glossiness** to **0.6**, **Glossy Samples** to **16**, and **IOR** to **1.5**. On the **BRDF** rollout, choose **By IOR (fresnel reflections)**.

On the **Advanced Transparency Options** group, choose **Thin-walled (can use single face)** option for **Glass / Translucency treat objects as**. Also, turn on **Transparency propagates Alpha channel** and then take a render [see Figure E7].

If you want to create strong blur, adjust the values of **Transparency** and **Glossiness** in the **Refraction** group. Also, enable **Translucency**. On the **Refraction** group, set **Transparency** to **0.8**, **Glossiness** to **0.8**, and **Glossy Samples** to **16**. Check **Translucency** and set **Weight** to **0.2** and then take a render [see Figure E8].

E7   E8

Exercise 5: Creating the Water Material
In this exercise, we are going to create the water material [see Figure E3].

The following table summarizes the exercise.

Table E5: Creating the leather material	
Topics in this section:	• Getting Ready • Creating the Water Material
Skill Level	Intermediate
Project Folder	**unit-mt3**
Start File	**umt3-hoe1to8-start.max**
Final Exercise File	**umt3-hoe5-end.max**
Time to Complete	20 Minutes

Getting Ready
Open the **umt3-hoe1to8-start.max**.

Creating the Water Material
Apply an **Arch & Design** material to **geo1**, **geo2**, and **geo3** in the scene. On the **Parameter Editor | Main material parameters** rollout | **Diffuse** group, set **Color** to the following RGB values: **0.0, 0.058**, and **0.019**. On the **Reflection** group, set **Reflectivity** to **1**. On the **Refraction** group, set **IOR** to **1.3**. On the **BRDF** rollout, choose **By IOR (fresnel reflections)**. Now, take a test render [see Figure E1].

On the **Special Purpose Maps** rollout of the material, set **Bump** to **0.1** and then click **Bump's None** button. On the **Material/Map Browser | Maps | mental ray** rollout, double-click **Ocean**. Take a test render [see Figure E2].

You need to adjust the values for ocean parameters to get a nice bump. On the **Ocean Parameters** rollout, set **Largest** to **0.5**, **Smallest** to **0.25**, **Quantity** to **3**, and **Steepness** to **1** and then take a render [see Figure E3].

| E1 | E2 | E3 |

Save the scene with the name **umt3-hoe5-end.max**.

In this exercise, we're going to create the sofa fabric material [see Figure E1]. The following table summarizes the exercise.

Table E6: Creating the sofa fabric material	
Topics in this section:	• Getting Ready • Creating the Sofa Fabric Material
Skill Level	Intermediate
Project Folder	**unit-mt3**
Start File	**umt3-hoe1to8-start.max**
Final Exercise File	**umt3-hoe6-end.max**
Time to Complete	20 Minutes

Getting Ready
Open the **umt3-hoe1to8-start.max**.

Creating the Sofa Fabric Material
Apply an **Arch & Design** material to the teapot geometry in the scene. Rename the material as **sofaFabricMat**. On the **Main material parameters** rollout, click **Color's** button. On the **Material/Map Browser | Maps | General** rollout, double-click **Bitmap**. On the **Select Bitmap Image File** dialog, choose **sofaFabricDif.jpg**. Also, set gamma override to **2.2**. Also, set **Diffuse Level** to **0.7**.

E1

On the **Coordinates** rollout, set **Blur** to **0.2**. On the **Parameter Editor | sofaFabricMat | Main material parameters** rollout | **Reflection** group, set **Reflectivity** to **0.08**, **Glossiness** to **0.5**, and **Glossy Samples** to **16**. On the **BRDF** rollout, set **0 deg. refl**, **90 deg. refl**, and **Curve shape** to **0.1**, **0.3**, and **2**, respectively. On the **Special Purpose Maps** rollout of the material, click **Bump's None** button. On the **Material/ Map Browser | Maps | General** rollout, double-click **Bitmap**. On the **Select Bitmap Image File** dialog, choose **sofaFabricBump.jpg**.

On the **Coordinates** rollout, set **Blur** to **0.2**. On the **Special Purpose Maps** rollout of the material, set **Bump** to **0.4** and take a render [see Figure E1]. Save the scene with the name **umt3-hoe6-end.max**.

Exercise 7: Creating the Wooden Cabinet Material

In this exercise, we are going to create the wooden cabinet material [see Figure E1].

The following table summarizes the exercise.

Table E7: Creating the leather material	
Topics in this section:	Getting Ready Creating the Wooden Cabinet Material
Skill Level	Intermediate
Project Folder	**unit-mt3**
Start File	**umt3-hoe1to8-start.max**
Final Exercise File	**umt3-hoe7-end.max**
Time to Complete	20 Minutes

Getting Ready

Open the **umt3-hoe1to8-start.max**.

Creating the Wooden Cabinet Material

Apply an **Arch & Design** material to **geo1**, **geo2**, and **geo3** in the scene. Rename the material as **woodCabinetMat**. On the **Main material parameters** rollout | **Diffuse** group, click **Color's** button. On the **Material/Map Browser | Maps | General** rollout, double-click **Bitmap**.

On the Select **Bitmap Image File** dialog, choose **woodCabinetDiff. png**. Also, set gamma override to **2.2**. On the **Coordinates** rollout, set **U** and **V** to **2** in **Tiling** column. Also, set **Blur** to **0.2**. On the **Parameter Editor | woodCabinetMat | Main material parameters** rollout | **Reflection** group, set **Reflectivity** to **0.4**, **Glossiness** to **0.7**, and **Glossy Samples** to **32**. On the **Main material parameters** rollout | **Reflection** group, click **Glossiness** button. On the **Material/Map** E1 **Browser | Maps | General** rollout, double-click **Bitmap**.

On the **Select Bitmap Image File** dialog, choose **woodCabinetGloss.png**. On the **Coordinates** rollout, set **U** and **V** to **2** in **Tiling** column. Also, set **Blur** to **0.2**. Now, take a test render.

On the **Special Purpose Maps** rollout of the material, click **Bump's None** button. On the **Material/Map Browser | Maps | General** rollout, double-click **Bitmap**. On the **Select Bitmap Image File** dialog, choose **woodCabinetBump.png**. Also, set **U Tiling**, **V Tiling**, and **Blur** values as done earlier.

Take a render [see Figure E1]. Save the scene with the name **umt3-hoe7-end.max**.

In this exercise, we're going to create parquet material for the floor [see Figure E1].

The following table summarizes the exercise.

Table E8: Creating the leather material	
Topics in this section:	• Getting Ready • Creating the Parquet Material
Skill Level	Intermediate
Project Folder	**unit-mt3**
Start File	**umt3-hoe1to8-start.max**
Final Exercise File	**umt3-hoe8-end.max**
Time to Complete	20 Minutes

Getting Ready
Open the **umt3-hoe1to8-start.max**.

Creating the Parquet Material
Apply an **Arch & Design** material to the teapot geometry in the scene. Rename the material as **woodParquetMat**. On the **Main material parameters** rollout | **Diffuse** group, click **Color's** button. On the **Material/Map Browser** | **Maps** | **General** rollout, double-click **Bitmap**. On the **Select Bitmap Image File** dialog, choose **floorParquetDiff.png**. Also, set gamma override to **2.2**.

E1

On the **Coordinates** rollout, set **Blur** to **0.2**. On the **Parameter Editor** | **Main material parameters** rollout | **Reflection** group, set **Reflectivity** to **0.7**, **Glossiness** to **0.7**, and **Glossy Samples** to **16**. On the **Main material parameters** rollout | **Reflection** group, click **Color's** button. On the **Material/Map Browser** | **Maps** | **General** rollout, double-click **Bitmap**. On the **Select Bitmap Image File** dialog, choose **floorParquetRef.png**. On the **Coordinates** rollout, set **Blur** to **0.2**.

On the **Special Purpose Maps** rollout of the material, click **Bump's None** button. On the **Material/Map Browser** | **Maps** | **General** rollout, double-click **Bitmap**. On the **Select Bitmap Image File** dialog, choose **floorParquetBump.png**. On the **Coordinates** rollout, set **Blur** to **0.2**. On the **Special Purpose Maps** rollout of the material, set **Bump** to **0.4** and take a render [see Figure E1].

Save the scene with the name **umt3-hoe8-end.max**.

Exercise 9: Creating Glossy Varnished Wood
In this exercise, we're going to create a varnished glossy wood material using the **Physical** material [see Figure E1].

The following table summarizes the exercise.

Table E9: Creating Glossy Varnished Wood	
Topics in this section:	• Getting Ready • Creating the Material
Skill Level	Intermediate
Project Folder	**unit-mt3**
Start File	**umt3-physical-mat-start.max**
Final Exercise File	**umt3-hoe9-end.max, umt3-hoe9-end-2.max**
Time to Complete	20 Minutes

Getting Ready
Open the **umt3-physical-mat-start**.

Creating the Material
Apply a **Physical** material to the **geo1**, **geo2**, and **geo3** geometries in the scene. Rename the material as **glossyVarnishedMat**. On the **Parameter Editor | Presets** rollout, select **Advanced** from the **Material mode** drop-down. On the **Parameter Editor | glossyVarnishedMat | Basic Parameters** rollout | **Base Color and Reflections** section, click **Base Color's** button.

On the **Material/Map Browser | Maps | General** rollout, double-click **Bitmap**. On the **Select Bitmap Image File** dialog, choose **wooden-plank-1.jpeg**. Also, set gamma override to **2.2**.

The first spinner in the **Base Color and Reflections** section is **Weight**, the relative measurement of the base color. The value in this spinner participate in the energy conversion. Click the button next to **Weight** to assign a map to it.

The Color swatch next to the **Weight** button is the base color of the material. For non-metals, this swatch defines the diffuse color. For metals, it defines the color of the metal itself. Click on the button next to the swatch to assign a color to it.

Take a test render [see Figure E2].

Notice the render in Figure E2, the wood is highly reflective, we need to add some roughness to the reflection and transparency components.

On the **Reflections** section, set **Roughness** to **0.9** and then take a test render [see Figure E3]. Notice that setting **Roughness** to **0.9**, the material has lost its gloss and looks very flat. Glossiness is the effectively the inverse of the roughness. If you enable the **Inv** switch corresponding to the **Roughness** parameter, it will yield glossy material. The **Roughness** parameter lets you control the roughness of the material. A higher **Roughness** value yields a blurrier result. You can lower the **Roughness** value to make the mirror like material.

Enable the **Inv** switch and then set **IOR** to **1.7**.

The **IOR** parameter controls the index of refraction level of the material. If defines how much rays bend when they enter a medium. It also affects the angular dependency of the reflectivity when set to the default **Fresnel** mode [see the **Advanced Reflectance Parameters** rollout].

On the **Transparency** section, click the **Lock** icon and then set **Roughness** to **1**. Also, enable the **Inv** switch. Take a test render [see Figure E4].

By default, roughness values of reflectivity and transparency are locked together. You can unlink them clicking the **Lock** icon.

On the **Anisotropy** rollout, select **Map channel** and then set **Channel** to **1**. Set **Anisotropy** and **Rotation** to **0.4**, and **0.3**, respectively. Take a test Render [see Figure E5].

The **Anisotropy** parameter controls the U-direction roughness in relation to the V-direction roughness. The **Rotation** parameter controls the anisotropy angle. This control ranges from **0** to **1** which represents one full revolution. The **Auto** option automatically orients the anisotropy whereas the **Map channel** option orients the anisotropy based on a given texture space.

Now, we will create a bump map using the **Noise** map as done in Exercise 3.

Drag a **Noise** map to the active view. On the **Parameter Editor | Noise map | Coordinates** rollout, set **Source** to **Explicit Map Channel** and ensure **Map Channel** is set to **1**. Set **Tiling U, V**, and **W** to **0.5, 200**, and **100**, respectively. On the **Noise Parameters** rollout, set **Size** to **0.2** [see Figure E6].

Set **Color #1** to **RGB[180, 180, 180]**. Drag a **Mix** map to the active view. Connect **Noise** map to the **Color 1** port of the **Mix** map and **Bitmap** to the **Color 2** port. Connect the **Mix** map to the **Bump Map** port of **glossyVarnishedMat** [see Figure E7]. On the **Parameter Editor** | **Mix** map | **Mix Parameters** rollout, set **Mix Amount** to **30**.

E6

E7

Take the final render [see Figure E1]. Now, if you want to create a less glossy satin varnished wood material, you need to lower down the reflection **Roughness** and **IOR** values [see Figure E8].

Check the **umt3-hoe9-end-2.max** file for the satin varnished material.

E8

Exercise 10: Creating Glass Materials

In this exercise, we're going to create a glass materials using the **Physical** material.

The following table summarizes the exercise.

Table E10: Creating the Glass Materials	
Topics in this section:	• Getting Ready • Creating the Materials
Skill Level	Intermediate
Project Folder	**unit-mt3**
Start File	**umt3-physical-mat-start.max**
Final Exercise File	**umt3-hoe10-end.max**
Time to Complete	20 Minutes

Open the **umt3-physical-mat-start.max** file.

Creating the Materials

Apply a **Physical** material to **Geo1**, **Geo2**, and **Geo3** in the scene. Rename the material as **glassMat**. On the **Parameter Editor | glassMat** material | **Presets** rollout, choose **Advanced** from the **Material mode** drop-down.

There are two types of modes available for the **Physical** material: **Standard** and **Advanced**. When you choose the **Standard** mode, you get access to the parameters that you can use to create most physically plausible materials. The **Advanced** mode gives you access to advanced reflection, roughness, and weight parameters. You can use these parameters to create advanced materials.

On the **glassMat** material | **Basic Parameters** rollout | **Base Color** section, set **Base Color** weight to **0**. The material turns black. On the **Transparency** section, set the **Transparency** weight to **1** to make the glass completely transparent [see Figure E1]. On the **Reflections** section, set **IOR** to **1.7**.

The **IOR** value sets the Index of **Refraction** level. It controls how much rays bend when entering in a medium.

Turn on the **Thin-walled** box and take a test render [see Figure E2].

When this box is turned on, the object is considered to be made out of an infinitely thin transparent shell. This shell us not reflective. Also, the transparency depth is disabled and the sub-surface scattering is replaced by translucency.

Turn off the **Thin-walled** box.

You can create tinted glass by specifying a color for **Transparency** and specifying a depth. In the **Transparency** section, set color to **Red** and then set **Depth** to **0.05** and take a render [see Figure E3].

You can create some interesting effects by using sub-surface scattering option. On the **Sub-Surface Scattering** section, set color to yellow and take a test render. Notice that there is no change in the color of the glass. As discussed earlier, the sum of various shading components can not exceed 100%, therefore, you need to reduce weight of other parameter to see the effect of sub-surface scattering.

On the **Transparency** section, set **weight** to **0.85** and take a render [see Figure E4].

Exercise 11: Creating Metal Materials

In this exercise, we're going to create a metal materials using the **Physical** material.

The following table summarizes the exercise.

Table E11: Creating the Metal Materials	
Topics in this section:	• Getting Ready • Creating the Materials
Skill Level	Intermediate
Project Folder	**unit-mt3**
Start File	**umt3-physical-mat-start.max**
Final Exercise File	**umt3-hoe11-end.max**
Time to Complete	20 Minutes

Getting Ready

Open the **umt3-physical-mat-start.max** file.

Creating the Materials

Apply a **Physical** material to **Geo1**, **Geo2**, and **Geo3** in the scene. Rename the material as **metalMat**. On the **Parameter Editor** | **glassMat** material | **Presets** rollout, choose **Advanced** from the **Material mode** drop-down.

First, we will create highly reflective material. On the **glassMat** material | **Basic Parameters** rollout | **Base Color** section, set **Base Color** weight to **0**. On the **Reflections** section, set **IOR** to **48** and then take a test render [see Figure E1]. The reflection in the material is coming from the gray background. If you want more reflections in the metal, use a reflection map.

Now, if you want to create a material like aluminium, blur the reflections by adding some roughness to the metal. On the **Reflections** section, set **Roughness** to **0.3** and take a render [see Figure E2]. You can make the metal darker by darkening the **Reflection** color. Set it to medium gray and take a render [see Figure E3].

If you want to add of the weight of the base color to the material, it will have no effect because of the high **IOR** value. If you use low **IOR** values, you loose the metal look. To compensate for this, you can use the **Metalness** parameter. If you set **Metalness** to **1**, you do not see the base layer, just the colored reflections.

On the **Parameter Editor** | **metalMat** | **Basic Parameters** rollout | **Base Color** section, set base color to **RGB[0.82, 0.416, and 0.099]** and weight to **0.3**. On the **Reflections** section, set reflection color to **RGB[0.584, 0.584, 0.584]**, weight to **0.7**, **Roughness** to **0.3**, **Metalness** to **0.5**, and **IOR** to **6**. Take a render [see Figure E4].

Summary

The unit covered the following topics:

- Autodesk Materials
- Arch & Design Material
- Physical Material

Index

This page is intentionally left blank

Other Books Published by Rising Polygon

Rising Polygon Publishing

[Best Textbooks at Lower Prices]

Modeling Techniques
with
3ds Max 2016 and CINEMA 4D R17 Studio
The Ultimate Beginner's Guide

@risingpolygon
www.risingpolygon.co

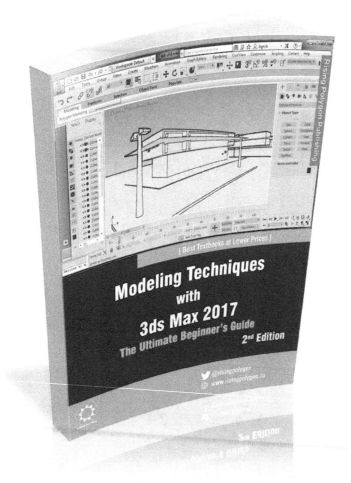

| Best Textbooks at Lower Prices |

Modeling Techniques
with
3ds Max 2017
The Ultimate Beginner's Guide
2nd Edition

@risingpolygon
www.risingpolygon.co

[Best Textbooks at Lower Prices]

Modeling Techniques
with
CINEMA 4D R17 Studio
The Ultimate Beginner's Guide
2nd Edition

@risingpolygon
www.risingpolygon.co

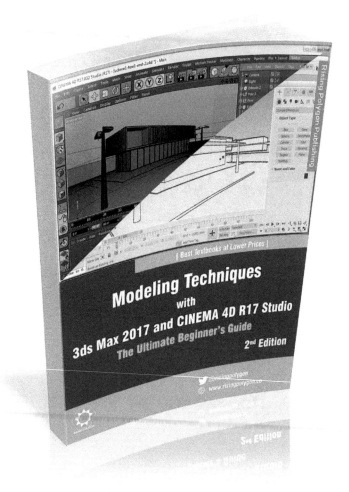

[Best Textbooks at Lower Prices]

Modeling Techniques
with
3ds Max 2017 and CINEMA 4D R17 Studio
The Ultimate Beginner's Guide

2nd Edition

risingpolygon
www.risingpolygon.co

Rising Polygon Publishing

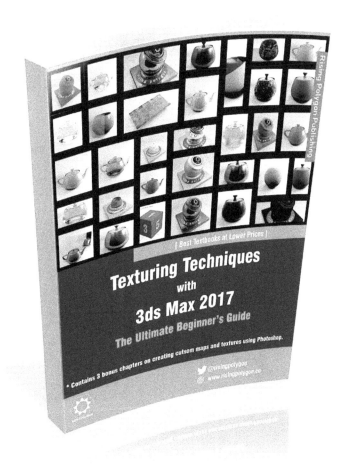

[Best Textbooks at Lower Prices]

Texturing Techniques
with
3ds Max 2017
The Ultimate Beginner's Guide

Contains 3 bonus chapters on creating cutsom maps and textures using Photoshop.

@risingpolygon
www.risingpolygon.co

Rising Polygon Publishing

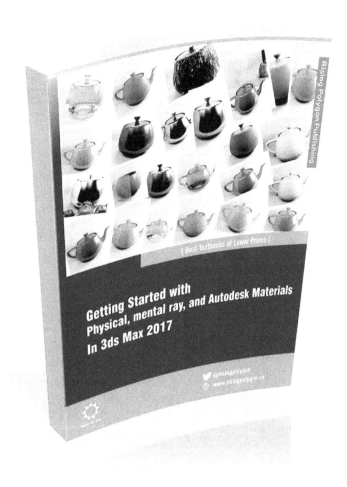

Getting Started with
Physical, mental ray, and Autodesk Materials
In 3ds Max 2017

Rising Polygon Publishing

| Best Textbooks at Lower Prices |

@risingpolygon
www.risingpolygon.co

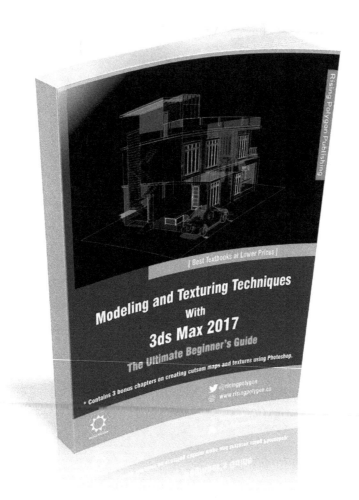

[Best Textbooks at Lower Prices]

Modeling and Texturing Techniques

With

3ds Max 2017

The Ultimate Beginner's Guide

▸ Contains 3 bonus chapters on creating cutsom maps and textures using Photoshop.

🐦 @risingpolygon
🌐 www.risingpolygon.co

Rising Polygon Publishing

www.ingramcontent.com/pod-product-compliance
Lightning Source LLC
LaVergne TN
LVHW062301060326
832902LV00013B/1990